INTERNATIONAL SERIES OF MONOGRAPHS IN
HEATING, VENTILATION AND REFRIGERATION

GENERAL EDITORS: N. S. BILLINGTON AND E. OWER

VOLUME 6

TOTAL ENERGY

OTHER TITLES IN THE SERIES IN
HEATING, VENTILATION AND REFRIGERATION

Vol. 1. Osborne—Fans
Vol. 2. Ede—An Introduction to Heat Transfer Principles and Calculations
Vol. 3. Kut—Heating and Hot Water Services in Buildings
Vol. 4. Angus—The Control of Indoor Climate
Vol. 5. Down—Heating and Cooling Load Calculations

TOTAL ENERGY

BY

R. M. E. DIAMANT
M.Sc., Dip.Chem.E., A.M.Inst.F.

Lecturer in Chemical Engineering,
the University of Salford

PERGAMON PRESS

Oxford · New York · Toronto
Sydney · Braunschweig

Pergamon Press Ltd., Headington Hill Hall, Oxford
Pergamon Press Inc., Maxwell House, Fairview Park, Elmsford, New York 10523
Pergamon of Canada Ltd., 207 Queen's Quay West, Toronto 1
Pergamon Press (Aust.) Pty. Ltd., 19a Boundary Street, Rushcutters Bay,
N.S.W. 2011, Australia
Vieweg & Sohn GmbH, Burgplatz 1, Braunschweig

First edition 1970

Library of Congress Catalog Card No. 70-102906

PRINTED IN GREAT BRITAIN BY PAGE BROTHERS (NORWICH) LTD.
08 006918 5

1532813

CONTENTS

Preface   vii

SI Units   ix

1. What is Total Energy?   1
2. Principal Prime Movers used in Total Energy Production.   25
3. Steam Turbines and Total Energy *by* A. C. VALENTINE (W. H. Allen Sons & Co. Ltd.)   53
4. Governor Systems for Industrial Steam Turbo-alternators *by* A. C. VALENTINE (W. H. Allen Sons & Co. Ltd.)   108
5. Open-cycle Gas Turbines and Total Energy *by* H. R. M. CRAIG (AEI Turbine-Generators Ltd.)   155
6. Closed-cycle Gas Turbines and Total Energy *by* H. U. FRUTSCHI, W. HAAS, C. KELLER and D. SCHMIDT (Escher-Wyss Ltd.)   209
7. Diesel and Gas Engines and Total Energy   251
8. The Fuel Cell and Total Energy *by* H. R. ESPIG (Energy Conversion Ltd.)   286
9. Refrigeration and Total Energy   299
10. District Heating and Total Energy   317
11. Existing Total Energy Schemes in North America   361
12. Economic Assessment of Total Energy *by* the Northern Natural Gas Co., Omaha, Nebraska, U.S.A.   405

Bibliography   419

Index   427

v

PREFACE

THE production and distribution of electricity today is an extremely wasteful process. During the conversion of fuel to electric power at centralised power stations more than 60% of the heat content of the fuel is thrown away in unsightly and expensive cooling towers. Distribution of energy in the form of electricity is by far the most expensive and least desirable way of distribution of any public utility due to the need to erect massive overhead powerlines.

It is far better to generate the power where it is wanted and to use the waste heat produced for useful purposes. This is what *Total Energy* is all about. It is a completely new concept. In 1950 the term was practically unknown. Yet every succeeding year now sees an increasing rate of expansion in this very sensible development. The large power-generating companies, too, are realising that they can no longer afford to throw away all their waste heat and they are starting to utilise it in the form of district heating, particularly in Europe.

This book is believed to be the first comprehensive textbook in this new field. Because it is hoped that it will have world-wide appeal, it was decided to give all units in the English system and in the new metric SI (Système International d'Unités). A table of SI conversions is included. To avoid confusion, all money values are given in U.S. dollars, with the date when they applied in brackets, except in one case where Canadian dollars are given instead.

The author would like to thank all the many organisations and firms whose help has made this book possible. He would particularly like to thank his co-authors for their valuable contributions.

University of Salford, England   R. M. E. DIAMANT

vii

SI UNITS

(Système International d'Unités)

THE following are conversion factors from English units to SI:

1 inch	$= 0.0254$ m
1 foot	$= 0.3048$ m
1 yard	$= 0.9144$ m
1 in^2	$= 645.16$ mm^2
1 ft^2	$= 0.0929$ m^2
1 yd^2	$= 0.836$ m^2
1 in^3	$= 1.638 \times 10^{-5}$ m^3
1 ft^3	$= 0.0283$ m^3
1 U.K. gallon (not used in this book)	
	$= 4.536$ dm^3
1 U.S. gallon	$= 3.785$ dm^3
1 lb	$= 0.4536$ kg
1 lb/ft^3	$= 16.019$ kg/m^3
1 lb/in^2	$= 6.8948$ kNm$^{-2} = 0.068948$ bar
1 psig	$= 0.068948$ bar $(g) = 6.8948$ kNm^{-2} (g)
1 Btu	$= 1.055$ kJ
1 therm	$= 100,000$ Btu $= 105.5$ MJ
1 hp	$= 745.7$ W
1°R	$= 5/9$ °K
t°F	$= 5/9 (t - 32)$ °C
1 Btu/ft^2-hr °F	$= 5.678$ W/m^2 °C
1 Btu/ft-hr °F	$= 1.7307$ W/m °C
1 Btu in./ft^2-hr °F	$= 0.1442$ W/m °C
1 Btu/ft^3	$= 37.258$ kJ/m^3
1 ton of refrigeration	$= 3.5169$ kW

CHAPTER 1

WHAT IS TOTAL ENERGY?

ELECTRICITY is the most convenient general form of energy. It can be converted at almost 100% efficiency into heat and also at very high efficiencies into mechanical energy, light energy and sound energy. Its great advantage is the ease with which the energy can be led exactly to the spot where it is needed, yet for many purposes such flexibility is scarcely needed.[82, 104]

However, the production of electricity from the combustion of natural fuels, or for that matter, from the heat produced in nuclear reactions is by no means efficient. In the chain of reactions:

Fuel→ Heat→ Mechanical energy→ Electrical energy,

the weakest link is in all cases the conversion from heat to mechanical energy. In even the most perfect system this is limited by Carnot's equation:

$$\text{Eff.} < \frac{T_2 - T_1}{T_2}$$

where T_2 and T_1 are the highest and the lowest temperatures of the system in degrees absolute respectively. In practice T_2 is represented by the maximum gas temperature achieved inside the diesel engine, gas engine or gas turbine, or the maximum saturation steam temperature inside a steam turbine, while T_1 is represented by the temperature of the exhaust gases of a diesel or gas plant, and by the temperature of the condenser water in the case of a steam plant. As exhaust gases in gas turbines and similar equipment emerge at around 1400°R (773°K) while the operating temperatures are seldom much in excess of 1950°R (1073°K) the thermodynamic limitation of efficiency of the heat-energy conversion process with such typical gas turbines is

$$\frac{1073 - 773}{1073} = 27 \cdot 8\%$$

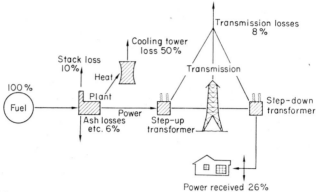

(a) Conventional power generation

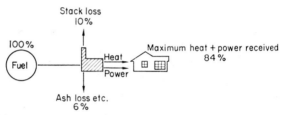

(b) Total energy power generation

Fig 1.1

It would no doubt be possible to design gas-turbines with somewhat lower exhaust temperatures and somewhat higher combustion-chamber temperatures, but improvements in the overall efficiency of operation would still be marginal.

Steam turbines operate under better conditions. Modern steam plants can operate with steam at up to 580°C (853°K) and exhaust the steam at a temperature as low as 30°C (303°K). The theoretical limit of the conversion of heat into energy with such a turbine is thus:

$$\frac{853 - 303}{853} = 64\cdot5\%$$

However, due to the facts that steam as a compressible gas deviates considerably from the ideal gas laws, that it is necessary to superheat the steam to avoid sedimentation and corrosion of turbine blades, and for many other reasons, the actual practical efficiencies of even the most modern steam plants seldom, if ever, exceed about 36–37%. Nor is there much likelihood of much improvement in the future. The lower limit is already set by the high vacuum operated on the exhaust side, which can hardly be improved upon. Better construction materials may make it possible to squeeze a few more pounds of pressure out of the steam boiler, so as to increase the inlet temperature somewhat. However, even this is unlikely to raise the overall efficiency of power generation by more than a few percent at the most.

As far as the older, low steam-pressure steam turbines were concerned their efficiencies were very poor. As recently as 1963 the Oxford power station, operating with a steam feed temperature and pressure of 640°F (340°C) and 250 psig (17·4 bar (g)) pressure, had an operating efficiency of only 8·07% while the Ribble A station, another low steam-temperature and pressure station, operated at 5·77% overall efficiency.

Yet, according to the first law of thermodynamics, the total heat input into a system must always equal the total heat (or other forms of energy) output. What has happened to the remaining energy contained in the fuel? It has been converted into heat. Some of this heat, such as the heat lost by radiation from the boiler plant, or lost as sensible and latent heat in the flue gases, it not easily regained, although later in this book we shall encounter a Russian technique of doing precisely this (p. 334). Most modern boiler plants work at efficiencies of 85% and above. In addition, there is a certain heat loss in the turbine bearings and in the conversion process from mechanical energy to electricity, but these factors remain small. By far the largest proportion of heat is lost to the atmosphere either directly, as when the exhaust gas from gas turbines, gas engines and diesel engines is released into the air, or indirectly. When seawater or river water coolers are used to abstract heat from the condenser in which the low-pressure steam from the exhaust side is reconverted into water, or when cooling towers are used to dissipate the heat, vast quantities of energy are wasted. In most cases the quantity of energy so wasted is much greater than the energy usefully converted to electricity. As the temperature of the water fed into the

cooling towers is quite low, it is virtually impossible to make use of
these large quantities of low grade heat.

TOTAL ENERGY operation seeks to obtain electricity in a way that
uses nearly all the energy contained in the fuel instead of only a small
fraction of this energy. There are several ways of doing this:[44, 45]

1. It is possible to use large existing power stations which are operated
on the ITOC (intermediate take-off condensing) principle so as to
obtain a flexible heat/electricity balance. Steam is bled off along the
turbine body and its latent heat is used to heat up circulating water to
any desired temperature between 200°F and 350°F (93–178°C).
Alternatively, the bled-off steam is used directly. The heat is then transported in the form of steam or hot water to urban areas and is used as
such for heating and air-conditioning purposes. Cooling towers or
other water coolers are still needed and, because of this, ITOC stations
do not operate at anything like full efficiency, but they are a good
deal more efficient than standard condensing turbines. In addition,
operating conditions are better from a general economic principle.

2. It is possible to abandon the grid system entirely and to build
small power generation plants as a part of the housing system or complex. These power generators can be small steam-driven back-pressure
plants, yielding hot water at a temperature of around 212°F (100°C).
This hot water can then be used for space heating or industrial purposes. Alternatively, the types of machines used may be diesel engines,
gas turbines, free piston gas engines or stationary aircraft jet engines,
which combine a reasonable efficiency of electricity generation with
high flue-gas output temperatures. The waste heat can be used for such
purposes as space heating, air conditioning, refrigeration, hot-water
supply, process heating, sea-water evaporation, etc.

The installation of such plant is particularly popular in the United
States where developments have been very rapid during the last few
years and where future developments promise to be even more startling.
At the end of 1964 there were only 175 schemes in operation in the
United States, but this figure rose to 300 by the end of 1966. It is estimated that by 1978 there will be at least 25,000 total energy systems
installed in America.

3. At the lowest level, it is even possible to provide total energy to
single dwellings. Such plant consists of a petrol-driven generator, or

may in the future be in the form of a natural gas-fired fuel cell, which produces electricity and enables the waste heat produced during the combustion processes to be used for space heating and the provision of domestic hot water.

ADVANTAGES AND DISADVANTAGES OF TOTAL ENERGY OPERATION

Cost of Transportation of Energy[107]

Long-distance transmission of electricity is one of the most expensive forms of transmission of energy known. If one assumes the transmission of the same quantity of energy over the same distance, and if one assigns to power transmission costs by means of an overhead 50 kV cable and auxiliaries such as transformers, switch gears, etc., an index figure of 100, the cost of transmission using other methods is as follows:

Oil in an underground pipeline, including cost of pumping stations, maintenance of pipes, etc. = 27.
Natural gas in underground pipeline = 31.
Hot water at a temperature of between 150 and 200°C using the Soviet single-pipe system including the cost of heat losses, pumping costs, etc. = 48.
Hot water using a flow and return pipeline employing a twin pipeline underground culvert, including heat losses, pumping costs, etc. = 67.

As can be seen, costs of transmission of energy in almost any other form are a fraction of the costs of equivalent electric power transmission. The reasons why electric power transmission is so dear are the following:

(a) It is necessary to use expensive step-up and step-down transformers at the beginning and at the end of the transmission lines, which waste a good deal of power in the form of heat.

(b) There are considerable power losses during the transmission of power. These are in the form of current leakages through insulation weaknesses, conversion of power into heat due to the resistance of the wires, thunderstorms, etc.

(c) The establishment of pylons ruins large areas of land for farming, and naturally compensation has to be paid for this. Underground pipelines do not interfere with farming at all.

(d) Erection costs and repair costs for overhead lines are very high, in contrast to buried lines which, once positioned, can usually be forgotten altogether.

If, however, electric power is to be transported not by means of overhead lines, but as is often suggested by many who object to enormous pylons on amenity grounds, by using buried cables, the cost figure would soar high above the index of 100 given. It has been stated that the cost of running underground high-voltage cables averages about $2·4 million per mile, roughly the cost of running an equal length of a six-lane motorway. Such costs are naturally prohibitive, and in consequence the only feasible way of transporting electric power over long distance would appear to be the overhead high-voltage cable, carried by large pylons. These pylons, apart from being unsightly, interfere with agriculture, constitute a hazard to aircraft, and are liable to being blown down during storms, causing interruption of services and possible hazards to the population. They also often interfere with television and radio reception.

Yet other types of energy can be transported completely conveniently underground, the pipes being virtually totally maintenance free and offering no trouble or hazards at all, except during the brief construction period.

Plant Cost

The individual plant cost of total energy equipment is often higher per unit power output than the cost of large-scale plant at a central electricity station. In addition, if connection to the grid system is to be avoided altogether, adequate stand-by facilities are needed, causing an increased capital expenditure. However, as the practice of total energy has expanded, there has been a trend for equipment to be made more economically, by rationalising some of the production processes. For example, the cost of gas turbines fell by 20% between 1960 and 1966. This trend is likely to continue so that the disadvantage of high capital cost should not weigh so heavily. On the other hand, although extra costs are incurred in providing premises such as a cellar or special substation for the total energy equipment, considerable savings can be made in reducing provisions for running power lines. As the erection of power lines is a mainly manual operation which is unlikely to be cheapened appreciably by mass-production techniques, and as such installations tend to become increasingly more expensive as the density of population increases, trends are again favourable to the total energy concept

Fuel Costs[48]

Small-scale consumers have to pay between 30% and 100% more for the purchase of basic fuels than the price which is charged to large undertakings, although there should be little difference in fuel costs charged to intermediate undertakings such as local authorities operating total energy stations for some of their housing estates, and large undertakings such as electricity boards. Smaller plants certainly do not utilise fuel as effectively as do larger plants. For example, a large, conventional gas-fired steam-generating plant uses 11 ft³ (0·31 m³) of natural gas per kWh of power generated, while small scale plants need between 12 ft³ (0·34m³) and 17·5 ft³ (0·50 m³) per kWh. On the other hand, there are better opportunities for small-scale plants to permit the proper utilisation of the waste heat for various purposes than there is for large plants. If a total energy plant is installed to supply both a housing estate and an industrial consumer, it is sometimes possible to obtain between 60% and 80% total utilisation of the heat present in the fuel. Some large-scale district heating gas turbines operate on such efficiencies, but figures like this are difficult to achieve with even highly efficient steam ITOC plants.

Independence from Grid System

The event which gave total energy its greatest boost in the United States was the catastrophic power breakdown in New York[2, 3] and the New England States on the 9 November 1965. One single faulty power relay at Queenston, Ontario, Canada, started the trouble. The total power flow of 1600 MW into Ontario was suddenly dumped upon

B

the New York system, knocking out the main east–west line of New York State. This caused the entire system to collapse affecting 83,000 square miles and 30 million people. The overall cost to the community of this very large power failure was enormous. Only small isolated areas operating total energy systems were immune and could go on normally. Questions have been asked whether modern grid systems are not becoming too large and involved so that such power failures may take place again. Total energy plants, with adequate stand-by facilities, have been considered to be probably more reliable than the enormous super grid systems, where the breakdown of one major component can affect the entire system.

The power failure particularly affected hospitals as only 75·6% had stand-by generators.

In the United States power lines are frequently blown down by hurricanes and tornadoes, thus interrupting vital power supplies. Total energy installations are almost immune against such natural disasters.

Actual Savings made by the Operation of Total Energy Installations[110]

It can be seen that it is always necessary to determine whether in the case in question total energy operation is more economical than the purchase of electricity from central electricity undertakings, which have the advantage of cheaper plant cost per unit power output and also lower fuel costs. There are three basic considerations which determine whether total energy is likely to be a viable proposition:

(a) The equipment must be employed as fully as possible.

(b) The recoverable heat must be utilised well.

(c) Adequate quantities of relatively low cost fuel must be available.

In general, it is not difficult to obtain at least as good and probably better utilisation figures for small total energy plant, as can be obtained for the plant owned by the large electricity undertakings. Much of the peak loading of centralised plant is due to the need to provide electric power for heating, which can be obtained much cheaper and easier in other ways. If electric power is only needed for purposes such as lighting, mechanical movers and other services, with the exception of heating and cooling, a much flatter power consumption curve is likely to be achieved than the one normal for large undertakings.

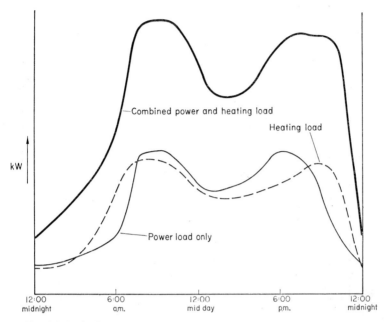

kW

Combined power and heating load

Heating load

Power load only

| 12:00 midnight | 6:00 a.m. | 12:00 mid day | 6:00 p.m. | 12:00 midnight |

FIG. 1.2. Daily fluctuations of power and heat demand in winter in the U.K.

Good utilisation of recoverable heat is a matter of rather greater difficulty especially in Northern Europe. In the United States this matter is facilitated by the fact that the energy requirements for heating needed in winter are almost balanced by the energy requirements during the summer for air-conditioning equipment.[150] In countries which do not need air conditioning during the summer, such as most Northern European countries, the problem is not quite so easy to solve. Definite steps must be taken to find consumers for the waste heat produced during the summer months. Such consumers may be various industrial undertakings, laundries, dyeworks, chemical works, etc. During the winter months such undertakings would be operating their own boiler plant, to obtain process heat, while during the summer they may be persuaded to purchase waste heat from the total energy plant, provided this waste heat is sold at a price which is lower than the cost of fuel to the undertaking.

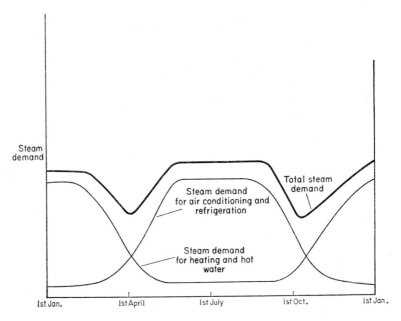

FIG. 1.3. Pattern of steam demand at a typical midcontinental, U.S. location.

Effect of the Fuel Cost upon the Relative Economy of Total Energy vs. Bought Electricity

In order to obtain a true cost analysis for the fuel used, it is necessary in all cases to consider the actual cost of this per kWh of electricity produced, and therm (GJ) of heat supplied. Normally power is bought from the central electricity generating authority at a given cost per kWh which is very high when considered in terms of net heating capacity. In most countries the cost of power charged to industrial and domestic consumers varies between 1 and 2 cents per kWh, or between 38 and 76 cents per therm (100,000 Btu) ($4·02–8·04 per GJ). The cost of crude fuel when bought directly, whether in the form of coal, oil or gas, is a small fraction of this, and seldom amounts to more than around 3–4 cents/therm (32–42 cents per GJ) while in the United States prime fuel costs well below this figure are quite common.

One of the reaons why bought electricity costs are so high is the very low efficiency of utilisation of the heat contained in the primary fuel. Total energy plants usually have a very much higher overall utilisation figure and therefore the fraction of cost represented by fuel charges is much lower.

Table 1.1 gives the heat content of the fuel used in combustion appliances.

TABLE 1.1. CALORIFIC VALUE OF VARIOUS FUELS

	Btu/lb	kJ/kg
Peat	1000–3000	2300–6900
Oil shales	1700–5000	3900–11,500
Lignites	5000–9000	11,500–20,700
Bituminous coals	10,200–14,500	23,500–33,400
Anthracite	14,900–15,200	34,400–35,000
Bunker C oil	18,300 gross	42,000 gross
Diesel oil	19,200 gross	44,000 gross
Petrol (gasolene)	20,500 gross	47,100 gross

The net values for the liquid fuels are about 6% less.

Fuel gases	Btu/ft^3	kJ/m^3
Blast furnace gas	90	3350
Producer gas (coke)	130	4840
Producer gas (coal)	160	5950
Blue watergas	290	10,800
Carburetted water gas, coal gas	450	16,700
Coke oven gas	525	19,500
Natural gas	950–1050	35,300–39,200
Acetylene	1550	58,000
Refinery tail gases	2750	65,300
Butane	3200	119,500

When bought electricity and directly purchased fuel are used for the power and heating/cooling requirements of a building it is possible to separate these two costs. This is very difficult to do with total energy equipment, where the fuel does several jobs at the same time. In addition, the utilisation of the fuel does not remain static. During periods of maximum utilisation, when

$$\frac{\text{electricity demand}}{\text{heat demand}}$$

is very large, total energy systems may be operating at an overall efficiency rating of up to 80%. During other periods, when there is a very low demand for the heat produced a very much lower utilisation, perhaps only between 40–50% may be expected.

From this it can be seen that no total energy system can be economical, unless a steady and high heat load can be satisfied from the system.

General Aspects of Importance to Assess Feasibility of Total Energy[88]

It would be a mistake to state that total energy is likely to be a success under all circumstances. It is most likely to succeed when

(a) Power prices are high due to the need for very long distribution lines, awkward sites or isolation of the consumers.

(b) Fuel prices are low. With the widespread development of natural gas supply networks in the U.S.A. and Europe the cost of gas especially as delivered to the consumer becomes very competitive.

(c) Steady demand for heat. In Northern Europe and certain places in America too, where the summer air-conditioning load is small or negligible, heat can be utilised by industrial undertakings and for such purposes as operating seawater evaporators, a use which is likely to become of increasing importance as the demand for drinking and industrial water increases.

(d) The stand-by requirement should be fairly low, and at any rate it should not exceed 100%. Most total energy systems operate without stand-by connections to the central power undertakings, but this is by no means excluded, even though the consumer is likely to be charged a rather higher price for such stand-by electricity from central undertakings. In municipal total energy/district heating systems, such as those which are used in Western Europe, a careful balance of power generation/heating requirements is always carried out.

Advantages of Central Generation of Electricity over Total Energy

These can be summarised as the following:[75]

(a) Low initial capital investment is needed by the developer.

(b) There is virtually no extra investment needed when the capacity needed increases.

(c) There is a minimum penalty when the load shrinks, as against total energy, where production costs per unit rise considerably.

(d) Total energy installations usually need some skilled personnel, none are needed in conventional connection to a central power undertaking.

(e) There is no noise, vibration, smoke or fuel-storage problem with central power generation and transmission to the consumer. This is probably the strongest argument against the installation of total energy appliances. The problems are, however, far from insoluble.

(f) Costs of central power generation are completely predictable, as against total energy schemes where a lot has still to be taken on trust, and where costs cannot be foreseen with any degree of accuracy.

Heating Costs Applicable in the United Kingdom at the End of 1967

A. E. Haseler of the British Ministry of Works has assessed comparative heating costs in the United Kingdom on the basis of an average dwelling which is heated at the rate of 675 therms per annum (71 GJ). These charges are given in Table 1.2 in dollars and cents per week.

TABLE 1.2

	$
On-peak electricity	3·96
Off-peak electricity uncontrolled	3·73
Off-peak electricity controlled	2·73
Coke	2·60
Gas	2·21
Oil	1·68
Anthracite	1·62
District heating: new city 60% connected to thermal station	1·33
District heating; new city 60% connected to combined power/heat (total energy) station	0·96

Essential Components of a Total Energy System

A total energy system has the following components:

(a) A prime mover which has an output consisting of shaft power together with heat energy. As an alternative the prime mover may be replaced by a fuel cell, where the output is in the form of electric power plus heat energy. As mechanical power can be converted into electrical energy at almost no thermodynamic loss, it can be seen that these two types of systems are quite comparable.

(b) A device which converts the mechanical energy into electrical energy. This is normally an alternator, which is of completely conventional design. Details as to the method of running alternators are given in Chapter 4.

(c) Methods of making the waste-heat energy usable. These include exhaust heat boilers, drying equipment, absorption air conditioners, etc. In addition a total energy installation must have the appropriate control and safety devices needed to run the plant effectively.

High-frequency Current Generation[66]

One of the advantages of producing one's own electricity is that one can supply power at a variety of supply voltages and frequencies, or alternatively produce d.c. electricity if so needed. Gas turbines rotate at a very high speed and can thus produce a.c. electricity at a high frequency. Such a form of electricity is useful for the following purposes:

High-frequency induction furnaces for metal treatment, fluorescent lighting, dielectric heating, etc.

Fluorescent lighting, particularly, is operated best at frequencies of up to 850 hertz. If such power is used, there is a much smaller heat/light ratio thus reducing the load on air conditioning equipment, lighting costs, and increasing the life of the lamps by up to 50%. While the standard frequency of power supply from grid systems is usually 50 hertz in Europe and 60 hertz in the U.S.A., it is possible to obtain high-frequency current at up to 3000 hertz in privately run total-energy systems, if so needed.

To indicate the marked saving in current possible with high-frequency power, it is stated that at the McAllen High School in Texas 452 kW of power were required to supply classroom lighting with grid current at 60 hertz. When the switch was made to high-frequency lighting using current produced by a gas turbine total energy system and employing a frequency of 840 hertz, only 350 kW were needed to supply the same lighting load.

Noise of Gas Turbine Equipment

One of the objections to the installation of total energy systems, in particular gas turbines, is the noise produced by such installations. By carefully examining the problem, these objections can largely be overcome.

The sources of noise with gas turbines are the following:

(a) *Compressor noise.* This is of high frequency and directional, and can be eliminated by the use of sound-absorbing linings in the inlet ducts. Two 90° bends in the duct also markedly reduce the noise and help considerably, but care must be taken that they do not produce pressure-loss difficulties. Sound attenuating baffles are placed in the inlet duct adjacent to the air filters.

(b) *Mechanical and gearing noises.* In the case of gas turbines such noises are not particularly important because of the absence of vibration. In the case of gas engines and diesel engines they are of greater importance but can be reduced very markedly by the incorporation of flexible mountings. Usually there is quite enough thermal insulation around the body of turbine plant to act as sound attenuators. If not, it is easy to enclose the turbine and line the enclosure with sound absorbing material.

(c) *Exhaust noise* is usually of a relatively low frequency. Exhaust heat recovery usually provides all the attenuation needed, except when by-pass operation is practiced. In such cases exhaust silencers mounted on the stack can be used.

USEFUL APPLICATIONS OF EXHAUST HEAT RECOVERY FROM PRIME MOVERS

(a) Coupling of Steam Turbines to Gas Turbines

In such a compound engines system where the gas turbine exhaust heat is made use of to produce steam for a condensing steam turbine the following characteristics may apply:

Gas turbine inlet temperature	1500°F (820°C)
Exhaust stack temperature	370°F (188°C)
Exhaust stack loss	37·3%
Condenser loss	27·2%
Overall efficiency	32·5%

B*

This contrasts with the following data which are applicable to the same gas turbine operating without steam turbine coupling. In this case the exhaust stack temperature was

750°F (400°C)

Exhaust stack loss	74·5%
Overall efficiency	23·5%

Coupling of a steam turbine to the gas turbine thus increases the efficiency of electricity generation of the latter by approximately 9%.

(b) *Process Steam Supply*

Waste heat from prime movers can be converted into process steam which is used by a wide variety of industries. Paper mills use large quantities of such steam, but they usually require it at varying pressures and at odd times. Demand can usually best be served by the storage of steam in an accumulator. The chemical industry uses enormous quantities of process steam for distillation, fractionation, evaporation and other unit processes. Breweries use large quantities of process steam as do food processing industries, laundries, gas works, hospitals and many other undertakings. All these are ready consumers of waste heat produced in prime movers.

(c) *Direct Drying*

There are a number of industrial processes, such as the manufacture of bricks, tiles, ceramics, glass and leather, where exhaust gases from small prime mover plants can be used directly for drying purposes. In June 1962 a British Ruston and Hornsby gas turbine was installed in a brickworks at Macon, Georgia, U.S.A., to provide lighting and power to the plant and also to supply some 17×10^6 Btu (18 GJ) per hour in order to operate the dryer furnaces. In this case the exhaust gases could be used directly. It was found that the system showed an overall saving of 16% in the first year over previous operational costs where electricity and fuel were purchased separately.

Direct drying is also used extensively in agricultural establishments for such purposes as vegetable drying, haymaking, grass drying, etc.

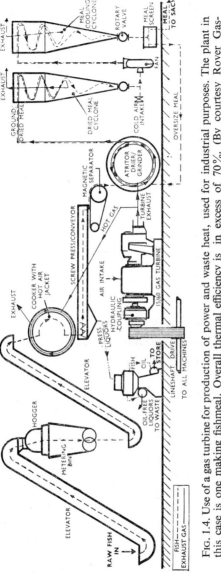

FIG. 1.4. Use of a gas turbine for production of power and waste heat, used for industrial purposes. The plant in this case is one making fishmeal. Overall thermal efficiency is in excess of 70%. (By courtesy Rover Gas-turbines Ltd.)

Another Ruston and Hornsby plant operates in St. Cloud, Florida, U.S.A., giving off 300 kW of power and supplying heat for the crop-drying plant.

(d) *Provision of District Heating to Communities*

District heating is usually provided by either large steam turbines operating on the ITOC or back-pressure cycle, or by large gas turbines. The matter will be dealt with fully in Chapter 10.

(e) *Provision of all Services to Housing Complexes*

The waste heat from prime movers is made use of widely in the U.S.A. for the provision of the following services to shopping centres, offices, hotels, schools, apartment blocks, etc. Space heating using low pressure steam or hot water; air conditioning and refrigeration using absorption plant or low pressure steam plant; provision of hot water for consumption purposes, and process steam where needed for swimming-bath heating, etc. In the United States of America total energy installations are often the property of natural-gas companies who operate and maintain the plant, and simply charge the owner of the complex a rental charge and for the fuel used. Because of the overall efficiency of such a plant, the sum of rental charge and fuel cost paid is usually a good deal lower than the owner would have had to pay, if he had bought his electricity and his fuel for other purposes separately.

(f) *Sewage Disposal* [116-17]

Gas turbines can be usefully driven by sewage methane which is produced at sewage works. At Beakton, Essex, England, there is a plant consisting of eight gas turbines which operate both blowers and electric generators, and are driven by waste methane. They provide the air flow used to activate the sewage and provide electric power for the works. The waste heat is utilised to digest the sludge and to produce the methane from it. The plant has been operating for over $\frac{1}{4}$ million hours with complete satisfaction and saves $1,200 per day in fuel costs.

(g) *Flash Evaporation as a Method of Waste Heat Utilisation*[115, 140, 148]

The provision of adequate quantities of fresh water to urban and industrial communities is a matter of increasing difficulty. One of the most promising ways of using the waste heat produced during various power generation processes is for the purpose of flash distillation of salt water and brackish water. The information which is given here has been supplied by Weir Westgarth Ltd. of Glasgow, Scotland.

Flash distillation consists of a technique of allowing the seawater to boil successively in a large number of chambers, each of which is maintained at a lower pressure than the one before to match the lower temperature of the water. The method of flash distillation of seawater is particularly promising with regard to the use of waste heat produced in nuclear power stations. For example, it would be feasible to design a nuclear power station operating on the total energy principle to produce 400 MW of electricity and 10 million cubic feet of water (283,000 m³) of fresh water per day. Assuming a cost of electricity of 0·43 cents per kWh (1968 costs), then the cost of production of water would be of the order of 44 cents per 1000 U.S. gallons (11 cents per m³) which includes all capital and running costs. Such costs are coming within reach of the costs which apply for traditional methods of collecting and storing rainwater.

OPERATING CYCLE OF A FLASH EVAPORATOR

The flash evaporator can consist of twenty to fifty chambers, each operating at a lower pressure than the preceding one. As heated brine flows from one chamber to the next, some of it flashes off into water droplets of brine. It then condenses on colder condenser tubes and drops as distillate into trays, from which it is then led away into storage. The brine, in passing from chamber to chamber, becomes progressively cooler and it is this same brine which is then pumped back through the condenser tubes to act as the coolant in the condenser section of each chamber. It becomes progressively hotter as it does this. In consequence, when it reaches the heat input section, and before re-entering the first flash chamber, its temperature need only be raised a few degrees to allow the vapour released in the flash chamber to condense on the condenser tubes. The heat is normally supplied by low-pressure steam

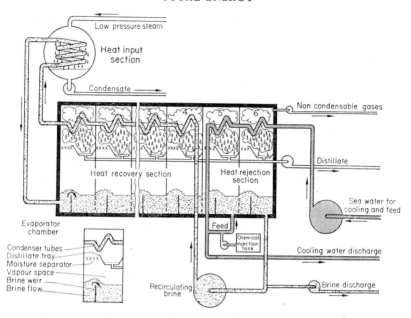

Fig. 1.5. Flow sheet of a flash evaporator. (By courtesy: Weir-Westgarth Ltd.)

which in its turn is readily obtained by the utilisation of waste heat from prime movers. As can be seen from Fig. 1.5 the heated brine passes from the heat input section to the first flash chamber (1) and from there successively through all the chambers down to the coolest one (6), flashing off a certain amount of water vapour at each stage. It is then extracted by the brine circulator pump and pumped back to the tubes of the heat recovery section at point (4). In the last few stages, the heat rejection section (5 and 6), cold crude seawater is pumped through the tubes. This allows condensation to take place in these stages and also extracts an amount of heat equal to that put into the evaporator at the heat input section, thus permitting a continuous cycle of operation. Some of the seawater, after being chemically dosed to prevent scale formation, is added to the circulating brine to make up for the distillate extracted and for brine which must be discarded in order to keep the brine concentration in the evaporator within the required limits. When seawater is heated, gases such as oxygen, carbon dioxide, etc., are given off. These are extracted by a vacuum pump or ejector system.

The heat which is required in a flash evaporator to produce unit weight of distillate is given by the following equation.

It equals:
$$\frac{(t_e - t_l)L}{(t_e - t_f)} \quad \frac{Btu}{lb} \quad \frac{(kJ)}{(kg)}$$

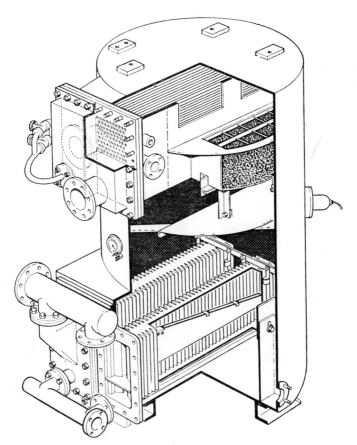

FIG. 1.6. Small packaged fresh-water generator designed to utilise waste heat from prime mover equipment. (By courtesy: Weir-Westgarth Ltd.)

where t_e is the temperature of the water entering the flash stage in
°F (°C),

t_l is the temperature of the water leaving the tube system in
°F (°C),

t_f is the temperature of the water leaving the last flash stage in
°F (°C),

L is the latent heat of flashed vapour in Btu/lb (kJ/kg).

Capital costs for typical evaporator plants depend upon the operating
efficiency. Low-efficiency plants have a

$$\frac{(t_e - t_l)}{(t_e - t_f)}\text{ratio of }0.25,$$

while the ratio for high-efficiency plants is of the order of 0·1 or less.
Thus low-efficiency plants have a fuel consumption which is $2\frac{1}{2}$ times
as high as that of high-efficiency plants. Typical cost figures quoted for
1967 are as follows, including associated boiler and turbo-alternator:

FIG. 1.7. Artist's impression of large flash evaporation plant. (By courtesy:
Weir-Westgarth Ltd.)

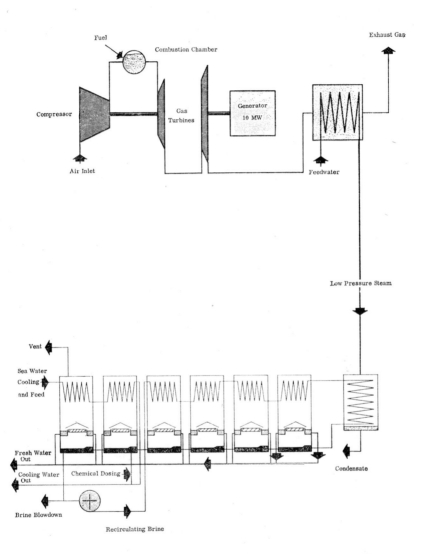

FIG. 1.8. Flash evaporation plant as part of a total energy system. (By courtesy: Weir-Westgarth Ltd.)

	Low-eff. plant	High-eff. plant
32,000 ft³/day (900 m³/day)	$430,000	$570,000
80,000 ft³/day (2250 m³/day)	$720,000	$900,000
160,000 ft³/day (4500 m³/day)	$1,240,000	$1,440,000

When fuel costs are high, it is obviously better to use a high-efficiency plant in spite of the increased capital costs of such a plant, while when fuel costs are low, as in the case when waste heat is being utilised, low-efficiency plants are better from the commercial point of view.

CHAPTER 2

PRINCIPAL PRIME MOVERS USED IN TOTAL ENERGY PRODUCTION

FOR many aspects of total energy production, one tends to use smaller plants than are generally used for the large-scale production of electricity for which the steam turbine reigns supreme. The following summarise the main prime movers used for total energy production.

A. THE DIESEL ENGINE[92, 105]

The diesel engine is available in almost any size, and during 1965 at least two companies, Sulzer Bros. of Switzerland and Götaverken of Sweden, brought out diesel generating units with capacities of around 1000 horsepower (0·746 MW) per cylinder so that an 18-cylinder diesel of this type produces no less than 13 MW. Most diesel engines use light distillate oils, but high and medium engines can be run on fuel gases. Under such circumstances it is common to call the engine a "gas engine". Diesel engines can be started quickly, have a low first cost and are both efficient and reliable.

They are commonly subdivided into low-speed, medium-speed and high-speed units.

Low-speed units with up to 300 rpm weigh about 100 lb/bhp (60 kg/kW), have the highest efficiencies, lowest oil consumption and wear rate, and incur the least expenditure on repair and maintenance.

High-speed diesel sets generally run at between 700 rpm and 1800 rpm and may weigh as little as 12 lb/bhp (7·4 kg/kW). Such sets can now be used for capacities of up to 2·5 MW and the trend is nowadays for the number of revolutions/minute to go up. The biggest plants of all tend to run at intermediate speeds, use heavy fuel oil and give extremely good characteristics from the point of view of long periods between

25

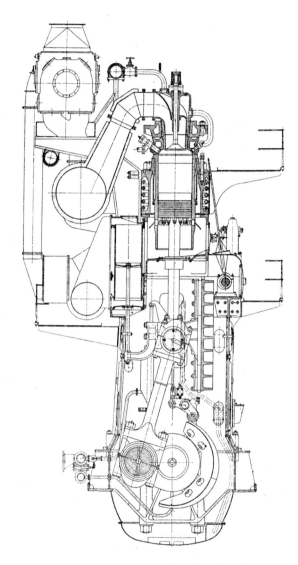

Fig. 2.1. Section through an 850-mm bore diesel engine. (By courtesy:
Gotaverken AB, Sweden).

refits. For emergency duties, where compactness of design and low capital costs are of the greatest importance, one tends to use very high speeds, 1800 rpm not being uncommon.

Diesel engines run on either a two-stroke or on a four-stroke cycle. The former is the simpler and reduces the space requirements and capital costs, but at the expense of lower running efficiency. Two-stroke engines are almost universally adopted for very large units, as in such a case there is very little difference in overall efficiency.

The engines are either naturally aspirated or supercharged. Supercharging and the fitting of an air cooler can increase the power output from an engine by 50% and improves the efficiency by up to 4%. Almost all diesel engines of 1000 kW and more are supercharged nowadays.

Efficiency of Diesel Engines[145]

Diesel engines are less efficient when used at high altitudes and also if the cooling fluid, whether air or water, is warmer than usual.

The mean electricity generating efficiency of an average diesel plant is between 31% and 37% provided the plant is of a reasonable size. Small diesel engines are less efficient, a 30 kW plant usually averaging about 25%. In general, for medium-size plants, a two-stroke engine is 4–5% less efficient than a four-stroke engine. For every 1000 ft above 500 ft elevation (300 m above 150 m) 3·5% is deducted from the efficiency of naturally aspirated engines and 2·5% is deducted from the efficiency of supercharged engines.

Similarly, an increase of 9°F (5°C) in the temperature of the cooling water above 80°F (27°C) causes a reduction in efficiency of between 2% and 3% depending upon degree of supercharging used.

Space requirements vary between 1 ft²/kW installed (0·1 m²/kW), and 20 ft³ (0·56 m³) for larger installations and up to 3 ft²/kW (0·3 m²/kW) with the same volume requirement for very small installations.

Costs

The capital cost of diesel generating sets per kW output falls as the

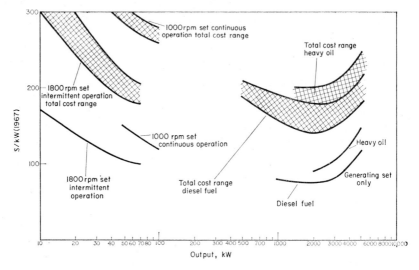

Fig. 2.2. Typical costs of diesel generating plant (1967).

size of the plant increases, but only up to a point. The lowest cost is found with sets between 1 and 3MW capacity, where the cost in 1967 was about $75–90 per kW output. Larger sets are more expensive per kW output, as are sets which use bunker C fuel (heavy oil) instead of diesel oil (Fig. 2.2). Typical costs of complete plants including buildings but excluding interest during construction are as follows (1967).

(a) 1800 rpm set running intermittently with a capacity of 10,000 kW, $300–380 per kW.

(b) 1800 rpm set as before but with a capacity of 70,000 kW, $180–200 per kW.

(c) 1000 rpm set operated continuously with a acapacity of 70,000 kW, $270–300 per kW.

(d) 2 MW set burning diesel oil $140–180 per kW.

(e) 2 MW set burning heavy oil (Bunker C), $180–200 per kW.

Most diesel engines are written off in between 10 and 20 years, the shorter period applying to high-speed engines. Most of the running costs are direct fuel charges, as maintenance charges, especially on slow-running diesels, are not high.

B. PETROL-(GASOLENE) DRIVEN PLANTS

Such plants are not widely used for current generation purposes, as their only real advantages are initial cheapness and light weight. They, however, suffer from so many disadvantages as against diesel engines that these are readily discounted.

    (a) The efficiency of petrol engines is only about half of that of an equivalent diesel engine.

    (b) Fuel costs are higher due to heavy taxation in most countries.

    (c) It is generally necessary to have a complete overhaul of the engine after 3000 hours of use and to scrap it after 6000 hours.

    (d) It requires better cooling than equivalent diesel engines.

    (e) The fuel is much more inflammable than diesel fuel and in consequence great care must be taken in storage.

Petrol engines are therefore only generally used for prime-mover purposes when low weight is of the overriding importance, and when the load factor is very low, i.e. for very rare stand-by purposes.

C. GAS TURBINE GENERATING PLANTS[40, 85, 106, 122, 128-9, 131]

The gas turbine is able to use a wide variety of fuels, is much more compact than an equivalent diesel engine and in consequence needs less money spending on foundations and buildings. Gas turbines do not need any cooling water and for this reason such engines are more suitable for arid countries than diesel engines, which are generally water cooled. The smallest gas turbines are no bigger than equivalent diesel plants, but it is also possible to manufacture gas turbines in sizes of 100 MW and bigger.

Gas turbines fall into two basic categories, the "open"-cycle gas turbine and the "closed"-cycle variety. In the former the combustion gases from the burning of the fuel pass through the different parts of the equipment, while in the latter, the turbine is driven by a separate circuit of gases, which are simply heated by the combustion gases via a heat exchanger.

The advantages of open-cycle gas turbines are very much lower capital cost, while closed-gas turbines have special applications where it is absolutely essential to keep the turbine free from contaminating deposits. Such gas turbines are often used in connection with nuclear power generation, and will be treated in detail in Chapter 6. Closed-cycle gas turbines are also used for firing such fuels as solid fuel, pulverised coal or peat.

The normal gas turbine used is, however, the open-cycle type. Waste-heat recovery on such turbines can be as high as 75%, using waste-heat boilers on the exhaust side.

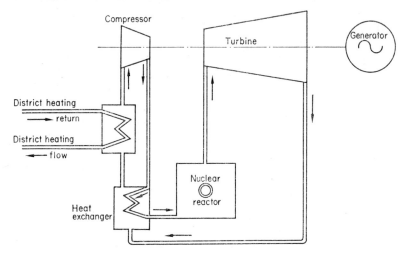

FIG. 2.3. Closed-cycle gas turbine with nuclear energy heating.

The output and the efficiency of gas turbines is improved considerably by the installation of certain auxiliary components such as reheating of the exhausted gases and cooling of the partially compressed gases. Part of the heat of the exhaust gases may be recuperated in a heat exchanger and returned to the air before it enters the compression chamber. Generally speaking, most of these refinements are only used with sets rather bigger than the average. Recuperation also affects the time taken for start-up. A simple open-cycle gas turbine can be started up in between 5–12 minutes while a recuperative type of plant may need up to half an hour to obtain peak output.

Gas turbines are made in single- and multiple-shaft types. In the former both turbine and compressor are mounted on a single shaft, and the electrical generator is driven directly from this shaft. In the

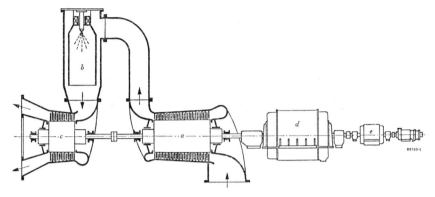

FIG. 2.4. Section through a single shaft gas turbine. (By courtesy: Brown-Boveri Ltd.)

two-shaft turbines one turbine unit is coupled to the air compressor and the other turbine is coupled to the electrical generator. The former is simpler and cheaper while the latter has a higher efficiency.

In the concentric shaft-drive system two compressors and their turbines are mounted coaxially on two shafts. One passes through the other so that the external turbine drives the external compressor and the internal turbine drives the inner compressor.

Gas turbines usually run at up to 27,000 rpm, so that it is usually necessary to provide gearing for driving the electrical generating equipment. Fuels used in gas turbines vary widely: they can be run on natural gas, methane, waste industrial gases, sewage methane, light oil distillate and heavy-grade oils. Any liquid fuels must always be converted into gases by preburning them in a combustion chamber.

When liquid fuels are used, the presence of vanadium, sodium and sulphur must be avoided, as these elements cause damage to turbine blades. High ash content of fuel oils is also harmful as the ash may be deposited on the blades. This effect can be minimised sometimes by adding silicon to the fuel as "Perolin" to raise the melting point of the ash.

Efficiency of Gas Turbines[26, 30]

A gas turbine works at its most efficient when the temperature of

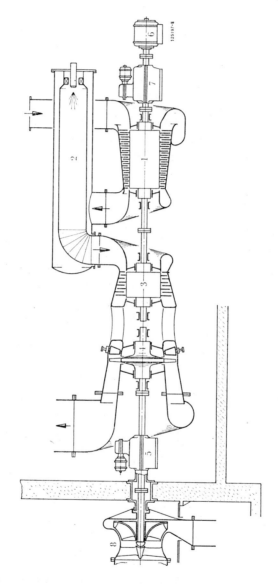

FIG. 2.5. Section through a split-shaft gas turbine; 1 = Compressor; 2 = Combustion chamber; 3 = Turbine; 4 = Power turbine; 5 and 7 = Bearing pedestals, barring gear, oil pump and the speed regulator drive; 6 = Starting motor; 8 = Pump. (By courtesy: Brown-Boveri Ltd.)

heat intake is high and the temperature of heat rejection is low. The limit of heat intake lies in the nature of the metals from which the turbine blades are constructed. For continuously operating plants the inlet temperature is usually no more than 1300–1470°F (700–800°C), but for plants which work on intermittent cycles, higher temperatures may be permitted. These can work with inlet temperatures of between 1650–1800°F (900°C and 980°C). The turbine inlet temperatures are also affected by the compression ratio of the air compressor, which operates at 44–88 psig (3–6 bar (g)) for single-shaft turbines and from 145–290 psig (10–20 bar(g)) for two-shaft turbines. The amount of air that is compressed is usually between 4 and 5 times the stoichiometric quantity required for the combustion of the fuel. Closed-cycle gas turbines work at much higher pressures than open-cycle gas turbines. Inlet temperatures are usually around 1300°F (700°C) and inlet pressures are around 730 psig (59 bar(g)) with an exhaust pressure of around 75 psig (5 bar(g)). The following efficiencies are normally quoted for typical gas turbines:

Simple open-cycle gas plants: 15–23%.

Recuperative open-cycle gas plants: 21–27%.

Two-shaft plants with intercoolers, recuperators and reheat: 32–33%.

Closed-cycle gas turbines: 30–33%.

The efficiency is subject to derating, as the above values are given for ambient air temperatures of 59°F (15°C) and sea level. For every 1000 ft (300 m) above sea level the turbine is derated by $3\frac{1}{2}$% and for every °C above 59°F (15°C) the turbine is derated by approximately 1%.

The principal factor which affects the useful life of a gas turbine is the "creep" in the turbine blades. The life is estimated at anything between 10,000 hours and 100,000 hours depending upon operating conditions. In general, turbines used continuously should be run at a lower speed than turbines which are used intermittently. On the other hand, repeated starting and stopping of gas turbines affects the number of hours between major overhauls.

Gas turbines, in general, require about quarter to half the floor space required by an equivalent diesel engine.

Capital costs vary considerably and the range of costs per kW output applying in 1967 is given in Fig. 2.6. In addition one must add about 10% to the cost of a plant using heavy oil. Continuously loaded plants cost about 10% more and peak-load plants cost about 10% less than the standard price.

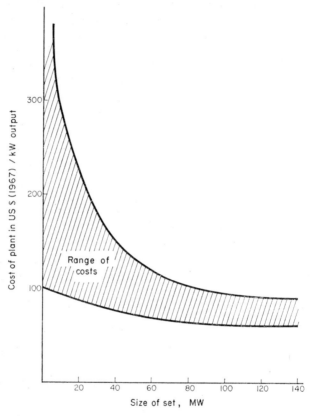

FIG. 2.6. Cost of gas turbine power generating plant (complete) (1967).

The life expectancy of a gas turbine is about the same as that of a diesel engine, namely about 15 to 20 years, continuously loaded plants usually last longer than intermittent service plants. The biggest factor in the running costs is fuel, but reblading, which has to be carried out at regular intervals, is also an expensive item. This is often carried out by the manufacturer of the turbine at a fixed annual charge.

D. FREE PISTON GENERATING PLANTS

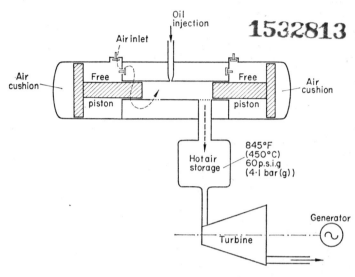

Fig. 2.7. Free-piston gas engine.

In the case of the free-piston generating plant, there are two loose pistons, which take the place of the compressor and combustion chamber of a gas turbine to convert all kinds of fuels into hot gases able to drive an associated gas turbine. In consequence the free-piston gas engine takes the place of the compressor and combustion chamber of a more conventional gas turbine. A combined free-piston generating plant and gas turbine has about the same efficiency as a diesel engine, which is higher than that of a straight-run gas turbine, yet its weight and cost picture is closer to that of a gas turbine. In the free-piston gas generator there are no connecting rods, cranks, etc., and the pistons act directly upon cushions of air. There is normally a degree of super-charge of between 44 and 73 psig (3 and 5 bar(g)) and in consequence there is sometimes trouble with piston rings and lubricants. In general, a free-piston generator needs the same amount of money spending on repairs as a normal diesel engine, but the oil consumption is higher due to the absence of a sump. Free-piston plants have been made in sizes between 1 and 26 MW, but the small plants do not usually compete effectively with diesel engines. A typical 6 MW gas turbine can be fed by between 8 to 9 gasifiers and, for example, at Chartres, France, twelve large twin-piston gasifiers serve a single turbine which is rated at 20 MW for continuous operation. Free-piston gas generators operate at piston speeds 1450–2130 ft/min (450–650 m/min), which corresponds to about 350 cycles per minute when idling to 600 c/min under full load with a typical 14 in. (340 mm) bore unit.

Gas turbines which are fed by free-piston generators operate at a lower temperature than straight gas turbines, i.e. at around 930°F (500°C) instead of up to 1300°F (700°C) as is usual with normal gas turbines. In consequence it is possible to use fuel adulterated with some sulphur, sodium and vanadium, which would be quite impossible to use in straight gas turbines. Up to 5% sulphur in fuel is permitted and can be used without any adverse affect upon the turbine blades.

Free-piston engines use water-cooled cylinders and compression heads, while pistons are oil cooled. The total water requirement is about 40 ft³ (1·1 m³) of water per minute per megawatt of plant rating, using an inlet water temperature of 86°F (30°C). The total amount of heat to be removed by the cooling system equals about one-seventh of the heat content of the fuel. This heat can naturally be used for total energy purposes.

Efficiency of Free Piston/Gas Turbine Plant

The efficiency of a free-piston/gas turbine plant at full load may reach 38%, or 36% if expressed in terms of electricity actually produced, considering the net calorific value of the fuel. Smaller plants have efficiencies of between 32–34%. A free-piston gas engine is derated in exactly the same way as a normal diesel plant with respect to altitude and temperature. Space requirements of free piston/gas turbines are between those of diesel engines and straight gas turbines. In many other respects too they occupy a similar in-between position between diesels and gas turbines.

Costs in the case of free-piston/gas turbine plants are rather higher than those applying to straight gas turbine plants especially when the plant is small, when they also cannot compete with diesel engines.

At large capacities, i.e. above about 2 MW, the free-piston/gas turbine plant has the edge over diesel engines, although it is more expensive than a gas turbine on its own. As, however, the free-piston unit has a higher efficiency, and is able to burn poorer fuel, this is probably its best applicability. The range of costs (1967 prices) is given in Fig. 2.8.

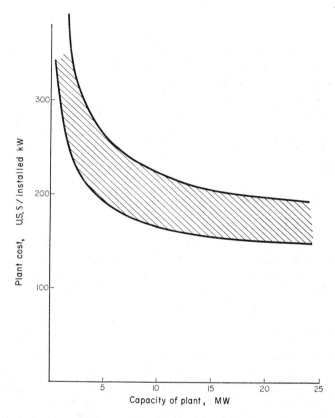

Fig. 2.8. Range of costs of complete free-piston/gas turbine installation (1967).

The top line corresponds to a single turbo set, while the bottom line corresponds to a triple turbo set. If the plant is to be used with heavy oil (Bunker C) the costs rise by about 6%.

In general, the free-piston gasifiers are considered to have the same life expectancy as medium-speed highly supercharged diesels. This means that they will have to be written off in somewhat under 15 years. The gas turbines have a life expectancy of about 20 years so that the write-off period of the combined plant is usually assumed as being 17 years.

E.   THE STIRLING ENGINE[108-9]

Although the principle of the Stirling engine was first invented by the Rev. Robert Stirling in 1816, comparatively little work had been done on this important principle until a few years ago. Development is proceeding at present at the Philips Research Laboratories, Eindhoven, Holland, to develop units with power outputs of up to 400 brake horse power (300 kW) and more per cylinder. The author herewith acknowledges the aid given to him by the Philips organisation in writing this section.

Method of Operation

In the Stirling engine thermal energy is converted into mechanical energy by first compressing an enclosed quantity of working gas at a low temperature, and after heating it allowing it to expand at a high temperature (around 1400°F (700°C)). As the piston which closes the gas-filled working space needs to do less work to compress the gas at a lower temperature than is liberated when the gas expands at a higher temperature, there is a net gain in mechanical energy from the engine.

The difference in temperature of the gas is obtained by dividing the working space into a cold and a hot section, between which the gas is moved by the displacer piston (Fig. 2.9). The two spaces communicate with each other through a number of channels, which are heated on the hot side of the engine, and cooled on the cold side. When the gas flows from the hot space to the cold space, the heat contained in the gas would be lost if there were no regenerator between the two heat exchangers. The regenerator consists of a porous fine-meshed metal mass and serves to store this heat to be given up again when the gas reverses its direction. Thus it now only becomes necessary to provide heat to the heater and to remove heat from the cooler to obtain continuous operation of the

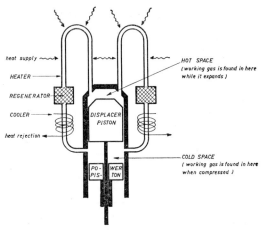

FIG. 2.9. Principle of displacer type Stirling engine, (By courtesy: Philips, Eindhoven.)

process. As the system is a closed cycle process, any source of heat can be used for the purpose. Sources of heat which might be usefully employed in the Stirling cycle include fossil fuels, nuclear and solar energy, or other sources of heat. The movement of the working piston and displacer govern the course of the Stirling process, which is shown in Fig. 2.10.

Stage 1. All the gas is contained in the cold space.

Stage 2. The working piston has been displaced and the gas has been compressed at low temperature.

Stage 3. The displacer has shifted the gas from the cold to the hot space.

Stage 4. The hot gas has expanded. Once this has happened, the displacer causes the gas to flow back to the cold space thus returning to the starting situation.

This then is the basic principle which was established by Stirling, the realization of which only lead to bulky and inefficient engines until a few years ago.

Practical Details of the Philips Stirling Engine[125, 147]

In order to overcome the inherent difficulties associated with the engine, the so-called "rhombic drive" method was developed. This

C

TOTAL ENERGY

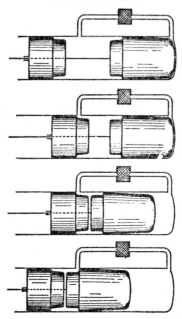

FIG. 2.10. Cycle of Stirling engine. (By courtesy: Philips, Eindhoven.)

drive allows the piston system to be used in combination with a crank-case at atmospheric pressure. In order to relieve the drive of dead forces, a buffer space of about constant mean pressure may be added underneath the power piston. The linear movement of the coaxial piston and displacer rods is also a favourable factor with respect to the sealing. The rhombic drive provides a further advantage in that even a single-cylinder engine is perfectly balanced. The low noise level conferred by continuous combustion and the gradual pressure cycle, which is almost sinusoidal, combine to make the engine very smooth running indeed. The working gas used is either hydrogen or helium, because these gases are close to ideality and are the most favourable as flow losses are least, while heat-transfer characteristics are good. The average pressure inside the engine is 1600 psig (110 bar (g)) and the cyclic variation which takes place is between 2000 psig (140 bar(g)) and 1150 psig (80 bar(g)). External heat exchangers are used. Figure 2.13 shows a section through a typical prototype engine.

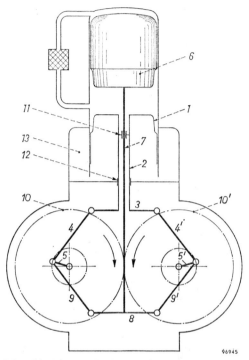

FIG. 2.11. Rhombic drive mechanism. Basic principle. 1 = power piston; 6 = displacer piston; 5-5′ = cranks in two shafts rotating in opposite senses and coupled by gears 10-10′; 4-4′ = con-rods pivoted from ends of yoke 3 fixed to the hollow power-piston rod 2; 9-9′ = con-rods pivoted from ends of yoke 8 fixed to displacer-piston rod, which runs through the hollow power-piston rod. 11 and 12 = gas-tight stuffing-boxes; 13 = buffer space containing gas at high buffer pressure. (By courtesy: Philips, Eindhoven.)

Sealing

One of the most difficult problems to be solved was the question of piston sealing. The Philips prototype engine uses a so-called "roll sock" consisting of an elastic rolling diaphragm A (Fig. 2.14) mounted between the piston rod B (or piston) and the bottom C (or wall) of the cylinder. The roll sock is sustained by oil, whose pressure P_0 is regulated by the regulating valve E at about 73 psig (5 bar(g)) below the varying

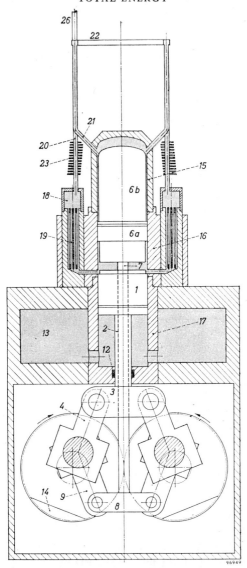

FIG. 2.12. Rhombic drive mechanism. Engineering design. Hydrogen-filled
sections shaded. Burner and preheater absent. 1 = power piston; 6a and
6b = displacer piston and insulating dome; 12 = power-piston stuffing-
box. 13 = buffer chamber. 14 = counterweights. 15, 16, 17 = cylinder in
which power piston and displacer piston move. 18 = regenerator compart-
ments; 19 = cooler compartment; 20, 21, 22 = heater tubes; 23 = fins;
26 = tube for temperature probe. Other figures as in Fig. 2.11. (By
courtesy: Philips, Eindhoven.)

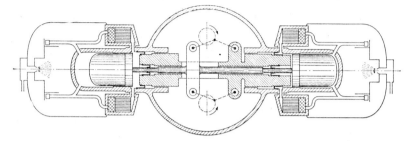

FIG. 2.13. Section through horizontally opposed Stirling engine. (By courtesy: Philips, Eindhoven.)

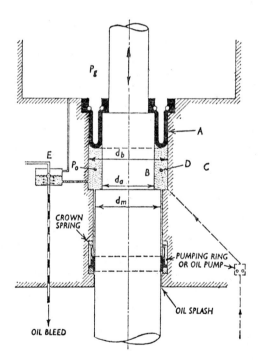

FIG. 2.14. Rollsock rolling diaphragm used with Stirling engine. (By courtesy, Philips, Eindhoven.)

gas pressure Pg which acts on the upper side. In order to avoid extra elongation of the roll sock with a constant oil volume, the diameters are chosen so that $d^2 = \frac{1}{2}d_a^2 + d_b^2$. The displacement of the bottom area of space D compensates the displacement of the roll sock A, which carries out only half the piston stroke. The pump arrangement provides

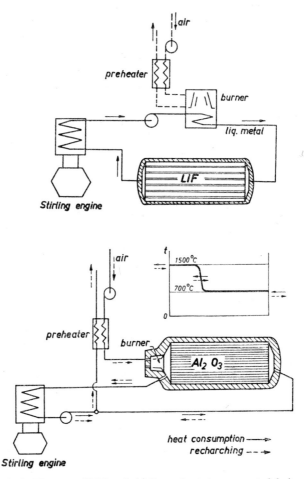

FIG. 2.15. The use of LiF and Al₂O₃ as heat-storage materials in conjunction with Stirling engine. (By courtesy: Philips, Eindhoven.)

oil refreshment and the possibility of regulating the pressure difference by bleeding oil via the regulating valve. With such seals reproducible lifetimes of more than 10,000 hours at 1500 rpm can be obtained.

Efficiency of Stirling Engine

Assuming that standard 18·8 chromium nickel steels are used for the hot parts which limits the temperature and pressure conditions to 1300°F and 1600 psig (700°C and 110 bar(g)), a 670 kW Stirling engine running at 525 rpm has an overall efficiency of 43·5% as against around 30% of a similar diesel engine. At the same time the Stirling engine only occupies approximately 60% of the space occupied by the diesel. With newer creep and heat-resisting alloys it is possible to operate the engine at temperatures up to 1470°F and 3200 psig (800°C and 220 bar(g)). Under such circumstances efficiencies of up to 50% may well be obtainable.

Stirling Engine Combined with Heat Storage

Because of the fact that the Stirling engine uses a closed cycle, it is possible to provide the heat to drive it from a variety of sources. A promising use of the engine is to operate it together with a heat-storage system. The heat-storage system uses either aluminium oxide or lithium fluoride. Aluminium oxide is capable of being heated to a very high temperature without fusing. In the case of lithium fluoride a combination of sensible heat and heat of fusion can be used. In addition, the heat-transfer medium, usually molten metal or salt, has a considerable heat-storage capacity as well. It has been calculated that the energy storage capacity of such a system is roughly 10 times that of the lead accumulator, weight for weight. The scope for systems such as these is obviously very wide.

Other Advantages of the Stirling Engine

(a) It requires no lubricating oil.
(b) The exhaust gases from the Stirling engine are much cleaner than those from a diesel engine due to the fact that combustion takes

place continuously at atmospheric pressure and between hot walls.

(c) The engine can be run at a wide range of speeds, with a virtually constant torque.

(d) The Stirling engine starts very reliably.

(e) The engine has no gyroscopic effect, and the engine-power control is well suited either to control the speed or to control the power even to negative values giving a considerable braking effect.

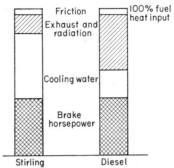

FIG. 2.16. Heat balance comparison between diesel engine and Stirling engine. (By courtesy: Philips, Eindhoven.)

The Use of the Stirling Engine for Total Energy Purposes

The engine has to be cooled efficiently, in that all heat dissipation required for thermodynamic purposes is done by the cooling water. It is obvious that the Stirling engine can be used even more economically if a good use is found for this waste heat. Space heating, space cooling, domestic and industrial hot-water supply all offer such uses. In the diesel engine only some 20% of the heat content of the fuel is passed to the cooling water as against 35% which is driven off with the exhaust gases and which is collected from these only with difficulty. The Stirling engine has 40% of the heat in the form of jacket heat and just over 10% as exhaust heat, obviously making it easier to use for total energy purposes than the diesel.

F. STEAM TURBINES

In a steam turbine feedwater is preheated using bleed heating from the turbine itself, and the preheated feedwater is then passed into the boiler where it is heated using a wide variety of fuels. Steam boilers are today fuelled by solid coal, pulverised coal, pulverised and dried peat, burning refuse, oil, gas, geothermic heat and nuclear power. In comparison with other types of generating plant the steam turbine has the advantage of extreme reliability, much lower repair and maintenance costs per kWh than for either diesels or gas turbines, and a longer expectation of life than is found for competing plant.

On the other hand, a steam turbine takes much longer to build than either a gas turbine or diesels, and it takes a very long time to put into operation. Finally, its greatest disadvantage is its requirements of very large quantities of cooling water. This means that unless a site close to a river, a lake or the sea is available, one needs to build cooling towers or spray ponds. Small steam turbines are extremely inefficient and have very high capital costs. Only when steam turbines become very large does the efficiency and capital cost per kW come within the range of competing plants. Basically, therefore steam plants are at their best when made in very large units, the bigger the better. The biggest unit currently in production is the AEI[1] condensing turbine proposed

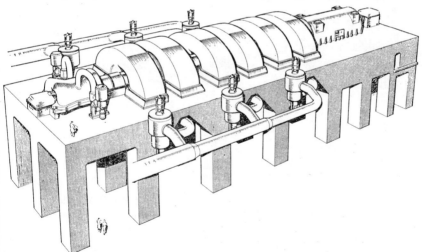

FIG. 2.17. Artists' impression of AEI 1100 MW, 1800 rpm single-axis turbine generator for Consolidated Edison Company, New York. (By courtesy: AEI Ltd., Manchester, England.)

C*

for the Consolidated Edison Company of New York. This turbine
has an output of 1100 MW operating at 1800 rpm and 60 cycles. Its
steam conditions are 950 psig (65 bar(g)) (saturated). The turbine has a
double-flow high-pressure cylinder followed by three double-flow

FIG. 2.18. Baumann exhaust system as used with the AEI 1100 MW steam
turbine. (By courtesy: AEI Ltd., Manchester, England.)

low-pressure cylinders. Owing to the fact that wet steam is being produced in the nuclear reactor, which gives rise to erosion problems, the
peripheral blade tip speeds of the last stages are reduced. Water is
removed from the steam by external water separators. Figure 2.18

shows the Baumann multi-exhaust system used. The cost of the turbine itself, less buildings and other auxiliaries, is only $20 per kW (1968), which is a much lower cost than could be achieved using gas turbines, even if it were possible to build a gas turbine of such an enormous size. This turbine is intended to be fed by steam from a boiling-water nuclear reactor.

For the generation of alternating current the speed of direct coupled turbines is dependent upon the cycle employed. For a 50-cycle supply the turbine speed is usually either 3000 or 1500 rpm, while for a 60-cycle supply 3600 or 1800 rpm are used. For sets with a capacity below about 5000 kW, gearing is used and the number of revolutions by minute are increased. Speeds of between 5000 and 10,000 rpm are then quite usual.

With most conventional steam turbines there is a so-called "stator" which has fixed blades and a "rotor" which possesses movable blades. As the steam passes from the high-pressure end of the turbine to the low-pressure end it flows alternatively through fixed and moving blades. A special design, developed by the Swede Ljungström, uses no stators but two sets of rotors which run in opposite directions. In this the steam enters the turbine blade system from the middle, and flows radially outwards, The effects of this is to double the relative rotational speed between the blade systems, thus giving a far more compact and efficient design than the more conventional stator/rotor system.

Steam Conditions and their Effect on Efficiencies

To obtain the maximum current-generating efficiency in a steam turbine system it is essential to work with as high an input pressure as possible, exhausting the steam at the condensing side at the lowest practical pressure and temperature.

Unfortunately it is quite impracticable to use high steam temperatures and pressures with small turbine systems, As a rough approximation one can state that with any given machine the operating efficiency increases by 1% for every 29°F (16°C) rise in steam temperature and by 1% for every 10% increase in steam pressure. When given steam conditions apply, doubling of the set size improves the efficiency of generation by roughly ½%. In very large steam turbines reheating of steam after it has passed through the high-pressure stage of the turbine becomes feasible, which improves the efficiency of the turbine and also increases the life of the turbine blades. Reheating is, however, seldom carried out on sets with a capacity below 100 MW.

Table 2.1 gives the recommended British standards of steam conditions employed with 50 cycle turboalternator sets running at 3000 rpm.

TABLE 2.1

Turbine output, MW	Steam pressure psig. bar gauge		Steam temp./ maximum °F °C		Feed-water temp. °F °C	
10	400	(28)	810	(430)	300	(150)
20	600	(41)	850	(455)	340	(170)
60	900	(63)	910	(490)	375	(190)
100	1500	(103)	1060	(570)	410	(210)
200	2350	(163)	1060	(570)	460	(238)

The number of feedwater heaters varies from three for the smallest set, up to six for the sets with a capacity of 100 MW or more. With normal condensing sets the exhaust pressures are usually standardised at between 1 to 2 in. of mercury absolute (34–68 mbar). In the United States alternator sets usually run at 60 cycles and 3600 rpm. However, the average steam pressure and temperature conditions are fairly similar to the ones used in Great Britain. Most American turbines are exhausted at 1·5 in. of mercury absolute (50 mbar).

Cooling Water Requirements

In normal condensing stations the quantity of cooling water required varies between 180 ft³ (1150 litres) of water per minute per MW for very small plants (about 1 MW) down to 60 ft³ (385 litres) water per MW and minute for plants with a capacity in excess of 600 MW. When cooling towers are used, the cooling water is recycled and losses amount to about $1\frac{1}{2}$–$2\frac{1}{2}$% of the quantity circulated. Cooling using cooling towers or spray ponds is very much more expensive than using direct seawater or river-water cooling.

For all reasonably sized steam sets, small quantities of steam are bled off along the length of the turbine and used to heat up the feed-water. This is not, however, used with very small steam sets or where fuel is particularly cheap or the loading is very low.

The efficiency of a steam turbine is very markedly dependent upon the size of the set.

Table 2.2 gives the range of efficiencies of typical steam plants.

TABLE 2.2

Very large plants:	capacity in excess of 100 MW	31–40%
Large plants:	capacity between 50 and 100 MW	27–34%
Medium plants:	capacity between 10 and 50 MW	22–31%
Small plants:	capacity between 1 and 10 MW	17–24%

Plants smaller than this in capacity are largely obsolete now except for certain specialised cases where power generation is not the main purpose. In general, plants with a capacity below one megawatt have efficiencies between $7\frac{1}{2}\%$ and 19% depending upon size and nature of auxiliaries.

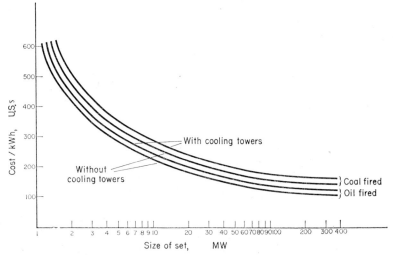

FIG. 2.19. Cost of construction of complete power stations using steam turbines (1967).

Cost of Steam Plants

The cost of a steam plant is given in Fig. 2.19. Gas firing of power stations costs about 2% less than oil firing, but to equip a station to use both gas and oil costs 2% more. Oil/coal dual-fired plants cost about 3% more than pure coal-fired stations.

The life expectation of an average steam plant is generally given as between 25 and 35 years, although the latter is rather optimistic in view of the fact that plant tends to become obsolete before it wears out.

CHAPTER 3

STEAM TURBINES AND TOTAL ENERGY

by

A. C. VALENTINE, C.Eng., A.M.I.Mech.E.

W. H. Allen Sons & Co. Ltd., Bedford, England

a member of Amalgamated Power Engineering Ltd.

POWER AS A BY-PRODUCT OF PROCESS STEAM

All factories use electric power and some form of heat. The quantity of each varies widely in different industries.

Many industries use vast quantities of low-pressure steam for heating purposes. Factories use steam because it has an outstanding ability to convey a large mass of heat from the heat producer or boiler to the heat consumer or processing plant. Steam has a high heat content which it can give up at a constant temperature. It gives up this 'heating heat', or latent heat, as the steam condenses back into water in the process heat exchanger. Most heat exchangers can make little or no use of superheat in the steam. Process steam is therefore normally only heated to temperatures giving, say, 20°F (11°C) superheat, to provide steam at a dry saturated state at the heat exchanger.

A modern industrial plant using low-pressure steam for process and heating can make efficient use of slightly more than 80% of the heat in the fuel, assuming the condensate returns from the process to the boiler feed system. This is because the latent heat is fully utilised.

The larger public power stations, on the other hand, cannot convert more than approximately 30% of the heat in the fuel into electrical power in condensing turbines. Allowing 12% losses in the boiler house, this means that 58%, or more than half the heat in the original fuel, passes into the condenser cooling water and is lost. This is really an oversimplification of the heat distribution, because modern power

53

stations have multi-stage feed-heating and re-heat cycles. However, it indicates that the greater part of the available heat is lost because a steam turbine cannot make appreciable use of the latent heat.

The overall thermal efficiency of generation by all the Central Electricity Generating Board stations in 1967 was only 27·87%. Even the latest design of very high-pressure stations incorporating 550-MW turbo-alternators have an overall cycle efficiency of only 39% at 100% load factor. This figure reduces to 37·5% when the stations are operating as base-load units.

All factories using reasonable quantities of low-pressure process steam can also use this steam as a power tool as well as a heating tool. The plant is quite straightforward. A new boiler raises steam at a substantially higher pressure than the factory heating process requires. This steam passes through a turbine where it expands, in several stages, from the boiler pressure to the exhaust pressure, which is determined by the process heating requirements. The turbine rotor converts the kinetic energy of expansion into mechanical energy. The rotor shaft drives an alternator which in turn changes the mechanical energy into electrical energy.

The turbine exhaust steam passes on to the heating process where it gives up its latent heat. This arrangement uses both the "power heat" and "heating heat" in the steam. With the combined cycle using a pure back-pressure turbine, part of the heat in the steam supplied to the turbine is converted into electrical energy in the turbo-alternator; the heat left in the exhaust steam is partly consumed in the process heat exchanger, the remainder returning to the cycle as condensate heat.

It will be appreciated that because the process consumes the latent heat in the exhaust steam, only combustion, mechanical, electrical and radiation losses occur in the cycle, which consequently has an overall efficiency of between 70% and 80% dependent upon the cycle conditions and particularly condensate recovery. The combined power and process steam plant is therefore more than twice as efficient as the condensing turbo-alternator plant.

Naturally, to accommodate the heat drop through the turbine, the high-pressure boiler uses more fuel than the low-pressure boiler supplying steam direct to the process. The value of the net power generated, allowing for the increased power consumed by auxiliary plant, more than offsets the cost of this additional fuel and shows a quick return on the capital expenditure of the power plant. In this way a factory can produce power at a very low cost; in most cases for a figure lower than it can purchase power from the public electricity supply authority.

BASIC THERMODYNAMICS

The supreme advantage of steam as a means of taking heat to a process is that it can give up all its relatively enormous latent or 'heating' heat at a single temperature. Also by controlling the process steam pressure, this temperature can be accurately fixed.

When steam gives up its heat in a coil or jacket it condenses and gives up its latent heat while the sensible heat is left in the condensate. Steam tables show that as the steam pressure falls, the latent heat increases and sensible or water heat reduces. As an example, steam at 50 psig (3.45 bar(g)) has a latent heat of 912 Btu/lb (2130 kJ/kg) while steam at 5 psig (0·345 bar(g)) has a latent heat of 961 Btu/lb (2245 kJ/kg). This lower pressure steam has 5·37% more Btu/lb of latent heat which it can readily give up to the process. This means that if the plant can accept heating steam at 5 psig (0·345 bar(g)) instead of 50 psig (3·45 bar(g)) it would use 5% less steam.

It follows that every effort should be made to use steam at the lowest possible pressure.

There are installations which cannot take advantage of this useful steam property. The heating surface in the plant may be too small to give a proper heat-transfer rate. Some processes require a certain minimum temperature and the pressure must be high enough to give such special temperature.

In plant employing direct contact heating the steam gives up both latent and sensible heat, and the pressure is fixed to give the desired final temperature of the mixture.

When considering power as a by-product from process steam, the same fundamental law applies to the steam turbine that applies to all other heat engines, i.e.

heat in steam entering turbine	=	heat in steam leaving turbine	+	heat equivalent of energy used in turbine

TOTAL ENERGY

The back-pressure steam turbine, which passes all its exhaust steam heat on to the process, is therefore unique among heat engines, because it generates power at nearly ideal efficiency. Internal losses in the turbine are only lost to power generation and pass on to process as increased heat in the exhaust steam.

The heat drop in the turbine represents energy converted into useful power plus the energy needed to make up the irrecoverable losses due to bearing friction, external leakages from casing glands, radiation, gear-

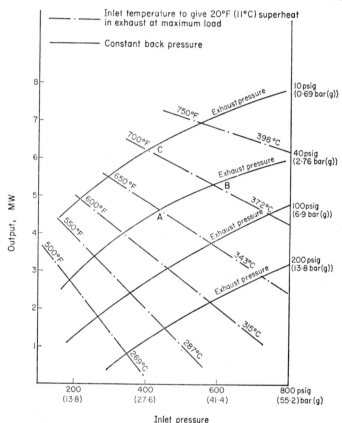

FIG. 3.1. Graph showing variation in inlet steam conditions with output to give 20°F (11°C) superheat in the exhaust with 120,000 lb/hr (54,400 kg/hr) flow.

ing and generation losses. The sum of these losses is nearly always less than 10%.

Although the back-pressure turbine generates power at nearly the ideal efficiency, the magnitude of that power obtainable from a given steam flow is rigidly determined by:

(a) supply steam temperature;
(b) supply steam pressure;
(c) exhaust or process steam pressure;
(d) turbine internal efficiency.

An increase in the ratio; supply steam pressure/exhaust steam pressure gives an increase in available power. These two pressures are of vital importance when designing a process steam installation. Sometimes one of the pressures is unalterably fixed by existing plant. At other times they can both be varied over wide limits subject to economic considerations.

The most obvious way of increasing the pressure ratio is to raise the supply pressure if a new boiler is being contemplated. However, a reduction of the exhaust pressure can produce a much greater gain.

This can readily be proved in theory with heat-drop diagrams on a Mollier (total heat/entropy) chart. However, as the average works engineer normally has little need to retain familiarity with the Mollier chart, this fact is illustrated graphically in Fig. 3.1. This graph shows how the output from a turbine designed to pass 120,000 lb/hr (54,500 kg/hr) varies with different inlet/exhaust pressure ratios, to give a constant 20°F (11°C) superheat in the exhaust steam.

At point A, representing inlet steam conditions of 400 psig (27·6 bar(g)), 630°F (332°C) and an exhaust pressure of 40 psig, (2·76 bar(g)) i.e. an absolute pressure ratio of 7·55, the turbo-alternator output is 4·450 kW. If the exhaust pressure remains unaltered but the inlet pressure increases to 600 psig (41·4 bar(g)), point B, with an absolute pressure ratio of 11·2, the turbo-alternator output increases to 5450 kW. However, if the inlet pressure remains at 400 psig (27·6 bar(g)) and the exhaust pressure reduces to 10 psig (0·69 bar(g)), point C, the absolute pressure ratio increases to 16·6 and the turbo-alternator output increases to 6200 kW.

It will be appreciated, therefore, that it is advantageous to both process heating and power generation to keep the turbine exhaust pressure as low as possible.

The power available from the turbine for a given pressure ratio is proportional to the inlet steam temperature. Although Fig. 3.1 does not illustrate this point directly, because it is drawn to provide a constant 20°F (11°C) superheat in the exhaust steam, it does illustrate another important point; namely, that as the inlet pressure increases, with a fixed exhaust pressure, the inlet temperature also increases to maintain the same exhaust condition. The ratio—steam supply temperature/steam exhaust temperature—remains constant for a given steam pressure ratio and a constant turbine efficiency. Therefore, an increase in the inlet steam temperature to produce more power, correspondingly increases the exhaust steam temperature. This results in higher superheat at the turbine exhaust branch, necessitating the addition of some desuperheating water to reduce the temperature to give 20°F (11°C) superheat. Although this has the effect of reducing the total steam flow through the back-pressure turbine by the volume of water added at the exhaust, there is a net gain in power generation.

The fourth factor—optimum turbine internal efficiency—is a function of rotor diameter, rotational speed and number of stages to suit the selected steam conditions. For a given set of steam conditions there is an optimum turbine rotational speed. The ratio—blade speed/steam speed—gives maximum efficiency for an impulse stage when it is between 0·48 and 0·54. The heat drop through the stage fixes the steam speed, but the blade speed depends on both the blading diameter and the rotor speed. A small rotor diameter and high rotational speed, in relation to volume flow, improves the turbine internal efficiency, by reducing internal steam leakages and, by the use of longer blades, increasing the blading efficiency. Such a turbine design utilises more of the heat in the supply steam and generates more power.

Although it is difficult to generalise due to the large permutations of steam pressures, temperatures and flows possible through a given turbine, a high-speed geared machine is usually more efficient than a direct-coupled machine for the smaller powers and exhaust volume flows. The gain in power more than offsets the gearing losses. At larger powers with larger exhaust volume flows, the direct-coupled sets become more efficient overall.

The following basic rules emerge for the generation of power from process steam:

(1) Use the highest practicable initial pressure and temperature.

(2) Use the lowest practicable exhaust or process pressure.

(3) Use the smallest size of turbine to give optimum internal efficiency.

(4) Never permit a large volume of steam to expand from one pressure to a lower pressure without getting some useful work from the expansion.

THE STEAM POWER RATIO

Industries fall roughly into three groups. Firstly, large steam users whose steam demand enables them to generate more than sufficient power for their needs. Secondly, factories whose process steam and power loads are approximately in balance. Thirdly, those industries whose power requirements are greater than can be met by using back-pressure turbo-alternators. Factories are constantly improving the efficiency of their steam-using processes and making labour-saving improvements which increase power demand. These factories move from the first and second groups to the second and third groups.

An urgent need thus develops for a reassessment of the power supply to the factory if manufacturing costs are to be kept to a minimum. Each individual factory calls for the closest investigation on its own merits to ensure the most economic installation.

TYPES AND COMBINATIONS OF POWER UNITS

There are several types of turbo-alternators available which can reconcile the widely varying steam and power demands of different factories. These can be used individually or in combination with each other or associated equipment.

The two extreme installations are the straight condensing turbine with an independent supply of process steam. Figures 3.2(a) and (b), and the straight back-pressure turbine Fig. 3.3.

(a) *Condensing Turbines*

A condensing turbine takes steam at boiler pressure and temperature and expands it through the nozzles and blading to a sub-atmospheric pressure or vacuum, where the condenser condenses it to water which

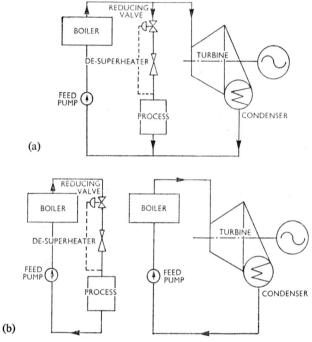

(a)

(b)

FIG. 3.2. Schematic arrangements of condensing turbine with reducing valve supplying process steam, (a) in parallel from a common boiler and (b) from two independent boilers

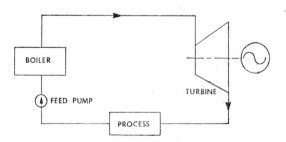

FIG. 3.3. Schematic arrangement of pure back-pressure turbine.

returns to the boiler. The process steam is supplied either from the same boiler, i.e. at a point in the system before the turbine, or from a separate boiler. Although such a system provides maximum flexibility for meeting varying process steam and electrical loads, it is the least efficient. Over 50% of the heat put into the steam entering the turbine is wasted as latent heat taken away in the boiler, and the process steam does no work in the turbine. This system is therefore normally never adopted in a modern works power plant. A possible exception is a plant which raises steam in boilers whose fuel is either waste process material or waste heat.

(b) *Back pressure Turbines*

As explained earlier, the straight back-pressure turbine takes steam from the boiler and produces power by expanding the steam through its stages, before finally exhausting the whole of the steam flow to the heating process. The supply of process steam is thus from a point in the system after the final turbine expansion. This system provides the maximum economy and the simplest installation.

An ideal back-pressure turbo-alternator installation is conditional upon the power demand corresponding to the output obtainable from the available steam flow. In cases where waste-heat boilers are used, it is also conditional upon the demand for low-pressure steam matching the production of high-pressure steam. Such ideals are seldom realised in practice. In fact, in a large number of factories the electrical load and process steam flow fluctuate widely and are out of step with each other. A fall in demand for one or other results of necessity in a deficit in the supply which is meeting the other. One, or a combination, of the following solutions will overcome this difficulty.

(c) *Parallel Operation with the Public Electricity Supply System*

The most flexible arrangement to balance process steam and electrical power demands is for the back-pressure turbo-alternator to run in parallel with the public electricity supply, provided the local electricity authority is agreeable (see Fig. 3.4).

The turbine is pressure-governed to maintain a constant steam pressure at the turbine exhaust branch, irrespective of fluctuation in process steam demand. The pressure governor automatically adjusts the opening of multiple inlet steam control valves, to pass a steam flow corresponding to the process steam demand. The process steam flow thus determines the output generated by the turbo-alternator at all times. When the turbo-alternator produces power in excess of the factory electrical load, the surplus is exported to the public supply system. Conversely, the factory imports any power deficiency.

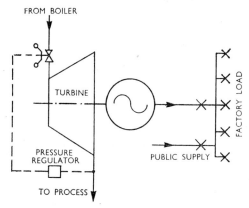

FIG. 3.4. Simple back-pressure turbine in parallel with public supply.

(d) *Back-pressure Turbine with Reducing and Surplus Steam Valves*

A factory using a straight back-pressure turbine to produce power from its process steam flow, but which does not operate in parallel with the public electricity supply system, can balance its steam and power demands with a pressure-reducing valve and/or a surplus steam valve. The reducing valve, with a desuperheater, is connected across the boiler and process steam mains, by-passing the turbine, and the surplus valve on the process steam main (see Fig. 3.5).

The turbine is speed-governed and passes a steam quantity corresponding to the electrical demand. The reducing valve makes up any process steam deficiency and the surplus valve 'blows-off' any surplus steam to atmosphere or to a "dump" condenser. The advantage of a dump condenser is that the surplus steam is condensed and returned to the feed system instead of being lost.

Surplus steam must never be allowed to find its own way out of the system through the exhaust main relief valve. A special surplus valve must be fitted to the exhaust pipework, designed to open and maintain a pressure only fractionally above the process system design pressure. This valve prevents the back pressure on the turbine rising to the relief

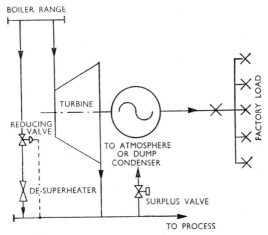

FIG. 3.5. Simple back-pressure turbine with reducing and surplus valves,

valve setting pressure. An increasing back pressure has a cumulative effect of further reducing the amount of power which the turbine generates from the available steam flow and places the system further out of balance.

The use of reducing and surplus valves is the cheapest and simplest method of covering sudden periods of out-of-balance of steam and electrical loads for limited duration. One example is when paper breaks on a paper-making machine; the power demand remains sensibly constant, but the steam demand reduces appreciably for a period of 10 or 15 minutes until the break has been rectified. At first this system may appear uneconomic. Although it is wasteful, it is not necessarily so wasteful as some of the other schemes. Each case must be investigated on its merits to assess costs of blowing off steam against the purchase of power, where this is possible. In cases where the peak out-of-balance is very infrequent and of short duration, it is possible to generate up to nearly one-third of the total power demand by this method at a lower cost than imported power. It is often cheaper than installing a pass-out turbine or separate condensing turbine with the consequent condenser losses.

(e) *Back-pressure Turbine with an Accumulator*

When there is an approximate balance of the mean power and the mean process steam demands, and the fluctuations are frequent and of short duration, consideration can be given to employing a steam accumulator to balance the demands. An accumulator is a large cylindrical vessel, nine-tenths filled with water. It stores steam by condensing it into water and gives up steam by flashing the heat stored in the water into steam at a lower pressure. The storage capacity of an accumulator is dependent upon the pressure difference between the charging and discharging mains.

This method of balancing the power and process steam demands is not used much in modern plants due to the cost and space requirements of the accumulators. The position of the accumulator in the steam system and the method of control of its charging and discharging valves vary widely to suit individual installations.

Figure 3.6 shows an accumulator operating in conjunction with a speed-governed pure back-pressure turbine. The accumulator absorbs steam when the process steam demand is low, and returns steam to the system to meet peak demands. It supplements the turbine exhaust-steam flow in a similar manner to a normal reducing valve, but draws on its storage capacity instead of imposing a peak demand on to the boiler. It thus provides an even boiler firing rate and deletes the necessity for designing the boiler and turbine for the peak process steam demand. The charging valve can be controlled by the pressure in the accumulator in addition to the pressure in the boiler range, to prevent a shortage of steam for the process.

Charging of the accumulator can take place either from the boiler range or an extraction point on the turbine. The latter arrangement is normally adopted for a large pressure ratio between boiler and process pressure, and allows some power to be generated in the turbine, by reducing the pressure drop across the accumulator.

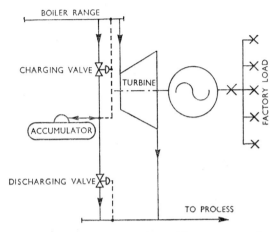

FIG. 3.6. Simple back-pressure turbine with steam accumulator.

(f) *Pass out Condensing Turbines* (*ITOC*)

When the process steam demand is small in relation to the electrical demand or it varies widely throughout the day, a pass-out condensing turbine may provide the best solution. This essentially consists of a combination in a single cylinder, of a back-pressure turbine taking steam at the boiler pressure and exhausting to the process pressure, followed by a condensing turbine taking additional steam at the process pressure to make up the total electrical load (see Fig. 3.7). The turbine is speed-governed and a pressure regulator maintains a constant steam pressure at the pass-out branch, irrespective of fluctuations in the demand for process steam, by varying the opening of a pass-through valve which controls the steam flow to the turbine exhaust.

The pass-out condensing turbine therefore has the advantage that it can simultaneously control the electrical power output and the pass-out pressure with both demands fluctuating. The turbine design can readily match the operating conditions. The selected inlet steam conditions should be as high as possible to enable the turbine to generate the maximum power from the available process steam flow and to keep the condenser losses low.

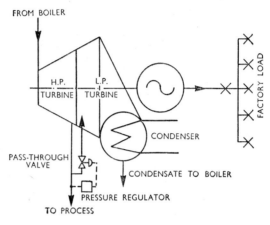

FIG. 3.7. Simple single-cylinder single pass-out condensing turbine.

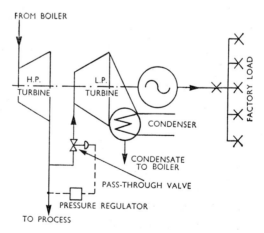

FIG. 3.8. Two-cylinder single pass-out condensing turbine.

When the process steam flow is large relative to the condenser flow, the turbine often comprises two separate cylinders having their steam flow in series (see Fig. 3.8). Such a twin-cylinder machine actually comprises a straight back-pressure turbine and a separate condensing turbine coupled together. The shafts may be connected in tandem, or side-by-side with two pinions meshing on to a common gear wheel. The first arrangement involves both rotors running at the same speed, but the latter gives complete freedom of choice of speed. This enables each cylinder to be designed for its most economic speed and results in an improved overall turbine efficiency.

When boilers burning waste fuel or receiving waste heat produce steam which exceeds the process steam demand, the pass–out condensing turbine provides the only economic solution, provided that there is a use for the additional power generated, or it can be exported.

(g) Back-pressure Turbine and Separate Condensing Turbine

In some factories the steam/power balance varies from winter to summer. Usually the steam demand is greatest in the winter to provide factory space heating in addition to process requirements. Such an installation may justify a back-pressure turbine for use alone in winter, with a separate condensing turbine running in parallel with it in summer to make up the power deficit due to seasonal drop in process steam demand. A converse out-of-balance often arises in tropical countries where seasonal irrigation loads occur due to the operation of motor-driven pumps.

The condensing turbine may take its supply steam from the process steam main or the boiler steam main. The former arrangement is called an exhaust condensing turbine. It has the same effect as the back end of a pass-out condensing machine, but has the advantage that when shut down in the winter it does not lower the efficiency of the back-pressure set through additional windage losses, ventilating or cooling steam, and the power consumed by the condensing plant auxiliaries. The capacity of the condensing turbine must be sufficient to meet the peak out-of-balance of power and process steam requirements.

The separate condensing turbine can also act as a reserve unit for the back-pressure turbine to keep essential plant in operation. It would then take its steam through a reducing valve arranged in parallel with the back-pressure turbine. This reducing valve would also supply the process steam demand (see Fig. 3.9). Compared with the pass-out condensing turbine, the separate condensing turbine has the disadvantage that during spring and autumn it must be started up every time the steam/power ratio requires it, whilst the condensing end of the pass-out set is available at all times. However, if a load programme can be adequately planned, this need not be a serious disadvantage.

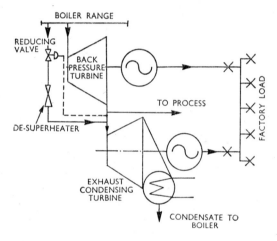

FIG. 3.9. Back-pressure turbine with exhaust condensing turbine.

A condensing turbine which takes steam from the same boiler range as the back-pressure turbine is known as a high-pressure condensing turbine (see Fig. 3.10). It is more expensive than an exhaust condensing turbine because it must be designed for the boiler steam conditions and it must be larger than the exhaust turbine for the same combined electrical output, since it must provide a larger share of the power. This is because the steam for an exhaust turbine previously passes through the back-pressure turbine, increasing its throttle flow and hence the power it develops, leaving a smaller deficit to be made up by the condensing turbine.

A back-pressure turbine, operating with an exhaust turbine, maintains a high throttle flow during both winter and summer; it therefore operates at a high efficiency throughout the whole year. In comparison a back-pressure turbine operating in parallel with a high-pressure condensing turbine, only passes a low throttle flow in the summer, as determined by the process steam demand; it therefore operates at a reduced efficiency during this period.

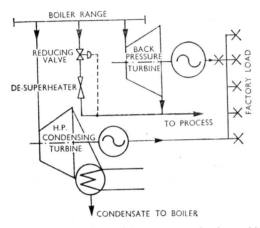

FIG. 3.10. Back-pressure turbine with separate condensing turbine taking high-pressure steam.

These facts result in the combined annual steam consumption of a back-pressure turbine running in parallel with a high-pressure condensing turbine, being higher than that for a unit operating with an exhaust condensing turbine.

(h) Back-pressure Turbine and Diesel Plant

An alternative to the separate condensing turbine or parallel operation with the public electricity supply to meet excess electrical demand, is the installation of diesel generating plant to run in parallel with the back-pressure turbine (see Fig. 3.11).

An attractive arrangement is possible if use can be made of the diesel engine jacket and exhaust heat for heating either boiler feed water or process water. Diesel generators can be the solution if there is difficulty in providing condenser cooling water, although air-cooled condensers are also available.

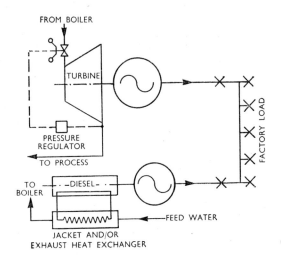

FIG. 3.11. Simple back-pressure turbine with diesel engine.

(i) *Topping Turbines*

Within a few years of installing new boiler and back-pressure generating plant, factory management may find that due to continuous improvement and economies in process machinery, their power demand has greatly outgrown the power available from their process steam flow.

The purchase of power is the simplest solution to this problem, but may be costly depending upon the type of electrical demand.

The alternative is to install additional power plant. In addition to the high-pressure condensing turbine working with a new boiler, or diesel plant, discussed above, consideration can be given to a new higher pressure boiler and a 'topping' turbine. This type of turbine is a back-pressure machine taking higher pressure steam and exhausting it to the inlet of the existing back-pressure turbine, i.e. the two turbines run in series thermally (see Fig. 3.12). The low-pressure boiler may be retained as a standby to give a reduced output from the existing turbine in an emergency.

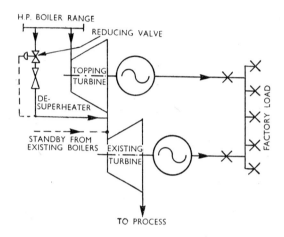

FIG. 3.12. Topping turbine exhausting to existing back-pressure turbine.

(j) *Pass-out Back-pressure and Double Pass-out Condensing Turbines*

Some industries require process steam at more than one pressure. Such cases call for a pass-out back-pressure turbine (Fig. 3.13) or a double pass-out condensing turbine (Fig. 3.14). The pass-out back-pressure set usually runs in parallel with the public electricity supply to balance electrical and steam demands. The double pass-out condensing set provides the balance independent of the outside electricity supply. Turbines passing out steam at more than two pressures are rare, due to the added complexity of the pressure control gear and increased manufacturing costs. If more than two process pressures are essential it is usual to provide the demand having the smallest power potential, via a reducing valve from one of the pass-out points or the boiler steam range.

D

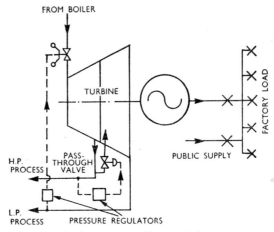

FIG. 3.13. Pass-out back-pressure turbine supplying two process pressures and running in parallel with the public supply.

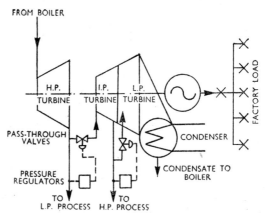

FIG. 3.14. Two-cylinder double pass-out condensing turbine.

(k) *Mixed-pressure Turbines*

A factory may already have steam-driven plant exhausting at a pressure appreciably in excess of the pressure necessary for the process heating temperature. A new power from process steam plant could utilise this exhaust steam in a mixed-pressure turbine. These turbines are like inverted pass-out turbines. In addition to taking high-pressure steam from the boiler, they pass-in steam at a stage of the turbine corresponding to the exhaust pressure of the other steam plant (see Fig. 3.15). A mixed-pressure turbine may exhaust to a back pressure or a condenser to suit the particular needs of a given installation. The control gear ensures that the turbine takes all the available low-pressure steam at all times and makes up with high-pressure steam to balance the demand for process heating steam, and also electrical power when a condenser is incorporated.

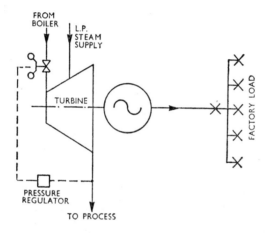

FIG. 3.15. Mixed pressure back-pressure turbine.

Feed-water Heating

High boiler conditions require careful treatment of the make-up water which replaces the process steam losses due to contamination of the condensate. The treatment usually includes de-aeration of the complete feed water supply to the boiler in a direct-contact pressure-type de-aerator feed heater. The steam supply to the de-aerator can be taken from the process steam main, to increase the available steam flow through the turbine for power generation, thereby improving the overall economy of the power plant installation. The economics of the feed-heating system require careful investigation. The choice of system depends on the size of the plant. For small industrial plant, it is not usual to raise the feedwater temperature above 240°F (116°C) at the boiler feed pump suction, because of technical and material considerations. Temperatures above this figure require one or more stages of high-pressure heating which are costly to provide and, in some cases, may prove rather too complex for small industrial plants. When required, the steam for high-pressure feed heaters is supplied from bleed points at suitable stages in the turbine or from a higher pressure process steam main, if available.

THE SELECTION OF STEAM CONDITIONS AND PRELIMINARY ASSESSMENT OF POWER OBTAINABLE

Choice of Exhaust or Pass-out Steam Conditions

The first detail to settle is the process pressure or pressures, which should be as low as possible. The steam gives up its latent heat to the process at the saturation temperature corresponding to its pressure. The plant design must therefore ensure that the processing temperatures are as low as possible. When the engineer has fixed the process temperature, he must determine how close the temperature of the heating steam must be to the processing temperature. When steam heats by direct injection, there may be no need for any temperature difference at all. When steam gives up its heat through a heating surface, the plant design must keep the temperature difference to a minimum. Finally, the size of the steam pipe between the turbine exhaust or pass-out branch and the process plant must give the minimum pressure drop. The economics of initial plant cost also influence the final choice of these last two design factors.

The turbine exhaust steam should be slightly superheated, for two reasons. It will lose a little heat in the pipe taking it to the process due to radiation, and dry saturated steam is usually desirable at the process; in addition, slight superheat will protect the last stages of the turbine and the pipework from corrosion and erosion. The usual value of this superheat is 20–30°F (11–16·5°C) at full steam flow. As the steam flow through the turbine reduces, the temperature of the exhaust steam will rise.

Choice of Boiler Pressure and Temperature

There are two basic methods of selecting the turbine inlet steam conditions; one is to obtain the maximum electrical output from the process steam flow, and the other is to provide a given exhaust or pass-out steam temperature. The former necessitates high boiler pressures and temperatures. However, there are practical limitations on the choice of high boiler conditions for the average industrial plant.

The need for more exacting feedwater treatment at pressures above about 600–650 psig (41·3–44·8 bar(g)) often influences the maximum pressure. At this steam pressure the treatment should preferably change from a simple base exchange system to complete demineralisation. The cost of chemicals for such a plant is approximately 3 times that for the base exchange system. This is an important factor for processes necessitating a high percentage of make-up water. The capital cost of the plant is much greater and it calls for a higher standard of operation by qualified staff.

The capital cost of boiler plant for steam pressures above 650 psig (44·8 bar(g)) is disproportionately high if the steam flow is small.

The specific volume of steam reduces as its pressure increases. This means that for a given steam flow the height of the first-stage turbine blades reduces with increase in steam pressure. A stage is finally reached where the turbine efficiency falls due to increased percentage losses in the blading.

High boiler steam temperatures also increase the capital cost of the plant by necessitating the use of alloy steels. The usual limit on steam temperature for the use of carbon steels in the boiler is 800°F (426°C) for superheater tubes, and up to 850°F (455°C) for headers and steam pipework, which is not integral with the boiler.

In the turbine, where the design must accommodate the movement of a high-speed rotor relative to the casing, this limit is 750°F (400°C) for most parts, except those like the rotor, which are highly stressed, where the materials change at a rather lower temperature.

Steam temperatures of 900–950°F (480–510°C) usually result in a special design of inserted steam belts in the turbine to prevent high temperature steam coming into contact with the main turbine cylinder.

Generally speaking, for normal industrial installations there is little to gain economically by raising the boiler steam pressure above 650 psig (56 bar(g)) or the steam temperature above 850°F (450°C) until the total steam flow exceeds 100,000 lb/hr (45,500 kg/hr).

If the engineer chooses boiler conditions to produce, say, 20°F (11°C) superheat at the turbine exhaust branch, he obtains a low turbine inlet steam temperature relative to the chosen pressure. This is particularly the case with high process steam pressures, which is illustrated in Fig. 3.1 and is discussed under basic thermodynamics. An increase in the boiler temperature would produce more power, but the exhaust steam would need desuperheating. However, if the process steam temperature is critical, some desuperheating will be necessary at partial loads, because the exhaust temperature rises as the steam flow decreases. It is usual to install a pressure-reducing valve and desuperheater in parallel with the back-pressure turbine to provide process steam when the turbine is out of operation, or to balance the heat and power demands. This desuperheater can be designed for a high turn-down factor and desuperheat the exhaust steam if required.

When a turbine provides steam at two process pressures, variations in steam temperature will occur at both pressures with variations in the steam flow to either or both of the processes. It is better to choose turbine inlet conditions to match the power requirements and desuperheat both process steam flows, than try to obtain the required process steam temperature by selection of boiler steam conditions.

Particularly for small turbines, the combination of high inlet steam pressure with relatively low inlet steam temperature is not very satisfactory, although it provides desirable exhaust conditions. This is because the specific volume of the steam reduces as its superheat decreases and necessitates small blade heights with resultant lower turbine efficiency, as explained above.

Although there are no officially recognised standard steam conditions, the following figures at the turbine stop valve appear to be traditional for power and process steam installations:

400 psig (27·6 bar(g)): 750°F (400°C)
600 psig (41·3 bar(g)): 800°F (426°C)
900 psig (62·0 bar(g)): 900°F (482°C)
1500 psig (103·5 bar(g)): 950°F (510°C)

All these conditions have at least 300°F (167°C) superheat, which is ideal for power generation purposes. It is not necessary to follow these conditions exactly. For example, the use of carbon steel in the turbine and simple feedwater treatment limits the maximum conditions to 600 psig (41·3 bar(g)) 750°F (400°C)

Finally, the use of dry saturated steam at the turbine inlet is not recommended. The steam becomes wet during its passage through the turbine and serious corrosion and erosion problems occur. The use of special materials such as stainless-steel nozzles and diaphragms and chromium plating of the rotor will overcome these problems, but these materials add appreciably to the cost of the turbine. It is preferable to use superheated steam, which at the same time provides a greater electrical output, and dry saturated steam at the process, as explained earlier.

Choice of Feed-water Temperature

The final feed-water temperature depends on many diverse factors. Traditionally, but not in all cases, small industrial plants having steam flows below 100,000 lb/hr (45,500 kg/hr) and boiler pressures below 600 psig (41·3 bar(g)) only incorporate low-pressure feed heating, i.e. before the boiler feed pump. It is not usual for the temperature at the feed pump suction to be above 230–240°F (110–115°C). This is to limit the net positive suction head required at the pump suction to prevent vaporisation of the hot feed water. For larger plants and/or higher boiler pressures, the final feedwater temperature may be raised in high-pressure feed heaters up to 70% of the saturation temperature corresponding to the boiler pressure.

It is advisable to discuss the selection of feedwater temperature with the boiler manufacturer, as it affects the design of the heat-recovery plant. It is desirable to design this plant for a final gas exit temperature of approximately 350°F (171°C) at maximum rating, to prevent corrosion in this part of the boiler. In a 400 psig (27·6 bar(g)) 750°F (400°C) cycle using a feedwater temperature of 230°F (110°C) a conventional economiser with cast-iron extended surface can be designed to meet this requirement. However, for a 900 psig (62·0 bar(g)) 900°F (482°C). cycle using high-pressure feedwater heating to a final temperature of, say, 340°F (171°C) a final gas temperature of 350°F (177°C) could not be obtained by using an economiser only. In this case the boiler manufacturer would normally provide an air heater.

The nature of the fuel to be burned, and the degree to which corrosion might occur on the cold end of the economiser or air heater, will also affect the design of the heat-recovery plant, and hence the selection of feedwater temperature.

An essential requirement with a water-tube boiler is the removal of oxygen from the feedwater to prevent corrosion. This is particularly important in a plant having a large percentage of make-up water added to the system, to replace process steam losses due to condensate contamination. This duty can be combined with feedwater heating in a direct contact pressure type de-aerator feed heater.

The steam for feed heating is normally taken from the process steam main. This increases the steam flow passing through the turbine and results in a larger turbo-alternator output. When there is more than one process pressure it is obvious that, in the interests of maximum power generation, the feed-heating steam should be taken from the lowest possible pressure consistent with the heating requirements. Certainly a de-aerator can always take heating steam from the low-pressure steam main. A high-pressure feed heater requires steam having a saturation temperature approximately 10°F (5·5°C) above the final feedwater temperature, for economic heat transfer in a tubular heater.

The final choice of feedwater temperature will probably be determined by personal preference for high overall plant efficiency or simplicity of plant operation. In a small industrial plant the chief engineer often decides against the added complication of high-pressure feed-heating plant. In the larger plants, the extra power generated by the heating steam usually pays off the additional capital expenditure quickly and shows a good profit for the additional fuel consumption.

Choice of Condenser Vacuum

The condenser vacuum for a turbine having a condensing section is normally chosen to provide the best turbine thermodynamic efficiency consistent with an economic capital expenditure. Figure 3.16 shows the recommended maximum vacuum at varying cooling-water inlet temperatures for pass-out condensing turbines for power and process steam installations. The dotted line indicates the vacuum which could be obtained from a well-designed condensing plant. However, it is rare for an industrial pass-out, condensing turbine to be designed for an exhaust vacuum higher than 28·75 in. Hg (97 kNm^{-2}) due to plant design considerations. The full line indicating the recommended maximum vacuum therefore levels off at this figure.

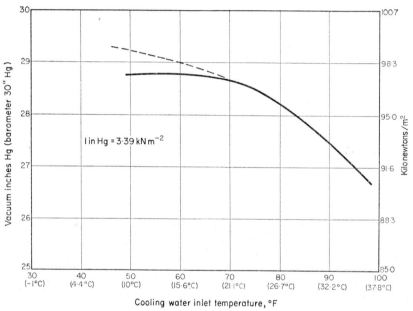

FIG. 3.16. Recommended maximum vacuum at various cooling water inlet temperatures.

The specific volume of steam increases rapidly at higher vacua, which consequently involve the use of long, highly stressed blades in the last few turbine stages, a large exhaust end casing and connecting pipe to the condenser, a large condenser cooling surface and/or a large cooling water flow, all of which increase the capital cost. Also the full theoretical gain in thermodynamic efficiency is not realised in practice, because of a relatively high exhaust loss, resulting from the tremendous specific volume and the increased moisture in the steam. The net gain from a vacuum in excess of 28·75 in. Hg (97 kNm^{-2}) on the type and size of turbines being considered is not usually sufficient to justify the additional capital expenditure.

When using Fig. 3.16, extreme variations in water temperature should be ignored, so that the plant is designed for conditions which apply over the greater part of a year. For a given condenser design and a constant steam flow, the vacuum will rise with a lower water temperature, and fall with a higher water temperature. Similarly, for a constant water temperature the vacuum will rise with the small steam flows occurring at partial loads.

Distribution Pipework

As explained earlier, the turbine exhaust or pass-out pressure should be as low as possible to provide maximum power from the available steam flow. This implies the minimum pressure drop in the distribution pipework between the turbine and the process plant. The process temperature determines the process pressure. If the plant designer then adds a nominal low pipeline pressure drop to the process pressure to determine the turbine exhaust or pass-out pressure, the diameter of the pipe will vary with the distance between the turbine and the process. Eventually a point is reached where it is cheaper to install a smaller diameter pipe and tolerate a larger pressure drop with the resultant drop in power output. The economics of all steam distribution systems therefore merit close investigation before the final plant design is settled.

A careful study of a pipe system will indicate that it has an economic steam velocity. This velocity will not vary much with pipe diameter for a given set of steam conditions. The plant designer must study each system on its own merits. He should equate the cost of the pipe work, lagging, heat loss and pressure drop against the cost of the available power energy lost in the steam main.

As a general guide for a preliminary assessment the following steam velocities may be used:

Superheated steam between boiler
and turbine   130–200 ft/sec (40–62 m/sec)
Dry saturated steam between turbine
and process plant   100–130 ft/sec (33–40 m/sec)

Exhaust steam when wet but above
  atmospheric pressure   70–100 ft/sec (21–33 m/sec)
Exhaust steam under moderate
  vacuum   150–200 ft/sec (46–62 m/sec)
Exhaust steam under high vacuum   200–350 ft/sec (62–105 m/sec)

It is obvious that the distribution pipework should be as straight and short as possible, consistent with adequate provision for thermal expansion. It should have the minimum number of bends and fittings; elbows should never be used if there is room for bends.

ASSESSMENT OF POWER OBTAINABLE FROM PROCESS STEAM FLOW

Having fixed the process steam pressure and flow and given preliminary thought to the boiler conditions, the next step is to assess the power obtainable from the process steam flow. If a straight back-pressure turbine cannot produce enough power to balance the power demand and the management do not contemplate parallel running with the public electricity supply, they should investigate the various combinations of power units previously discussed.

The charts, Figs. 3.17 and 3.18, provide a ready means of determining the relationship between the power obtainable and the steam flow for a given set of steam conditions. In the interests of simplicity these charts are only approximate. For the range of steam conditions given, they will normally give powers or flows within plus or minus 5% of the correct plant design. The charts also correlate inlet and exhaust temperatures.

The charts may be used within the following ranges:

Inlet pressure: 200–1000 psig (13·8 bar(g)–69 bar(g)).

Inlet temperature: 300–1000°F (149–540°C).

Any exhaust pressure including vacuum.

They can be used at lower inlet conditions than quoted, with some loss of accuracy.

Do not use the charts for:

Inlet conditions above 1000 psig, 1000°F. (69 bar(g), 540°C.)

Dry saturated or wet inlet steam.

Single-stage turbines.

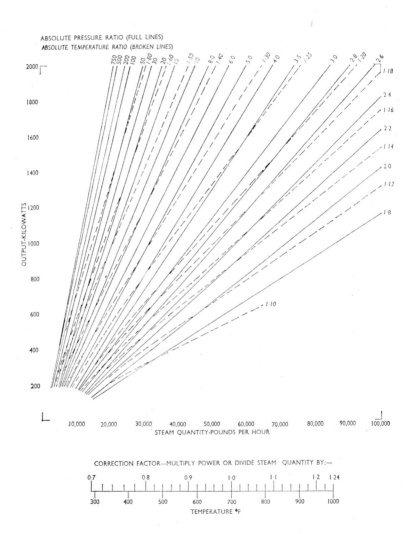

FIG. 3.17. Steam-consumption chart up to 100,000 lb/hr or 2000 kW (British units).

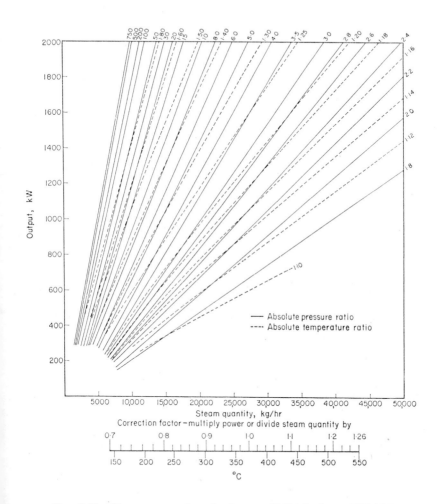

FIG. 3.17a. Steam-consumption chart up to 50,000 kg/hr or 2000 kW
(metric units).

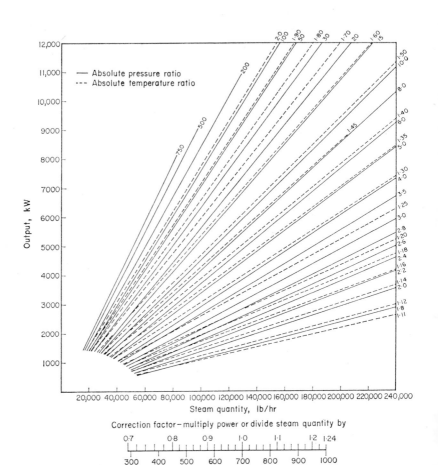

Fig. 3.18. Steam-consumption chart up to 240,000 lb/hr or 12,000 kW
(British units)

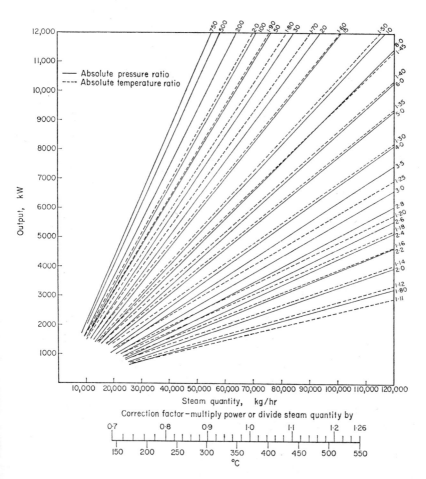

FIG. 3.18a. Steam-consumption chart up to 120,000 kg/hr or 12,000 kW
(metric units).

Figures 3.19 and 3.20 can be used to simplify the calculations. To use Figs. 3.17 and 3.18, divide the absolute inlet pressure by the absolute exhaust pressure to obtain the absolute pressure ratio, or use Fig. 3.19. Trace a line vertically from the available steam quantity on the bottom scale to the full line corresponding to the absolute pressure ratio. Note this point and proceed horizontally from it to the power obtainable on the vertical scale. Correct the output by multi-

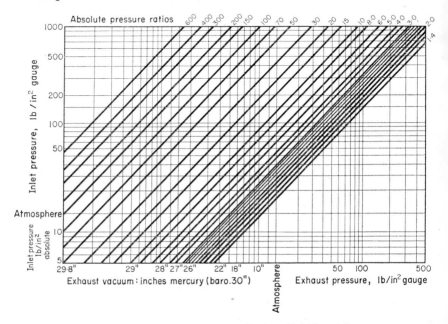

FIG. 3.19. Absolute pressure ratio chart (British units).

plying by the inlet temperature correction factor at the bottom of the chart. This gives the actual output obtainable. Conversely, the steam flow required to give a known output can be obtained by reversing the procedure and dividing the steam flow read from the bottom scale by the inlet temperature correction factor.

To obtain the exhaust temperature at full flow, read the absolute temperature ratio off the chart at the point of intersection on the pressure ratio line previously noted. The exhaust temperature may then be calculated from the known inlet temperature. Conversely, an inlet temperature may be calculated from a known exhaust temperature. This method of calculating inlet and exhaust temperatures only applies to superheated steam. It is possible to find the exhaust temperature if the steam is dry; otherwise, it is only possible to find out if the steam is wet or dry. (See example No. 1.)

It will be appreciated that any one point on the charts corresponding

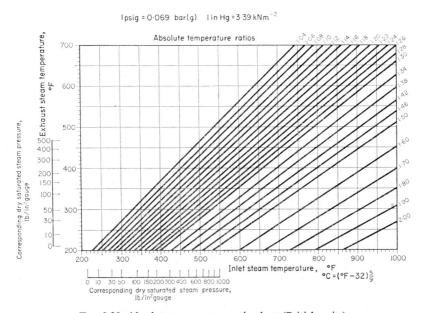

FIG. 3.20. Absolute temperature ratio chart (British units).

to a given steam flow or electrical load and pressure ratio can only represent one fixed turbo-alternator efficiency. The charts have been constructed using average full load efficiencies for the turbine, gear and alternator. Therefore they will only give accurate figures for loads or steam flows corresponding to the continuous maximum or design rating of the plant. At partial loads or flows the turbo-alternator efficiency falls, due to the no-load steam flow and the irrecoverable losses such as bearing friction, etc., accounting for a larger proportion of the steam flow. If used for partial load figures, the charts would consequently give optimistic figures. While this fact necessarily limits the use of the charts, they are only intended to enable a preliminary survey to be made in overall terms, to decide which one of several possible schemes merits further detailed investigation. Reference should then be made to the turbine designer for the part load performance of the plant.

When calculating figures for condensing turbines having absolute pressure ratios in excess of 750, use the maximum absolute pressure ratio line shown on the chart, i.e. 750.

The exhaust temperatures calculated from the charts also only apply at full steam flow. As the steam flow reduces at partial loads, and the turbine thermodynamic efficiency falls, the exhaust temperature rises because the turbine has extracted less heat from the steam during expansion.

The chart can be used for all types of turbine, but examples are only given for back-pressure and pass-out condensing machines.

There are two methods of working out the power obtainable from a pass-out turbine. The best method is to consider the pass-out turbine as two turbines, one operating between the inlet pressure and the pass-out pressure, passing the full steam quantity, the other operating between the pass-out pressure and the exhaust pressure, passing the exhaust steam quantity. The other method is to consider the pass-out turbine as two turbines, one operating between the inlet pressure and the pass-out pressure, passing the pass-out quantity, the other operating between the inlet pressure and the exhaust pressure, passing the exhaust quantity.

The second method is likely to be less accurate than the first, but may sometimes be more convenient. For example, if the inlet steam conditions, the pass-out flow and pressure, and the exhaust pressure are known together with the required electrical output, the power available from the pass-out steam can then be obtained, and the additional steam quantity calculated to give the total output.

When calculating the absolute pressure ratio it is important to make allowances for the pressure drop in the steam pipes between the boiler and the turbine and between the turbine and the process machinery. These pressure drops will depend upon the pipe lengths and steam velocities for each individual case. If no details are available, figures of the order of $2\frac{1}{2}\%$ of the boiler pressure may be taken between boiler and turbine and, say 3–5 psi (0·26–0·35 bar) between turbine and process assuming reasonably short pipe runs. Similarly, a temperature drop of 10°F (5·5°C) may be taken between the boiler and turbine stop valves, assuming close proximity of the boiler and the turbine.

Examples

The first example covers a simple back-pressure turbine. For convenience the second and third examples cover pass-out back-pressure and double pass-out condensing turbines.

The pass-out flows required from the turbine are calculated from a system heat balance which makes allowance for feed heating steam and desuperheater spray water. A preliminary assessment of the steam quantity required for feed heating can be obtained by assuming that each pound of steam gives up 1000 Btu (1055 kJ) of latent heat to the feed water. The heat required to raise the feed temperature is the product of the desired temperature rise of the mixture of process condensate return, make-up water, and also turbine condensate when a pass-out condensing turbine is incorporated, and the sum of these water quantities. This steam quantity is added to the process steam flow and the approximate pass-out temperature determined from the chart. Final adjustments are then made to the feed-heating steam and desuperheater water quantities to obtain a true heat balance. The turbine output is then calculated using the final steam flow figures.

EXAMPLE 1. What is the approximate steam consumption of a 1500 kW back-pressure turbo-alternator taking inlet steam at 585 psig (40·2 bar(g)) 750°F (400°C) and exhausting at 25 psig (1·75 bar(g))? What is the approximate exhaust temperature?

$$\text{The absolute pressure ratio} = \frac{585 + 15}{25 + 15} = \frac{600}{40} = 15.$$

From Fig. 3.17 the steam quantity required = 30,200 lb/hr
(13,700 kg/hr)
and the absolute temperature ratio = 1·54.

From the temperature correction scale at the bottom of Fig. 3.17, the correction for an inlet temperature of 750°F (400°C) is 1·04.

Therefore, the corrected steam quantity is

$$\frac{30,200}{1\cdot04} = 29,000 \text{ lb/hr } (13,200 \text{ kg/hr})$$

Absolute temperature ratio

$$1\cdot54 = \frac{750 + 460}{\text{Exhaust temperature} + 460}$$

Absolute exhaust temperature $= \dfrac{1210}{1\cdot54} = 785°\text{R } (436°\text{K}).$

Exhaust temperature at full flow

$$= 785 - 460 = 325°\text{F } (163°\text{C}).$$

Saturation temperature at 25 psig ($1\cdot75$ bar(g))

$$= 267°\text{F } (130°\text{C}).$$

Condition of exhaust steam $= 325 - 267 = 58°\text{F } (32°\text{C})$ superheat.
Now suppose the inlet temperature had been 600°F (316°C). Then absolute exhaust temperature

$$\frac{600 + 460}{1\cdot54} = \frac{1060}{1\cdot54} = 688°\text{R } (382°\text{K}).$$

Exhaust temperature at full flow

$$= 688 - 460 = 228°\text{F } (109°\text{C}).$$

Since the saturation temperature is 267°F (130°C) this indicates that the exhaust steam is wet but it will not give the dryness fraction.

EXAMPLE 2. A pass-out back-pressure turbine is required to provide 18,900 lb/hr (8600 kg/hr) of steam at 135 psig ($9\cdot35$ bar(g)) and 31,200 lb/hr (14,400 kg/hr) of steam at 33 psig ($2\cdot28$ bar(g)). The proposed inlet stop-valve conditions are 625 psig ($43\cdot4$ bar(g)), 750°F (400°C). What is the turbo-alternator output and what is the approximate condition of the pass-out and exhaust steam?

Consider the machine as two turbines, i.e. 50,100 lb/hr (22,800 kg/hr) from the inlet to pass-out and 31,200 lb/hr (14,200 kg/hr) from pass-out to exhaust.

Inlet to pass-out absolute pressure ratio

$$= \frac{625 + 15}{135 + 15} = \frac{640}{150} = 4 \cdot 26.$$

From Fig. 3.17 the output from 50,100 lb/hr (22,800 kg/hr)

$= 1485 \, kW$

and the absolute temperature ratio $= 1 \cdot 285$

Temperature correction for 750°F (400°C) $= 1 \cdot 04$

Corrected output $= 1485 \times 1 \cdot 04$ $= 1545 \, kW.$

Absolute pass-out temperature

$$= \frac{750 + 460}{1 \cdot 285} = \frac{1210}{1 \cdot 285} = 940°R \, (520°K).$$

Pass-out temperature at full flow

$$= 940 - 460 = 480°F \, (249°C).$$

Saturation temperature at 135 psig (9·35 bar(g)) = 358°F (181°C)

Condition of pass-out steam = 480 − 358 = 122°F (68°C) superheat.

Pass-out to exhaust absolute pressure ratio

$$= \frac{135 + 15}{33 + 15} = \frac{150}{48} = 3 \cdot 13.$$

From Fig. 3.17 the output from 31,200 lb/hr (14,200 kg/hr) = 695 kW

and the absolute temperature ratio $= 1 \cdot 2$

Temperature correction for 480°F (249°C) $= 0 \cdot 822$

Corrected output $= 695 \times 0 \cdot 822$ $= 570 \, kW.$

Absolute exhaust temperature

$$= \frac{480 + 460}{1 \cdot 2} = \frac{940}{1 \cdot 2} = 785°R \, (437°K).$$

Exhaust temperature at full flow

$$= 785 - 460 = 325°F \, (163°C).$$

Saturation temperature at 33 psig (2·3 bar(g)) = 278°F (137°C)

Condition of exhaust steam = 325 − 278 = 47°F (26°C) superheat.

Total output from turbine

$$= h.p. \text{ output} + l.p. \text{ output}$$
$$= 1545 + 570 = 2115 \, kW$$

EXAMPLE 3. A double pass-out condensing turbine is required to provide 19,000 lb/hr (8,650 kg/hr) of steam at 135 psig (9·3 bar(g)) and 34,500 lb/hr (15,700 kg/hr) of steam at 33 psig (2·3 bar(g)) and a power output of 4500 kW. The proposed inlet stop valve conditions are 625 psig (43 bar(g)) 750°F (400°C) and the exhaust vacuum is 28·5 in. (96 kNm^{-2}) mercury. What is the total throttle steam flow and what is the condition of the steam at both pass-out branches?

In this case the total steam flow is unknown, so it is necessary to treat the machine as three separate turbines with the steam flows in parallel, i.e. inlet to high pressure (h.p.) pass-out, inlet to low pressure (l.p.) pass-out and inlet to condenser. Calculate the power available from each pass-out flow and then find the additional steam necessary to make-up the deficiency between the power developed and 4500 kW. Use actual steam flow to each pass-out point to determine pass-out temperatures.

Inlet to h.p. pass-out absolute pressure ratio

$$= \frac{625 + 15}{135 + 15} = \frac{640}{150} = 4.26.$$

From Fig. 3.17 the output from 19,000 lb/hr (8650 kg/hr) = 485kW
Temperature correction for 750°F (400°C) = 1·04.
Corrected output = 485 × 1·04 = 505 kW.
Inlet to l.p. pass-out absolute pressure ratio

$$= \frac{625 + 15}{33 + 15} = \frac{640}{48} = 13.34.$$

From Fig. 3.17 the output from 34,500 lb/hr (15,700 kg/hr) =
1650 kW.
Corrected output = 1650 × 1·04 = 1715 kW.
Total power from process steam
$$= 505 + 1715 = 2220 \text{ kW}.$$
Extra power required by condensing steam
$$= 4500 - 2220 = 2280 \text{ kW}.$$
Inlet to condenser absolute pressure ratio

$$= \frac{625 + 15}{15 - (28.5/2)} = \frac{640}{0.75} = 855.$$

Note. Use maximum pressure ratio line of 750.
From Fig. 3.18 the steam flow for 2280 kW = 24,500 lb/hr
$$(11,150 \text{ kg/hr}).$$

Corrected steam flow $= \dfrac{24,500}{1\cdot04} = 23,500$ lb/hr (10,700 kg/hr).

Total throttle flow = high pressure (h.p.) pass-out + low pressure (l.p.)
pass-out + condenser flow

$$= 19,000 + 34,500 + 23,500 = 77,000 \text{ lb/hr (35,000 kg/hr)}.$$

Steam flow through turbine up to h.p.

pass-out branch = 77,000 lb/hr (35,000 kg/hr).

From Fig. 3.18 the absolute temperature ratio
   for a flow of 77,000 lb/hr. (35,000 kg/hr) and a pressure ratio of
   $4\cdot26 = 1\cdot295$.
Absolute h.p. pass-out temperature

$$= \frac{750 + 460}{1\cdot295} = \frac{1210}{1\cdot295} = 935°\text{R (519°K)}.$$

H.p. pass-out temperature at full flow

$$= 935 - 460 = 475°\text{F (246°C)}.$$

Saturation temperature at 135 psig (9·35 bar(g)) = 358°F (181°C).
Condition of h.p. pass-out steam

$$= 475 - 358 = 117°\text{F. (65°C). superheat.}$$

Steam flow through turbine up to l.p.

pass-out branch = 77,000 − 19,000 = 58,000 lb/hr (26,300 kg/hr).

From Fig. 3.18 the absolute temperature ratio for a flow of 58,000
lb/hr (26,300 kg/hr) and a pressure ratio of 13·3 = 1·52.
Absolute l.p. pass-out temperature

$$= \frac{750 + 460}{1\cdot52} = \frac{1210}{1\cdot52} = 795°\text{R (441°K)}.$$

L.p. pass-out temperature at full flow

$$= 795 - 460 = 335°\text{F (168°C)}.$$

Saturation temperature at 33 psig ($2\cdot3$ bar(g)) = 278°F (137°C).
Condition of l.p. pass-out steam

$$= 335 - 278 = 57°F (32°C) \text{ superheat.}$$

Figures 3.19 and 3.20 have not been used when working out these examples. However, they can simplify the arithmetic. Figure 3.19 provides a direct reading for the absolute pressure ratio from known inlet and exhaust steam pressures in lb/in² gauge (bar gauge) and/or inches of mercury (kN m^{-2}). Figure 3.20 provides a direct reading for either the exhaust or inlet steam temperature, in degrees Fahrenheit (Centigrade) when one of these temperatures and the absolute temperature ratio are known. Figure 3.20 also relates the pressure and temperature of dry saturated steam, enabling the condition of the exhaust steam to be determined without the use of steam tables.

STEAM COSTING

When a factory uses steam for heating purposes only, or for supplying a power generating machine only, there is no difficulty in costing the steam. The accountant assesses the total cost of steam generation per 1000 lb (kg) or other basic unit and charges it wholly to the steam user.

However, when the same steam is used firstly for power production and then for heating, the accountant must determine a fair means of dividing the cost between the two users.

Considerable controversy surrounds the method to be adopted. However, there are at least three basic systems generally accepted for the division of steam costs:

(a) *Heat basis*

The amount of heat put into the steam in the boiler is calculated. The heat content of the steam at the exhaust of the turbine and of the condensate returning from the heating process is determined, which enables the actual heat consumption of each to be ascertained and debited in suitable proportions. All heat units may be referred back to pounds (kilogrammes) of standardised steam from and at 212°F (100°C),or taken as British thermal units (kilojoules).

(b) *Adiabatic basis*

A sink or final temperature is taken and the adiabatic heat drop from the initial steam state to the final sink pressure is debited to power. The adiabatic heat drop from the turbine exhaust pressure (at the initial entropy) to the sink pressure is credited to power and debited to the heating process.

(c) *Available energy basis*

A reasonably attainable sink or final temperature is taken, and the adiabatic heat drop from the initial steam state to the final sink pressure is debited to power. The exhaust of the turbine is calorimetered and the adiabatic heat drop from the actual exhaust state (at its actual exhaust entropy) to the sink pressure is credited to power and debited to the heating process.

Each of these basic systems has its merits, depending upon the local circumstances and costing ideas of each individual factory. The heat basis gives the most accurate assessment of how the steam is actually being used to produce power and heat.

Whichever basis is adopted, the division of costs can be made quite simply for a straight back-pressure turbine, by finding the proportion of heat in 1 lb (kg) of steam, which is to be debited to power and heat. The total cost is then divided in these proportions. A pass-out turbine is not quite so simple because of the varying steam flows to pass-out and the condenser. The combined heat available per hour from the steam flow between the boiler and the process sink and the boiler and the condenser sink is determined. The heat content of the steam flow per hour from the turbine branch to the process sink is calculated and debited to the process. The difference between these two figures is debited to power and the total cost divided in these proportions.

Since a steam turbine is primarily installed to reduce power costs it is reasonable to argue that the power should only be charged with the "marginal" costs, i.e. those costs which are incurred to produce power, over and above the costs that would be incurred if process steam only were produced in the boilers. This can be done quite simply, but involves the calculation of a fictitious cost for the generation of process steam in low-pressure boilers, It is therefore not a true division of actual operating costs, but is a convenient method of comparing the economics of two schemes if a power unit cost is required in the planning stage.

COMPARISON OF ESTIMATED OPERATING COSTS

Whatever system of steam costing a factory may adopt, the simplest method of comparing the estimated operating costs of alternative new power and heating plants is to compare the total annual operating costs only. This method has the advantage that the final issue is not clouded by attempting to separate the cost of power from process heat, to enable the power unit costs to be compared with purchased power unit costs. After all, the total cost to the factory is all that really matters; the division of this cost between power and process heat is purely academic.

The total annual operating costs of both the generation of power and the provision of process steam by means of various high-pressure boiler and turbo-alternator plants, can be readily compared with the total annual cost of purchasing all the power from the public electricity supply authority and the provision of all process steam from low-pressure boilers.

If the capital cost of each high-pressure boiler and its associated turbine plant is divided by the annual savings the plant can achieve in annual operating costs, compared with the low-pressure boiler scheme with purchased power, a comparative "pay-off" period is obtained for each scheme.

The annual costs comprise:

(a) Boiler Fuel Cost

This cost is obtained by calculating the heat input to the boiler and dividing this value by the boiler efficiency and the calorific value of the fuel and multiplying by the cost of the fuel. When making this calculation using the gross calorific value of the fuel, it is important to ensure that the gross boiler efficiency is based on the gross and not the net calorific value.

The choice of coal or oil depends on the availability and purchase price of each at the factory site. Both should normally be investigated unless one is obviously unsuitable.

(b) Feed Water Cost

This is the cost of purchasing and treating the make-up feedwater. The quantity of make-up is determined by the sum of the process losses, the system losses and blowdown losses. If the blowdown is appreciable the make-up quantity can be credited with flash steam, provided a flash recovery system is included, and the steam is returned to the feed heaters.

(c) Capital Charges

These charges cover depreciation, interest and insurance. Depreciation is based on the anticipated life of the plant and is calculated by dividing 100 by the life in number of years. Although high-pressure boilers and turbo-alternator plant have a useful life of 30 years or more, they are generally given an economic life of between 10 and 20 years, according to the period over which the process plant they are feeding becomes obsolete. In some extreme cases, such as oil refinery plant, the period can be less than 10 years.

The interest charge is the average interest rate over the life of the plant and is calculated from the following formula:

$$\text{Average interest rate per cent} = \frac{N + 1}{2N} \times R$$

where N = life of plant in years;
R = interest rate per annum; this is usually 1% above current bank rate with a minimum of $5\frac{1}{2}\%$.

Insurance varies widely, depending upon the class of insurance required and the method adopted in each factory for costing insurances. It is usually omitted in preliminary surveys on the assumption that insurance is a factory overhead charge, but a figure of 1% could be used, if desired.

(d) Labour Charges

These charges cover the wages of the men employed on the plant throughout the year, and vary from factory to factory.

(e) Maintenance Charges

A figure is included to cover the average cost of maintenance over the life of the plant. This figure is based on experience of similar plant.

(f) Purchased Power Cost

These costs are based on the local Electricity Board's tariff which usually comprises the sum of a maximum demand charge, a unit charge and a fuel cost adjustment. Depending upon the circumstances there may also be a supply or standby charge.

SUMMARY OF ECONOMIC CONCLUSIONS TO BE DRAWN

The following conclusions emerge from a large number of economic assessments which the author has undertaken.

1. It is not always the plant with the lowest capital expenditure and pay-off period that provides the most economic plant.
2. The location of the factory and hence the local cost of coal and oil may seriously affect the economics of any scheme.
3. There is no fixed answer to any power and steam requirements; each must be considered on its own merits, including the use of different fuels.
4. An assessment of different schemes should be made, using total annual operating costs.
5. A new plant should not be selected by comparing an estimated figure for privately generated power unit costs with purchased electricity unit costs, without considering the corresponding cost of the process steam. If the adiabatic or available energy basis is used and provides a unit cost comparable with purchased power, it would obviously be wrong for management to decide on low-pressure boiler plant. The cost of the process steam would immediately increase approximately 100%.
6. If a division of steam costs is required in a plant which uses latent heat, the most accurate system is the heat basis.

RUNNING IN PARALLEL WITH THE PUBLIC ELECTRICITY
SUPPLY SYSTEM

If a factory requires additional power over and above that which a back-pressure turbine can produce from the process steam flow, one of the ways of balancing the steam and power demands is to purchase such additional power from the public electricity supply authority.

THE STANDARD INDUSTRIAL TARIFF

The public electricity supply authorities in Britain publish standard industrial tariffs which are designed to reflect the true average cost of providing and distributing the supply to the consumer, and to encourage the maintenance of a high utilisation factor.

The industrial tariff comprises two basic charges—a maximum demand charge and a running or unit charge. The maximum demand charge is usually measured in kilovolt-ampere-hours (kVAhr), which automatically accounts for variation in power factor. A few Electricity Boards measure the maximum demand in kilowatt-hours (kWhr), and apply a power factor adjustment clause which increases the standard maximum demand charge when the average lagging power factor is below a specified figure, usually 0·85 or 0·9. All Electricity Boards also apply a fuel adjustment clause which makes an increment addition or reduction to the unit charge to allow for variation in the cost of the fuel consumed at the generating station, from a specified figure. The values of the maximum demand and the unit charge decrease in three or more steps as the magnitude of the load increases. The number of units chargeable at each rate is a function of the maximum demand figure applying during the period.

Depending upon the particular circumstances of an installation, a fixed annual charge may also apply to cover rent of the public authority's equipment, used solely to supply power to the consumer's factory.

The Electricity Boards normally quote two tariffs, one for medium-voltage supply at voltages below 650, and an alternative for higher voltages above 650. The high-voltage tariff is appreciably cheaper, but the consumer must provide his own step-down transformers and, of course, generate at the higher voltage. Each scheme must be considered on its merits, but generally speaking all but the smallest users will find that the high voltage system proves the most economical. An added advantage is that the factory electrical distribution can be at high voltage with transformers placed at local load centres. The greatly reduced cost of high-voltage cables will often pay off the cost of the transformers. Above approximately 3000 kVA the capital cost of the alternator begins to reduce as voltage is raised.

Most Electricity Boards offer a choice between an annual or monthly maximum demand tariff. The annual tariff makes a constant scale of charges throughout the year, based on the peak demand during the 12 months. The monthly tariff varies the charges in accordance with the peak demand in each month. The price per kW or kVA of maximum demand occurring during a year is usually only ten times that charged per month. Therefore, unless the demand varies appreciably throughout the year, the annual tariff may work out cheaper than the monthly tariff.

Some monthly tariffs extend to different basic charges for specified summer and winter months, the winter charges being the highest. For some industries, such a tariff may be very attractive, as the difference between winter and summer charges is appreciable.

It is the usual practice for Electricity Boards to measure the maximum demand over half-hourly periods, the maximum demand being twice the largest number of units consumed during any half-hour during the month or year, depending upon whether the monthly or annual tariff applies. Since both the maximum demand charge and the unit charge are functions of this peak half-hour figure, the total price per kilowatt hour will be a minimum when the factory maintains the kilowatt demand constant, i.e. 100% utilisation factor.

Some Electricity Boards offer a reduction for "off-peak" or night units supplied between the hours of 11.00 p.m. and 7.00 a.m. provided the consumer pays an additional rental for the time switch and additional metering equipment necessary to calculate the rebate. Other Electricity Boards make a larger reduction in the last step of the unit charges, which gives a similar result, because the additional units used at night are all chargeable at the reduced rate. Also, where a consumer can arrange that his maximum demand in "off-peak" hours is higher than at other times, he may obtain a special agreement to a concession related to the demand in excess of that during peak periods.

The Electricity Boards will usually be willing to negotiate terms for a supplementary supply to standby private generating plant, in addition to the normal value of the imported power load. This takes the form of a fixed annual charge and is of the order of $3.00 — $3.60 (1967) per kVA for a high-voltage supply, with correspondingly higher figures for a low-voltage supply. Any units actually imported from this supplementary supply are chargeable at the same rate as the regular supply.

It will be obvious from the above that factory managements should discuss their detailed requirements with the local Electricity Board who will give impartial advice on the choice of the most suitable tariff, and negotiate special terms when the local conditions merit them.

USING A TURBO-ALTERNATOR TO REDUCE MAXIMUM DEMAND CHARGES

There are two basic methods of operating private turbo-generating plant when a factory imports power from the public electricity supply to balance its steam and electrical demands.

One method is to supply the factory loads through a double-busbar switchboard. One busbar is fed from the public supply and the other by the turbo-alternator. The outgoing feeder units are connected to either busbar as required to balance the steam and electrical loads, i.e. the two systems are kept completely independent of each other. It is impossible for the electrical load on the system fed by the private generating plant to balance exactly the power which the turbo-alternator produces from the process steam flow at all times of the day. This means either passing steam through a reducing valve to supplement the turbine flow to process; or conversely, passing exhaust steam from a back-pressure turbine to atmosphere through a surplus valve, or steam to a condenser in a pass-out turbine.

The second method is to connect both the public electricity supply and the privately generated supply on to common busbars which supply all out-going feeder units, i.e. the two supplies operate in parallel. Although in the past some public supply authorities did not favour parallel running with industrial power plant, most authorities are now willing to consider such an arrangement and, today, there are many factories where various types of turbo-alternator are operating successfully in parallel with the public electricity supply.

An industrial consumer can obtain some financial benefit from operating a turbo-alternator in this manner by reducing the maximum demand on the imported power supply. As explained above, the price consumers pay for imported power is a minimum when the electrical demand is maintained constant, i.e. 100% utilisation factor.

The utilisation factor of the imported power can be expressed as follows:

$$\text{Utilisation factor} = \frac{\text{kVA used in a given period}}{\text{total hours in the period} \times \text{maximum demand}}$$

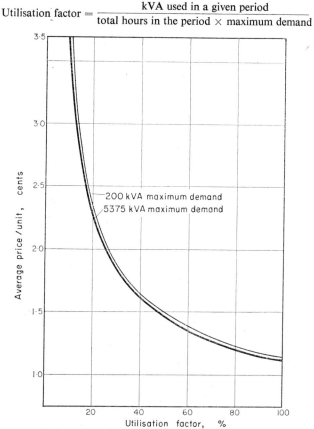

FIG. 3.21. Effect of utilisation factor on the average unit price calculated from a typical British Electricity Area Board industrial monthly tariff for maximum demands of 5375 kVA at 0·8 power factor, based on a month of 720 hours. (1965 prices)

For example, if the maximum demand is 5375 kVA in a month of 720 hours and the total kilowatt hours imported at 0·8 power factor in that month is 2,200,000, the utilisation factor is

$$\frac{2,200,000}{0\cdot8 \times 720 \times 5375} \times 100 = 71\%.$$

Figure 3.21 shows how the average price per unit increases as the utilisation factor decreases. It also shows that the average unit cost is marginally higher as the maximum demand decreases.

The financial penalty for a short-lived extravagance or factory mishap may be very considerable, especially if an annual tariff applies. The importance of restricting the peak kVA demand will be readily appreciated.

Industrial turbo-alternator control gear can be designed to maintain a constant kilowatt, and also kVA demand, on the public electricity supply and ensure that the turbo-alternator carries all peak variations. Pass-out condensing sets in particular can operate in this way. A back-pressure turbo-alternator can have control gear designed to open an exhaust surplus valve to pass additional steam through the turbine to meet peak demands, and thus limit the imported power to a preset maximum figure. The saving in purchased power costs can be much greater than the cost of the extra steam passed to atmosphere.

As explained later under technical considerations of parallel operation, a synchronous alternator may be used to improve the power factor of the load on the public electricity supply. This reduces the kVA maximum demand charge. The following figures illustrate this fact. Assume a consumer pays $19.20 per kVA per annum and the load is 1000 kVA at 0·7 power factor.

Actual kW loading = 1000 × 0·7 = 700 kW.
If the power factor is improved to 0·95

$$\text{kVA maximum demand} = \frac{700}{0\cdot95} = 737 \text{ kVA.}$$

Annual saving = 19·20 × (1000 − 737) = $5070
If the power factor is improved to unity, the kVA is 700.
Actual saving = 19·20 × (1000 − 700) = $5760.

E

The reduced maximum demand kVA also reduces the number of running units chargeable at the highest steps of the tariff.

A suitably designed synchronous alternator, having a low-rated power factor and a high kVA rating, is capable of improving an extra low factory power factor. This involves a larger frame size alternator, but the saving on imported power costs usually pays off the extra cost well within 2 years, the actual period depending upon the relationship of alternator output to imported power.

In some cases surplus electricity generated privately may be sold to the public supply authority, provided a reasonably continuous supply can be made available. This is an attractive proposition when power is produced by waste heat or fuel which is a by-product of the factory process, and the power generated is always in excess of the factory load.

A factory may have a constant electrical load with a process steam demand which is insufficient to meet the electrical load for part of the day, but is capable of producing excess power for the remainder of the day. In such a case the best arrangement is to run in parallel with the public electricity supply system on a two-way agreement. Part of the day the factory would export power to the public supply system and, at other times, it would import power.

The public supply authority will not pay the same price for power exported from the factory as it charges for the power it sells to the factory. It will probably offer approximately half the rate charged. This is because approximately half the cost of supplying electricity to the consumer is its distribution. Power exported by a factory only saves the authority's generating costs; it still has to be distributed. Also, power exported can rarely be maintained at a guaranteed constant figure, so the supply authority is obliged to provide stand-by capacity to meet other commitments. The public supply authorities are not usually interested in purchasing power that is only available during "off-peak" times, i.e. during the night.

Although the Electricity Boards in Great Britain are statutorily authorised to make special agreements of this nature, the final decision is left to the local Board concerned, who will carefully assess the particular circumstances applying to each individual case where it is possible to export power. Factory management must never assume that they will be able to export power to the public electricity supply system; or even that they may operate their private generating plant in parallel with the public supply until the whole matter has been discussed in detail with the Electricity Board's technical and commercial engineers. There may be local distribution system restrictions which prohibit such an arrangement.

TECHNICAL CONSIDERATIONS OF PARALLEL OPERATION

The public electricity supply in Great Britain is almost entirely a three-phase, 50-cycles system. Private industrial power-generating plant must be designed for the same system if parallel running is contemplated.

There are two basic types of alternator suitable for parallel operation with the public supply. They are:

1. *Synchronous Alternators*

This is the conventional type of alternator having its own rotating or static excitation equipment. When this type of machine operates independently of the public supply, an automatic voltage regulator maintains a constant generation voltage by control of the machine excitation. Once the machine is synchronised with the public supply, this supply determines the system voltage. Adjustment of the alternator excitation now alters the power factor.

An automatic voltage regulator can be arranged to maintain the load on the public supply at unity or any other desired power factor under all conditions of working, by controlling the excitation of a suitably designed synchronous alternator. The example quoted earlier shows how this reduces the kVA maximum demand charge to a minimum, and can produce a financial advantage in the case of a factory having a poor power factor. There are, of course, other methods of improving a poor power factor, the most common being the use of capacitors.

2. *Asynchronous or Induction Alternators*

This type of machine is really an induction motor driven above synchronous speed. It is a simple machine which is cheaper than a synchronous alternator for the same output. There is a generally held opinion that it is simpler to operate than the synchronous machine because no synchronising equipment is required. This is not strictly true. It is necessary to provide some visual indication that a speed close to synchronous speed has been reached. This common belief of simplicity could lead to serious mishaps due to the operating staff not taking the necessary care when paralleling the machine. They are more likely to take care with a synchronous machine which they know must be synchronised. In actual fact there is no difficulty whatsoever in training unskilled personnel to operate steam turbines and to paralleling synchronous alternators. The standard induction alternator is incapable of running alone becase it must draw its excitation current from the public supply to which it is connected. Failure of the public supply will therefore bring about the entire failure of the electricity supply in the factory. It is impossible to use this type of machine to correct the power factor on the imported power. In fact, the induction alternator actually helps to worsen the power factor by taking its excitation current from the public electricity system. This effect can be offset by the installation of capacitors.

In recent years manufacturers have developed compensated induction alternators. These machines have the advantage over the normal induction alternator of being self-exciting and can be operated independently of the public supply. The power factor of the load generated is adjusted by varying the position of the brushes on the commutator. However, their advantages over the normal induction alternator are more than outweighed by their relatively complicated design and high cost.

The synchronous alternator would normally provide the better and simpler installation.

When privately owned power-generating plant operates in parallel with the public electricity supply system, it virtually becomes part of that system. It must, therefore, comply with the relevant provisions of the various statutory regulations governing the supply of electricity. To ensure that parallel operation does not jeopardise either the public supply or the private supply within the factory, nor introduce hazards to the operating staff, certain operating rules must be agreed between the public supply authority and the factory.

The private consumer must provide satisfactory synchronising equipment at the point where his generator is connected to the public supply system. Also, the protective arrangements must ensure that if his generator becomes defective, it is immediately disconnected from the system. In addition to overload and earth leakage protection, alternators of 1000 kW and above usually have "balanced" or circulating current protection, which will disconnect them from the system much more rapidly than overload protection if an internal fault occurs on the alternator.

The neutral earthing arrangements must be agreed with the public supply authority, who will not permit the private alternator to be earthed when operating in parallel with their high-voltage system, as this system already has a neutral point earthed. However, when the alternator operates independently of the public system, its neutral point must be earthed, preferably through a resistance.

Reverse power relays can be fitted to prevent the public supply system motoring the alternator in the event of the steam supply being cut off, and also to prevent export of power to the public supply system unless an export agreement is operative. Alternatively, the turbo-alternator control gear can incorporate devices which achieve these objects.

The public supply authority must be satisfied that the method of operating the plant will not impose a short-circuit duty on the switchgear in excess of its assigned rating.

CHAPTER 4

GOVERNOR SYSTEMS FOR INDUSTRIAL STEAM TURBO-ALTERNATORS

by

A. C. VALENTINE, C.Eng., M.I.Mech.E.

W. H. Allen Sons & Co. Ltd., Bedford, England,

a member company of Amagamated Power Engineering Ltd.

GOVERNING systems control the steam flow through the turbine to achieve one or more of the following basic functions:

(a) Maintain a nominally constant shaft speed at all loads.

(b) Maintain a nominally constant steam flow through the turbine.

(c) Maintain a nominally constant pass-out steam pressure at all flows.

(d) Maintain a nominally constant inlet steam pressure at all flows.

(e) Maintain a nominally constant exhaust steam pressure at all flows.

(f) Prevent overloading the alternator.

(g) Limit the value of power imported from or exported to the public supply system.

The choice of governing system is largely influenced by the method of operating privately owned power generation plant, e.g. to provide a completely independent power supply to the factory, or to provide a joint supply in parallel with the public electricity supply system. The fundamental difference is that the speed of an independent turbo-alternator will vary with changes in load, while the machine running in parallel with a large external electrical system is automatically tied to the frequency of that system irrespective of load. The principles involved in these two methods of operation are discussed separately in the chapter.

TURBO-ALTERNATORS OPERATING INDEPENDENTLY OF THE PUBLIC ELECTRICITY SUPPLY SYSTEM SPEED-GOVERNING SYSTEMS

Principle of Operation

To ensure a steady frequency of the electricity supply feeding the motors in the factory, an independent turbo-alternator has governor gears to maintain a nominally constant rotational speed irrespective of any changes of electrical load. The turbo-alternator speed would remain constant, even without governor gear, if the electrical load, inlet steam valve opening and steam conditions all remain unchanged. However, should the load increase, with a constant inlet steam valve opening, the shaft speed would decrease because the turbine would not then receive enough steam. The steam valve must open wider to admit more steam to match the load before the speed will return to normal. Conversely, when the load decreases, the valve must reduce steam flow to maintain normal speed.

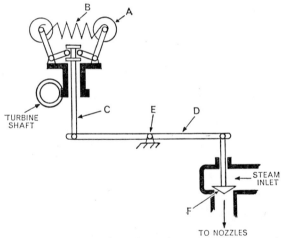

Fig. 4.1. Schematic diagram of simple speed governor without speeder gear.

A speed governor makes these changes automatically. Figure 4.1 shows a diagram of a simplified speed governor. Two flyweights A rotate on a vertical axis driven by the turbine shaft through a worm and wheel. The flyweights are pivoted so that as they move under centrifugal force they vary the load on spring B and move the spindle C which is

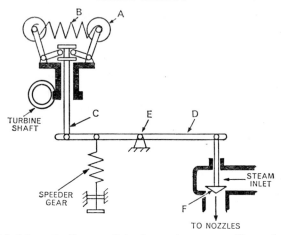

FIG. 4.2. Schematic diagram of simple speed governor with speeder gear.

connected via lever D and fulcrum E to the steam control valve F. A decrease in speed causes the weights to move in, spindle C to move down and valve F to open wider to admit more steam.

Most modern speed-governing systems incorporate oil relays which increase the power of the governor to move steam valves against high steam pressures while the speed governor itself, which only has to move the oil-relay pilot valve, can be made sensitive and conveniently small. Figure 4.3. illustrates the basic components of an oil-relay system.

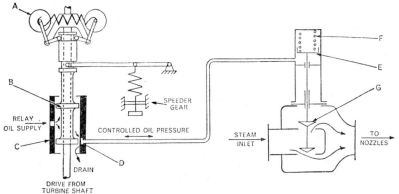

FIG. 4.3. Basic components of a simple oil-relay throttle-control speed governor system.

High-pressure relay oil enters the annular space surrounding pilot valve B and leaks past the edge of the pilot valve beat through the top opening of the port D into the relay cylinder; the oil also leaks to drain through the bottom opening of the port. The position of the pilot valve beat relative to the port therefore determines the oil pressure acting under relay piston E, against spring F, and controls the opening of the steam valve G. When an increase in electrical load occurs, the turbine speed decreases, the governor weights A move inwards and the pilot valve moves downwards, thus increasing the area of the port open to high-pressure oil and decreasing the area open to drain. The oil pressure under the relay piston increases and the steam valve opens wider to admit more steam to the turbine, which restores the speed to approximately its original value; this speed difference is discussed below. The increase in speed causes the pilot valve to move upwards again and a new position of equilibrium is reached with the turbine carrying the increased load. Conversely, when a decrease in electrical load occurs, the pilot valve moves upwards to decrease the oil pressure acting under the relay piston and reduce the steam valve opening.

The actual practical design of a speed governor varies with its particular application.

Performance

British Standard Specification No. 132 states that the permanent speed variation from "no load" to "full load" shall not exceed 4% of the rated speed. Also when operating at the rated speed, and the rated full load is thrown off, with the inlet steam pressure and temperature and the exhaust pressure remaining normal, the maximum temporary variation in speed shall not be sufficient to bring the emergency governor into operation. The latter is normally set at 10% above the rated speed and the temporary maximum speed variation is usually quoted as 8% for a condensing or back-pressure turbine, and 9% for a pass-out machine. The higher figure applies to a pass-out turbine because of the much greater variation in throttle steam flow which can occur from "no load, no pass-out" to "full load, full pass-out".

Speed Droop or Speed Regulation

The permanent speed variation due to load change is often referred to as the "speed droop" or "speed regulation". Figure 4.4 explains the need for a speed droop. For simplicity this figure is purely diagrammatic with the range of change in weight radius exaggerated. The centrifugal force of the governor weights depends upon their weight, their radius of movement and the square of their speed; larger radius or higher speed means greater force, i.e. the operating condition moves to the right or the top of the diagram respectively. Lines ON_1, ON_2, etc., are constant speed lines and pass through the origin O. The load on the governor springs depends upon their rate and the amount they are extended; larger weight radius means more spring extension and hence greater load. The load on the springs is equal and opposite to the centrifugal force of the weights when the governor is in equilibrium. It is known as the controlling force because it determines the equilibrium speed.

Consider what would happen if the spring rate exactly matched the increase in centrifugal force for each unit of change in weight radius. With the turbine operating at 100% rated speed, point C on line ON_3, assume a decrease in load occurred resulting in a 1% speed rise to line ON_2. The weights would develop more force than the spring over the change in weight radius and would fly to their "out" position, point D, shutting the inlet steam throttle valve. As the steam flow stops, the speed would decrease and at a speed slightly below 100%, point E, the spring force would exceed the weights force and move them to their "in" position, point F, opening the steam valve wide. Therefore, if the spring rate matched the rate of increase in centrifugal force, the system would hunt wildly from valve shut to valve wide open, without ever reaching a balance. Such a system is obviously quite useless for the control of a turbine.

To overcome this situation the spring force must increase faster than the weight force as the speed rises, i.e. the spring or controlling force, dotted line AB, must have a greater gradient than the centrifugal force speed lines ON_3, etc.

If the turbine is running at 100% speed, i.e. point C where the spring force line AB cuts the 100% speed line ON_3 and the load decreases,

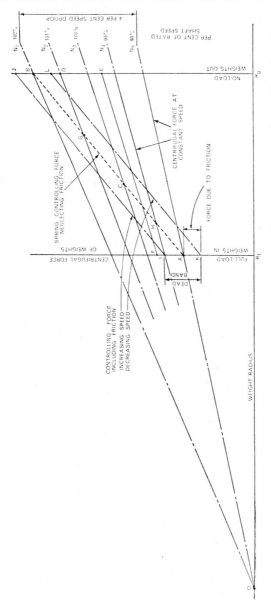

Fig. 4.4. Simplified representation of speed governor "speed droop" or "speed regulation" and "dead band".

the speed increases and the governor weights' centrifugal force momentarily exceeds the spring force so that they move outwards, raising the governor spindle to decrease the steam valve opening. Reduced steam flow limits the speed increase, so the spring force again balances the centrifugal force. The spring force prevents the weights flying to their "out" position and the governor takes up a new position of equilibrium at a higher speed, i.e. point G on the line ON_2. Conversely, for an increase in load the speed decreases, the spring force overcomes the reduced weight force so that the weights move inwards, lowering the governor spindle to increase the valve opening. Greater steam flow limits the speed fall and the governor system balances again at a lower speed, e.g. point H on line ON_4.

Figure 4.4 shows that for a definite change in speed the governor alters its position by a definite amount, i.e. for every speed it is able to take up a definite position; the governor is then said to be stable. The speed variation from no load to full load on the diagram is 4%. This is the governor droop or regulation.

Dead Band

So far it has been assumed that the governor is frictionless. Actually, friction is always present in the governor moving parts and in the mechanism which it operates. This friction tends to prevent the upward movement of the pilot valve, the outward movement of the weights and the closing movement of the steam throttle valve, when the shaft speed increases, and, conversely, it tends to prevent movements in the opposite directions when the speed decreases. Friction therefore increases the spring-controlling force when shaft speed increases, and decreases this force when speed decreases. This effect is indicated in Fig. 4.4 by chain-dotted lines IJ and KL, respectively, corresponding to a spring controlling force represented by line AB when friction is neglected. The vertical distance between these two lines is the governor's "dead band", i.e. change in speed which must take place before the controlling force moves the governor spindle to correct the steam valve opening. The shaft speed therefore varies between these two lines, depending on whether the load is increasing or decreasing.

If the governors of turbo-alternators operating in parallel have different dead bands, satisfactory load sharing will be adversely affected because the governors will not respond to load changes at the same speed change, i.e. one will begin to accept the load change before the other detects it.

System Stability

A speed governor is said to be stable when for each speed within its working range, it has only one radius of rotation for the governor weights at which it is in equilibrium, i.e. for a definite change in speed the governor alters its position by a definite amount. Figure 4.4 illustrates that a permanent speed droop due to load change is necessary for stable operation. The speed governor itself can be made stable with a relatively small speed droop. Unfortunately a stable governor does not ensure a stable speed-governing system. The complete system has a chain of stability involving additional factors, such as the time lag before the steam throttle valve moves in response to a speed change, the volume of steam entrained between the throttle valve and the nozzles, the inertia of the turbine rotor, gearing and alternator rotor, alternator excitation control, etc., all of which will affect the time lag before the speed recovers after a load change. To guarantee satisfactory operation the complete speed-governing system must be subjected to a stability analysis.

Speed/Output Adjustment

Figure 4.5 shows the relationship between shaft speed and power output of a turbo-alternator having a 4% speed droop. Lines A, B, C, D and E represent the effect of five different governor spring loads. Spring load A gives 100% speed at full load and 104% speed at no load. Spring loads B, C, D and E give 100% speed at 75, 50, 25% and no load, respectively. To maintain a constant supply frequency to the motors in the factory, it is usual to keep the speed at 100% irrespective of the value of the load. This is achieved with a speed-adjusting device known as a speeder gear (see Figs. 4.2 and 4.3), which applies an external force to increase or decrease the effective spring controlling force so that it is equivalent to a range of springs. The speeder gear is adjusted either by hand or by a remotely controlled motor to hold 100% speed at any

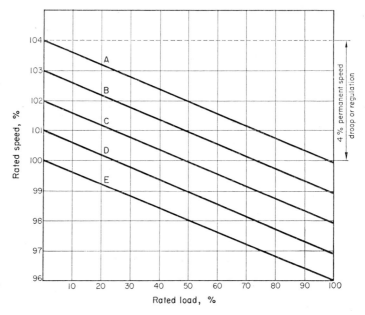

FIG. 4.5. Varying relationships between rated shaft speed and rated load for different settings of the speeder gear of a speed governing system having a 4% speed droop.

load by, in effect, moving the position of the speed droop, or controlling force, line on the diagram. The actual percentage speed droop varies slightly as the line moves up or down on the diagram, because the spring controlling force lines are parallel, while the centrifugal force speed lines diverge from the origin (see Fig. 4.4).

Isochronous Speed Governor

A speed governor having a zero permanent speed droop due to load changes is called an isochronous governor. It is fitted with a compensating device which acts as an automatic speeder gear. A load variation causes a transient change in shaft speed to which the governor weights respond and the governor pilot valve moves to adjust the opening of the steam throttle valve. The compensator receives a signal from the movement of the pilot valve and applies a load to the governor mechanism to adjust the controlling force, and gradually eliminates the speed change by repositioning the governor weights at 100% rated speed as the load steadies at its new value.

Normal industrial turbo-alternators rarely have isochronous governors. The ability to change load without changing permanent speed causes difficulties with load sharing between machines operating in parallel. A speed droop is necessary to prevent interchange of load between machines. In special cases one machine of a group may have an isochronous governor, as discussed below.

Parallel Operation and Load Sharing

When synchronous alternators operate in parallel with each other, but independently of the public supply system, they all run at the same speed, just as if they are coupled mechanically. When the load increases, the speed of the factory system falls until the revised total output of all the units matches the new load. The kW load is shared between the

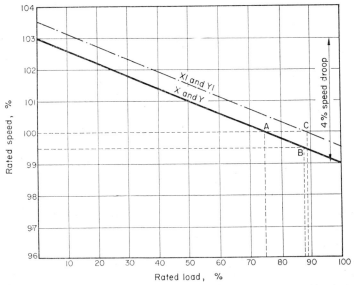

FIG. 4.6. Load sharing between two turbo-alternators having identical governor speed droops.

machines according to their rated outputs and to the governor speed droops of the turbines driving the alternators.

Consider two sets X and Y running in parallel; if both have the same speed droop they share load between them on an equal percentage basis, see Fig. 4.6. Each is set to carry 75% rated load at 100% rated

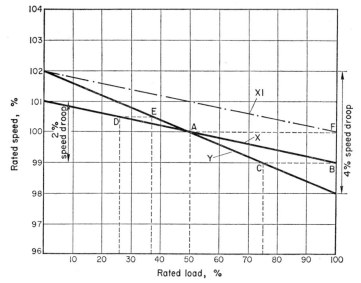

FIG. 4.7. Load sharing between two turbo-alternators having different governor speed droops.

speed, point A. As the load increases the speed will droop along the full line marked X and Y. If the speed droops to 99·5% each set will carry 88% rated load, point B. Depending upon the type of load, this fall in system frequency results in the actual connected load being slightly less than would be the case at normal frequency. Adjustment of the speeder gear on both sets restores the shaft speed, and hence system frequency, to 100%, by moving the speed droop line to the chain-dotted line marked X_1 and Y_1. The resultant rise in system frequency slightly increases the actual connected load to, say 89% point C.

Now assume both sets have different governor speed droops as represented by the two lines X and Y in Fig. 4.7. At a 100% speed, each set carries 50% rated load, point A. If the load increases until the speed falls to 99% set X will carry 100% load, point B, and set Y 75% load, point C. Conversely, if the load decreases until the speed rises to 100·5% set X will carry 26% load, point D, and set Y 37% load, point E. In each case the speed can be restored to 100% by the speeder gears. If both speed governors are adjusted the same amount, the sets each retain the revised percentages of load. However, one set can be made to accept all the load change if required, up to its rated capacity. Return to the 100% speed with each set carrying 50% load,

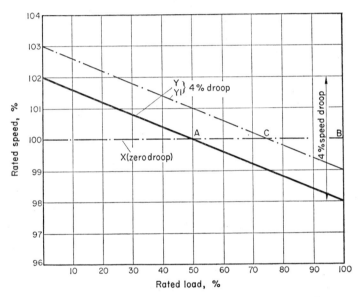

Fig. 4.8. Load sharing between two turbo-alternators, one having an isochronous governor and one having a governor with speed droop.

point A, then if the load increases by 50% of the output of the set with the smallest speed droop, i.e. set X, it will accept all this load if its speed droop is moved up to chain-dotted lines X_1 by the governor speeder gear, and the system speed will remain at 100% point F.

If one of the machines has an isochronous governor, while the other has a 4% speed droop, lines X and Y in Fig. 4.8, the set with the isochronous governor will take all load variations within its rated capacity, e.g. X can increase load from 50%, point A, to full load, point B, while Y continues to carry 50% load, and the speed remains at 100%. Such a system, i.e. varying load at constant frequency, is limited to load changes within the rating of the set having the isochronous governor and is therefore not employed very often. Greater load changes involve adjustment of the speeder gear of set Y to maintain 100% speed, e.g. line Y_1 for set Y carrying 75% load, point C.

It will be obvious from the above that the machine with the smallest speed droop will always take the largest share of any load variation. In fact, when turbo-alternators having different speed droops operate in parallel, there is always the danger that the unit having the smallest speed droop may become overloaded, unless load changes are carefully supervised. This is particularly so if one set has an isochronous governor.

While satisfactory sharing of the kW load between turbo-alternators operating in parallel depends upon the speed/kW characteristics, i.e. speed droops and dead bands of the turbine governors, satisfactory sharing of the kVAR load is dependent upon the voltage/kVAR characteristics of the automatic voltage regulators. This latter subject, while very important, is outside the scope of this book; it is sufficient to state here that curves of percentage rated voltage plotted against percentage rated kVAR load must have similar droops to those discussed for percentage rated speed against percentage rated kW load.

Methods of Speed Governing

There are three methods of speed governing commonly employed:
 (a) Throttle governing.
 (b) Nozzle control governing.
 (c) By-pass governing.

As explained earlier, all but the simplest forms of modern speed governor gear are of the oil relay-operated type; Fig. 4.3 illustrates a basic throttle governing system where the speed governor controls the opening of a single large throttle valve which passes the total steam flow to the turbine. This type of speed governor is simple and is quite satisfactory for a base-load condensing or back-pressure turbine which

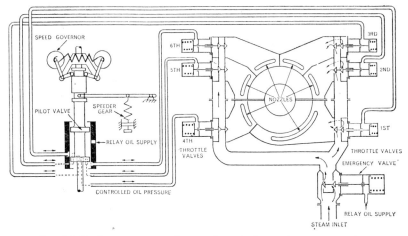

FIG. 4.9. Basic components of a nozzle control, speed governor system, incorporating fully automatic multi-throttle valves.

will run continuously at, or only slightly below, its maximum continuous rating. Throttle governing takes advantage of the fact that the quantity of steam passing through an orifice is proportional to the pressure upon it. At any flow below the maximum, the governor varies the steam pressure at the inlet to the turbine nozzles so that it is only

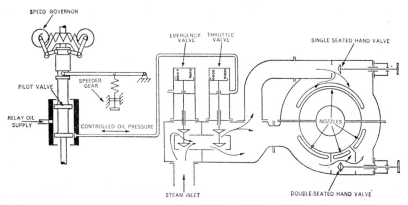

FIG. 4.10. Basic components of a nozzle control, speed-governing system, incorporating a single oil-relay throttle valve and multiple hand valves.

sufficient to pass the reduced flow through the full nozzle area.

The power obtainable from a quantity of steam depends on the available heat drop between inlet and exhaust conditions; also it is an intrinsic property of steam that this heat drop depends only on the initial temperature and the absolute pressure ratio. It follows that to obtain maximum efficiency at partial steam flows, the pressure at the inlet to the turbine nozzles must be maintained at the highest possible figure, i.e. avoid the excessive pressure drop across the throttle valve which is associated with simple throttle governing.

Nozzle control governing, which automatically adjusts the nozzle area to suit the steam flow, achieves this effect. The full nozzle area is divided into a number of small groups, each under the control of a separate throttle valve (see Fig. 4.9). The governor opens these valves consecutively to increase the nozzle area as the steam flow increases. Due to the small nozzle area and hence steam flow, controlled, the slight throttling loss across each automatic throttle valve is negligible in comparison with that on the total steam flow across a single large valve. This fact is of considerable importance in back-pressure turbines working with a small pressure ratio, and also is of some benefit to all turbines. Nozzle control governing is essential for efficient operation of back-pressure or pass-out turbines supplying process steam to a factory where both the process steam and electrical demands vary widely over very short periods. Allen turbines for this type of duty have four or six automatic throttle valves, depending upon the particular circumstances of the load variations to be accommodated.

In factories where steam consumption is not of prime importance due to an excess of cheap or waste fuel, e.g. cane-sugar factories burning bagasse, and a simple control system is required, steam turbines are still supplied with a single large throttle valve and a measure of nozzle control is achieved by hand-valves (see Fig. 4. 10). Usually one double-seated and one single-seated hand valve are employed. The operator sets these valves according to the load on the machine. However, the full benefits of nozzle control on steam economy can only be realised by fully automatic control of multiple throttle valves.

Some turbines have a specified maximum economical rating at 80% of the alternator maximum continuous rating; this constitutes the design point of the turbine. In the case of back-pressure turbines and the high-pressure cylinder of a twin-cylinder pass-out condensing machine, where the steam flow is large in relation to the blading mean diameter, it is usually desirable to distribute the available heat drop between inlet and exhaust, as evenly as possible over all the turbine stages at the 80% rating, in order to achieve the best possible efficiency. This makes it impracticable to pass the steam flow, corresponding to the alternator maximum continuous rating, through the turbine simply by increasing the area of the main inlet nozzles.

By-pass governing, in which the increased steam flow by-passes the inlet nozzles and enters the relatively larger area of the second or even the third stage nozzles, overcomes this difficulty. Usually two additional automatic governing valves, or by-pass valves, control the steam flow beyond that required for the maximum economical rating. Up to this point the multiple automatic throttle valves control the steam flow; when they are fully open and additional power is required from the turbine, the governor opens the by-pass valves to admit the total steam flow into the selected stage, completely by-passing the inlet nozzles. This redistributes the heat drop over less stages. The net result is a higher full-load steam rate but a lower steam rate at the 80% design rating, than a corresponding turbine which admits all its steam via the inlet nozzles.

A less complex method is to design the governing system so that the final throttle valve of a four- or six-valve system is just about to commence opening at the 80% rating, i.e. minimum throttle pressure drop and compromise the stage heat drops between the steam flow for 80% and 100% rating. This design produces a closer relationship between the 80% and full-load steam rates.

Typical System for Condensing Set

Figure 4.11 is a simplified block diagram for a speed-governed system for a straight condensing turbo-alternator. An oil pump provides oil at a pressure of 60 psig (4·15 bar (g)) to the governor relay oil system. The speed governor reduces this oil pressure across its pilot valve control beat to determine the opening of the single or multiple throttle steam valves. The relay supply oil also holds the emergency steam valve open and is connected to the emergency trip valve. In the event of unsafe

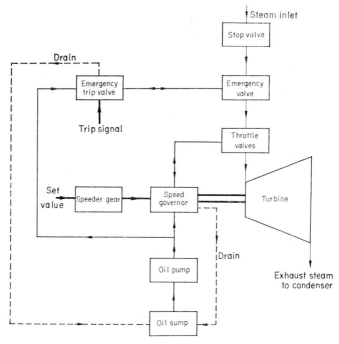

Fig. 4.11. Simplified block diagram of a speed-governing system for a straight condensing turbo-alternator.

operating conditions arising, protective devices operate the trip valve to destroy the relay oil pressure so that the emergency steam valve closes under spring action to cut off the steam supply.

Typical System for a Back-pressure Set

Figure 4.12 is a simplified block diagram of a simple speed governing system for a back-pressure turbine, including a reducing valve and a surplus valve to balance the process steam and power demands. The turbine is speed governed and passes a steam quantity corresponding to the electrical demand. The reducing valve makes up any process steam deficiency and the surplus valve "blows-off" any surplus steam to atmosphere or to a dump condenser. The advantage of a dump condenser is that the surplus steam is condensed and returned to the feed system instead of being lost. Surplus steam must not be allowed to find its own way out of the system through the exhaust main relief valve.

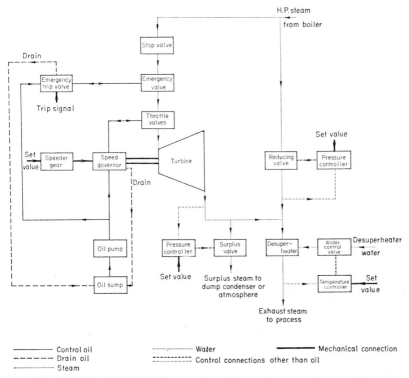

FIG. 4.12. Simplified block diagram of speed governing system for a straight back-pressure turbo-alternator with associated reducing valve and desuperheater. (The key to dotted and various thickness lines applies also to Fig. 4.11.)

A special surplus valve must be fitted to the exhaust pipework, designed to open and maintain a pressure only fractionally above the process system design pressure. This valve prevents the back pressure on the turbine rising to the relief valve setting pressure. This is important because an increasing back pressure has a cumulative effect of further reducing the amount of power which the turbine generates from the available steam flow and places the system further out of balance.

The reducing valve has a desuperheater to drop the temperature of the steam to, say, 20°F (11°C) above saturation temperature at the exhaust pressure. The turbine exhaust temperature increases with reducing throttle steam flow (see Fig. 4.13). If steam temperature is critical in the process, the reducing valve desuperheater can be used to maintain a constant steam temperature to the process irrespective of whether the steam is supplied from the turbine or the reducing valve, or from both simultaneously.

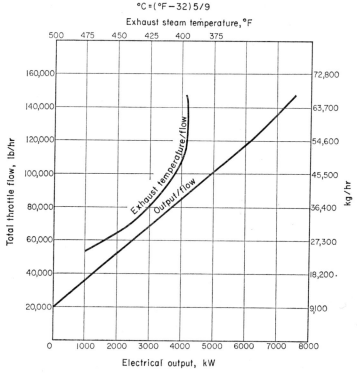

FIG. 4.13. Variation of exhaust steam temperature with throttle steam flow for a 7500 kW turbine having inlet steam conditions of 1250 psig (86 bar (g)), 850°F (455°C) and an exhaust pressure of 95 psig (6·55 bar (g)). (1 psig = 0·0069 bar (g)).

PASS OUT GOVERNING SYSTEMS

Principle of Operation

Pass-out turbines have a pressure governor which varies the steam flow passing out of the turbine to suit the changes in process steam demand. If the process requires more steam, with a constant pass-through valve opening, the pressure at the turbine pass-out branch falls, because not enough steam is available. The pass-through valve must close further to restrict the flow to the condenser and hence increase the flow to process to match the new demand, before the pressure returns to normal. Conversely, when the process demand decreases, the pass-through valve must open wider to pass more steam to the condenser and reduce the flow to pass-out, to maintain normal pressure.

A pass-out pressure governor makes these changes automatically. Figure 4.14(a) shows a diagram of a simplified pass-out pressure regulator system. The steam pressure at the pass-out branch A acts against a spring-opposed piston B, which is connected to the pass-through valve C via lever D and fulcrum E. An increase in steam pressure causes the piston B to move down and the pass through valve C to open to pass more steam to the condenser.

As with the speed governor, a hand adjustment is fitted to vary the value of the preset pressure by adjusting the load on the regulator spring (see Fig. 4.14(b)). Similarly, to increase the power of the regulator, it operates the pass-through valve via an oil relay (see Fig. 4.15); a bellow replaces the spring-opposed piston. The pilot valve is of the leak on/off type similar to that employed in the speed governor.

The control gear for an independent pass-out turbine must carry out the following two functions:

(a) Maintain the shaft speed nominally constant.

(b) Maintain the pass-out steam pressure nominally constant.

It must meet both these requirements irrespective of changes in both the electrical load and the process steam demand.

This is achieved by using a speed governor to control the admission of high-pressure steam through the throttle valves, and a pressure regulator to control the admission of steam to the low-pressure end of

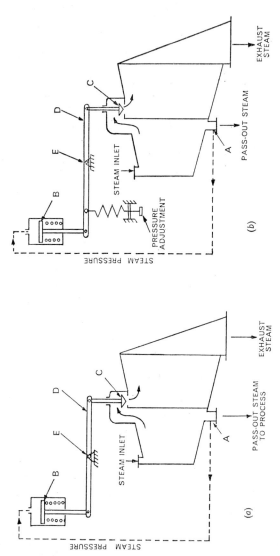

Fig. 4.14. Schematic diagram of simplified pass-out pressure regulator system: (a) without pressure adjustment, (b) with hand pressure adjustment.

the turbine through the pass-through valve. Multiple pass-through valves provide nozzle control on the low-pressure turbine when the steam flow is large. A variation in demand for either electricity or process steam causes both speed and pressure-governing systems to operate.

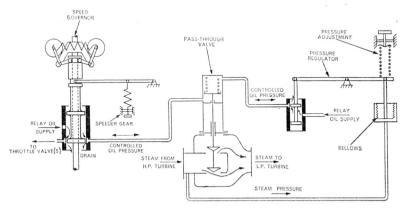

FIG. 4.15. Basic components of a pass-out pressure and speed governor oil-relay system interlinked from speed to pressure.

An increase in alternator load causes the speed to fall; the speed governor responds by opening the inlet throttle valves and allows more steam to enter the turbine. If the opening of the pass-through valve remained unaltered, the steam pressure at the pass-out branch would rise. The speed governor oil relay is therefore interlinked to the underside of the pass-through valve relay piston (see Fig. 4.15), so that a movement of the speed governor to open the throttle valves also opens the pass-through valve a corresponding amount to pass the additional steam to the low-pressure end of the turbine, leaving the pass-out steam conditions unaltered. Conversely, a decrease in alternator load results in both the throttle valves and the pass-through valves closing further, to reduce steam flow through the turbine.

An increase in process steam demand causes the pass-out pressure to fall; the pressure regulator responds by increasing the oil pressure acting on top of the pass-through valve relay piston, assisting the spring to close the valve further, thus restricting the steam flow to the low-pressure end of the turbine, and allowing more steam to pass out of the machine to process. The smaller steam flow through the low-pressure turbine stages reduces the power developed in these stages and results in the shaft speed falling. The speed governor then restores the power by increasing the steam flow through the turbine, as explained previously. The pressure regulator can be interlinked to the speed governor to obtain immediate adjustment of the throttle valves, but care is required with such a system to prevent the risk of hunting between the pressure and speed governors.

Performance

At present no British Standard Specification quotes performance figures for pressure regulators. The regulators fitted on Allen turbines maintain the steam pressure constant within plus or minus 1 psi (0·07 bar) or 2% of the nominal set pressure, whichever is the greater. This is the system "pressure droop" or "pressure regulation".

A handwheel permits the set pressure to be changed by varying the compression of a spring assisting the control bellows. This adjustment can be up to plus or minus 20% of the absolute nominal set pressure.

The regulator has an adjustable oil dashpot associated with its pilot valve, which provides stability under adverse conditions yet sensitive control with slow pressure variations. It slows up the reaction of the regulator to large sudden changes in steam pressure without requiring coarse spring ratings.

Typical System for Pass-out Condensing Set

Figure 4.16 is a simplified block diagram of a speed and pressure governing system for a pass-out condensing set having the speed governor interlinked to the pass-through valve. The temperature of the pass-out steam increases with reducing steam flow, and a desuperheater can be fitted as explained for the back-pressure turbine exhaust; for simplicity Fig. 4.16 does not indicate a desuperheater. As the operating range of throttle steam flow is large due to the pass-out steam require-

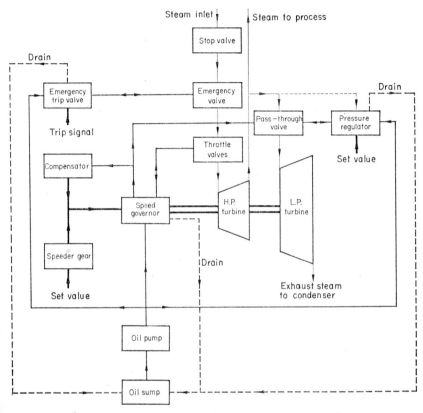

Fig. 4.16. Simplified block diagram of speed and pressure governing system for a pass-out condensing turbo-alternator.

ments, the speed governor is fitted with a compensator which reduces the permanent speed variation due to changes in steam and electrical load and hence throttle steam flow. This device applies the changes in controlled relay oil pressure, after a suitable delay, on to a spring-loaded piston connected to the speeder gear so that it changes the spring-controlling force. Simple adjustments vary the time delay before the compensation of the speed occurs and also the amount of compensation applied.

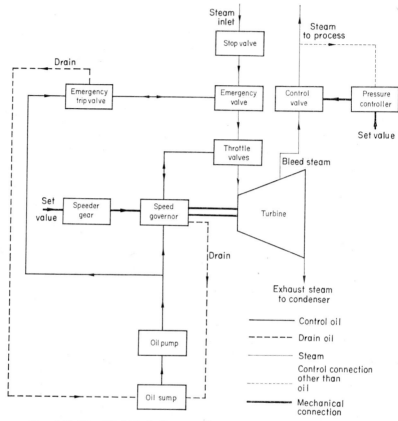

Fig. 4.17. Simplified block diagram of speed-governing system and pressure-control valve for a condensing turbine with a bleed steam branch. (The key to dotted and various thickness lines applies also to Fig. 4.16).

BLEED-POINT PRESSURE CONTROL

Principle of Operation

Steam passes out of a turbine bleed point at an uncontrolled pressure. The turbine has no pass-through steam valve; the steam passes straight through the turbine stages without leaving and re-entering the cylinder, the process steam bleeding out of a branch between two suitable stages. As the stage steam pressures fall with decreasing throttle steam flow, the pressure at the bleed branch will vary with steam flow. The bleed branch must therefore be placed at a point where the stage pressure will be sufficiently high for the process needs at the minimum anticipated steam flow. It follows that at higher steam flows the bleed pressure will be higher than is actually required. If the process cannot accept this higher pressure, an external pressure control valve, which is completely independent of the turbine governing system, reduces it to a constant figure at all steam flows.

This arrangement simplifies the turbine governor system when the process steam demand is small relative to the total throttle steam flow. The higher pressure necessary at maximum steam flow results in a loss of potential power from the process steam. Each case must be considered on its merits to determine whether this loss is greater than that due to the pressure drop across a pass-through valve.

Typical System

Figure 4.17 is a block diagram of a speed-governing system with a pressure-control valve for a condensing turbine having a bleed steam branch supplying steam to process.

TURBO-ALTERNATORS OPERATING IN PARALLEL WITH THE PUBLIC ELECTRICITY SUPPLY SYSTEM

Machines Having Normal Speed Governor Gear

Straight condensing turbo-alternator

A straight condensing turbo-alternator rarely operates in parallel with the public electricity supply system because it is usually cheaper to purchase all the required electric power from the public supply authority. This is because large central power stations can generate condensing power much more efficiently than is possible with a small independent condensing turbo-alternator, assuming that a factory purchases fuel for its boilers. However, if a factory has large quantities of waste material available from its main production process, which has no commercial value but is suitable for use as fuel for a boiler, the factory can raise cheap steam. Then, if the process requires very little or no steam, it may be economically worth while to use the steam in condensing turbo-alternators to reduce the value of the imported power supply.

Since the power output of a privately owned generating set is negligible compared with the capacity of the public electricity supply system, it is incapable of influencing the frequency of that system when operating in parallel with it. This means that the shaft speed of the private generating set will follow the public supply system frequency. While this frequency remains constant the turbine speed governor is incapable of varying the steam flow to the nozzles because the governor weights do not move. The governor spring-controlling force must change before the weights will move; the speed-adjusting gear is used to change this force. When synchronising the private machine with the incoming supply, the speeder gear adjusts the controlling force so that the turbo-alternator's shaft speed at no-load corresponds to the external system frequency. In Fig. 4.18, line F represents the normal system frequency and line D the no-load governor speeder gear setting. The speed governor has a controlling force equivalent to a 4% "speed-droop" characteristic over its no-load to full-load travel, when operating independently. When the set is paralleled with the incoming supply, the steam flow increases as the speeder gear applies less force, and the controlling force line progressively moves through positions C, B and A. The machine accepts load corresponding to the point where this line crosses the system frequency line.

Because the shaft speed cannot droop when tied to the public supply frequency, the speed governor in effect becomes a load governor, or, more literally, a steam flow governor, i.e. for a given setting of the speeder gear, with a constant system frequency, the turbine will pass a constant steam flow and hence have a constant power output, assuming the steam conditions remain fixed. Consequently, once the governor is set, the public supply system will accept all variations in the factory electric power demand. To limit the maximum demand on the imported supply to a given value, the turbine driver alters the speeder gear setting so that the turbine accepts more load, e.g. if set to line B on Fig. 4.18, the turbine carries 75% load, point X, but if the setting is increased to

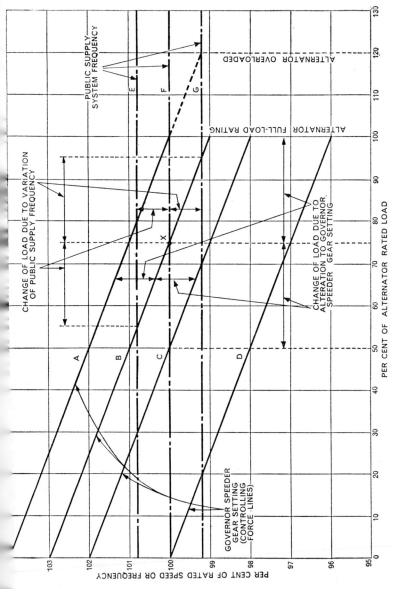

Fig. 4.18. Chart showing change of kilowatt load carried by a condensing turbo-alternator having normal speed-governor gear and operating in parallel with the public supply system, due to variation of speeder gear setting or system frequency.

line *A*, the turbine carries 100% load; conversely, if set to line *C*, it carries 50% load.

If the public supply frequency falls, the turbine speed governor responds to the fall in speed, automatically opening the throttle valves wider, and the turbine accepts a larger share of the load, e.g. if frequency falls from line *F* to line *G* on Fig. 4.18 with the governor set to line *B*, the turbine load increases from 75% to 95%. Conversely, if frequency rises to line *E*, the turbine load decreases to 55%. If the governor is set to line *A*, and the frequency falls to line *G*, the alternator would be overloaded 20%, i.e. point *Y*, provided sufficient steam can pass the nozzles.

The turbine driver can counteract this automatic procedure by adjusting the speeder gear. The danger of overloading the alternator, while operating with constant inlet steam conditions, can be avoided by fitting a positive stop to limit the governor travel in the direction which opens the inlet throttle steam valves.

This is the method of operating condensing sets which are supplied with steam under the control of the turbine driver. However, if the steam comes from waste-heat boilers which receive their heat at varying rates from the process, the turbine is normally fitted with an automatic inlet pressure governing system, described later.

Pass-out condensing turbo-alternator

A pass-out condensing turbine fitted with a normal speed and pass-out pressure governing system will run satisfactorily in parallel with the public supply system, provided that a competent driver is always available to deal with certain circumstances which may arise. Special automatic devices can meet some of these circumstances.

A pass-out turbine develops a constant load while the pass-out demand and public supply frequency both remain constant, i.e. the public supply accepts all load variations. Provided the pass-out demand remains constant, the machine behaves similarly to a condensing machine.

However, an increase in pass-out steam demand reduces the electrical load carried by the turbine, while a decrease in steam demand increases the electrical load. The turbine driver can correct these effects by adjusting the speeder gear setting. If the variations in process steam demand are rapid and frequent, it is unreasonable to expect him always to accept responsibility for protecting the turbo-alternator from extreme conditions.

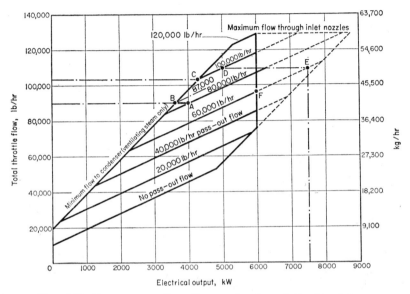

FIG. 4.19. Steam-consumption diagram showing relationship between steam flow and electrical output, for a 6000-kW pass-out condensing turbo-alternator having inlet steam conditions of 600 psig (41·3 bar (g)), 800°F (426°C) a pass-out steam pressure of 60 psig (4.15 bar (g)) and an exhaust vacuum of 28 in. Hg (94·5 kNm⁻²). The diagram shows the effect of changes in pass-out steam demand when operating in parallel with the public supply system with fixed speeder gear settings.

If an increase in pass-out steam demand occurs when the steam flow through the inlet steam throttle valves is set at a low figure, the normal governor gear may not be able to maintain a constant steam pressure at the pass-out branch. Figure 4.19 illustrates this condition. Assume the machine is operating at point A, passing out 80,000 lb/hr (36,300 kg/hr) with 4000 kW electrical load, and the process steam demand increases to 100,000 lb/hr (45,500 kg/hr). The pass-out regulator closes the pass-through valve to limit the steam flow to the condenser, but because the frequency does not fall, the speed governor makes no altera-tion to the inlet steam valve opening, so the operating point moves horizontally to point B at constant inlet flow of 90,000 lb/hr (41,000 kg/hr). The minimum ventilating steam flow to condenser is 3000 lb/hr (1360 kg/hr), so the pass-out flow is limited to 87,000 lb/hr (39,640 kg/hr), and the process pressure falls. The pressure regulator can be interlinked to the speed governor via a control cylinder to adjust the governor controlling force automatically, so that the inlet valves open to increase the flow to 103,000 lb/hr (46,800 kg/hr), point C, with 100,000 lb/hr (45,500 kg/hr) passing out. When the pass-through valve is completely closed (i.e. only ventilating steam passing through holes in the valve beats) and the pass-out pressure falls, a control beat in the pressure regulator admits relay oil on top of a piston in the control cylinder to apply a force to the speed governor pilot valve in the direc-tion to increase the relay oil pressure acting on the inlet throttle valves. If the pass-out demand then decreases again, the operating point moves down the minimum flow to condenser line until it reaches point B, and then moves horizontally at 90,000 lb/hr (41,000 kg/hr) as the pass-out regulator removes the force from the speed governor and controls the steam pressure by adjusting the opening of the pass-through valve.

At the other extreme, if a decrease in pass-out steam demand occurs when the steam flow through the inlet steam throttle valves is set to a high figure, there is a positive danger that a turbo-alternator with normal governor gear may be overloaded electrically. Figure 4.19 again illustrates this condition. Assume the machine carrying an electri-cal load of 5000 kW and a pass-out demand of 100,000 lb/hr (45,500 kg/hr) point D, when the latter demand decreases to 60,000 lb/hr (27,300 kg/hr). As the frequency does not rise the speed governor does not alter the inlet steam valve opening, and the operating point moves horizontally to intersect the 60,000 lb/hr (27,300 kg/hr) pass-out line at point E. At this point the turbine can produce 7500 kW, which is equivalent to an overload of 25% on the alternator. An automatic alternator load-limiting device, initiated from the alternator phase current, can override the speed governor setting and reduce the total steam flow to 96,000 lb/hr (43,600 kg/hr) point F, corresponding to 60,000 lb/hr (27,300 kg/hr) pass-out at the alternator full-load rating.

Alternator load limiter

Figure 4.20 is a schematic diagram of an alternator load limiter circuit. Current transformers *A*, fitted in the alternator phase connections provide a signal proportional to the alternator load. The signal passes through the three-phase variable-ratio transformer *B* and a three-phase rectifier *C*, to a control coil *D* in the load-limiter body *E*. The control coil energises a magnetic core *H*, which attracts a spring-loaded armature *G*. Movement of the armature causes pilot valve *F* to move down. While the alternator current is less than its full-load value, the relay oil passes the pilot valve control beat *J* without restriction, but as soon as the current exceeds this value, the armature movement is sufficient for the pilot valve control beat to decrease the port opening to pressure oil and increase the opening to drain. The relay oil passing the load-limiter pilot valve is connected to a spring-loaded piston in an attachment on the speed governor. Movement of this piston automatically overrides the setting of the governor speeder gear and adjusts the governor controlling force. When the load limiter decreases the opening of control port *J* to pressure oil, it reduces the oil pressure acting on the governor attachment piston, which adjusts the position of the speed governor pilot valve. This action reduces the governed oil pressure in the throttle steam valve oil relays, causing the valves to close further and restrict the steam flow to that corresponding to the alternator maximum continuous rating at the reduced pass-out flow. When the pass-out demand is restored, the turbine output falls and the load limiter removes the restriction.

The variable-ratio transformer provides adjustment of the current value at which the restriction occurs. The load-limiter pilot valve has an adjustable dashpot which provides stability under adverse conditions.

Typical system for a pass-out set

Figure 4.21 is a simplified block diagram of a speed and pass-out pressure governing system incorporating a governor attachment and an alternator load limiter.

The load limiter is isolated when the machine operates independently of the public supply system. The governor attachment also houses a compensating device which reduces the permanent speed variation

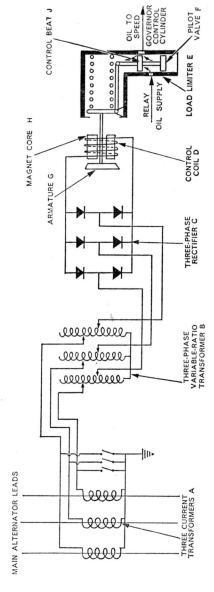

Fig. 4.20. Schematic diagram for alternator electrical load limiting device.

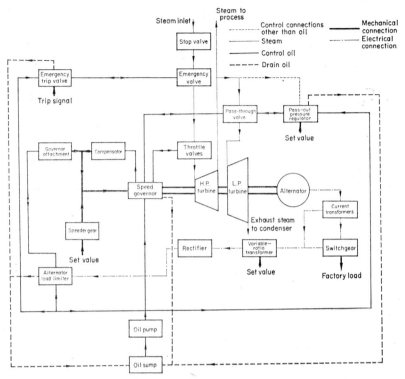

FIG. 4.21. Simplified block diagram of normal speed and pass-out pressure governing system, incorporating a governor attachment and an alternator load limiter for a pass-out condensing turbo-alternator operating in parallel with the public supply system.

due to load changes when the turbo-alternator operates under normal speed-governing conditions. This device uses the relay oil pressure to change the governor controlling force, as explained earlier.

Inlet-Pressure Governing System

Principle of operation

When a factory has vast quantities of waste heat which can be utilised to raise steam, the most economical power plant installation is usually one which uses all the steam in a high-efficiency turbo-alternator and employs as many electric motor drives as possible. Usually the boiler capacity is in excess of the factory process steam demand and a pass-out condensing turbine is required to absorb the excess steam. The surplus power which is often available can then be sold to the public electricity authority.

As there is normally no control over the quantity of steam available from waste-heat boilers, satisfactory governing of the turbine presents certain problems. As restriction of the boiler output is not acceptable, the waste-heat boiler cannot generate steam to suit the electrical demand; also, because the turbine speed is tied to the public supply frequency, the normal speed governor cannot control the turbine. The primary function of the governing system for this type of installation is to extract the maximum amount of electrical power from the available steam. This is achieved by inlet pressure governing, incorporating automatic nozzle control with multiple throttle valves.

The inlet pressure governor maintains a nominally constant steam pressure at the turbine stop valve, and hence a constant maximum heat drop across the turbine, by automatically adjusting the area of high-pressure nozzles open to steam to suit the steam quantity available from the boiler. In addition to maximum system efficiency, this method of control also provides incidental but important advantages, such as preventing the turbine robbing vital auxiliary machinery of steam and preventing priming due to reduced boiler pressure.

Figure 4.22 is a simplified diagram of the basic components of an inlet pressure governing system. It uses the speed governor pilot valve A to control the opening of the inlet throttle steam valves under both speed and inlet pressure governing conditions. The turbo-alternator is paralleled with the public supply system under the control of the speed governor and speeder gear B in the usual way, with the oil relay connection from the pressure regulator isolated. When the machine has been paralleled with the outside system, the speed governor alone is incapable of controlling the valve openings. The inlet pressure regulator is now put into circuit and controls the movement of the speed governor pilot valve A in conjunction with the pressure control cylinder D and lever C. The inlet pressure regulator is of similar construction to the pass-out regulator, having a spring-opposed bellows, connected to the steam supply to the turbine, controlling a leak on/off pilot valve.

Fluctuations in steam flow from the waste-heat boiler either increase or decrease the supply steam pressure to the turbine. The regulator bellows *F* responds to these pressure variations and moves pilot valve *E* to vary the oil pressure acting on the piston in control cylinder *D*. This

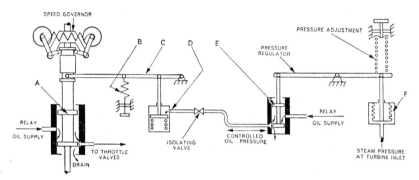

FIG. 4.22. Basic components of an inlet-pressure governing system showing interconnection between the pressure regulator and the speed-governor pilot valve.

piston applies a load to the speed governor pilot valve *A*, which is reflected in variations in oil pressure acting under the throttle steam valve pistons, resulting in appropriate changes in valve openings to pass the available steam flow. The bottom beat of pilot valve *E* controls the regulator relay oil pressure, so that an increase in supply steam pressure causes the throttle valves to open further and a decrease in pressure closes the valves further.

Performance

The inlet pressure regulator maintains the supply steam pressure constant within plus or minus 2% of the nominal pressure. Provision is made for adjusting the set pressure, and the regulator has an adjustable dashpot which ensures both stability and sensitive control.

Typical system for pass-out condensing set

Figure 4.23 is a block diagram of an inlet-pressure governing system for a pass-out condensing turbo-alternator. It incorporates a pass-out

F*

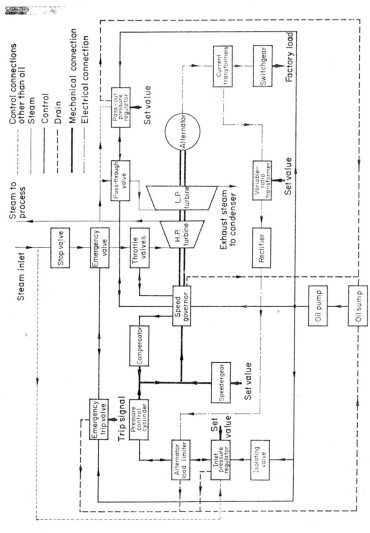

Fig. 4.23. Simplified block diagram of an inlet-pressure governing system, incorporating an alternator load-limiter, for a pass-out condensing turbo-alternator operating in parallel with the public supply system.

steam pressure regulator which acts identically to that described for a speed governed machine. Also an electrical load-limiting device is included to override the inlet pressure regulator, and to prevent more than full load being generated, should an abnormally large steam flow to the condenser result. This may be due to a sudden reduction in pass-out demand, when the turbine is operating with a large total throttle flow from the waste-heat boiler.

The turbo-alternator can operate as a normal speed-governed machine independently of the public supply system with the inlet pressure regulator and load limiter isolated. The governor attachment which embodies the inlet-pressure control cylinder also houses a compensating device which reduces the permanent speed variation due to load changes, when operating under normal speed-governing conditions.

Back-Pressure Governing System

Principle of operation

The most common application of a privately owned turbo-alternator operating in parallel with the public supply electricity system is the case of a back-pressure turbine providing process steam from high-pressure boilers. As the electrical power demand in a factory seldom corresponds to the output which the turbo-alternator can produce from the process steam flow, this arrangement allows the public supply system to make-up any deficiency of power or to absorb any surplus of power; assuming, of course, that satisfactory technical and commercial arrangements can be negotiated with the local electricity authority. Some installations operate a one-way agreement, i.e. either import or export power only, while others operate a two-way agreement, both importing and exporting power at different times of the day or night to suit the heat/power balance applying in the factory.

Again the primary function of the governing system for this type of installation is to extract the maximum amount of electrical power from the available steam flow, which, in this instance, is determined by the process steam requirements. This is achieved by back-pressure governing, incorporating automatic nozzle control with multiple throttle valves.

The back-pressure governor maintains a nominally constant steam pressure at the turbine exhaust branch, irrespective of variations in process steam demand, by automatically adjusting the opening of the multiple throttle valves to pass a steam flow corresponding to the process steam demand. The process steam flow thus determines the output generated by the turbo-alternator at all times.

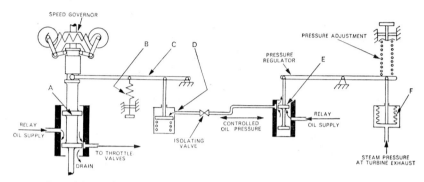

FIG. 4.24. Basic components of a back-pressure governing system showing interconnections between the pressure regulator and the speed governor pilot valve.

Figure 4.24 is a simplified diagram of the basic components of back-pressure governing system. It is very similar to the inlet-pressure governing system, and uses the speed governor pilot valve A to control the opening of the inlet throttle steam valves under both speed and back-pressure governing conditions. The fundamental difference is that the back-pressure regulator uses the top beat of its pilot valve E to control the relay oil pressure acting in the control cylinder, while the inlet pressure regulator uses the bottom beat. After the machine is paralleled on the speed governor, the back-pressure regulator is put into circuit. Fluctuations in process steam demand either increase or decrease the steam pressure at the turbine exhaust branch. The regulator bellows F responds to these pressure variations and the system adjusts the position of the speed governor pilot valve A to cause appropriate changes in the throttle steam valve openings to pass the steam flow required in the process. Because the top beat of pilot valve E controls the regulator relay oil pressure, an increase in process steam pressure causes the throttle valves to close further and a decrease in pressure opens the valves further.

A danger of overloading the alternator arises if the turbine operates with a range of inlet and/or exhaust pressure to suit varying plant requirements. The heat drop across the turbine, and hence power developed, is proportional to the ratio of inlet and exhaust steam pressures. It follows that if the alternator is rated for a normal exhaust pressure which is not the lowest of the range or an inlet pressure which is not the highest of the range of pressures, the turbine is capable of developing sufficient power to overload the alternator at full steam flow. A load limiter is then fitted to override the back-pressure regulator and restrict the steam flow to that corresponding to the alternator full-load rating.

Performance

The back-pressure regulator maintains the exhaust steam pressure constant within plus or minus 1 psi (0·07 bar) or 2% of the nominal pressure, whichever is the greater. Provision is made for adjusting the set pressure up to plus or minus 20% of the nominal absolute set pressure, and the regulator has an adjustable dashpot which ensures both stability and sensitive control.

When a purchaser anticipates taking full advantage of the 20% pressure adjustment, this should be stated when tenders are called for, in order to ensure that the last rows of blading are designed for the maximum stress conditions which can arise.

Typical systems

The typical system diagrams are intentionally complex to enable them to illustrate all the devices discussed. All back-pressure governing systems do not necessarily include all these devices; each scheme is considered on the particular conditions applying in the factory.

Figure 4.25 is a block diagram of a back-pressure governing system, including an export power controller. This device is discussed later. A reducing valve is usually installed in parallel with the back-pressure turbine, both to act as a standby and often to meet peak process steam demands if these are of short duration, so that the turbo-alternator rating matches the normal maximum steam demand only.

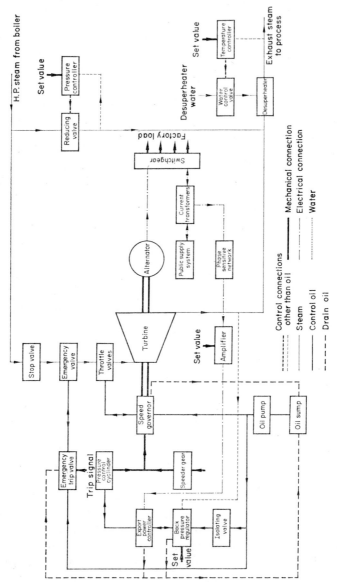

Fig. 4.25. Simplified block diagram of a back-pressure governing system for a straight back-pressure turbo-alternator operating in parallel with the public supply system, and incorporating an export power controller and a stand-by reducing valve.

Figure 4.26 is a block diagram of a pass-out, back-pressure governing system incorporating an alternator load limiter. This type of turbine provides process steam at two pressures and maintains both pressures nominally constant, irrespective of fluctuations in demand at either pressure or both pressures simultaneously. The back-pressure regulator acts, via a control cylinder, on the speed governor pilot valve to control the admission of high-pressure steam through the throttle valves, and the pass-out regulator controls the admission of steam to the low-pressure end of the turbine through the pass-through valves.

An increase in low-pressure process steam demand causes the exhaust pressure to fall; the back-pressure regulator responds by opening the inlet throttle valves and allows more steam to enter the turbine. The back-pressure/speed governor oil relay is interlinked to the underside of the pass-through valve relay piston in a similar manner to that described for the pass-out condensing turbine, so that the pass-through valve opens a corresponding amount to pass the additional steam to the low-pressure end of the turbine, leaving the pass-out conditions unaltered. Conversely, a decrease in low-pressure process steam demand results in both the throttle valves and the pass-through valves closing further to reduce the steam flow through the turbine. An increase in high-pressure process steam demand causes the pass-out pressure to fall; the pass-out pressure regulator responds by closing the pass-through valve further and allowing more steam to pass-out of the turbine. The reduced steam flow to the low-pressure end of the turbine is now insufficient to meet the low-pressure process demand, so that the exhaust pressure falls. The back-pressure governor then restores the steam flow by increasing the total flow through the throttle valves, as explained previously. Conversely, a decrease in high-pressure process steam demand again results in pass-through valve and throttle valves closing further.

A compensator is fitted to the speed governor to give close speed control under speed-governing conditions. The back-pressure regulator is then isolated but the pass-out regulator still maintains a nominally constant high-pressure process steam pressure. The exhaust pressure varies to suit the steam flow necessary to meet the electrical demand unless an automatic by-pass reducing valve and a surplus valve are installed.

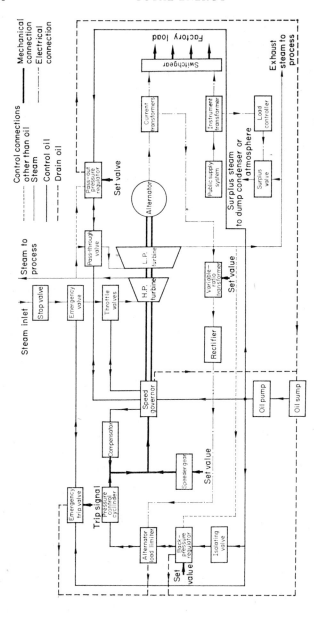

Fig. 4.26. Simplified block diagram of a back-pressure and pass-out pressure governing system, incorporating an alternator load limiter and an electrically-operated exhaust steam dump valve, for a pass-out back-pressure turbo-alternator operating in parallel with the public supply system.

The electrically operated exhaust steam dump valve limits the value of imported power.

Control of Imported or Exported Power

When a privately owned turbo-alternator operates in parallel with the public electricity supply system, the local supply authority may impose a limit to the power which a factory can import or export. In any event the tariff for the purchased power encourages a high utilisation factor, i.e. an average running demand nearly equal to the maximum demand. An excessively high maximum demand for only half an hour will greatly increase the cost of all power purchased during the accounting period. The private turbo-alternator must therefore carry the peak-load when it arises, to ensure that the imported power maximum demand does not exceed an acceptable figure. The standard governing systems described above do not do this automatically.

When the imported maximum demand reaches a predetermined figure, electrical instruments can sound an alarm to inform the turbine driver that he must either adjust the turbine governor speeder gear setting to accept more load, or, alternatively, shed certain unessential electrical loads. Various automatic systems can make these adjustments, depending upon circumstances.

Electrical governor

An electrical governor, whose primary function is to maintain, automatically, a nominally constant value of the electrical power either imported from, or exported to, the public supply system, has not received favour and has not been developed in detail. In principle, this type of governor takes a signal from the current passing through the connection to the public supply system and compares this value with a reference set value. Any difference in these values results in an adjustment of the speed governor controlling force to vary the steam flow through the turbine. The system thus ensures that the turbo-alternator accepts all factory load variations.

A selector switch determines whether the system controls import or export of power at a particular time, when both are required at different times. With the electrical control system isolated, the speed governor controls the shaft speed in the usual way.

If this type of governing system is fitted to a back-pressure turbine, a reducing valve and a surplus valve maintain a constant process steam pressure.

Exhaust steam dump valve

When power is imported only, and a turbo-alternator has a back-pressure governing system, it is possible to limit the imported power by fitting an exhaust steam dump valve. When, due to a change in a factory steam/power balance, the imported power reaches a predetermined value, a wattmeter, or a maximum-demand control meter, fitted in the public supply connection, sends a signal to a power-operated dump valve on the exhaust steam main. The valve opens to pass steam either to a dump condenser or to atmosphere, thus increasing the low-pressure steam demand. The back-pressure governor responds and increases the steam flow through the turbine, enabling it to generate additional power. Conversely, as the electrical demand falls, the dump valve closes and the system returns to normal pressure control. The saving in purchased power costs can be much greater than the cost of the extra steam dumped.

Preferential electrical load shedding

A similar effect is obtained by using the signal to operate a preferential electrical tripping relay to shed unessential load until the peak load diminishes.

Occasionally a dump steam valve and load shedding are used in series.

Export power controller

A factory operating a two-way agreement, or exporting power only, may wish to limit the value of the power exported to a predetermined figure. An export power controller overrides the pressure governor, in a similar manner to the alternator load limiter when a high steam demand occurs coincidental with a low factory electrical power demand.

Referring to Fig. 4.25 current transformers, fitted in the connection to the public supply system, send a signal proportional to the current flowing in the connection through a phase sensitive network to an amplifier which compares it with an internal reference set value. The amplifier only acts on a unidirectional input signal, corresponding to export of power to the public supply system, and an error signal only develops when the preset export value occurs. The amplifier then sends a signal to the control coil of the electro/hydraulic controller so that it attracts a spring-loaded armature. As the current in the coil increases, the movement of the armature causes a pilot valve to move so that its control beat decreases the port opening to relay oil from the back-pressure regulator and increases the opening to drain. This decreases the oil pressure acting in the pressure-control cylinder on the speed governor, and consequently reduces the throttle valve relay oil pressure so that the valves close sufficiently to restrict the steam flow to that corresponding to the factory electrical load plus the maximum permitted export load. Conversely, as the factory electrical load increases, or steam load decreases the export power controller removes the restriction and the machine returns to normal control.

While the power controller is restricting the steam flow, a reducing valve in parallel with the turbine automatically cuts in to make up the deficiency, and maintains the process steam pressure at a slightly reduced pressure.

Loss of Public Supply Connection

Although the public electricity supply is generally reliable, it does fail occasionally under various circumstances. The local electricity authority therefore insists that a factory takes adequate precautions to protect both its own and the authority's equipment should the two supplies become disconnected. These precautions are dependent upon the particular conditions prevailing at the point of connection.

The major danger occurs if a public supply system circuit-breaker, remote from the factory trips, leaving the privately owned generating plant connected to an isolated network. It is essential to ensure that the public supply breaker in the factory trips immediately, to prevent the possibility of the public supply being reconnected out of phase with the privately owned plant. Depending upon the circumstances this is achieved by a reverse power relay, an overload relay or a rate of change of frequency relay fitted on the public supply connection at the factory.

After the public supply connection opens, a straight condensing or pass-out condensing machine returns to normal speed governing; the factory frequency depends upon the speeder gear setting and the factory load. In the case of a pressure-governed machine, the frequency depends upon the turbine exhaust conditions and the factory load. If these are widely out of balance, the pressure regulator should be taken out of circuit or steps taken to balance the steam flows; each case is considered on its merits.

In all cases, if the factory is exporting power when the public supply circuit-breaker opens, the factory frequency rises; if it is importing power the frequency falls. In the latter case, a preferential tripping relay can disconnect selected feeder breakers until the load corresponds to the alternator full-load rating.

Prevention of Motoring

A turbo-alternator, running independently, automatically stops when its emergency trip gear operates. This is not the case when the machine operates in parallel with the public supply system. When the throttle steam flow falls below no-load flow, the alternator takes power from the outside system and acts as a motor driving the reduction gear and turbine rotor. This is undesirable, as windage inside the cylinder could overheat the rotor.

A reverse power relay on the alternator circuit-breaker can trip the breaker when power flows into the alternator. A time delay relay is incorporated to prevent the relay operating should a temporary reverse flow occur when the alternator is synchronised with the public supply.

Alternatively, a limit switch on the turbine emergency steam valve can trip the alternator circuit-breaker immediately the valve shuts to cut-off the steam supply.

Should the steam supply to an inlet-pressure governed turbine fail completely, the regulator would close the throttle steam valves and the turbine would cease to generate power. To prevent the alternator motoring the turbine, a pressure switch connected upstream of the throttle valves can trip the alternator circuit-breaker when the steam pressure falls to a preset figure.

CHAPTER 5

OPEN-CYCLE GAS TURBINES AND TOTAL ENERGY

by

H. R. M. Craig, B.Sc., C.Eng., F.I.Mech.E.

Advance Turbine Development, AEI Turbine-Generators Limited

GENERAL CHARACTERISTICS OF THE OPEN-CYCLE GAS TURBINE

In its simplest form the open-cycle gas turbine is a machine where air is taken from the atmosphere, compressed, heated at constant pressure (usually by combustion of fuel in the air) and expanded in the turbine. The work produced by the turbine is used to drive the compressor in the cycle and the balance provides the useful output of the machine. This balance is typically one third to one half of the total expansion work.

The efficiency obtained from a simple machine of this type depends on three main parameters. It depends upon the aerodynamic efficiency of the compressors and of the turbines: 1% in compressor and turbine efficiency producing 3–5% change in output for a given fuel input. It depends upon the maximum temperature of the cycle, higher temperatures always producing higher efficiencies, all other factors being equal. Lastly it depends upon the pressure ratio of the cycle. As the pressure ratio is increased from unity the turbine is able to extract from the hot gas a higher proportion of its total energy, and less heat is rejected to atmosphere so that in general efficiency increases with increasing pressure ratio. If this process is continued too far two effects modify the argument. Firstly, the efficiency of the compression process drops since the air being compressed at the high-pressure end of the cycle is already hot, and secondly in the limit the outlet temperature from the compressor equals the maximum temperature of the cycle and by this point no fuel energy can be added and the cycle output would become zero even if there were no aerodynamic losses. The general picture therefore is of a cycle efficiency which rises with pressure ratio

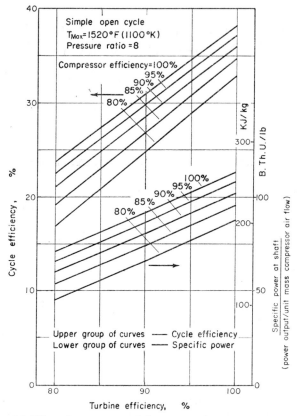

FIG. 5.1. Effect of component efficiency on typical cycle performance.

to an optimum and then declines (Figs. 5.1 and 5.2). It should also be noted that the fraction of total turbine work which is available as output diminishes as the pressure ratio increases. The higher pressure ratio cycles are therefore the more sensitive to component efficiency.

A cycle of this type is the simplest form of gas turbine but it suffers from the disadvantage that its efficiency tends to be only moderate. A number of simple additions can therefore be made to the cycle which, at the expense of some increase in complexity, increase either its efficiency or its specific output.

Three of these are important:

1. It is possible to divide the compression into two or more stages and to provide intercooling between each stage. This has the effect of increasing the optimum pressure ratio of the cycle and its

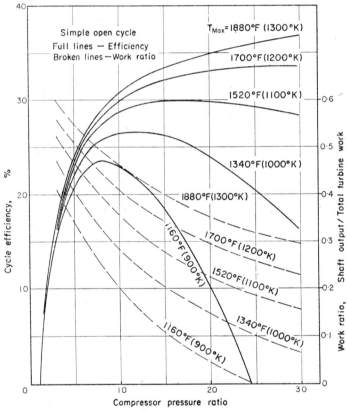

FIG. 5.2. Effect of pressure ratio and temperature on typical cycle performance.

specific output, and in addition it provides a useful addition to the efficiency of the cycle. The optimum position for intercooling varies somewhat according to whether the optimum specific output or optimum efficiency is required, but in either case is earlier in the cycle than the geometric mean of pressures (which would be the best if the heat in the gas at outlet from the high pressure compressor is not used) (Figs. 5.4, 5.5).

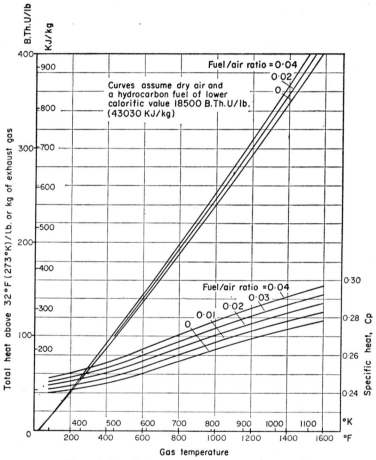

FIG. 5.3. Specific heat and total heat of exhaust gas.

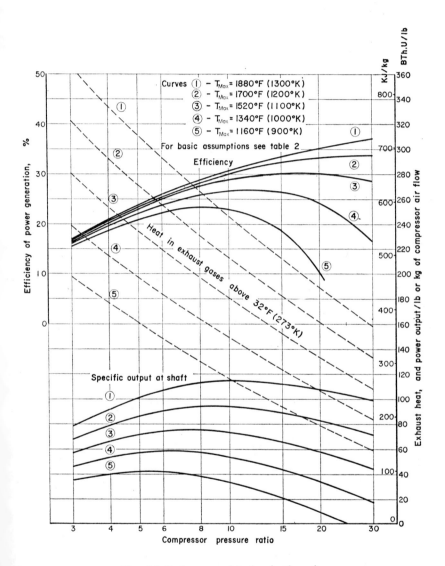

FIG. 5.4. Performance data for simple cycle.

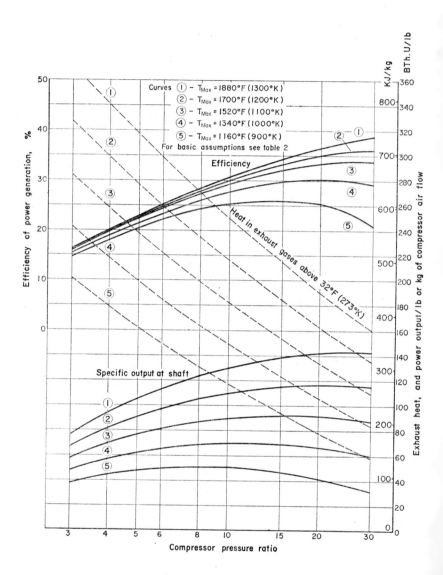

FIG. 5.5. Performance data for intercooled cycle.

2. In like manner the turbine can be split into two or more stages and heat added between the turbines in order to increase the work output from the lower pressure end of the expansion cycle. This has the effect of considerably increasing the specific output of the cycle but the effect on the efficiency is usually small and sometimes detrimental unless some method of waste heat recovery is also used (Fig. 5.6).

3. Means may be provided for recovering the waste heat in the turbine exhaust. Two such means are fairly common. The first is to provide a heat exchanger whereby the heat in the gas at outlet from the turbine is used to preheat the air at outlet from the compressor before fuel is added in the combustion chamber. This effectively reduces the fuel input to the machine for what is substantially the same power output (although some loss in power is involved due to the pressure drops in the heat exchanger and associated duct work reducing the available expansion pressure ratio for a given compressor pressure ratio). The amount of heat which can be so exchanged in this manner diminishes as the pressure ratio of the cycle increases because of the increasing compressor outlet temperature and the decreasing turbine outlet temperature. Simple cycles to which a heat exchanger is added therefore have a low optimum pressure ratio (around 4 to 6) (Fig. 5.7). The second means is to provide a waste heat boiler in the exhaust and to raise steam which can then be used for a variety of purposes. This is the scheme which is employed in the majority of total energy plants.[4, 100, 123, 120]

It will be clear, of course, that these changes in the cycle are not alternatives and cycles can be produced with heat exchangers and intercoolers, and re-heat (Figs. 5.8, 5.9, 5.10, 5.11). Other changes are achieved by varying the layout of shafts and the method of controlling them. For instance, the power output shaft may be controlled to run at constant speed for electrical power generation, or at varying speeds for other applications. The turbine driving the compressor and that driving the load may be the same turbine, or they may consist of two turbines either in series or in parallel. Where intercooling is employed the low-pressure compressor may be driven by the low-pressure turbine, and the high-pressure compressor by the high-pressure turbine

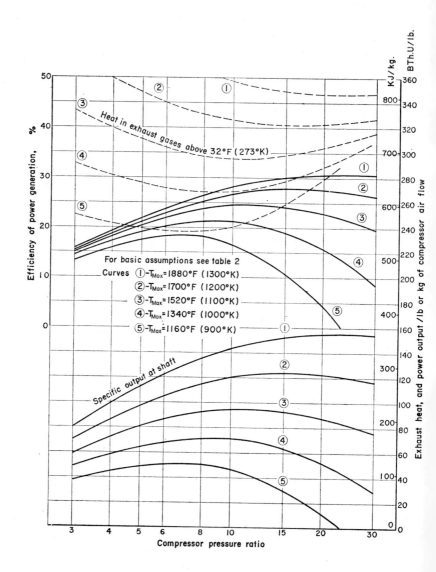

5.6. Performance data for cycle with reheat.

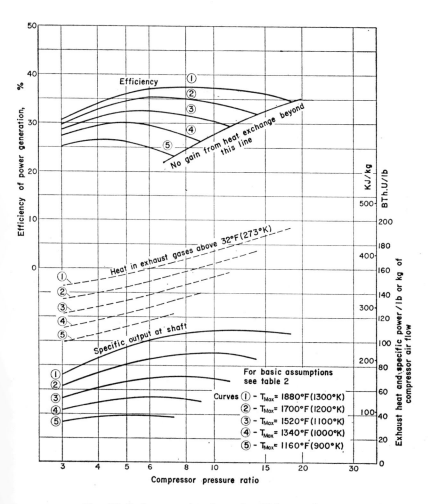

Fig. 5.7. Performance data for cycle with heat exchange.

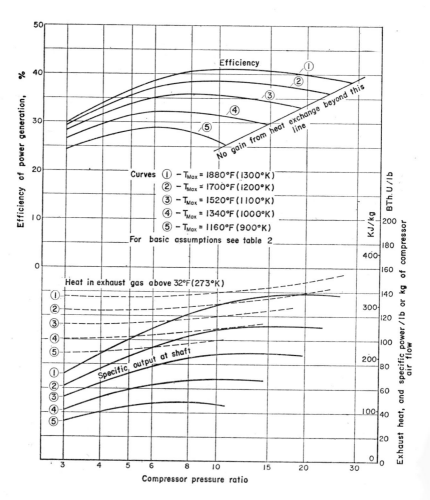

FIG. 5.8. Performance data for cycle with intercooling and heat exchange.

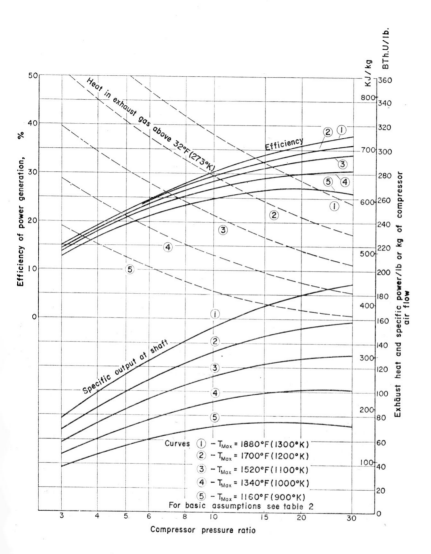

FIG. 5.9. Performance data for cycle with intercooling and reheat.

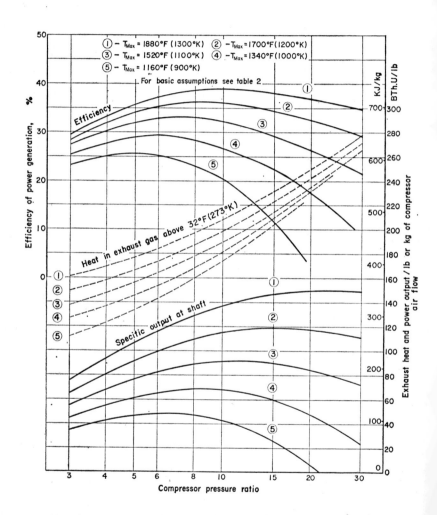

FIG. 5.10. Performance data for cycle with reheat and heat exchange.

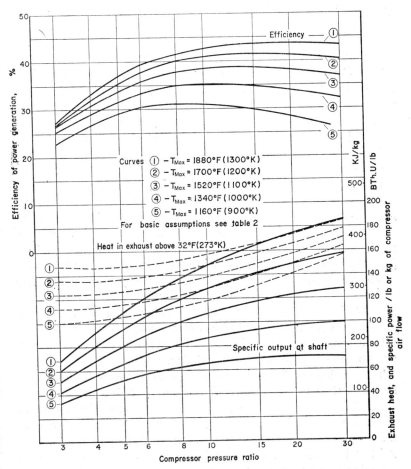

FIG. 5.11. Performance data for cycle with intercooling reheat and heat exchange.

in series with it, or vice versa; and the load-producing turbine may be a third turbine or may be combined with either of the two compressor-driving turbines. Enough has perhaps been said to show that a very wide variety of machines can be designed and constructed under the general title of open-cycle gas turbines, each with differing characteristics (particularly in respect of part load performance) which make some cycles much more suited than others to particular applications.

Off-design Performance

The off-design performance of an open-cycle gas turbine is sensitive to the atmospheric temperature and pressure, to the cycle chosen, and to the method of control. To attempt a detailed examination of all the issues involved is outside the scope of this chapter, but some general observations may be of use to those not greatly familiar with the characteristics of such machines.

For given temperature conditions, the air throughput and hence output of a gas turbine is directly proportional to the atmospheric pressure and the machines therefore are fairly sensitive to altitude. At a given atmospheric pressure the non-dimensional power output, (power/$P\sqrt{T}$) is a unique function for most cycles of the ratio of the maximum cycle temperature to the atmospheric temperature. This generally means that the output of a gas turbine drops with increasing ambient temperature fairly rapidly, a loss of 1–$1\frac{1}{2}\%$ output for every $1\,°C$ increase of temperature being not untypical. Similarly the output available increases on cold days, but a limit may be reached to this process either by choking of the inlet blades of the compressor at some value dependent on the precise design of the machine or, alternatively, by some stress consideration in the design.

The part-load performance is also affected by the cycle chosen and by the method by which its shafts are controlled[97]. For instance, a single-shaft machine controlled to operate at constant speed for power generation tends to have a poor part-load performance as at low loads the compressor is forced to operate at full speed at a part of its characteristic where it is not too efficient. The same machine operating with a variable-speed load may slow down at part load and remain operating at an efficient part of its compressor characteristic and hence give rather better part-load performance. Machines designed above their optimum pressure ratio tend to give better part-load performance than those designed well below it, and machines with waste-heat recovery or heat exchangers always tend to give better part-load performance than machines without them.

However, the problem of part-load performance is not simply one of efficiency. In multiple-shaft arrangements it is important, at off-design conditions, not only that the compressors shall not move into a very inefficient region of operation (especially as this sometimes involves risk of blade failure) but also that the compressors shall not surge. Surging is a condition where the flow through the compressor becomes very unstable and is associated with the attempt to pass too small a flow through the machine at a given speed. For this reason some cycles which at full load appear attractive are, in fact, impracticable. For instance, a compound cycle with the power take-off from the high-pressure shaft is very likely to surge at part load if the load varies with the cube of the speed, but it is a practicable arrangement with a constant-speed load. Considerations of this type are, of course, very much taken into account by manufacturers whose advice must be sought on the part-load characteristics of their particular machines; and great care is taken to see that those cycles which are marketed are thoroughly reliable in this respect.

Choice of Fuels and Maximum Temperature

The early development of gas turbines was hindered by the non-availability of alloys for the blading which could withstand centrifugal stress at temperatures in excess of 1112°F (600°C). Alloys, however, have become available in the last 30 years which have allowed the maximum temperature for which a gas turbine can be designed to be increased to well over 1472°F (800°C) for long-life applications and somewhat higher for short–life. The use of blade cooling by passing air delivered from the compressor through passages within the blade profiles offers means of increasing temperatures even higher. This has been of considerable use in the aircraft field where such cooling need only be applied to the first few blade rows of a turbine to increase take-off ratings, but is of rather less value for long-life sets since in this case the cooling may have to be extended to longer, more complex blade shapes where adequate cooling is harder to apply effectively.

Temperatures in the upper range (which produce the higher efficiencies) are of interest where the fuel is distillate oil or natural (or other clean) gas. In the case of heavy oil (or any oil containing appreciable traces of vanadium or sodium) the temperature has to be limited severely. Heavy oils tend to cause fouling of the turbine due to deposits of the ash on the turbine blading. If, however, the oil contains vanadium, vanadium pentoxide is produced by combustion, and this is very highly corrosive at its dewpoint of 1238 °F (670 °C) (a temperature which may be somewhat modified in the presence of other ash components). It is therefore normal practice in the case of gas turbines burning heavy oil to limit the maximum cycle temperature to around 1202 °F (650 °C), to control the specification closely so as to preclude the use of the more virulent oils, to use methods of washing the oil, and to use additives which contain the deposition problem within acceptable limits. If action along these lines is taken, heavy-oil-burning gas turbines can be made to operate very satisfactorily.

Low-calorific value gases can also be burnt, but it should be noted that where the calorific value is significantly lower than, say, 500 Btu/ft³ (18·6 MJ/m³) the volume of the gas added in the combustion chamber starts to become significant and may affect the matching of the compressor and turbine size. In addition, if the gas is not available at a higher pressure than the maximum pressure of the gas turbine cycle (plus some allowances for control) an additional gas compressor is required, and this may require a significant power to drive it, and may introduce installational problems.

In the early days of gas turbines some enthusiasm was shown (mainly by those not engaged in the design of the machines) for burning of unusual fuels in gas turbines such as coal, peat, cotton stalks, upcast ventilation air from mines, etc. Those fuels which had high ash contents generally led to unacceptable deposition or erosion problems. The others were mainly unattractive commercially. Development in some of these fields continues, and may yet be successful.

Heavy oil as a fuel for gas turbines has been mainly attractive on the grounds of its low price. In the United States there is currently an attempt to provide a universal fuel which will be vanadium and sodium free to be marketed throughout the world at a price intermediate between ordinary distillate and heavy fuel oil. If this is, in fact, achieved it will provide a substantial fillip to high-temperature gas turbines.

Dual fuel engines (usually distillate/natural gas) present little difficulty. It is normal practice to run heavy oil burning gas turbines on distillate oil at start-up and shut-down so as to avoid the "freezing" of heavy oil in the pipelines when standing in a cold condition.

Construction and Reliability

The very early gas turbines (and to some extent some of the machines operating at a low temperature of 1202°F (650°C)) utilised principles of construction based on steam turbine experience. The use of tempera-

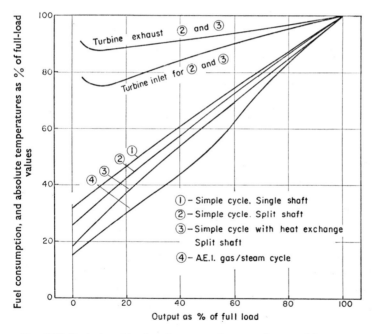

FIG. 5.12. Typical part-load performance of open-cycle gas turbines.

tures substantially in excess of this figure forced what was in any case a desirable development, namely the use of construction methods which separated the temperature-bearing components from the stress-bearing components so far as was possible and provided components which would have the maximum freedom of movement and minimum of distortion under transient temperature conditions. Provision is made of cooling air passages between relatively heavy pressure bearing components and liners whose main function is to contain hot gas and withstand oxidation. Wide use is made of unsplit casing constructions which minimise distortion; or alternatively the provision of water cooling with split casings to achieve the same result. Air cooling of blade roots, turbine discs and casings has become standard practice. Well-designed open-cycle gas turbines of this type have an unequalled record of reliability and freedom from maintenance. This reliability is one of their principal advantages, and offsets to a significant extent the relatively high fuel costs which the gas turbine usually incurs where waste-heat recovery is not available. In addition such machines can be started quickly, accept rapid changes of load, are highly manoeuvreable, and are therefore free from the disadvantages sometimes associated with large diesel engines, high-pressure steam machinery or the air heaters of closed-cycle gas turbines.

Aircraft Engines for Industrial Purposes

The ability to start and change load rapidly has been developed most strongly in aircraft gas turbines where the incentive is greatest, and use has been made of these machines increasingly for peak-load applications. One or more aircraft jet engines are discharged into a single power turbine designed for the purpose; and units of this type can readily be made to reach full load within 2 minutes of a cold start. Such machines require the somewhat more frequent maintenance associated with aircraft gas turbines unless they are significantly de-rated; and it is therefore normal to use them at a power output less than that for which they would be supplied for short life aircraft applications, in order to restrict maintenance costs to a level nearer to that of industrial gas-turbine designs. Usual sizes are in the 10–60 MW range. (Figs. 5.13, 5.14).

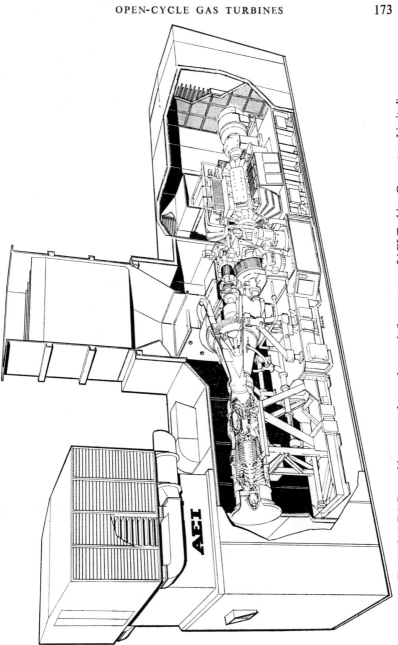

FIG. 5.13. A.P.1 Gas turbine arranged as package unit (by courtesy of AEI Turbine-Generators Limited).

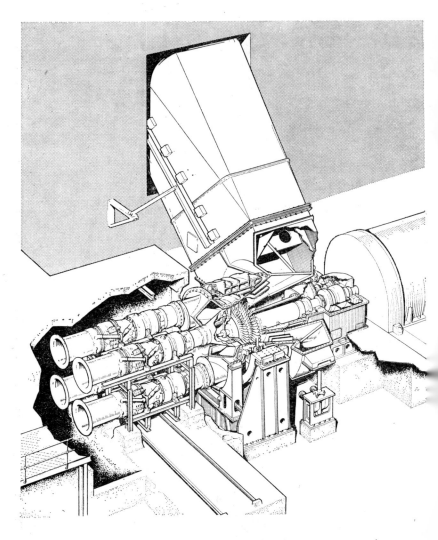

5.14. AEI multi-aircraft engine installation as used in U.K. power station
(by courtesy of AEI Turbine-Generators Limited).

Applications of Open-cycle Gas Turbines

The primary use of open-cycle gas turbines to date has been, of course, in the aircraft field. Since the development of the jet engine in Great Britain and Germany during the Second World War the pure jet engine rapidly took over virtually all military aircraft requirements. On the civil side first the prop-jet, then the pure jet, and later various types of by-pass jet engines have dominated the field.

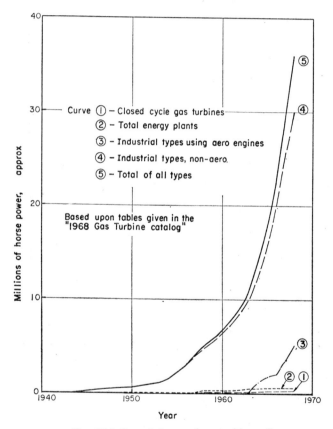

Fig. 5.15. Growth in use of gas turbines—I.
(1 hp = 746 W)

G*

In the industrial field progress has been slower. The first gas turbines were produced before the Second World War, but the market was very small until the development of materials in the early 1940s made higher temperatures feasible. A great deal of development activity was carried out after the Second World War and the main applications were for power generation, or for driving pumps or compressors in areas where suitable fuels were available at low prices (such as, for instance, oil fields where natural gas was burned to waste). Here the

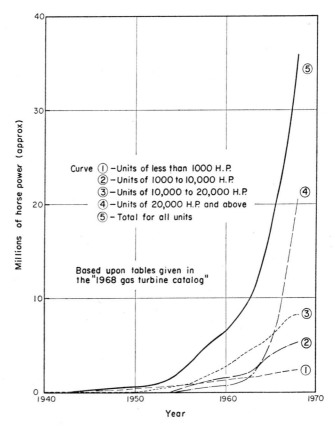

5.16. Growth in use of gas turbines—II.
(1 hp = 746 W)

low capital cost of the gas turbine proved particularly attractive, together with its ease of maintenance and high reliability. In addition sets were supplied for peak-load applications where the relatively high cost of fuel was unimportant. A limited application was also found in the marine field, although initially such projects were in order to gain seagoing experience rather than because they were commercially justified. For naval applications the gas turbine found higher favour due to its low weight and compact design. A limited number of units were also employed for railway traction and were particularly competitive where sustained high powers were required. Since about 1950 there has been a very considerable growth in the use of open-cycle gas turbines of all types in industrial applications (Figs. 5.15, 5.16) encouraged by their low capital costs, rapid starting and proved low maintenance costs and high availability; the total power installed almost doubling every 3 years, and the general trend being towards larger frame sizes.

Small Machines

In addition to large gas turbine units, there has also been considerable development activity in producing very small units. These have been developed for applications where high output from a small weight and size is of importance, such as provision of portable gas turbines for driving pumps, for fire-fighting applications, for use in automobiles or heavy lorries, for military purposes and for total energy schemes where only small power loads have to be met. Producing small power outputs from a gas turbine efficiently presents significant problems. The most efficient type of compressor is generally the axial-flow machine, but this inherently provides a large throughput of air, and if only small powers be required the designer has to use very high rotational speeds, the blading is extremely small, requires very fine tolerances and becomes virtually a watchmaking job. In addition, axial flow compressors are particularly sensitive to Reynolds number effects in the lower Reynolds number range and performance deteriorates rapidly if the Reynolds number of the blading (based on chord) drops below about 150,000. Small gas turbines therefore almost invariably utilise centrifugal compressors which run at rather lower rotational speeds, more easily handle lower throughputs and are easier and cheaper to manufacture in small sizes. Likewise the turbine is sometimes, though less frequently, made as a centripetal design (which is essentially a 50% reaction turbine and which gives performance comparable with an axial design of the same reaction and blading aspect ratio).[37]

OPEN-CYCLE GAS TURBINES FOR TOTAL ENERGY SCHEMES

In total energy schemes, the heat rejected from the gas turbine is utilised, and it is therefore sometimes thought that the efficiency of the gas turbine is of no importance. It ought, however, to be realised that the quest of the gas turbine designer for high efficiency is not necessarily because he regards efficiency as an end in itself. For a given cycle once the mass flow of a gas turbine is fixed then basically the size of the gas turbine is fixed. Once its maximum temperature is decided then basically the costliness of the construction for a given size is settled. These two factors therefore determine to a first approximation the cost of the gas turbine and they also determine its fuel consumption. The efficiency represents the useful work done by the machine and therefore, within limits, it is true to argue that the efficiency of the gas turbine is inversely proportional to the cost per kW. The quest for high efficiency is also a quest for low capital cost of the plant.[83, 84, 151]

However, it will be realised that in total energy schemes the efficiency of the gas turbine is not necessarily, *per se*, an important factor. Two types of total energy schemes, however, have at this stage to be distinguished. First, there are those schemes in which the waste-heat recovery from the gas turbine can be efficiently utilised irrespective of how much there is. In its simplest form this might mean a scheme where waste heat was converted into steam or hot water (or both) which were then fed into the steam and water mains of some process plant, and all that the gas turbine could conceivably produce could be efficiently utilised in the outlet from those mains.[53] In such a scheme the efficiency of the gas turbine is mainly relevant in so far as it affects the capital cost of the turbo machinery. The second type of scheme is that wherein a specified amount of waste heat only can be efficiently utilised, such as schemes where the rejected heat is supplied to a distillation plant, or an absorption type refrigerator, or some process which has a defined required heat input.[18, 62] Excess heat provided by the gas turbine might then be rejected by the control system of the other plant. If in these schemes there is also a well-defined power output requirement of the gas turbine it follows that one gas turbine efficiency will produce a better balanced plant than any other. In practice, situations rigidly of this type are not likely to occur frequently, and most schemes where waste heat recovery is deemed important should have sufficient flexibility built into them to permit efficient use of varying power load and/or the efficient use of varying quantities of exhaust heat. In such cases, cycles with good part-load performance may be particularly attractive.

The gas turbine is particularly suitable for total energy schemes in that practically all the heat not turned into shaft power is available in the exhaust gas for other uses.[56] With a diesel engine perhaps 36% of the input energy becomes shaft work, about another 36% is available in the exhaust gas, and nearly 30% goes into oil coolers, engine-cooling water and radiation, etc., from where it cannot usually be readily recovered. In the gas turbine, losses to oil coolers, radiation, etc., may be only 1 or 2% of the total heat input, though this figure, of course, rises with intercooled cycles. Use of the exhaust gas may also be limited by dewpoint corrosion where sulphur-bearing fuels are involved (see p. 170) but this limitation also applies to the diesel engine.

Total energy schemes can also be distinguished in two other ways. First, a distinction may be drawn between those schemes where the primary requirement of the whole plant is for shaft power,[25] (and the waste heat from the gas turbine is utilised primarily as a means by which that shaft power can be augmented), and those schemes wherein the energy in the exhaust is required primarily for some heating process (for instance, district heating, process, distillation or refrigeration schemes). Secondly, distinction may be made between those schemes where the heat in the exhaust of the gas turbine is used to produce steam or hot water (which represents the large majority), and those cases where the waste heat is utilised for heating some other fluid. With these distinctions in mind we shall now turn to consider the application of gas turbines to such total energy schemes.

TOTAL ENERGY SCHEMES TO AUGMENT SHAFT POWER

The gas turbine as a prime mover is a machine which burns fuel, turns perhaps something like 20–40% of its total energy into useful shaft power and rejects 60–80% of its energy as hot gas at atmospheric pressure. There are two ways in which this rejected hot gas can be turned into further shaft work. It can be presented to another prime mover which would find large quantities of hot gas at atmospheric pressure useful. In such schemes the bulk of the shaft power tends to be produced in the other prime mover, the bulk of the heat being added in the total cycle somewhere other than in the gas-turbine combustion chamber. Alternatively, the gas turbine combustion chamber can be seen as the only, or certainly the primary, place where fuel is added and the waste heat can be utilised in a steam or other cycle to provide some auxiliary power. The first gives rise to what for convenience we shall call steam/gas cycles (where the bulk of the power is normally produced in the steam turbine), the latter to what we shall call gas/steam cycles where the bulk of the power is normally produced in the gas turbine.

Steam/Gas Cycles

In steam/gas cycles the basic concept arises from the fact that the boiler of a conventional steam-turbine plant can utilise efficiently large quantities of preheated air from the gas turbine exhaust which still contains easily enough oxygen to permit further burning of fuel. In its simplest form the gas turbine discharges into the boiler air intake and as far as the gas turbine is concerned its waste heat is utilised with complete efficiency. Alternatively, the gas-turbine exhaust heat is used for feed-heating the steam plant. The total efficiency of the cycle depends of course, on the inherent efficiency of the steam cycle employed, but it is likely to be about 2% better than the steam cycle without the gas turbine. The gas turbine efficiency suffers only in so far as the boiler imposes a back pressure on its turbine. A typical cycle diagram is shown in Fig. 5.17. Plants of this type have been installed, for instance, at Hohe Wand in Austria[18] and Riverton (Kansas).[19] An important variant of this scheme seeks to utilise the high pressure which is available in the gas turbine cycle. Modern steam turbine boilers are extremely large and their size dominates most conventional steam-turbine stations. For instance, the boiler of a 660-MW oil-fired steam turbine station is likely to be about 200 ft (60 m) high and occupy a plan area of about 8000 ft² (750 m²). The tubing and steam drums may weigh about 5000 tons (or tonnes). Now the heat-transfer coefficient on the water side of the tubes is high, but on the gas side of the tubes the convective portion is directly proportional to the 0·8 power

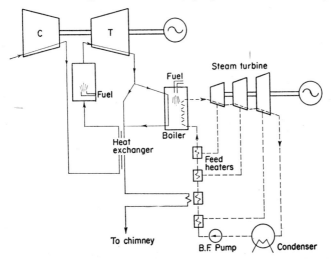

FIG. 5.17. Steam/gas cycles: simplified cycle diagram for plant using un-pressurised boiler.

of the absolute pressure. If, for instance, the gas was raised in a gas turbine to 88 psig (6 bar (g)) pressure the volume, and mass of convective tube, would be reduced five-fold approximately. Accordingly a number of cycles have been proposed in which the boiler is pressurised by the gas-turbine compressor and the boiler combustion space and the gas-turbine combustion space are made one and the same.[137] In cycles of this sort some schemes envisage the gas turbine still producing shaft power, but in others its function is simply to be self-driving and provide the pressurisation of the combustion space. A typical example of schemes of this sort is shown in Fig. 5.18. Here again the cycle efficiency is raised by about 2%. In this case, however, preheat is given to the combustion air by the work done on the gas in the compressor and the gas-turbine exhaust cannot be utilised in the same way. It can, however, be used in the steam cycle as a means of feed-heating. The saving in cost of the boiler heat transfer surface has to be balanced against the fact that the still large boiler has now to be contained within a pressure vessel, and if heavy fuel is utilised in the boiler, restriction of the tem-

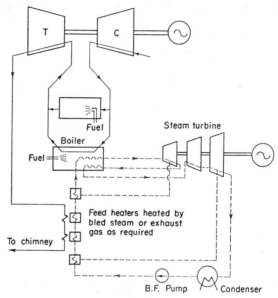

FIG. 5.18. Steam/gas cycles: simplified cycle diagram for plant using pressurised boiler.

perature of the gas in the turbine will apply, together with such treatment of the fuel as may be necessary to contain deposition and corrosion in the turbine within acceptable limits. Boiler deposition problems tend to be aggravated by the reduction in heat transfer surface area.

Gas Steam Cycles

In cycles where the gas turbine is the primary source of power the waste heat can be passed into a boiler. The steam raised can then be utilised in three ways:

1. The steam may be raised at high pressure, fed through a back pressure turbine, and rejected either to some process or in the manner given in the section below. This permits a high efficiency of utilisation of the higher temperature part of the waste heat but, on the other hand, it should be noted that the higher the pressure at which the steam is raised the higher is the temperature of rejection of the gas-turbine exhaust gas, and therefore the higher efficiency is partly illusory unless

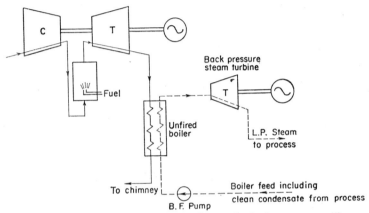

5.19. Gas/steam cycles: simplified cycle diagram for back-pressure auxiliary steam cycle.

some sort of dual pressure cycle is employed. It should be noted that conventional high-pressure steam turbines do not have the capacity to accept frequent rapid starts and stops in the manner of a gas turbine. Furthermore, the steam turbine in this case will generally run at a higher speed than other shafts in the system, and gearing will normally be needed. (Figs. 5.19, 5.20 and 5.21).

2. A second method is to raise steam at a pressure rather higher than the maximum pressure of the gas-turbine cycle, and to inject it into the gas turbine itself. Steam at the same pressure as air has approximately half the density and twice the specific heat of air. Roughly speaking, therefore, it will pass quite happily through a turbine designed to operate on air and produce about the same power per unit volume. The added mass flow through the turbine produces a marked increase

in the net output of the turbine, and since no additional rotating machinery is employed the scheme has significant attractions. On the other hand, it should be noted that if water or steam is to be passed through the turbine in significant quantities, a high purity of water is required and only a small proportion of that water can be recovered from the exhaust; so the scheme has almost invariably to be associated with a distillation plant which can be fitted into the cycle after the waste-heat boiler. A

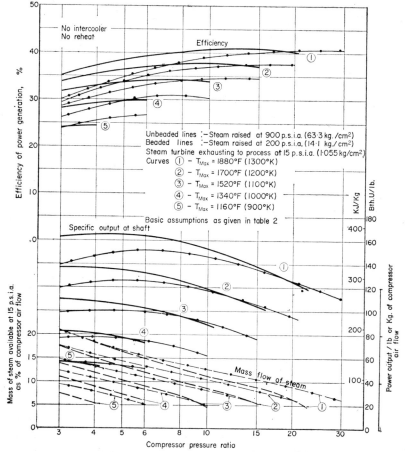

FIG. 5.20. Performance data for back-pressure gas/steam cycle—I.
(15 psi = 1.035 bar)

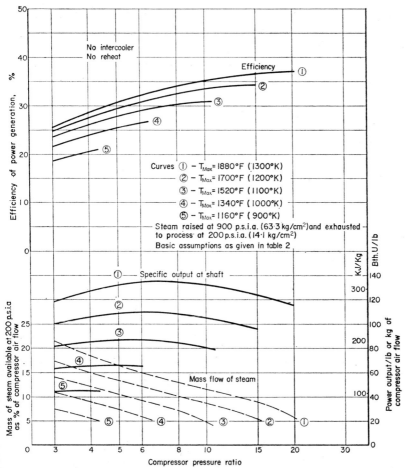

FIG. 5.21. Performance data for back-pressure gas/steam cycle—II.
(200 psi = 13.8 bar)

moderate yield evaporator is sufficient to supply the requirements. To offset the undoubted advantages of the cycle we have, therefore, the disadvantage of the loss of a great deal of high purity water and probably the complication and cost of providing an evaporator and linking the availability of the cycle with the availability of the evaporator. It should be noted that as the turbine has to be designed to accept the higher mass flow with steam it will not run satisfactorily if the steam is for any reason not available. This is particularly true if the steam being injected is used for cooling of any of the high temperature parts of the turbine (Fig. 5.22 and 5.23).

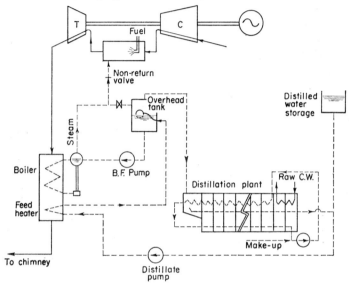

FIG. 5.22. Gas/steam cycles: simplified cycle diagram for plant using steam injection.

3. The third method of utilising steam from the waste heat boiler to produce shaft power is to generate steam at low pressure (100–200 psi, 7–15 bar) with superheat, and to pass this through a conventional condensing steam turbine. The steam pressure is maintained at a lowish figure in order to extract as much waste heat as possible from the system (unless a dual pressure system is used, which gives an increase in thermal efficiency at the cost of some added complexity). This type of cycle raises the thermal efficiency of the turbo-machinery producing useful power to about 40% (with a maximum cycle temperature of, say, 1600°F (1150°K)) and is competitive with the more complicated pure gas turbine cycles that can produce the same efficiency. It does not require large quantities of pure water; and because the steam turbine machinery is at

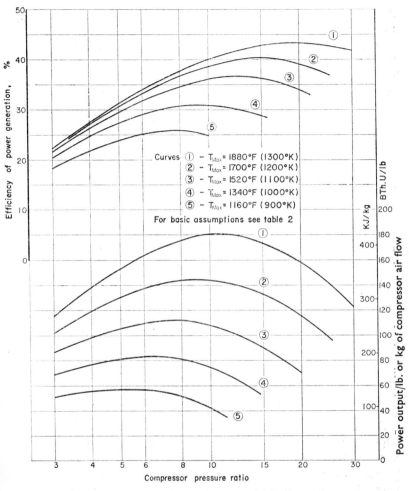

FIG. 5.23. Performance data for steam-injection cycle.

low temperature and pressure it can respond to load changes and quick start-ups in the same manner as the gas turbine. The only difference in the characteristic of the steam machinery from the gas-turbine machinery in this respect is that because of the weight of metal and water in the boiler some delay occurs before the waste-heat boiler will produce load from a cold start. This can be dealt with, if required, either by arranging for the steam machinery to operate under vacuum, or not to run until steam is available or, alternatively, by making arrangements for the waste-heat boiler to be kept warm or for the initial heating to be provided by a steam accumulator. A plant of this general type has been installed, for instance, at Neuchatel.[160] A typical cycle diagram is shown in Fig. 5.24 and cycle data is given in Fig. 5.25.

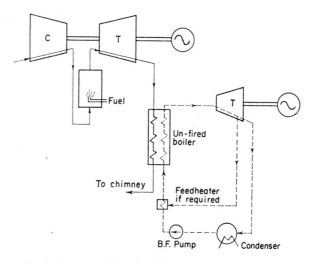

FIG. 5.24. Gas/steam cycles: simplified cycle diagram for plant using condensing auxiliary steam cycle.

All those cycles which embody waste heat recovery in steam boilers require, of course, a small quantity of water for boiler make-up. Some of them require significant quantities either for distillation purposes (if the steam is to be injected) or for condenser cooling or intercoolers; and this provides a certain limitation on one of the advantages of the gas turbine, namely, that it can be used in sites where water is scarce. However, the cooling water requirements of a combined gas/steam cycle as in paragraph (3) above are about one-third of that for an equivalent steam station, so that a significant part of the advantage is maintained. One attractive application of such schemes where natural gas or some other suitable fuel is available is to replace existing

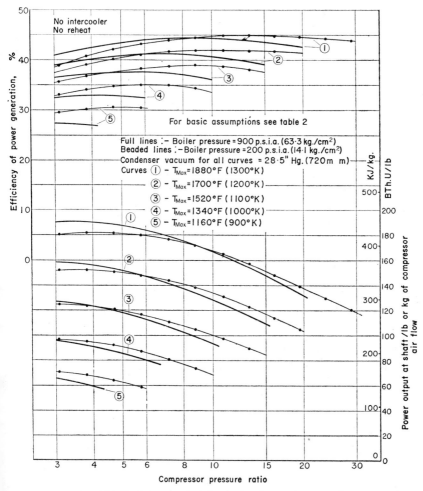

FIG. 5.25. Performance data for condensing gas/steam cycle.

steam power stations in urban areas where water supplies are restricted. Use can be made of the existing water supplies and the output of the station trebled with a possible improvement in thermal efficiency.

Variations on the schemes above can also be made by the addition of auxiliary firing between the gas-turbine exhaust and the waste-heat boiler. This is attractive in order to meet abnormal loads required on the steam system or some emergency load condition, but for normal operation tends to be wasteful. Proposals have been made that this objection can be overcome by the use of low-grade fuel for after-burning, the cheaper price of the fuel offsetting the reduced efficiency of the cycle. By this means the scheme described in paragraph (3) above can be, in the limit, converted to a cycle which is predominantly a steam turbine with the gas turbine providing preheat to a boiler on the lines of the scheme outlined on pages 180-181. If this can be done, of course, the steam turbine is no longer a flexible instrument which can follow the load changes of the gas turbine, but has become a conventional piece of high-pressure steam machinery complete with feed heaters, etc., and the boiler becomes a fired boiler capable of burning heavy fuel. By this means part of the advantage of scheme (3) in providing power efficiently at a low capital cost per kilowatt is lost.

An interesting variation of scheme (3) above has been proposed by A.E.I, Turbine-Generators Limited where the waste heat boiler produces steam at 200 psi and 700°F (14 bar, 370°C) operating on the exhaust gas from a simple open-cycle gas turbine with one stage of intercooling. The low-pressure compressor is provided with variable-stagger stator blading so that its pressure ratio can be varied at will. The cycle is free from matching troubles and provides an excellent part-load performance giving substantially constant efficiency between

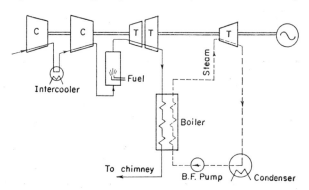

Fig. 5.26. AEI gas/steam cycle diagram (by courtesy of AEI Turbine-Generators Limited).

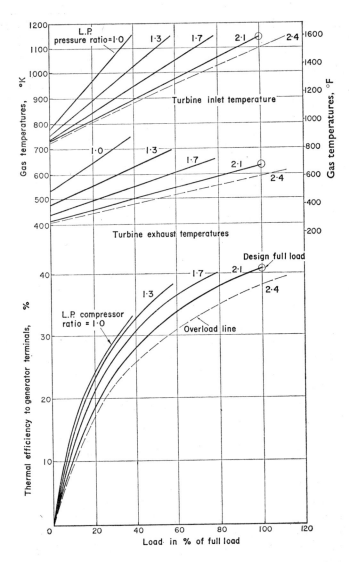

FIG. 5.27. Performance data for AEI gas/steam cycle (by courtesy of AEI Turbine-Generators Limited).

full load and half load (or even 30% load if required). This is achieved by maintaining the maximum temperature at part load and recovering the additional heat rejected from the gas turbine with the steam cycle. Gas-turbine cycles which maintain high temperature at part load are usually efficient but unusable because of the very drastic drop-off in load with increasing ambient temperature. In this case, however, adjustment of the l.p. compressor blade stagger can be made to compensate for changes in ambient temperature so that the drop-off of load with ambient temperature is no greater than that of a straight intercooled open-cycle machine.

The variation of the l.p. compressor stator blade stagger also permits some variation at will of the quantity of exhaust heat produced for a given power output, and this unusual flexibility has some value for total energy schemes, where some or all of the steam is required for purposes other than power generation (Figs. 5.26 and 5.27).

OTHER TOTAL ENERGY SCHEMES

Outside the range of power generation the energy in the exhaust gas of an open-cycle gas turbine can be used for any of the other purposes which are described elsewhere in this book. In addition a certain quantity of low-grade heat is available from the intercoolers of such cycles as employ them, and there is no insurmountable difficulty in designing these intercoolers to take smaller quantities of water than is normal with a higher temperature rise where this is advantageous.

Four principal uses can be described briefly:

1. The waste heat may be used as the heat input source for distillation plant. In the case of large distillation schemes this is likely to take the form of a multi-stage flash evaporator of the type pioneered by Richardsons Westgarth in Great Britain and by Westinghouse in the United States (Chapter 1).

2. A second use of the exhaust heat of the gas turbine is in connection with process plant where the gas turbine is integrated into some process which has power requirements and also the need for heat to be supplied. Probably the most common of such schemes are those where steam is raised in the waste heat boiler and supplied into a steam main and utilised elsewhere in the process (Fig. 5.28). There are, however, cases

Fig. 5.28. A.P.1 gas turbine with waste-heat recovery installed in U.K. refinery (by courtesy of AEI Turbine-Generators Limited).

where the chemical process involves some exothermic reaction which replaces or supplements the combustion chamber of the gas turbine and where the gas turbine's ability to provide pressurised air is also utilised in the chemical process involved (Fig. 5.29).

3. The exhaust heat is also utilised—particularly in the U.S.A.—in providing the heat source for an absorption-type refrigerator itself employed either in an air-conditioning scheme or for the purposes of pure refrigeration. The absorption type refrigerator is a natural choice in such schemes as it requires virtually no energy input apart from heat.

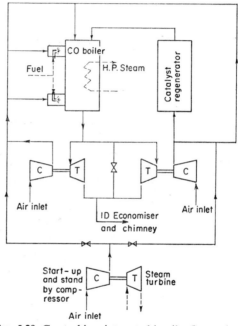

FIG. 5.29. Gas turbines integrated in oil-refinery plant.

4. The last of these uses is for district or other heating. The waste heat is usually converted into either steam or hot water in a waste-heat boiler, and this is employed directly for heating. Where the need arises the steam raised may be supplied to both a heating system and to an air-conditioning refrigerator to provide complete air conditioning (Fig. 5.30).

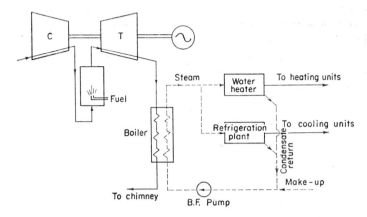

FIG. 5.30. Use of gas turbine exhaust heat for air conditioning.

USE OF FLUIDS OTHER THAN WATER

In all the foregoing it has been assumed that the recovery of waste heat from the gas turbine has been either by direct use of the hot exhaust gases or by transfer of this heat into hot water or steam. There are, however, other fluids besides water which merit consideration. For instance, it has been proposed, particularly with regard to gas/steam cycles, that instead of using steam the subsidiary cycle should utilise a fluor carbon such as freon or hexafluorobenzene. Fluids of this type raise questions which cannot be adequately discussed in a chapter of this length, but the following brief comments may be relevant:

1. Subject to what is stated below, in most cases the alternative fluids offer little or no advantage over the use of water either in terms of efficiency or in terms of the size and cost of heat-exchange equipment.

2. The alternative fluids do offer a significant advantage in terms of the size and inherent cost of the turbines in power-generation schemes; but to achieve lower costs in practice a sufficient number of similar machines would have to be produced to recover the development costs involved.

3. Some of the fluids are relatively expensive, and some are toxic, so that adequate seals must be provided and maintained.

4. As a rough guide it can be said that the preliminary assessment of any total energy scheme can be carried out using water as the second fluid, and this will not normally give significantly misleading results. Once a scheme has been assessed as at least marginally worth while employing water, then it is advantageous to see if any of the less common fluids would provide a worthwhile advantage.

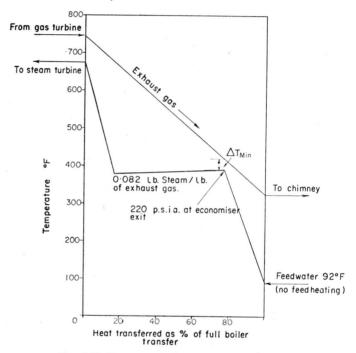

FIG. 5.31. Temperature diagram for steam boiler.
(220 psi = 15.18 bar)

5. In one case, however, the use of some of these fluids does offer a worth while advantage in terms of efficiency. Usually in intercooled cycles there is no obvious use for the heat rejected in the intercooler, as this is very lowgrade heat, and the limit to heat recovery in the exhaust is usually at the 'pinchpoint' (evaporator minimum temperature difference) in the waste-heat boiler. Below this temperature there is

more heat available in the exhaust gas than is needed to provide sensible heat for all the water that can be evaporated. With, for instance, freon 21—which has high sensible heat and whose top temperature is limited to about 330°F (165°C) on grounds of stability, the heat rejected in the intercooler can be employed for feed heating purposes in the freon cycle, with beneficial results to cycle efficiency (Figs. 5.31 and 5.32).

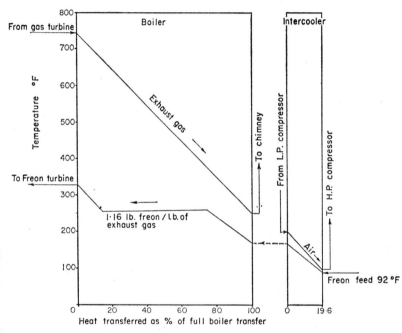

FIG. 5.32. Temperature diagram for Freon boiler.
°C = 5/9 (°F − 32))

DESIGN OF HEAT EXCHANGERS AND WASTE-HEAT BOILERS

Most total energy schemes employ heat exchangers or waste-heat boilers.[143] Such equipment is inherently simple, and provided reasonable care is taken in its design should provide trouble-free service.[53, 137]

Waste-heat boilers, for instance, are significantly simpler than conventional fired steam boilers, partly on account of the absence of any radiant surface, partly on account of the absence of the need for any forced- or induced-draught fans, and partly on account of the low steam pressures generally involved. In plants which start and change load slowly no real constructional difficulties are involved; but in plants where rapid starts or load changes are envisaged it is necessary to see that thermal stresses are not set up under transient conditions by a structure which redundantly links parts of unequal thicknesses—otherwise cracking and failure can occur.

It is also important to protect the heat-exchange surface from the condition where combustion chambers fail to ignite on start-up, and the very large surface area can be sprayed with fuel—otherwise catastrophic fires can be started. Reliable ignition, the turning off of fuel promptly if ignition fails, and a period of purging before relighting are the essential safeguards needed.

Where heavy oil fuel is used it is important to provide means of cleaning the gas side at periodic intervals, and even using distillate fuels or natural gas the provision of means of cleaning is desirable unless rigorous steps are taken to see that combustion is really clean at all times. With clean gas or distillate, cleaning should only be necessary exceptionally.

Where fuels contain any sulphur there is a risk of dewpoint corrosion (due to the formation of sulphuric acid from the water and oxides of sulphur resulting from combustion). The dewpoint of sulphuric acid in the exhaust gas is somewhat above 212°F (100°C) the attack being worst near this value. The severity of attack reduces as temperatures increase, and no attack is experienced at surface temperatures of about 300°F (150°C). Extraction of exhaust heat has therefore to be limited (in the case of sulphur-bearing fuels), and the design of the low-temperature end of the boiler adapted, to ensure that the metal surfaces are certainly above 250°F (120°C) and preferably above 300°F (150°C). Materials particularly susceptible to acid attack should be avoided. Prolonged starting-up and shutting-down periods should be eliminated, and water washing of the gas surfaces employed before prolonged shut downs.

Four main types of heat exchange equipment may be employed.

1. Gas/Air Heat Exchangers—Recuperative

These are employed where the exhaust heat is used to preheat combustion air, or possibly air for some drying or other process. Usually they are of fairly simple construction employing plain circular tubes, and are situated as near as possible to the turbine exhaust. Tubing may well be of mild steel up to metal temperatures of about 900°F (480°C) and stainless steel thereafter. These heat exchangers are usually large in comparison with the rotating machinery; and where space is at a premium more compact surfaces can be devised though usually at some extra cost. The problem is not one of simply providing a heat-transfer surface with better heat-transfer coefficients; it is also one of ducting the gas and air in and out of the heat exchanger in a compact manner compatible with good distribution and minimum loss. An example of a compact heat exchanger designed specifically for a gas turbine purpose is given in Fig. 5.33.

For most simple cycle applications which run reasonably continuously at full load it is not economical to provide a thermal ratio of more than about 70–75% and the economics generally dictate a total pressure drop (sum of the two sides) of about 4–5%,

2. Gas/Air Heat Exchangers—Regenerative

In an attempt to provide lightweight, compact heat exchangers with a high thermal ratio considerable development (particularly in the automotive field) has been carried out on various types of regenerative heat exchangers; usually consisting of a rotating matrix which by its rotation has each part alternately immersed in the hot gas and cooler air. Thermal ratios of 90% are claimed, with modest pressure drop. The problem, particularly at high temperatures, is the provision of a really reliable long-life seal, and for this reason few such plants have so far found commercial service. Some are now being produced for automotive applications.

3. Gas/Hot-water Heat Exchangers

These are most common with small power installations of, say, 5 MW capacity for trading or housing estates or hospitals for use with district

H

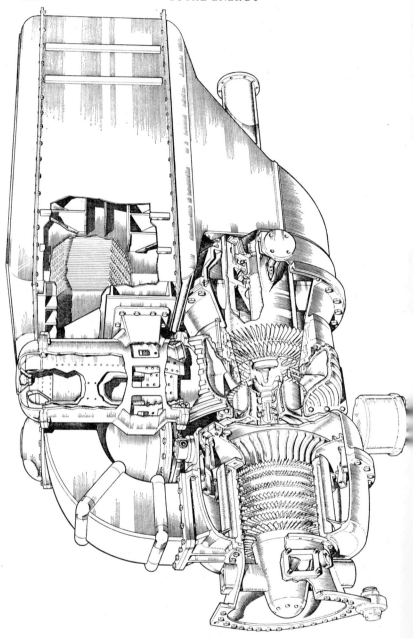

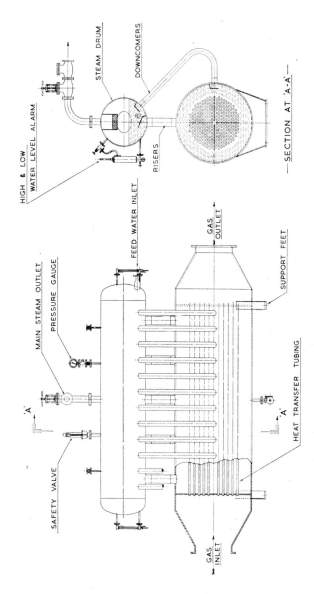

FIG. 5.34. Typical arrangement of a fire tube waste-heat boiler (by courtesy of Clarke, Chapman and Company Limited).

and space heating. Like the first case, the most usual arrangement is for tube coils or nests inserted in the turbine exhaust. Care has to be taken that water does not boil in the tubes, but in general the all-water exchanger is least liable to damage during a rapid start-up. Provision of secondary surface on the gas side is often advantageous.

4. *Waste-heat Boilers*

Waste-heat boilers may be either of the shell or water tube type. Shell (or fire tube) boilers are basically a shell full of water with gas-bearing tubes interconnecting the tube plates. Such designs are limited by pressure, by rate of evaporation, and are restricted to producing saturated steam (Fig. 5.34).

Water-tube boilers (where the water passes through the tubes) are not subject to the above restrictions, and can be supplied with natural circulation, controlled circulation, or forced circulation.

Natural circulation types consist of two or more drums interconnected by tubing through which the water circulates by natural convection. They are normally designed to give a 50% volume mixture of steam and water at riser exit; this mixture being separated in the drum, and the steam passing to a superheater if required (Fig. 5.35).

Controlled or assisted circulation boilers are similar to the natural convection ones, except that a pump is provided to give the necessary circulation. Only a single drum (for separation) is required. A circulation ratio of from 2·8:1 to 6:1 is customary, the upper limit being determined by pumping power.

Once-through, or forced circulation boilers require no drums, and the feed pump supplies the necessary head for overcoming friction losses in the tubing (Fig. 5.36).

The choice of unit for any application depends upon a number of factors including the space available, the power consumption permissible, and the need to accept rapid load changes. Natural circulation units have essentially vertical tubes, require no electric power (other than the feed pump), and on account of the large masses of water and metal take least readily to sudden load changes. Assisted circulation boilers do not have to have vertical tubes, require more power, but have smaller masses of metal and water. Once-through boilers take most power,

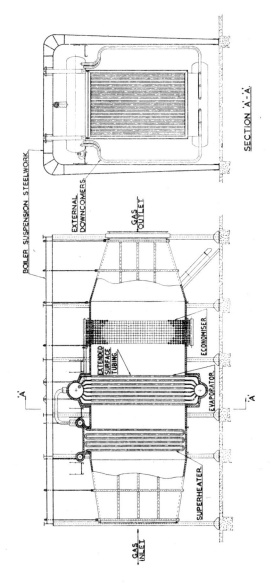

Fig. 5.35. Typical arrangement of natural circulation water-tube waste heat boiler (by courtesy of Clarke, Chapman and Company Limited).

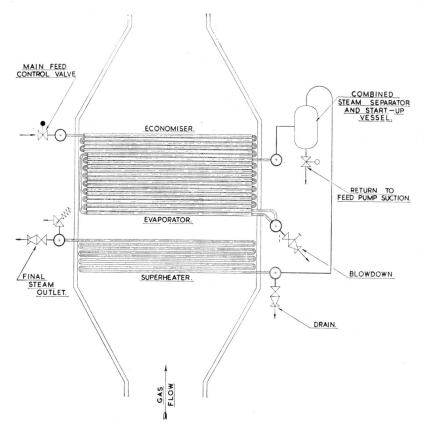

FIG. 5.36. Typical arrangement of a "once-through" waste-heat boiler (by
courtesy of Clarke, Chapman and Company Limited).

least space, and respond most readily to sudden changes of demand.

The waste-heat boiler has virtually no option but to turn the heat
from the exhaust gas into steam (except in so far as a by-pass is fitted)
and control of the boiler must essentially be integrated with the control
of the gas turbine. Indeed it is important to engineer the entire plant as
a whole. This also applies to the choice of pressure drop through the
boiler—high-pressure drops resulting in a reduction of boiler size and
cost, but also a decrease in the gas-turbine power output. With distillate

fuels, and continuous operation at full power, economic sums on their own indicate an allowable pressure drop of only about 4–6 in. w.g. (10–15 mb) in the boiler gas side; and it should be recognised that this results in boilers very much larger than the rotating plant. With cheaper fuels, with lower utilisation, and to some extent with higher pressure-ratio cycles it becomes economic to use higher boiler-pressure drops, and this tendency is increased if the size of equipment is important. For instance, for a naval project where size and weight were important, and the economics centred on running at around 25% power, a full-load pressure drop (with a high-pressure ratio cycle) of about 60–70 in. w.g. (15–18 kNm^{-2}) might be justified. At such high-pressure drops steps have to be taken to eliminate or control tube vibration.

The use of secondary surface is usually justified in the economiser and evaporation sections of the boiler, but in the superheater section plain tubes may often be justified. A high degree of secondary surface is especially appropriate with distillate or clean gaseous fuels, where fouling may be neglected. The diameter of tubing employed has a major effect on the weight of the heat-transfer surface and the weight of water contained, and there is therefore a strong case for using as small diameter tubing as possible. This temptation must be resisted where there is any doubt about the purity of the boiler water, as small-bore tubes are the more liable to deposition, blockage, and failure. Usual commercial practice is for 1 in. to 1½ in. (2·5–4·0 cm) diameter tubes, but smaller diameters may be used if water purity is carefully controlled.

Feedwater must be treated to remove temporary and permanent hardness and dissolved solids. Demineralisation is the best way to do this, and the resultant feedwater should have a maximum total dissolved solids level of less than 1 ppm. Oxygen must also be removed in a de-aerator, and because they are self-venting, boiler manufacturers usually prefer the pressure type. This, however, limits the boiler feed temperature to about 228°F (109°C), and for a given boiler pressure limits the amount of exhaust heat which is extracted from the gas turbine and therefore may slightly reduce the efficiency of the plant compared to a vacuum type de-aerator with steam ejectors for venting. Oxygen level should be kept to below 0·01 cc per litre for units up to about 900 psi pressure (62 bar).

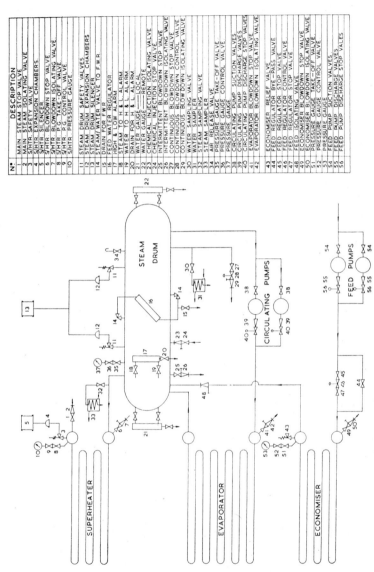

Fig. 5.37. Typical diagrammatic arrangement of valves and fittings for a drum-type waste-heat boiler (by courtesy of Clarke, Chapman and Company Limited.)

N°	DESCRIPTION
1	MAIN STEAM STOP VALVE
2	MAIN STEAM ISOLATING VALVE
3	S/HTR SAFETY VALVE
4	S/HTR EXPANSION CHAMBERS
5	S/HTR SILENCER
6	S/HTR BLOWDOWN STOP VALVE
7	S/HTR PG TAKE-OFF VALVE
8	S/HTR BLOWDOWN ISOLATING VALVE
9	S/HTR PG CONTROL VALVE
10	S/HTR PRESSURE GAUGE
11	STEAM DRUM SAFETY VALVES
12	STEAM DRUM EXPANSION CHAMBERS
13	STEAM DRUM SILENCER
14	STEAM WATER VALVE TO F.W.R
15	DRAIN FOR F.W.R
16	FEED WATER REGULATOR
17	HIGH & LOW ALARM
18	STEAM TO H & L ALARM
19	WATER TO H & L ALARM
20	DRAIN FOR H & L ALARM
21	WATER GAUGE — LOCAL
22	WATER GAUGE — REMOTE
23	CHEMICAL INJECTION ISOLATING VALVE
24	CHEMICAL INJECTION VALVE
25	INTERMITTENT BLOWDOWN STOP VALVE
26	INTERMITTENT BLOWDOWN ISOLATING VALVE
27	CONTINUOUS BLOWDOWN STOP VALVE
28	CONTINUOUS BLOWDOWN CONTROL VALVE
29	CONTINUOUS BLOWDOWN ISOLATING VALVE
30	WATER SAMPLING VALVE
31	WATER SAMPLER
32	STEAM SAMPLING VALVE
33	STEAM SAMPLER
34	STEAM RELEASE VALVE
35	PRESSURE GAUGE TAKE-OFF VALVE
36	PRESSURE GAUGE CONTROL VALVE
37	PRESSURE GAUGE
38	CIRCULATING PUMP SUCTION VALVES
39	CIRCULATING PUMP DISCHARGE VALVES
40	CIRCULATING PUMP DISCHARGE STOP VALVES
41	EVAPORATOR BLOWDOWN STOP VALVE
42	EVAPORATOR BLOWDOWN ISOLATING VALVE
43	ECONOMISER RELIEF VALVE
44	FEED REGULATOR BYE-PASS VALVE
45	FEED REGULATOR STOP VALVE
46	FEED REGULATOR CONTROL VALVE
47	FEED REGULATOR STOP VALVE
48	FEED ISOLATING VALVE
49	ECONOMISER BLOWDOWN STOP VALVE
50	ECONOMISER BLOWDOWN ISOLATING VALVE
51	PRESSURE GAUGE TAKE-OFF VALVE
52	PRESSURE GAUGE CONTROL VALVE
53	PRESSURE GAUGE
54	FEED PUMP SUCTION VALVES
55	FEED PUMP DISCHARGE VALVES
56	FEED PUMP DISCHARGE STOP VALVES

The pH value of the boiler water must also be controlled usually by chemical dosing with hydrazine either at the suction side of the boiler feed pump, or direct into the de-aerated water storage tank. In the latter case further dosing will be required after the feed pump, the object being to keep the pH value between 8 and 8·5.

TABLE 5.1. RECOMMENDED MAXIMUM CONCENTRATION FOR WATER IN
WASTE-HEAT BOILERS

Data taken from a private communication to the author from Mr. F. C. Bligh of the Permutit Company Limited and reproduced with his permission.

Boiler pressure	932°F (500°C) Gas			1832°F (1000°C) Gas			
	Total dissolved solids	Alkalinity	Silica	Total dissolved solids	Alkalinity	Silica	Iron and copper
psi (bar)	ppm	ppm	ppm	ppm	ppm	ppm	ppm
150 (10·3)	5000	1200	200	4000	1000	200	*
400 (27·6)	3000	600	100	2000	400	50	*
600 (41·5)	2000	400	40	1500	300	30	0·05
900 (62·1)				†	10	5	0·02

* No specific limit but water should be obviously clean.

† Low solid demineralised or distilled water make-up should be used.
Each boiler installation should be considered on its merits. The above figures largely coincide with figures published by British, American and German authorities but are modified for typical waste-heat boilers.

In boilers with recirculation the solids build up and are controlled by blowdown. Table 5.1 gives data on the maximum concentration permissible. Figure 5.37 shows a diagrammatic arrangement of the valves and fittings generally necessary to satisfy safety requirements for a drum-type waste-heat boiler.

TABLE 5.2. ASSUMPTIONS USED FOR ESTIMATES OF PERFORMANCES

The data given in Figs. 5.4–11, 20, 22 and 23 are based on the following assumptions:

Compressor polytropic efficiency	89%
Turbine polytropic efficiency	88%
Pressure losses (total, based on lower pressure)	
Inlet and outlet ducting, total	1%
Each casing diffuser, total	2%
Combustion or re-heat chamber	2%
Intercooler	2%
Heat exchanger (sum of two sides)	5%
Intercooler thermal ratio	90%
Heat exchanger thermal ratio	70%
Atmospheric and cooling-water temperature	15 °C
Fuel-gas oil—lower calorific value	43·1 MJ/kg
	18,500 Btu/lb

In intercooled cycles the high pressure compression ratio is assumed to be the square of the low pressure compression ratio. This is not far removed from the position for maximum efficiency or from the position for maximum specific power. In reheat cycles the reheat position is assumed to be after a high-pressure turbine which drives the only or the high-pressure compressor, This is not the optimum position in the cycle, but the most likely practical position. Reheat temperature is assumed equal to cycle maximum temperature.

As indicated in Fig. 5.1. the performance of a gas turbine cycle is highly sensitive to the component performance. The values cited here are typical of higher efficiency machines, though significantly different values may be obtained from some machines commercially available. In particular lower component performance may be expected from very small machines.

Waste-heat values are given above 0°C and may be corrected to other values approximately by using the data of Fig. 5.3. In steam-raising applications, the useful waste heat is roughly that available above the evaporation temperature of the steam (Fig. 5.31).

Data on steam/gas and gas/steam cycles should be taken as approximate only as significant variations occur according to the extent to which feed heating is employed; and the steam turbine efficiency may vary appreciably depending on whether it is required to run at the same speed as another shaft in the cycle or not.

All cycle efficiencies are based on the lower calorific value of the fuel.

CHAPTER 6

CLOSED-CYCLE GAS TURBINES AND TOTAL ENERGY*

by

H. U. FRUTSCHI, W. HAAS, C. KELLER and D. SCHMIDT

Escher-Wyss Ltd., Zurich, Switzerland

I. AIR HEATERS[59-61, 63-65, 130, 156]

1. *General Principles for Design and Construction*

In a closed-cycle gas-turbine plant the air heater plays a similar part to the boiler of a steam turbine plant. The transmission of heat from fuel to working medium is indirect, i.e. through heat-transfer surfaces by radiation and convection, so that the combustion gases do not come into contact with the turbine and heat exchanger.

Table 6.1 gives data of a few selected stations. Although the externa structure of the air heater as well as the firing equipment and other auxiliary installations are similar to those of a boiler, it differs essentially from the latter and can best be compared to a directly fired super-heater. It is generally of a two-pass, vertically arranged design.

The combustion chamber with top-mounted burners constitutes the first downwards pass. A single-row tube cage forms the radiation section. In the second, generally upwards gas pass, the heat-transfer surface of the convection section is located and above it is the air pre-heater. The circulating air flows first in cross counter-current to the combustion gases through the convection section and reaches the inlet headers of the combustion chamber through pipes outside the air heater.

---

* The closed-cycle gas turbine system is a Swiss proposal by Ackeret and Keller from 1936. It has been promoted and pioneered by Escher Wyss Ltd. and its licensees, both for conventional aed nuclear fuel. A summary of the development work is given in the Escher Wyss news 1966, No. 1, volume 39, and 1967 No. 3, volume 40.

From there it flows downwards through the radiation section parallel to the gases and, after reaching its final temperature, it arrives at the outlet header and from there at the pipe leading to the turbine. This arrangement of the heat-transfer surfaces gives the shortest connection pipes without many intermediate headers.

TABLE 6.1. DATA OF TYPICAL CLOSED-CYCLE GAS TURBINE INSTALLATIONS (51, 78)

	Ravens-burg, Germany	(112) Toyotomi, Japan	Haus Aden, Germany	Nippon Kokan, Japan	Novoka-shirsk USSR
Capacity (MW)	2·30	2·00	6·37	12	12
Fuel	coal	natural gas	coal mine gas	blast furnace gas	brown coal
No. of burners	3	1	5	4	6
Air flow lb/sec	54·5	53	146	226	220
(kg/sec)	(24·8)	(24·2)	(66·6)	(101·7)	(101·2)
Outlet temp., °F	1220	1220	1270	1270	1270
(°C)	(660)	(630)	(680)	(680)	(680)
Pressure drop, %	3·5	3·0	4·2	3·5	3·2
Combustion chamber heat release rate, Btu/ft³hr	1400	2540	1550	1850	1270
(kJ/m³ hr)	(51,700)	(96,000)	(57,000)	(68,000)	(46,500)
Gas temperature at outlet, °F	1760	1830	1920	2070	1780
(°C)	(960)	(1000)	(1050)	(1130)	(970)
Gas temperature at outlet of convection section, °F	870	970	940	910	840
(°C)	(470)	(520)	(500)	(485)	(450)

The design of an air heater is rather complex as many different and mostly interrelated factors must be taken into consideration. These do not depend upon the cycle alone, but also upon the nature of the fuel and the general layout. The convection surface resembles in principle the superheater section of a boiler and is normally made of various heat-resisting ferritic materials graduated according to the temperature used. On the other hand, for the radiant-heat transfer surface in the combustion chamber austenitic materials are needed.

The higher the inlet temperature of the turbine, the better their quality must be. At a given outlet temperature the allowable pressure drop of the circulating air has a decisive influence on the amount of tubing required and consequently on the price of the air heater. The higher the internal heat-transfer coefficient, the more the surface loading can be increased or the heating surface reduced without exceeding the design wall temperature of the tubes.

The high cycle pressure level leads to a favourable heat-transfer coefficient (a). It depends on pressure (p) and velocity (c) according to $a = k\,(c.p.)^{0.8}$. For instance, at 710 psig (50 bar(g)) a is approximately 23 times higher than at atmospheric pressure at the same velocity. Heat-transfer coefficients in the range of $a = 205$ Btu/ft²-hr-°F (1·16 MW/m² deg C) are used in heater tubes. Wall temperatures can be brought to only 90–126°F (50–70°C) above maximum cycle temperature. Tube diameters of 1–1¾ in. (25–46 mm) are normal. Tube wall thickness is 0·08–0·16 in. (2–4 mm), while stresses are from 2150 to 3600 psig (150–250 bar(g)) only. These low values add to the life of the plant.

Fuel is another factor that influences the layout and design of the furnace and of the whole air heater. Its chemical and combustion qualities have an important effect on the size and shape of the combustion chamber, as they necessitate the adherence to definite sectional and volumetric loads for satisfactory operation.

For solid fuels the height of the combustion chamber is also influenced by the burnout duration of the individual pulverised particles. Moreover, the furnace and the heat-transfer surface must be so designed, that combustion is completed before the flue gases reach the outlet, and the temperature of the gases is not inadmissibly high at the inlet to the convection section. For solid fuels this temperature must be sufficiently below the fusion point of the ashes to avoid slagging of the convection surfaces. For gaseous and liquid fuels the dimensions of the combustion chamber are determined primarily by the maximum wall temperature of the tubes.

2. Air Heaters for Solid Fuels[19, 20]

The newer development in air heaters, characterised mainly by the adoption of radiant heat transfer surfaces and the establishing of the final heating stage in the combustion chamber, was pioneered in the

2300 kW plant at Ravensburg. This first industrial closed-cycle gas-turbine plant with pulverized coal firing was put into service at the beginning of 1956 in the works of Escher Wyss GmbH, Ravensburg, and from then on has supplied electric power and heat to the factories

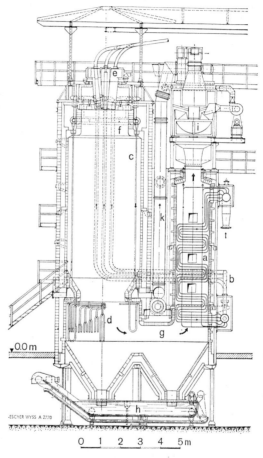

FIG. 6.1. Industrial air heater with pulverised fuel firing for the 2300 kW Ravensburg plant. a = convection section, b = connection pipes, c = radiation section, d = final heating stage, e = burner, f = ignition muffle, g = connection channel, h = ash extractor, i = combustion air preheater, k = duct to forced draught fan.

and office buildings with a high degree of reliability. The air heater, an external design, is shown in Fig. 6.1. The circulating air, enters the header at the upper end of the convection section (a) and flows downwards in cross counter-current to the combustion gases through the tube banks. These are suspended from straight supporting tubes which are also air-cooled. From the common outlet manifold of the convection section, six connecting pipes (b) located outside the air heater lead to the same number of inlet heaters of the combustion chamber. These are disposed annularly on top of the air heater and, like all the parts mentioned so far, are made from ferritic materials. The air then flows first parallel to the combustion gases through the single row cylindrical tubing assembly of the radiation section (c), then through the end heater (d), and finally reaches the two straight laterally placed end manifolds. The tubes of the radiation section and of the final heater as well as the end headers are made of austenitic material with 16Cr 13Ni 1Nb. The upper end of the combustion chamber is built as an uncooled, cylindrical ignition muffle (f) with a diameter of 7·8 ft (2·4 m) and a height of 3·9 ft (1·2m). On top of this muffle, three burners for pulverised coal (e) are placed and in their centre is the light-oil ignition burner. The gas connection part is uncooled and provided with two ash hoppers. Because of the right angle deflection of the gas before and after the channel, about 20% of the suspended ash particles drop into the hoppers and are conveyed by a common wet ash extractor (h) to a lorry. After the convection section the combustion gases pass first through a Ljungström air preheater (i) and then through a mechanical dust separator (multi-cyclone). The grinding of the coal takes place in two direct-injecting impact-type mills. One of these meets 72% of the maximum fuel requirement and the other, half this figure, i.e. 36%. Each pulveriser is supplied with coal from a separate concrete bunker by an infinitely variable feeder. Drying of the coal takes place during the grinding operation by hot air at about 810°F (430°C), bled off after the air preheater. Two mills and three burners are installed, giving the system its necessary flexibility of operation. Depending on the fuel consumption, either both mills are in service, or only one of them with its corresponding burner. Thus, for example, it is possible to run the air heater even at only 20% of the full load on coal alone without auxiliary fuel oil. To keep the radiation tubes clean six retractable soot blowers are installed at two levels in the combustion chamber. These are operated by compressed air at 140 psi (10 bar) and put into action once a day. The Ravensburg air heater has given good results over a long operating period. For pulverised coal firing, a heater of this size is, economically, obviously the smallest permissible. Its external dimensions and the manufacturing costs for the auxiliary installations are not much less than those of the air heater for the 6600-kW Municipal Power Plant at Coburg (Germany), in which similar type coal is burnt. This air heater, like all those built after Ravensburg, has no separate final heating stage. It differs from the first design at Ravensburg by having an octagonal combustion chamber. Thus it is possible to build the radiant surface in separate elements as eight equal walls each, with an inlet and an outlet header, preassembled in the workshop. Apart from the tubes of the combustion chamber and the 8 outlet headers made of steel with 16 Cr 16Ni 2Mo and 1Nb, the lower part of the convection section of this air heater is also austenitic, but of a slightly lower quality.

The adaptability of solid fuels[33] for air heaters of closed-cycle gas turbines is not limited to the high-grade bituminous coals used in the plants mentioned so far. For example, in Scotland in 1959 a 2000-kW plant for peat firing was installed at Altnabreac and in 1960 a similar sized plant with slurring firing at the Rothes colliery. At Altnabreac the peat, hand-cut and delivered with a water content of 55%, was dried during the grinding process by flue gases bled off after the air preheater. After separating off the steam in cyclones, the pulverised peat with a 30% moisture content was conveyed to the burners. The coal slurry burnt in the air heater at Rothes contained 24% ash and 26% water, and had a net calorific value of 6400 Btu/lb (14·65 MJ/kg). Both air heaters gave good service after some initial difficulties. Unfortunately both plants are no longer in operation, the digging of peat as well as the coal production being stopped in 1962 as uneconomical. During the past few years extensive research has been carried out in a test plant in Japan to ascertain how far and under what conditions the high-ash bituminous coal that is common there can be fired in pulverised form in air heaters. These types of coal contain 2–8% water, 46–55% ash, and have a net calorific value between 4570–6970 Btu/lb (10·4–15·8 MJ/kg). They tend to wear the milling and firing equipment because of the high percentage of quartz in the ash (more than 50% SiO_2). The results of numerous investigations have shown that even these low-grade fuels can be used in closed-cycle gas turbine plants, if

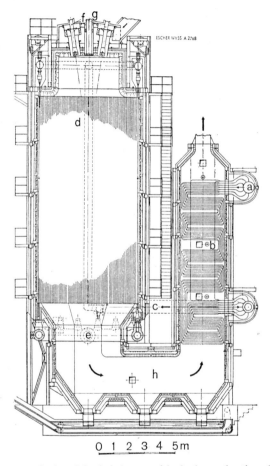

FIG. 6.2. Pulverised coal-fired air heater with single combustion chamber. Maximum continuous output 14,300 kW, air outlet temperature 1324°F (720°C). a = air inlet header, b = convection section, c = connection pipes, d = combustion chamber, e = air outlet header, f = PF burner, g = ignition gas burner, h = fluegas duct and ash hoppers.

their combustion properties are taken into due consideration in the design and construction of air heater and auxiliary equipment.

3. *Air Heaters for Gaseous and Liquid Fuels*

For gaseous and liquid fuels the manufacturing costs of the whole air heater installation are naturally smaller then for solid fuels. Also with low grades of fuel costs are higher. Whereas the various fuel oils

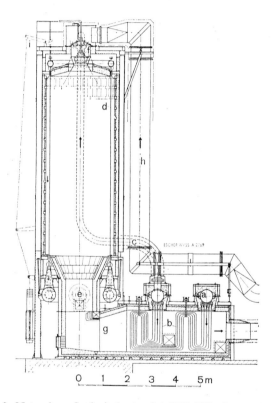

FIG. 6.3. Natural-gas-fired air heater for 2000 kW plant at Toyotomi (Japan). a = air inlet header, b = convection section, c = connection pipes, d = combustion chamber, e = air outlet header, f = burner, g = gas channel, h = air duct, i = support of radiant tubing.

are similar in their calorific values, the heating capacity of the industrial gases varies considerably according to their origin. These differences have an influence not only on the firing equipment, but also on the size of the air heater and the auxiliary installations. The total expenditure is lowest when a high-grade gas is available. This, for example, is the case in the 2000-kW plant that has been in operation since 1957 at Toyotomi in the north of Hokaido Island (Japan). The natural gas-fired air heater of this plant can be seen in Fig. 6.3 which shows a cross-section. It is characterised by its compact construction and differs from the Ravensburg air heater in the arrangement of the convection section which is horizontal in this case. To avoid the use of austenitic materials the air flow in its final stage is parallel to the gas. From the convection section (b) two connecting pipes (c) lead to the annular inlet header of the furnace. After flowing through the cylindrical tube bundle (d) of the furnace the air reaches the eight outlet headers and from there the internally insulated annular manifold (e) that discharges into the pipe leading to the turbine. The horizontal arrangement of the convection section facilitates the suspension of the tubing. Apart from the tubes of the combustion chamber, only the eight small outlet headers and the thin guide tube of the internally insulated annular manifold are made of austenitic material with 16Cr 13Ni and 1Nb. All other tubes and headers are ferritic.

This compact construction is also used for oil-fired air heaters. As distillates offer no difficulties, special measures must be taken to prevent high-temperature corrosion when burning residual oils, with ashes containing considerable quantities of vanadium and sodium. Extensive laboratory tests in the following years have shown that corrosion can best be prevented by certain additives which transform the low-melting Va and Na compounds into others with a higher melting point than that of the metallic materials. A heavy oil with the following chemical properties was burnt in a test plant: Viscosity 3430 sec Redwood No.1 at 100°F (38°C), sulphur 3%, ash 0.12%, containing 76% V_2O_5 and 7% Na_2O. Commercially milled dolomite powder CaMg $(CO_3)_2$ suspended in light oil was added to the fuel. It was injected immediately in front of the burner and metered so that the dolomite content was about 1% in weight of the oil. After a test period of about 1000 hours and tube wall temperatures between 1200–1480°F (650–800°C) no corrosion could be found. Based on these results a large-scale experiment was carried out under normal working conditions in the plant at Ravensburg in 1960 with residual oil and the addition of dolomite. It lasted 3200 hours. A heavy commercial fuel oil was used, containing about 1–3% sulphur, 110–570 ppm ash, 20–55 ppm vanadium and 17–50 ppm sodium. The dolomite powder was blown in with the combustion air. The addition was made by a shaking device regulating the weight to about 1% of the amount of the oil. From the economic point of view this quantity was quite permissible, as it amounted to only 0·7% of the fuel costs. As examinations undertaken after this experiment showed neither high-temperature nor low-temperature corrosion had occurred.

Another gaseous fuel is used in the 6500-kW plant at Haus Aden (Germany) supplying a colliery in the Ruhr-area with power, air and heat. The air heater of this plant is designed for combined firing of mine gas and bituminous coal. Its principal data can be found in Table 1. The gas is sucked out underground before mining the coal. It contains on average about 1·5% CO_2, 13% O_2. 36·5% CH_4, and 49% N_2. As its quantity and also its calorific value vary considerably, bituminous coal had to be provided as stand-by fuel. Moreover, to carburise the gas flame, i.e. to increase its intensity of radiation, a small quantity of pulverised coal corresponding to about 10% of the fuel input is added. The coal is ground in two mills, one of which is designed especially for carburisation and has a throughput of only 0·4 t/hr. Five burners for the combined firing of mine gas and pulverised coal are arranged in the roof of the combustion chamber.

The wide range of various fuels that have been used so far is completed by blast-furnace gas, used in the air heater of the 12-MW plant at Nippon Kokan, Japan. In this air-heater, blast-furnace gas produced by this steel works is fired without any additional fuel. The octagonal combustion chamber is equipped with a small ignition muffle, with three blast-furnace gas burners fitted in its roof. The tubing of the combustion chamber is of austenitic material with 16Cr 16Ni 2Mo 1Nb. Owing to the high temperature of the gases leaving the combustion chamber, the two lower bundles of the convection tubes are also of austenitic material but of a lesser quality.

II. HEAT EXCHANGERS

The characteristic items of a heat exchanger that determine thermodynamically the whole behaviour of a gas turbine are the heat recovery and the pressure drop, factors that also influence the size and manufacturing cost of the apparatus itself. In a closed-cycle gas turbine the heat transmitted from the low-pressure to the high-pressure air in the recuperator is approximately equal to the heat supplied to the cycle by fuel in the air heater. The air leaving the compressor with a pressure of 430–510 psig (30–36 bar(g)) is thereby preheated from about 195–750°F (90–400°C) and that discharged from the turbine with a pressure of 93–106 psig (6·5–7·5 bar(g)) is cooled from about 810°–248F (430–120°C). Any plant operates most economically if this heat exchange takes place with temperature difference and pressure drop kept as small as possible. The heat exchanger of the plants in service have efficiencies of 90–92% and pressure drops of between 2·5% and 3·5%. In spite of these high values of heat recovery the dimensions and weights of these heat exchangers are not very large compared with recuperators of open-cycle gas turbines, due to the higher pressure level and better heat-transfer coefficients. As surfaces are kept clean in closed-cycle equipment, it is possible to use heat-transfer elements with very small flow areas resulting in compact design. Such an effective element consists of a thin-walled tube with 0·2 in. (5 mm) wide and 0·014–0·02 in. (0·035 or 0·5 mm) thick corrugated steel strips wound internally and externally, and brazed with hard solder. By having a staggered arrangement of the fins, favourable heat-transfer coefficients, characteristic for a turbulent flow, are obtained. The brazing is done by induction heating in an inert-gas atmosphere. For the manufacture of these tubes a special band winding-machine was built. In the tubes to the right, the high-pressure air flows through the inner finning, that is, in the space between the supporting tube and the heat-transfer tube, while the low-pressure air passes in counter current through the outer finning. In the tubes of the bundle to the left, the opposite takes place. Both types of tubes are set in an equilateral triangle arrangement. To prevent by-pass flows it is necessary to fill the spaces between the tubes and on the circumference with profiled triangular aluminium bars. The design of a 2300-kW heat exchanger

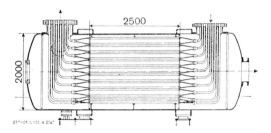

FIG. 6.4. Heat exchanger for 2300 kW plant. Corrugated strip finnned
tubes. Internal high pressure type.

with corrugated strip fin tubes is shown in Fig. 6.4. It consists of tubes
in which low-pressure air passes through the outer finning. In this
design nineteen tubes are gathered into one bundle. For improved
performance, it is sometimes more economical to use the type of tubes
in which the low pressure air flows inside. Figure 6.5 shows such a
heat exchanger in service in two 6500-kW plants in Germany. The

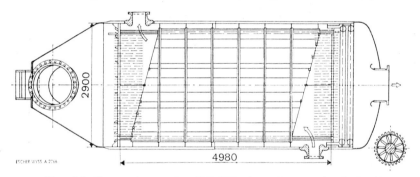

FIG. 6.5. Heat exchanger for 6370 kW plant. Corrugated strip finned
tubes. External high-pressure type.

separate tubes are rolled directly into the tube plates. One of the plates
is welded to the shell and the other is mounted movably with 2 "Torus"
expansion joints. This kind of construction was also used for a 12,000-
kW plant fired with blast-furnace gas in Japan. All these units have
proved satisfactory in service. The heat exchangers with corrugated
strip fin tubes are characterised by simple design, in particular short

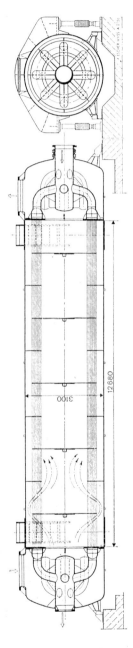

FIG. 6.6. Heat exchanger for 12,000 kW with single pass and smooth tubes.

tube-lengths and compact arrangement with short connecting pipes. In the case of larger equipment these tubes lead to plant diameters that are sometimes not acceptable for reasons of transportation. In such cases the heat exchangers are built with smooth, narrow tubes. An example of this design for a 12,000 kW plant is shown in Fig. 6.6. It is of cross counter-current type. The heating surface consists of steel tubes 0·32 in. (8 mm) in diameter, in annular arrangement for single pass flow of the high-pressure air. To obtain better heat-transfer coefficients, the low-pressure air is led in cross current to the tubes and deflected repeatedly by transverse baffles. On the high-pressure side the tubes open out at both ends into ring headers. To obtain a more even distribution of the air, these are joined by eight tubes to the axially placed inlet and outlet manifolds. At the cold end of the apparatus an expansion joint is fitted to compensate for the different thermal expansions between tubes and shell. In principle, the heat exchangers of gas-turbine plants are horizontally arranged and placed directly beneath the machine. This ensures the most favourable general arrangement and the shortest pipe connections.

III. COOLERS

Cooling of the cycle air to an economically low temperature before it enters the compressors takes place in a precooler and, depending upon the purpose of the plant, in one or two compressor intercoolers. The dimensions and the manufacturing costs of these units depend largely on the chosen log, mean temperature difference and the allowable pressure drop of the cycle air. In general, the coolers are designed for a temperature difference between air and cooling water of 13–18°F (7–10°C) at the cold end and a relative pressure drop of about 1–0·5% depending on whether they are used to supply hot water for heating purposes or not. If so, the heat-transfer surface is divided into a hot water and a fresh water part. Both are placed in a common shell with one-way air flow. The cooling water required by a CCGT plant is considerably less than that for a comparable steam-turbine plant. The temperature level usually allows the use of non-ferrous tubes with soft soldered copper fins. The flow area between the fins may be reduced if desired, as there is no danger of fouling.

There are essentially two different types of coolers built. In the one, of generally applicable and orthodox design, the heat exchange surface consists of conventional spirally finned tubes through which the water flows. The construction of such a cooler is shown in Fig. 6.7. It consists of a cylindrical shell with the air to be cooled flowing in the direction of its longitudinal axis. The finned tubes are gathered into bundles

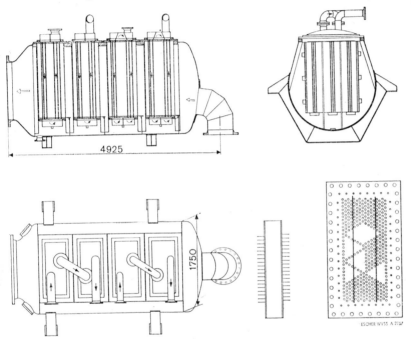

FIG. 6.7. Precooler for a 2300-kW gas turbine. The cooling water flows inside the tubes.

and set at right angles to the air stream. This cooler for a 2,000 kW plant has a heating water and a fresh water part. The water passing through the tubes flows, in both, counter current to the circulating-air and is deflected several times. This design is also well suited for not very clean cooling water. The internal diameter of the tubes was also chosen to facilitate mechanical cleaning. In the other cooler design the water passes in cross-current flow to the tubes. Tubes with corrugated strip fins inside constitute the heating surface. The fins are of 0·2 in. (5 mm) wide and 0·014 in. (0·25 mm) thick copper strips and are soft soldered to the non-ferrous metal tubing. The air flows in the space between the small supporting tube and the heat transfer tube. Figure 6.8 shows such a cooler. It is a pre-cooler for a helium closed-cycle gas turbine plant. The tubes are set in triangular arrangement, and are rolled into the tube plates, one of which has a flexible fastening. Baffles deflect cooling water several times. The same design may also be used for air coolers. This very compact construction is most suitable for

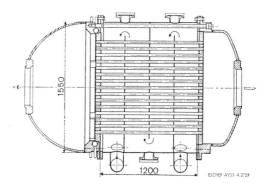

FIG. 6.8. Precooler for helium closed-cycle gas turbine plant. The cooling water flows outside the tubes. Single-pass design for 10×10^6 Btu/hr (10·5 GJ/hr) and temperature difference at cold end of 10°F (5·5°C).

closed-cycle cooling water, clean cooling water, or where chemical cleaning is sufficient. It is space saving and thus very suitable, for example, for marine propulsion units.

The Helium Gas Turbine for Nuclear Power Plants[17, 19, 70, 74, 93–95]

In all known power plants with water-cooled reactors, only the steam turbine is used to convert the reactor heat into mechanical work. With the recent development of gas-cooled high-temperature reactors and gas turbines, the latter will start to compete with steam plants. The gases, which have high outlet temperatures of over 1290°F (700°C), can drive a gas turbine in a direct circuit and can thus be utilised

without additional pressure and temperature losses such as are inevitable in the case of intermediate heat exchangers (Fig. 6.9). This not
only improves fuel economy, but also appreciably reduces capital
costs and simplifies the plant as a whole. As more than two-thirds of
the price of the power supplied by present-day nuclear plants is due to
the high plant cost, it is especially desirable to reduce this cost factor.
More complex fuel cycles designed to improve efficiency and better fuel

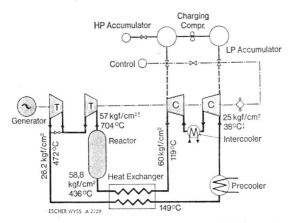

FIG. 6.9. Circuit of gas-cooled nuclear reactor and helium closed-cycle
gas turbine.

utilisation merely affect the fuel cost, which is low anyway, but do not
appreciably influence the overall power production price.

On completion of the 25 MWe prototype power plant of this kind in
Geesthacht (Schleswig Holstein), in co-operation with the German
Atomic Energy Authority, the gas turbine will for the first time super-
sede the steam turbine on an industrial scale in the nuclear field.

Although the direct circuit is very simple, this first plant will, with a
gas-inlet temperature into the turbine of 1340°F (730°C), reach an
overall efficiency of over 37%. This is quite remarkable in view of the
small plant capacity and already suggests that in future larger plants
the efficiency rates will far surpass those of present-day atomic plants
equipped with water-cooled reactors, which are operated with steam
temperatures of 570–750°F (300–400°C). The high efficiency is also

the result of the progress made in aerodynamics, which is especially marked in a gas circuit with permanently clean working medium.

High plant efficiency is sought not only for reduced fuel consumption, but also for the associated reduction in the size of the plant components.

The whole circuit—reactor and attached gas turbine system—is adjusted to the load by varying the pressure level at constant temperature in front of the turbine, as is the practice in conventional closed-cycle systems. This results in practically constant plant efficiency throughout a very wide load range. In consequence, the plant can be operated advantageously to cater not only for the base load, as is the case with most existing nuclear power plants, but also for variable loads (Fig. 6.10). For this reason it is also suitable for marine propul-

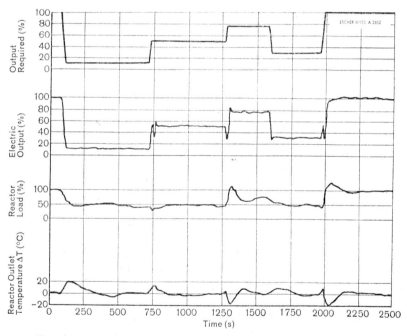

FIG. 6.10. Behaviour of a nuclear power set with gas-cooled reactor at variable load. The pressure-level control permits the reactor outlet temperature to be kept constant.

sion. Another most important fact is that, owing to the physical properties of gas circuits, the amount of cooling water required is only one third to one-fifth that of a corresponding steam plant. As the waste heat from this cycle process has a higher temperature level than in steam plants, the cooling water can be heated to over 212°F (100°C) and is thus used directly for heating purposes. The sale of the waste heat can help appreciably to reduce the fuel cost per kWh (by about 0·1 cent/kWh). In such a combined heating-and-power plant, as in conventional closed-cycle power plants, up to 85% of the energy contained in the fuel can be utilised.

In steam plants with conventional and nuclear heating, rises in temperature above 1110°F (600°C) are no longer economical. By contrast, the gas turbine opens the way to far higher medium temperatures of 1470–2190°F (800–1200°C) and thus to plant efficiencies of over 50%, without becoming over complex. Reactor construction and material development have today reached such a stage, that the combination of a high-temperature reactor with a closed-cycle gas turbine, as proposed by Ackeret and Keller 25 years ago, can be made feasible with the present proved means of gas turbine engineering. Not even temperatures over 1470°F (980°C) present any difficulties with helium-cooled graphite-moderated reactors with ceramic fuels (Dragon, Peach Bottom). In modern jet planes gas turbines are being run at over 1830°F (1000°C) without trouble. This also applies to the closed-cycle versions, which, owing to their smaller dimensions, are subject to less heavy stress.

It is generally assumed that gas turbines cannot be built in sizes above 50 MW, but this is not so. Closed-cycle helium gas turbines can be built in any size, from very small units up to 600 MW. All recent studies have shown that there is virtually no size limit. The back pressure is about 360 psig (25 bar(g)) and therefore the medium throughput can still be handled with small blades. There is no difficulty as with steam plants, that a low back pressure requires very large outlet sections. The efficiency of the helium cycle is independent of the working pressure, so that it is possible to choose this taking into consideration only the most favourable dimensions of the equipment. Unlike steam plants even very large capacities of 600 MW$_e$ do not need pressures in excess of 950 psig (62 bar(g)).

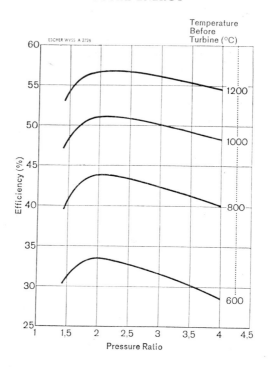

Fig. 6.11. Plant efficiency of the He cycle as a function of pressure ratio and the inlet temperature of the turbine, allowing for energy losses.

The Influence of the Physical Data of Helium in Comparison to those of Air [9-13, 89]

The main physical data of helium are given in Table 6.2. Using basic thermodynamics, some very important relationships useful in the design of helium circuits can be derived. Helium circuits are just as simple as air circuits, and quite equal in efficiency. All that is needed is that the maximum and minimum circuit temperatures remain the same, or in other words, that the compression of the medium on one side, and its expansion in the turbine on the other take place within the same temperature range (derivation from the Carnot cycle).

TABLE 6.2. COMPARISON OF PHYSICAL DATA OF AIR AND HELIUM

$A = 14 \cdot 2$ psi and $68°F$ (1 bar and $20°C$)
$B = 425$ psi and $1110°F$ (30 bar and $600°C$)

		Air	Helium
Molecular weight		29	4
Specific heat, C_p	A	0·24 (1·02)	1·242 (5·2) Btu/lb°F
	B	0·267 (1·13)	1·242 (5·2) (kJ/kg °C)
Adiabatic coefficient,	A	1·4	1·665
$x = C_p/C_v$	B	1·36	1·665
Thermal conductivity,	A	0·0148 (0·025)	0·085 (0·148) Btu/ft-hr°F
k	B	0·033 (0·058)	(0·180 (0·31) W/m°C)
Viscosity,	A	$3·7 \times 10^{-5} (1·85 \times 10^{-6})$	4×10^{-5} lb/ft²
			$(2 \times 10^{-6}$ kg/m²)
η	B	$8·0 \times 10^{-5}$ (4×10^{-6})	$8·5 \times 10^{-5}$ lb/ft²
			$(4·24 \times 10^{-6}$ kg/m²)

Heat Drop

The specific heat of helium is 5 times as high as that of air. Thus when the temperature limits are the same, the work done per unit weight circulating in the helium machine is 5 times that done in the air machine.

Pressure ratio

$$\pi = \frac{P_1}{P_2} = \left(\frac{T_1}{T_2}\right) exp \; \frac{x}{x-1} \qquad (1)$$

where:

x = ratio of specific heats at constant pressure and constant volume, i.e. C_p/C_v (dimensionless),

P = pressure in psi (Nm^{-2}),

T = absolute temperature, °R (°K),

V = volume, ft³ (m³),

ρ = density, lb-ft^{-3} (kg-m^{-3})

η = dynamic viscosity, lb/ft² (kg/m²),

d = pipe diameter in ft (m),

G = mass flow rate in lb-sec^{-1} (kg-sec^{-1}),

c = fluid flow rate in ft-sec^{-1} (m-sec^{-1}),
r = pipeline resistance in lb-ft^{-2} (kg-m^{-2}),
R = gas constant, ft-lb-mole^{-1}-°F^{-1} (kg-m mole^{-1}°C^{-1}),
F = pipeline friction in lb-ft^{-2} (kg-m^{-2}),
k = thermal conductivity Btu-hr^{-1}-ft^{-1}-°F^{-1} (W/m°C),
α = surface conductivity Btu-hr^{-1}-ft^{-2}-°F^{-1} (W/m^2°C).

For a specified temperature ratio T_1/T_2 the pressure ratio becomes much smaller in helium than in air (see Fig. 6.11).

Volume ratio

$$\frac{V_2}{V_1} = \left(\frac{T_1}{T_2}\right) exp \, \frac{1}{x-1}$$

This is also smaller for helium than for air. For example during expansion from 1330°F to 747°F (720°C to 398°C).

	Air	Helium
Pressure ratio	4.4	2·66
Volume ratio	3·0	1·80

Energy Losses in Pipes, Bends, Enlargements, etc.

The effect of these losses on the cycle may be taken to consist in the reduction of the expansion work in the turbine at a given compression ratio. The gas state at the turbine outlet may then be taken as P_2' and T_2' instead of P_2 and T_2. Therefore the relative pressure loss is equal to:

$$\beta = \frac{P_2' - P_2}{P_2}$$

with

$$\frac{T_2'}{T_2} = \left(\frac{P_2'}{P_2}\right) exp \, \frac{x-1}{x},$$

and assuming equal temperatures for air (labelled (A)) and helium (labelled (H)), we obtain that

$$(1 + \epsilon_H) \, exp\left(\frac{x-1}{x}\right)_H = (1 + \epsilon_A) \, exp\left(\frac{x-1}{x}\right)_A$$

for the same energy losses or as a first approximation,

$$\left(\frac{x-1}{x}\right)_{\mathrm{H}} \epsilon_{\mathrm{H}} = \left(\frac{x-1}{x}\right)_{\mathrm{A}} \epsilon_{\mathrm{A}}$$

and, with the values from Table 6.3.

TABLE 6.3. CHARACTERISTICS OF MACHINE WITH HELIUM AS WORKING MEDIUM

Capacity in MW	25	250	600
Mass flow, kg/sec	38	400	780
Mass flow, lb/sec	84	880	1720
Turbine inlet temp., °F	1340	1200	1380
°C	730	700	750
Turbine inlet pressure, psig	365	880	1008
bar(g)	25	60	71
Speed, rpm	10,000	3000 to 4200	3600
Number of stages	8 or 9	7 to	12
Maximum diameter, mm	800	1940	1740
Maximum blade length, mm	130	280	222

But $\epsilon_{\mathrm{H}} = 0.67 \ \epsilon_{\mathrm{A}}$

$$\epsilon = \frac{\Delta p}{P} \propto \frac{c^2}{r}$$

Assuming equal temperatures and equal resistance coefficients

$$\frac{\epsilon_{\mathrm{H}}}{\epsilon_{\mathrm{A}}} = \left(\frac{c_{\mathrm{H}}}{c_{\mathrm{A}}}\right)^2 \frac{r_{\mathrm{A}}}{r_{\mathrm{H}}}$$

or $\quad \dfrac{c_{\mathrm{H}}}{c_{\mathrm{A}}} = (0.67 \ r_{\mathrm{H}}/r_{\mathrm{A}})^{\frac{1}{2}} = 2.2$

Therefore, if, for example, velocities of 82–148 ft/sec (25–45 m/sec) are used in an air cycle, values of 180–328 ft/sec (55–100 m/sec) are permissible in a helium cycle.

Pipeline cross-sections

$$F = \frac{GV}{c}$$

I

and as $PV = RT$, we can write that:

$$F = \frac{GRT}{cP}$$

On calculating for air and helium we get:

$$\frac{F_H}{F_A} = 0.66 \frac{P_H}{P_A}$$

If the pressures chosen in front of the turbine are the same for air and helium, and there is a pressure ratio of 4·4 for air and one of 2·66 for helium, the following pipeline cross-section ratios are obtained for helium and air.

High-pressure part: 1:1·5
Low-pressure part: 1:2·5

This greatly simplifies the construction of large-capacity helium plants.

Mach Number

The velocity of sound in helium is 3 times as high as in air so that the maximum permissible speed of the compressor rotor does not depend on the Mach number as in the case of air. Peripheral speeds about double those permissible in air can be allowed. As the heat drop is about 5 times greater in the case of helium, the number of stages only increases in the ratio of $5/2^2 = 1·25$.

Heat Exchanger Surfaces

Assuming equivalent air and helium cycles, the same quantity of useful power involves the conversion of equal heat quantities in the equipment (recuperators and coolers). If the temperature difference is also the same, the only factor which requires special treatment is the heat transfer coefficient.

$$Nu = \frac{ad}{k} = 0.024 \, (Re)^{0.8} \, Pr^b$$

where Nu is the Nusselt number, Pr is the Prandtl number and Re is the Reynolds number.

For similar Prandtl numbers:

$$\frac{Re_H}{Re_A} = \frac{2 \cdot 2}{7 \cdot 2 \times 1 \cdot 07} = 0 \cdot 29 \quad \text{or} \quad \left(\frac{Re_H}{Re_A}\right)^{0.8} = 0 \cdot 37$$

$$\frac{a_H}{a_A} = 0 \cdot 37 \times \frac{k_A}{k_H} = 2 \cdot 00.$$

It can therefore be seen that the heat exchanger equipment of a helium plant need only be half the size of that of a comparable air plant. When it is further considered that the velocity can be a good deal higher as the flow path is shortened, the recuperator area required will only be about one third of that in air plants.

1. Sealing of Casings and Pipes

Helium, as is known, penetrates porous spots more easily than air. Even so, it is possible to achieve practically absolute sealing by consistent application of all-welded construction. To make quite sure, the flanges are provided with thin welding lips, which are only welded together before commencing industrial service.

2. Sealing of Machine Shaft

Use is made of a helium and oil-sealing system in which the pressure in the sealing-oil tank automatically follows the variations of the circuit pressure (low-pressure side) (Fig. 6.12). In this the lubricating and sealing-oil flow, which may contain helium, is not mixed with the oil returning from the outer bearings, which contains air, so as to ensure that no air can enter the circuit. On the other hand, the helium returned from the pressure oil tank to the circuit passes through a separator, which absorbs the traces of oil. These precautions are necessary to prevent the escape of radio active particles.

As in many other nuclear power plants, the heat developed in the reactor is transferred through a CO_2 primary circuit to the secondary steam circuit, it seemed obvious to design the CO_2 circuit as the working circuit. Such a solution is, however, beset by the basic drawback that any further development up to high temperatures is prevented by the nuclear properties of CO_2. That is why the solutions sought today aim, for example, at designing a CO_2 circuit in such a way that partial condensation takes place. Admittedly, such solutions have to discard the intriguing simplicity of the helium circuit with its ideal controllability.

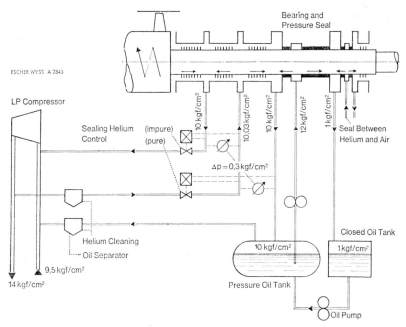

FIG. 6.12. Oil-sealing system used with helium closed-cycle gas turbine.

Combined Heat and Power Production[14, 86, 87, 101, 134]

In a closed-cycle gas turbine plant, the heat which has to be rejected from the lower end of the thermodynamic process is transmitted to the cooling water by pre- and intercoolers. In contrast to the steam cycle, the heat rejection is not an isothermal change of state (condensation)

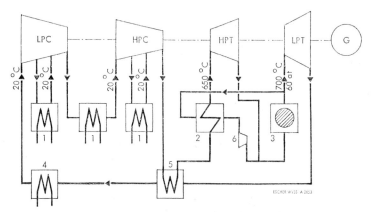

FIG. 6.13. Circuit of helium cycle using reheating outside reactor, 1 = intercooler, 2 = reheater, 3 = high temperature reactor, 4 = precooler, 5 = recuperator, 6 = circulator.

but an adiabatic one. It is thus possible to obtain such high cooling water outlet temperatures, that the rejected heat, or at least part of it, can be used for district heating purposes with the usual water supply and return temperatures. The fuel utilisation in such a case is double that of conventionally fired plants without waste heat recovery.

When the gas in the pre- and intercoolers is cooled by fresh water to the lowest possible compressor inlet temperature, the maximum possible mechanical or electrical output is obtained. When, however, district heating is practiced in connection with the plant, the electrical output is lowered, but up to 85% of the fuel heat and up to 95% of the reactor heat can be obtained as useful energy, taking the combined power and heat output.

Figure 6.15 shows two-cycle diagrams with differing cooler arrangements. The pre- and intercoolers in diagram A are provided with separate heating water and fresh water elements. Thus the gas is cooled down, for example, from 250°F to 140°F (120°C to 60°C) when passing the heating water element, and the water temperature will be raised in the counterflow heat exchanger from 122°F to 212°F (50°C to 100°C). The fresh water which follows causes a drop in the gas temperature down to that of the compressor inlet level, for example down to 68°F (20°C) with 50°F (10°C) cooling water. This heat which is subsequently

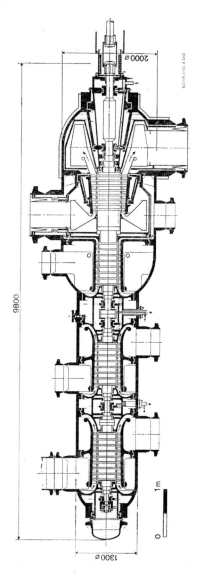

Fig. 6.14. Section through 25 MW$_e$ helium nuclear power plant.

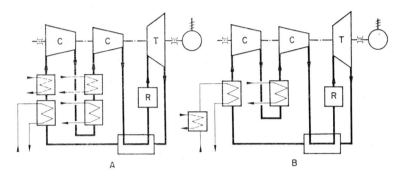

FIG. 6.15. Two typical flow sheets of closed-cycle systems.

rejected is lost, as the temperature level is too low. Another system of cooling-water flow is shown in Fig. 6.15B. In this case only heating water flows through the pre- and intercoolers. The return water from the district heating system having a relatively low temperature, passes through a heating water aftercooler before entering the pre- and intercooler of the gas turbine. If high-power production is desired and the heat requirements are low, the effect of the heating water after-cooler can be increased by opening the fresh-water flow. On the other hand, fresh water is throttled if the heat requirement is greater. When there is no water flow, all waste heat can be used at a suitable temperature level, so that the highest possible total efficiency—power and heat together—is obtained.

For the following discussion, in accordance with present-day practice, a turbine inlet temperature of 1325°F (720°C) for air and 1290°F (700°C) for helium is taken as a base. Machine efficiencies, pressure losses and gas heater efficiencies are in conformity with the newest plants in operation. The same assumption is made for the mechanical and electrical losses.

It is well known that for each cycle design there exists one optimum expansion ratio with regard to thermal efficiency and another, a higher value, for the largest output with a given gas mass flow.

If conditions of optimum combined heat and power production are desired the expansion ratio should be carefully selected.

Figure 6.16 shows these relations for two different cycle arrangements, namely with simple and with double intercooling of the compressed gases. The diagram on the left is valid for air and the other one for helium as the working medium. In both cases, a compressor inlet temperature of 68°F (20°C) is assumed. The two diagrams show, as function of the expansion ratio (π_{exp}), the most important parameters having an influence on the power–heat behaviour, e.g. fuel consumption,

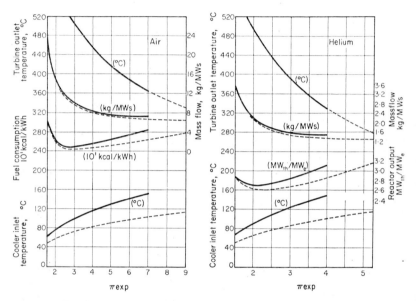

FIG. 6.16. Typical properties of air and helium in systems with one and two intercoolers. Full lines = one intercooler. Broken lines = two intercoolers. 1 kcal = 4·0 Btu = 4·2 kJ.

the specific mass flow passing through the machines and apparatus, the average gas-inlet temperature in pre- and intercooler and the turbine outlet temperature. The latter should not be higher than about 845°F (450°C), otherwise, more expensive alloys would be needed for the heat exchanger. In the case of helium (right-hand figure) the necessary specific thermal reactor output is plotted instead of the fuel consumption.

As an example, let us assume we need to generate an electric output of 30 MW and to find the usable waste heat production. The water temperatures are to be 212°F. (100°C) outlet, and 122°F (50°C) in the return pipe. In this case, the following cycle design for air as working medium may be chosen.

In order to obtain normal cooler dimensions, it is necessary to use a logarithmic mean temperature difference between gas and water not lower than about 36°F (20°C). Values of 18°F (10°C) at the cold end and 54°F (30°C) at the hot end are chosen. The mean value of the cooler inlet temperature in this case must be about 270°F (130°C). A cycle with only one intercooler is suitable as the left-hand diagram shows, with an expansion ratio of $\pi_{exp} = 5$. The corresponding fuel consumption can be taken as 10,550 Btu/kWh (11,200 kJ/kWh) which will be $3 \cdot 20 \times 10^8$ Btu/hr ($3 \cdot 38 \times 10^8$ kJ/hr). The thermal efficiency of the electric power production is extremely good, namely, 32·2%. As specific mass flow we obtain 17 lb/MWsec (7·7 kg/MWsec) so that 508 lb/sec (231 kg/sec) are needed, if an output of 30 MW is to be generated.

As the heating water enters the hot water element of the coolers with a return temperature of 122°F (50°C) the air will be cooled down from 270°F to 140°F (130°C–60°C) (temperature difference of 18°F (10°C) at cold end). For the two coolers, pre- and intercooler, the usable hot-water production will be: $2 \times 508 \times 0 \cdot 24 \times (270 - 140) \times 3600 = 1 \cdot 15 \times 10^8$ Btu/hr ($1 \cdot 21 \times 10^8$ kJ/hr) in which the specific heat of the air is 0·24 Btu/lb °F (1·03 kJ/kg °C). This usable hot water furthermore represents 35% of the fuel heat, so that the total efficiency becomes

$$= 32 \cdot 2 + 35 = 67 \cdot 2\%.$$

With a smaller expansion ratio, say $\pi_{exp} = 4$, a lower fuel consumption could be achieved, but the lower logarithmic mean temperature difference between air and hot water needs larger coolers. The higher outlet temperature of the turbine, in connection with a bigger mass flow needs a large heat exchanger and, moreover, the compressor outlet temperature, which is about 18°F (10°C) lower, gives a smaller usable hot-water production. As another example, the 30 MW is to be generated by a nuclear closed-cycle gas turbine plant, and as high a portion of the waste heat as possible is to be used in a district heating system with the same water temperatures as before, namely 212°F (100°C) outlet and 122°F (50°C) return temperature. As cycle medium, helium must be used. Figure 6.14 shows the corresponding curves on the right-hand side. The same considerations as we have made in case of air call for an expansion ratio of $\pi_{exp} = 3.15$. A specific reactor output of 2·92 MW_{th}/MW_e is necessary and the thermal efficiency (electric) will be $\pi_{exp} = 34.2\%$.

The reactor output is then $30 \times 2.92 = 87.6$ MW_{th}, and a specific mass flow of 3·5 lb/MWsec (1·6 kg/MWsec) is needed, which gives 105 lb/sec (48 kg/sec) for 30 MW generated at the generator terminals. The usable heat in the form of hot water is

$$Q = 2 \times 106 \times 1.25 \, (270{-}140) \times 3600$$

$$= 1.21 \times 10^8 \text{ Btu/hr } (1.27 \times 10^8 \text{ kJ/hr}).$$

The specific heat of helium is 1·25 Btu/lb °F (5·23 kJ/kg °C). This heating water production represents 34·4% of the thermal reactor output so that an overall efficiency for this district heating plant with a nuclear closed gas turbine cycle of $\eta_{tot} = 34.2 + 34.4 = 68.6\%$ is obtained. This result is of great importance, on account of the extremely high utilization of the reactor output made possible, and also with regard to the purity of the air in our towns. In this discussion we have devoted primary attention to the matter of power production neglecting the possibility of using the second intercooler. This means that we have only used the waste heat absorbed by the heating water at a return temperature of 122°F (50°C). However, it can be seen that an increase in gas-inlet temperature in the compressors will make more usable heat available because the temperature level of the heat rejection from the closed cycle is higher. Finally, if we turn the fresh water in the heating water aftercooler off completely, so that the cooling effect is obtained only from the heating water, the maximum fuel economy is obtained. In the preceding example with 122°F (50°C) heating water return temperature, a gas inlet temperature in the compressor stages of 140°F (60°C) would result. The highest return temperatures used in district heating hot-water networks are about 158°F (70°C). This requires, in the case of total combined power–heat production, gas temperature of 176°F (80°C) in the compressor inlet.

Figure 6.17 shows the pressure ratio and efficiency characteristics for the low-pressure and high-pressure compressor of a closed-air-cycle gas turbine as a function of the suction volumes for 68°F, 122°F and 176°F (20°, 50° and 80°C) inlet temperature. It can be seen that the low-pressure compressor characteristic is shifted in the direction of the partial load with about constant adiabatic efficiency. The high-pressure compressor characteristic is displaced in the direction of overload and its adiabatic efficiency decreases somewhat. These distortions represent

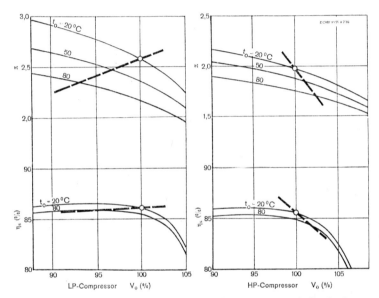

FIG. 6.17. Pressure ratio and adiabatic efficiency characteristics for low-pressure and high-pressure axial flow compressors of a closed-cycle gas turbine plant.

allowable variations in the pressure-volume behaviour for axial flow compressors with more than 100% reaction.

Thus higher compressor inlet temperatures lead to a lower expansion ratio in a given closed cycle. This causes variations in the closed cycle behaviour, as shown in Fig. 6.18. By way of an example, at constant power output at the generator terminals, the compressor inlet tem-

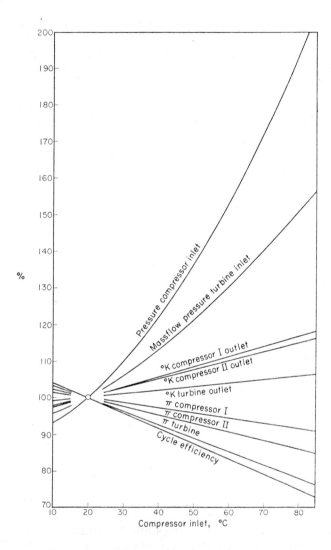

Fig. 6.18. Cycle behaviour for different compressor inlet temperatures. When the compressor suction temperature is 68°F (20°C) all values are at 100%. The lines drawn are applicable for conditions of constant power.

peratures are displaced from 68°F to 140°C (20°C to 60°C). The inlet pressure of the low-pressure compressor rises to 153%, the turbine inlet pressure and the mass flow to approximately 130%. The absolute compressor or outlet temperatures and the cooler inlet temperature increase to 111% and 110% respectively. The absolute turbine outlet temperature rises to 104% while the expansion ratio drops to 85%. Finally the cycle efficiency and thus the thermal efficiency of the plant (power/fuel) falls to 83%. This displacement of cycle behaviour is shown on Fig. 6.19 for 68°F (20°C) and 176°F (80°C) compressor inlet temperatures. The turbine inlet temperature, however, is constant.

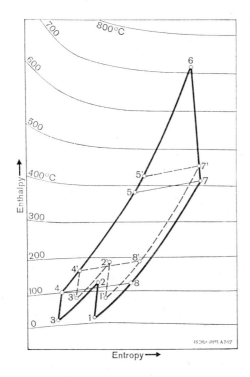

FIG. 6.19. Enthalpy–entropy diagram operating between 68°F (20°C) and 176°F (80°C).

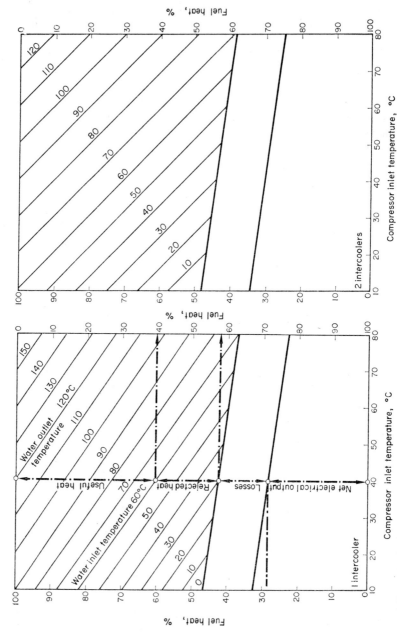

FIG. 6.20. Heat balances of closed-cycle gas turbines. Left-hand side: one intercooler. Right-hand side: two intercoolers.

Diagrams such as Fig. 6.16 can now be constructed for all compressor inlet temperatures between 50°F and 176°F (10°C and 80°C) if one converts according to Fig. 6.18. On the basis of exact calculations, the two heat and energy balances for closed-gas-turbine cycles with one or two intercoolers have been worked out (Fig. 6.20), compressor inlet temperatures are plotted on the x-axis while percentage heat content of the fuel is shown on the y-axis.

The lower part contains the electrical output for each compressor inlet temperature on the y-axis. The central part contains the unavoidable losses of air heaters, electrical and mechanical losses, auxiliary machinery requirements and thermal radiation. At the top the y-axis gives the total rejected heat in the coolers, which is contained in the heating and fresh water of the pre- and intercoolers, according to the flow diagram Fig. 6.15B. This upper range has the isothermal lines for the water. These show at the bottom end the water inlet temperature required, which is 18°F (10°C) lower than the equivalent compressor inlet temperature. At their top end, vertically above the compressor inlet temperature previously considered, the water-outlet temperature is given. This gives the maximum value, but lower values may be obtained by mixing the outgoing water with the return water from the heating network outside the coolers.

The example shows that, when the air temperature is 104°F (40°C) in front of the compressors, the net electrical output is 29%, and 57·5% heat must be rejected in the coolers. The water must enter the coolers at 86°F (30°C) and leave them at a temperature of 248°F (120°C). If the return temperature from the district heating network were 140°F (60°C), only 39% of the rejected heat could be used. The difference, namely 57·5 − 39·0 = 18·5%, is lost in the fresh water of the heating water after cooler. The total efficiency, 29% power and 39% heat, amounts to 68%.

It can be seen that with a compressor inlet temperature of 158°F (70°C), the whole of the rejected heat could be used. In this case 24·5% electrical power plus 61·5% heat gives a total efficiency of 86%. The graph on the right-hand side shows the heat balance for such a plant with two intercoolers. The net result is a higher power production figure, but about 86°F (30°C) lower heating water outlet temperatures. They are, however, quite high enough for most purposes. This remark-

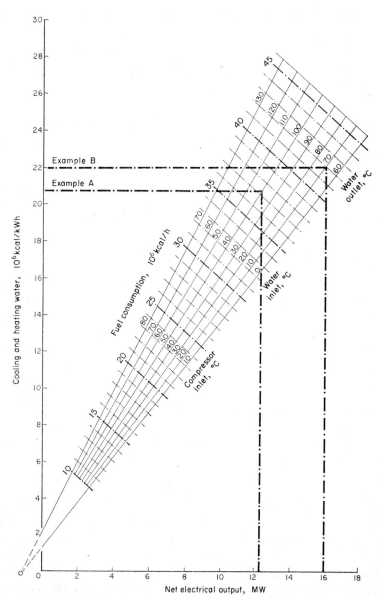

FIG. 6.21. Characteristics of combined power and heat production with a 15,000 kW closed-cycle gas turbine with two intercoolers for the entire range.

able result of 25% net power and 61% hot-water supply at 268°F (130°C) outlet and 158°F (70°C) return temperature is possible with plant which is only in the 15-MW size range. With steam turbines such results can only be achieved with plants in the 60–100 MW range, using very high pressures—2100–2860 psig (150–200 bar (g)) and reheating.

Figure 6.20 gives the operating data of a wide range of closed-cycle gas turbines. Figure 6.21 shows the power/heat characteristics of a 15-MW installation with two intercoolers over the entire practicable range. Using a system of coordinates with the generated electric net output on the x-axis and the total heat rejected in the coolers on the y-axis, lines of constant compressor inlet temperatures from 50°F to 176°F (10°C to 80°C) are drawn. The required water-inlet temperatures and outlet temperatures are marked on these lines, and as yet another parameter, the calorific value of the fuel is plotted. The two examples show how the diagram is used.

A type of design with one intercooler is required if a high heating water temperature is desired, and therefore a lower power production figure is acceptable.

Figure 6.22 shows the power/heat ratio, i.e. the generated electric net power output with respect to the useful heat production without heat rejection in the heating water aftercooler. The figure applies to a 15,000-kW closed-cycle gas turbine, fitted in this case with one and with two intercoolers. The heat production is plotted as the abscissa, and the power heat ratio together with the various heating water temperatures (outlet/return) and total efficiency as the ordinates. If coal is used as a fuel instead of oil or natural gas, the total efficiency is about 2% lower. These power/heat ratios make is possible to read off the optimum power production data, when operating a district heating programme.

To conclude, a heating programme adequate for a small town in Switzerland can be met by a 15,000-kW closed-cycle gas turbine with only one intercooler. A heating-water outlet temperature of 284°F (140°C) and a return temperature of 122°F (50°C) have been assumed.

This heating programme is shown on the left-hand side of Fig. 6.23 with power production when no heat rejection occurs in the after cooler, i.e. total power–heat production with maximum fuel economy. It can be seen that even at the heating limit of $2 \cdot 8 \times 10^7$ Btu/hr ($2 \cdot 94 \times 10^7$

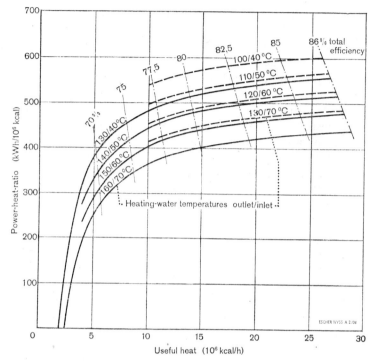

FIG. 6.22. Power–heat ratios of 15,000 kW closed-cycle gas turbine plants used in combined heat and power production. One or two intercoolers employing varying heating water outlet and return temperatures. Heating water after-coolers inoperative.

kJ/hr) (corresponding to 57°F (14°C) outdoor temperature), more than 2500 kW could be generated.

The power production increases with increasing heat requirements and reaches, at the maximum possible heat production of $1·1 \times 10^8$ Btu/hr ($1·15 \times 10^8$ kJ/hr), the very high value of 14,000 kW. The heat requirement in excess of this value (shaded peak) has to be covered by an additional boiler.

Figure 6.23 shows on the right-hand side the same heating programme with exactly the same turbine plant. But in this case, the maximum possible power production will be achieved. At a heat requirement below $1·1 \times 10^8$ Btu/hr ($1·15 \times 10^8$ kJ/hr) the compressor inlet

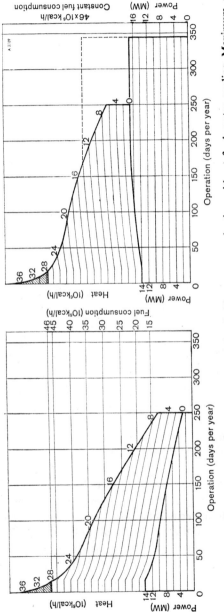

Fig. 6.23. Combined power and heat production. Left-hand side: power production without fresh-water cooling. Maximum fuel economy is obtained. Right-hand side: same heating programme but with maximum possible power production. Fuel consumption stays constant.

temperature is cooled down by the heating water aftercooler as far as possible, so that with maximum fuel consumption the required heat can always be produced. At less than $5 \cdot 6 \times 10^7$ Btu/hr ($5 \cdot 9 \times 10^7$ kJ/hr) a compressor inlet temperature of $68\,°F$ ($20\,°C$) is possible, which is about the lowest temperature limit for fresh-water cooling in winter time. The power production has reached 17,000 kW. This heat, namely $5 \cdot 6 \times 10^7$ Btu/hr ($5 \cdot 9 \times 10^6$ kJ/hr), will be obtained at practically no expenditure. Not all of it will be needed at the end of the heating period. The power production, however, will still remain constant at 17,000 kW and, if required, the $5 \cdot 6 \times 10^7$ Btu/hr ($5 \cdot 9 \times 10^7$ kJ/hr) waste heat which is at a useful temperature level could be absorbed. Examples of such summer-time heat requirements are swimming pools, absorption refrigeration plants, distillation of water (flash principle), etc.

The right-hand side of Fig. 6.23, in contrast to the left-hand side of the diagram, takes scaled water temperatures into consideration. These would be $284/122\,°F$ ($140/50\,°C$) outlet/return between $1 \cdot 44 \times 10^8$ and $1 \cdot 1 \times 10^8$ Btu/hr ($1 \cdot 52 \times 10^8$ and $1 \cdot 15 \times 10^8$ kJ/hr). These fall in proportion with the heat required to $212/122\,°F$ ($100/50\,°C$) when $5 \cdot 6 \times 10^7$ Btu/hr ($5 \cdot 9 \times 10^7$ kJ/hr) are reached. Below 4×10^7 Btu/hr ($4 \cdot 2 \times 10^7$ kJ/hr) the lowest temperatures which are $212\,°F/122\,°F$ ($100/50\,°C$) remain constant.

It is possible, for example, to produce combined heat and power according to Fig. 6.23a, i.e. with optimum fuel economy. If a demand arises for covering daily peaks, or if there is a period during which hydroelectric power production has fallen off, it is very easily possible to change over to maximum power production, i.e. to the plan as outlined in Fig. 6.23B. If in such a case there is a short period of heat deficiency, one can use peak boilers or employ hot-water storage facilities. The closed-cycle gas turbine therefore permits an extremely flexible combined power and heat production, gives very high power/ heat ratios when operating without aftercooling with fresh water, and even supplies heat when operated with a view to maximum power production with the highest thermal efficiency by using the maximum amount of aftercooling. Because of this even small units with a capacity above 6000 kW can be as economic as condensing steam turbine plants (without heat production) with an output of over 100 MW. Minimum costs are achieved with closed-cycle gas turbines in excess of 15 MW capacity.

CHAPTER 7

DIESEL AND GAS ENGINES
AND TOTAL ENERGY [23, 121, 159]

THE bulk of this chapter is based upon material published by Mirrlees National Ltd. of Stockport, England, in the journal of the Diesel Engineers and Users Association. The author herewith acknowledges his indebtedness to both these organisations and to Humphreys and Glasgow Ltd. of London, who provided him with the material on the Aldershot system.

With modern diesel and gas engines, where higher operating temperatures are employed both for cooling water and for exhaust gases, it becomes possible to utilise the waste heat produced in the form of steam or hot water, or both. The data given in this chapter refer to a typical pressure charged engine, the Mirrlees KVSS 12 which has the following characteristics:

Bore:	15 in. (38 cm)
Stroke:	18 in. (46 cm)
No. of cylinders:	12 in two banks of 6 cylinders each in Vee formation
Mean engine pressure:	154 psig (10·4 bar (g))
Speed:	428 rpm
Power output:	3168 brake horsepower (2360 kW)

HEAT BALANCE

Whilst diesel engines have a very high thermal efficiency, a large proportion of the heat supplied is rejected, only about 39% being converted into useful work. Figures 7.2 and 7.3 show the full load heat balance for the typical engine under consideration, the only difference being that under latent heat cooling, more heat is lost to radiation than

251

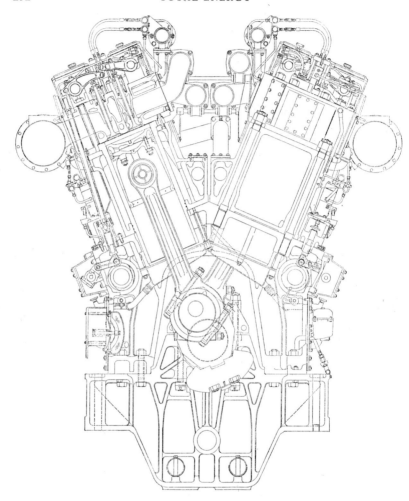

Fig. 7.1. Section through Mirrlees KDV engine.

with heat exchanger cooling, and thus less heat is rejected to the jacket water; this is due to the higher operating temperature.

There are three sources from which heat can be recovered, namely, jacket water, exhaust gases and lubricating oil.

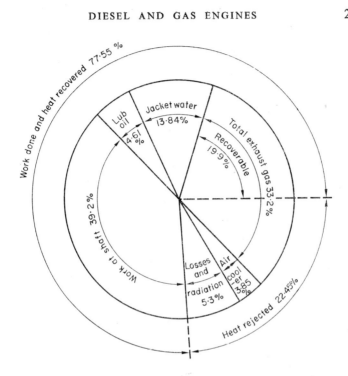

FIG. 7.2. Diagrammatic representation of heat balance with heat exchanger cooling.

(a) *Exhaust Gases*

For highly turbo-charged, four-stroke engines, the exhaust mass flow is approximately 13 lb hp⁻¹ hr⁻¹ (7·9 kg kW⁻¹ hr⁻¹) and the temperature approximately 750°F (400°C) after the turbocharger, both at full load. Heat can be extracted from the exhaust gases by passing them through the tubes of a boiler or water heater, the minimum gas outlet temperature being 350°F (177°C). For steam boilers, the exhaust outlet temperature should be approximately 70°F (39°C) higher than the saturation temperature; this maintains the tube lengths within economic limits and reduces corrosion troubles at low engine loads when exhaust temperatures fall.

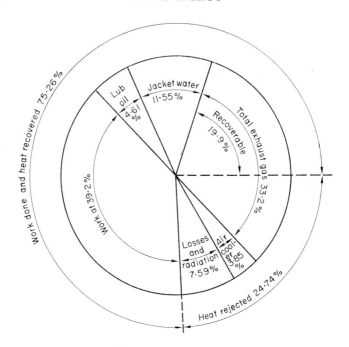

FIG. 7.3. Diagrammatic representation of heat balance with latent heat cooling.

It will be seen, therefore, that the maximum quantity of heat that can be recovered from exhaust gases is: 13×0.25 (750–350) = 1300 Btu hp^{-1} hr^{-1} (1830 kJ kW^{-1} hr^{-1}) at full load where 0.25 is the specific heat of the gases.

There are two types of exhaust gas boilers or water heater, vertical and horizontal. Both consist of gas inlet and outlet boxes, and a section containing tubes immersed in water. In a station containing three or less steam boilers, a feed pump would supply each boiler. Stand-by pumps are also present. These pumps are started and stopped by float-level controllers in the boilers, which are also fitted with alarms. In a station containing a large number of boilers, a better arrangement is to have one or two continuously running feed pumps supplying a pressurised feed main, from which water is admitted to the individual boilers by feed controllers.

Two engines can feed a common boiler of the double inlet, double outlet type, in which the gas sections are entirely separate, but the water section is common. It is not recommended that the exhaust gases of two or more engines are mixed, as this can lead to difficulties with back pressures and also with the necessary gas isolating valves.

The exhaust gas outlet temperature from a boiler increases with rising steam pressure, and in consequence the gas temperature drop over the boiler decreases, thus reducing the quantity of steam produced. For this reason, steam pressures above 100 psig (6·9 bar (g)) for heating loads, and 250 psig (17 bar(g)) for power loads are rarely used. A further disadvantage of high pressures it that steam production falls off rapidly with a reduction in engine load due to the falling exhaust gas temperatures.

When operating at full load the engine would produce the following quantities of dry saturated steam, with feedwater at 160°F (71°C) (see Table 7.1).

TABLE 7.1.

Steam pressure				
psig	15	50	100	250
(bar(g))	1·03	3·43	6·9	17·0
Steam quantity				
lb/hr	3980	3730	3300	2950
(kg/hr)	1810	1700	1500	1180

If an exhaust-gas water heater is installed, the maximum water temperature is fixed by the system pressure, and is generally about 200°F (93°C). If the heat input to a water heater is constant (assuming steady load), a given water flow rate will produce a fixed temperature rise. However, should the heat input vary, the constant-flow rate will result in a variable temperature, and this must be taken into consideration when planning the circuit.

It should be remembered, however, that the steam output from a boiler is purely a function of engine load and not steam demand. If, therefore, the steam demand fluctuates, some means must be found of condensing the surplus, assuming that it is undesirable to blow this off to waste. Almost all engines require a raw water supply for the oil cooler and possibly the air charge cooler, and this raw water can be passed through a tube condenser to which steam is admitted through a surplus valve. This arrangement is shown in Fig. 7.4.

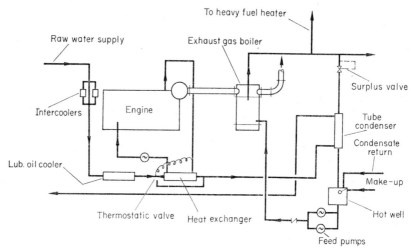

FIG. 7.4. Arrangement of auxiliary equipment to utilise engine waste heat.

If the output from a boiler or water heater is insufficient to meet the heating requirements when the engine is on full load, this must be allowed for at the planning stage. Provision can be made for a separate oil-fired section within the boiler, which can be controlled automatically by heat demand.

Where an engine is in operation on heavy fuel, this system is advantageous as the fuel oil supply is common.

(b) Lubricating Oil

A full-load temperature of 160°F (71°C) can safely be maintained for lubricating oil leaving an engine, and therefore a secondary water temperature of approximately 135°F (57°C) can be obtained at the oil cooler outlet. Engines fitted with oil-cooled pistons reject approximately 300 Btu hp^{-1} hr^{-1} (422 KJ kW^{-1} hr^{-1}) which, for the typical engine under consideration, amounts to 950,000 Btu/hr (1 GJ/hr). Because it is of a relatively low grade, this heat can only be used for warming up small quantities of cold water, or maintaining the temperature of water used for floor heating. Heat recovery from lubricating oil is not normally resorted to unless maximum recovery is being aimed at, as the quantity of heat available is relatively small and the cost of large auxiliary oil coolers is high.

(c) *Jacket Water with Heat Exchanger Cooling*

To provide, through an auxiliary heat exchanger, secondary water at as high a temperature as possible, the engine jacket water outlet is set at 180°F (82°C) which can give secondary water at 170°F (77°C). To cater for occasions when hot secondary water is not required, jacket water must be passed through the main heat exchanger which is fed by raw water from the cooling system. A thermostatic diverter valve must be fitted in the raw water circuit, controlled by the jacket water inlet temperature to the engine; this is necessary to prevent under-or over-

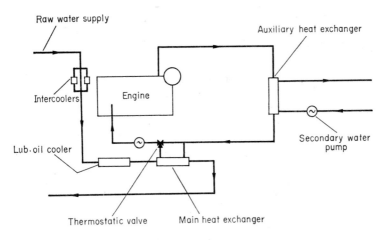

FIG. 7.5. Heat-exchanger cooling of jacket water.

cooling due to variations in secondary water flow rate, temperature, or engine load. For the typical engine, operating at full load, 2,850,000 Btu/hr (3 GJ/hr) could be recovered this way. The scheme is shown in Fig. 7.5. It is the simplest arrangement for recovering the heat dissipated to the engine jacket cooling water and will quickly recover the small additional capital expenditure.

The primary fresh water circuit should be made as compact as possible by positioning the auxiliary heat exchanger near to the engine; this ensures freedom in planning pipework, pumps and valves for the secondary circuit.

(d) *Jacket Water with Latent Heat Cooling*

The term latent heat cooling is used to describe a cooling system in which heat rejected by the engine jackets produces low-pressure steam which is flashed off directly from the jacket water. The circuit is pressurised, the maximum pressure so far used being 15 psig (1·03 (bar (*g*)) giving a water outlet temperature of 250 °F (121 °C). This system, which is illustrated in Fig. 7.6 operates as follows:

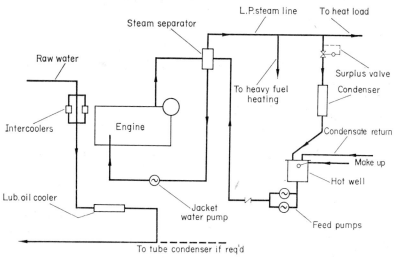

FIG. 7.6. Latent heat cooling of engine jacket water.

Jacket water circulates through the engine, up to a steam separator, and back to the engine. The circulation is generally effected by a pump, but it can be thermo syphonic. The steam separator must be mounted well above the water outlet level (about 8–10 ft) (2·4–3 m) so that the pressure in the engine will be greater than in the separator. As heat is rejected by the engine, the jacket water temperature gradually rises until it reaches about 210°F (99°C), when, for the first time, turbulence is visible.

The water temperature continues to rise until it reaches the saturation temperature of the system pressure, after which steam is flashed off from the separator. With a thermo-syphonic system, no circulation takes place until the outlet temperature reaches 180°F (82°C) the inlet still being cold, i.e. about 90°F (32°C).

The actual cooling of the engine is affected indirectly by condensing the steam, and this can be carried out by either supplying the steam to a heat load or directly to a condenser. The condensate must be returned to a hot well, from which it is pumped back into the separator by a flat-controlled feed pump which runs intermittently. If the heat load cannot be guaranteed to condense the total steam output under all conditions, then a condenser must be included in the system, to which the steam is fed through a surplus steam valve.

The surplus steam can be condensed in the following manner:

(1) *In a tube condenser.* This requires a raw water supply and some means of ultimately dissipating the heat, either to atmosphere or a large water mass. It should be remembered that all engines require a raw water supply to the lubricating oil cooler, and some engines a supply to the air charge cooler, and this water is very suitable.

(2) *In an air-blast condenser.* This type of unit is essentially a conventional radiator, except that it has a device at the condensate discharge to ensure that all steam is properly condensed and subcooled. Compared with a radiator, which cools jacket water from 180°F (82°C), an air blast condenser is smaller, cheaper and the fan power is much lower.

(3) *In a steam turbine-driven air-blast condenser.* This unit consists of a small axial-flow turbine, through which the steam passes, leaving at a pressure slightly above atmospheric and entering finned condenser tubes. The turbine drives a fan which draws air over the condensing

tubes and, in consequence, no power need be supplied to the unit. Compared with tube or motor-driven air-blast condensers, they are expensive.

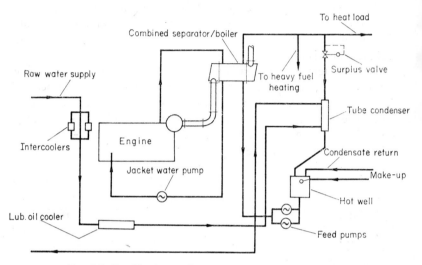

FIG. 7.7. Combined steam separator and exhaust gas boiler.

If the demand for steam is greater than can be met from the jacket heat, then a combined separator and exhaust gas boiler can be used. In such a unit, illustrated in Fig. 7.7, the jacket water flows over the horizontal gas tubes and steam is flashed off from jacket water which receives further latent heat from the exhaust gases. The pressure in the system is, of course, limited to 15 psig (1·03 bar(g)). Should higher pressures be required, it would be necessary to use a separate exhaust gas boiler.

It is considered that the advantages of latent heat cooling are as follows:

(a) The engine jackets are maintained at a high temperature. The high cost of distillate fuel oils is forcing more and more operators of large diesel engines to consider the use of cheaper residual fuel oils. All residual fuels contain sulphur, which when burned turns to sulphur dioxide and sulphur trioxide. The first of these is only slightly soluble in water, but the second dissolves in water to form sulphuric acid, which gives rise to excessive cylinder liner wear and lubricating oil contamination. It has been well established that the dew point of the products of combustion is approximately 195°F (90·5°C). At this temperature they become saturated with water which tends to condense on the inside of the cylinder liner. By maintaining the jackets above the dew point, therefore, condensation and the consequent formation of sulphuric acid is prevented, thus limiting the wear rates on liners, pistons and rings to those experienced with distillate fuel oils.

(b) The engine jackets are maintained at a constant temperature, and the rise in water temperature across the engine is small. Unless a thermostatic water diversion valve is used, a conventionally cooled engine has fluctuating jacket water temperatures due to changes in load, raw water temperature (heat exchanger cooling) and ambient air temperature (radiator cooling).

As the jacket temperature is purely a function of steam pressure, it should remain constant and thereby reduce thermal stresses.

(c) Lubricating oil tends to remain free from water, acid and sludge.

(d) Fuel consumptions tend to improve slightly.

(e) Live steam at pressures up to 15 psig (1·03 bar(g)) can be produced directly from the engine, and almost every installation can find some use or other for this heat.

Design of engine recovery system[31]

In general one can reckon on 2000 Btu hp^{-1} hr^{-1} (2800 kJ kW^{-1} hr^{-1}) jacket heat rejection for diesel engines and 2500 Btu hp^{-1} hr^{-1} (3500 kJ kW^{-1} hr^{-1}) heat rejection for gasolene engines if such engines are turbocharged. The quantities of heat evolved for naturally aspirated engines are some 600 Btu hp^{-1} hr^{-1} (700 kJ kW^{-1} hr^{-1}) lower.

As already mentioned, there are two methods of abstracting the heat, one consisting of the substitution of a heat load for the standard engine cooling system, and the other in permitting the engine-cooling system to boil and to obtain the low pressure steam produced.

Steam separator

The steam separator must be so designed that:

(a) the steam is of good quality;

(b) the water which returns to the engine is free from air bubbles;

(c) it does not cause an excessive pressure loss in the system;

(d) there is enough water storage to cater for fluctuations in engine loading.

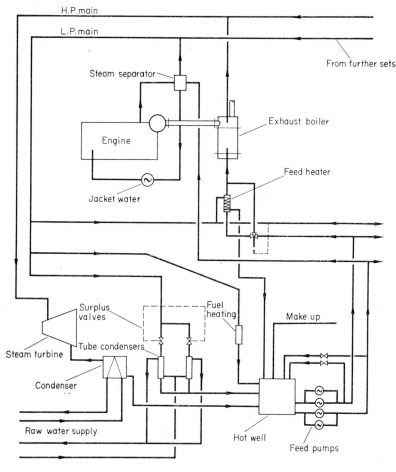

FIG. 7.8. Layout of complete engine heat-recovery system.

Standard steam scrubbing techniques are used and the layout is shown in Fig. 7.8. Because it is necessary to produce steam in order to cool the engine, all the steam produced must be condensed even if there should not be any heat demand at the time being. For this reason a control condenser is included in the circuit.

The nature of the piping between engine and steam separator is important. If the system is a natural circulation type the flow is produced by the difference in the density between the fluid in the rising pipes and the down pipes. The circulation rate increases with increased heat output to a maximum and then falls, as shown in Fig. 7.9. The reason for this is that as the heat input increases, the density differential also increases, but at the same time there is also an increase in the frictional losses in both circuits. After the maximum in Fig. 7.9 has been reached these losses outweigh the flow increase due to density differences.

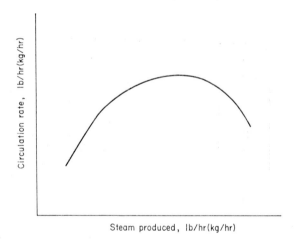

Fig. 7.9. Graph showing steam produced per hour as a function of the circulation rate.

To design an adequate system it is essential to have risers with as little frictional resistance as possible. It is usual to size them to cater for a maximum steam velocity of 6,000 ft/min (1830 m/min). In the down tube most troubles occur when the engine is running at no or small

K

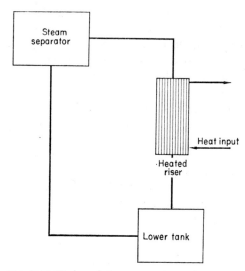

Fig. 7.10. Design of steam-separator system.

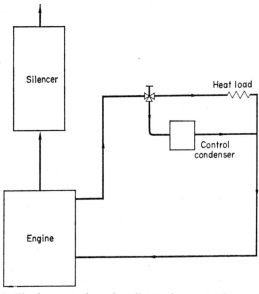

Fig. 7.11. The incorporation of a silencer into a total energy circuit.

loads. It should be designed to handle approximately 20 times the maximum full-load steam production at a maximum velocity of 300 ft/min (92 m/min). The steam separator should be positioned in such a way that the water level in it is a good deal higher than the highest point of the engine water system, and if the separator is some distance away from the engine its height should be increased to allow for pipeline friction. If a pump is installed, the separator height is no longer critical. The advantages of a forced circulation system are the following:

(a) one can use smaller pipe sizes;

(b) one can put the separator where one wishes.

Its disadvantages are:

(a) increased capital and running cost;

(b) pump failure may damage the system;

(c) the pump work must be subtracted from the overall efficiency.

UTILISATION OF WASTE HEAT FROM DIESEL ENGINES

(a) Space Heating

Most factories require a considerable amount of winter heating for both works and offices. If a factory generates its own power using a diesel engine, then large quantities of heat would become available. The form in which the heat is supplied, i.e. steam or hot water, depends on the installation. It should be remembered that in the U.K. the space heating load would fall off or become non-existent in the summer, and, therefore, some alternative duty for the heat should be found. It is impossible to be specific on the subject of space heating because each industry presents its own problems. In addition, engines are frequently installed in old factories which already have a heating system installed.

(b) Process Work

The requirement of a particular industry will decide whether steam or hot water is required. Recovered heat can be used to full advantage within the limits of water temperature and steam pressure previously referred to. It is essential, however, to ensure that a closed circuit is adopted in all cases and that heat dissipation is effected indirectly, keeping the primary circuit free from any contamination that could take place by the introduction of large quantities of make-up water.

(c) *Additional Power*

Diesel-engined power stations with total outputs of the order of 15–20 MW are becoming more common with the advent of sets having individual outputs in the 3–5 MW bracket. This popularity of large diesel alternator sets is due to the fact that quick deliveries can be obtained for the first few sets, the subsequent units being added to the station as load increases. There are two basic types of load which such a station is required to meet, namely a domestic load which fluctuates over 24 hours, and an industrial load, such as in an aluminium smelting plant, which is substantially constant over most of the year. With either type of load, but with the second in particular, recovered waste heat can be used to generate additional power, the system being illustrated in Fig. 7.8.

Each engine exhausts into a boiler, where superheated steam is raised. Typical steam conditions would be 240/280 psig 600/650°F (16·5–19 bar(g) (315–343°C)). The engines operate on latent heat cooling, the 15 psig (1·03 bar (g)) 250°F (121°C), steam being used for heating the feed to the exhaust gas boilers from 100°F (38°C) to 235°F (113°C) and for heating heavy fuel oil, which would almost certainly be used to reduce fuel costs. The h.p. steam feeds a turbine, which exhausts at about 28 in. (0·94 bar) vacuum into a condenser.

With the above steam conditions, the kW outputs of a turbine are about 5–7½%. of the total installed diesel capacity. For relatively small additional power sets, a reciprocating steam engine is very suitable as it is inexpensive; its steam consumption would be higher than for a turbine.

(d) *Main Boiler Feed Heating*

A commonly accepted rule is that for every 11°F (60°C) by which the feedwater temperature to a boiler is raised, there is a saving of 1% in fuel costs. The feedwater leaving the condenser of a condensing

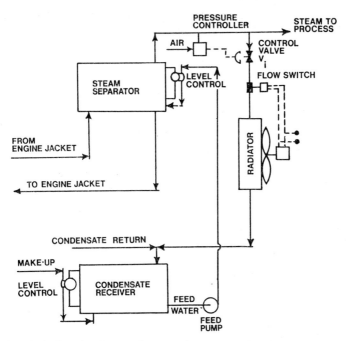

FIG. 7.12. Complete layout of an American system of utilising waste heat
from diesel engines. (By courtesy: Baird Inc., Shreveport Ltd.)

turbine is generally at a temperature of 100–110°F (38°–43°C). If
engine jacket water at 180°F (82°C) is used, the feedwater can be heated
to 170°F (77°C). If 15 psig (1·03 bar (g)) steam is used, the feedwater
can be heated to 235°F (113°C). These represent boiler fuel reductions
of 5·5% and 11·4% respectively. It is not always possible, however,
to heat the feed to these temperatures with existing installations, as
steam may be bled from the turbine for feed heating.

If the turbine steam consumption is 10 lb/kWhr (4·54 kg/kWhr),
the 15 psig (1·03 bar (g)) steam output from an engine operating on
latent heat with a combined boiler is 1·8 lb/bhphr (1·1 kg/kWhr) at
full load, and if main boiler feed water is heated from 110°F (43°C)
to 235°F (113°C) then the ideal ratio of turbine kW to engine kW is
1:1.

In many industries, condensate is not returned to the boiler house, but is used in process work or goes to waste. Under these conditions, with cold feed water, even larger temperature rises are possible.

(e) *Sea Water Distillation*

In many parts of the world there is a shortage of fresh water and heat normally wasted from a diesel engine can be harnessed in a distilling plant which can produce distillate of high purity. A recently developed form of distillation plant employs a multi-effect flash mechanism. (Fig. 7.13). The system is described in detail in Chapter 1,

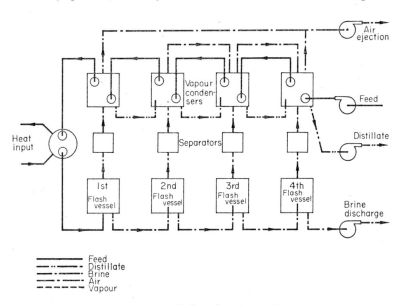

FIG. 7.13. Layout of a multi-effect flash installation using waste heat from diesel engines.

pages 19–24. The reason why this type of plant is so suitable for coupling to an engine cooling system is that it can readily be arranged to utilise heat at any relatively low temperature down to a feasible minimum of approximately 150°F (65·5°C).

The typical engine dissipates 900 Btu hp^{-1} hr^{-1} (1270 kJ kW^{-1} hr^{-1}) to the jacket water at full load with heat exchanger cooling and therefore 2,850,000 Btu/hr (3 GJ/hr) are available. The quantity of distillate which could be produced from this heat depends on the size and cost of the plant employed. In simple terms, it can be considered that the greater the installed vapour condenser surface, and hence the greater the cost, the greater will be the distillate production due to the better condensing efficiency. The performance efficiency of this type of unit is expressed in pounds of distillate per 1000 Btu (kg/MJ) of operating heat. A relatively inefficient plant of low cost would produce 2 lb per 1000 Btu (0·95 kg/MJ) so that in the example considered it would be possible to produce 5700 lb/hr (2560 kg/hr) of pure water from sea water.

Apart from the waste heat the only energy input to the plant is in the form of pump drives, of which there are four; feed, brine, distillate and air extraction, and their power requirements would total approximately 20 hp (15 kW).

It is emphasised that it is possible to cater in design for a much higher performance efficiency, 5 lb per 1000 Btu (2·38 kg/MJ) being possible, but this would be at the expense of first cost.

Because 15 psig (1·03 bar (g)) steam is hotter than jacket water at 180°F (82°C) the heat input section can be made smaller and cheaper. Again considering the typical engine, but this time operating on latent heat cooling, and making use of the exhaust gas heat, the heat available at full load is 5·7 × 10^6 Btu/hr (6 GJ/hr). If a distiller has a performance efficiency of 3 lb /1000 Btu (1·43 kg/MJ), then 17,100 lb/hr (7800 kg/hr) of distillate could be produced, or 183 tons/24 hr.

(f) Heavy Fuel Heating

As previously mentioned, the use of residual fuel oils is becoming increasingly more widespread, as diesel users are forced, by the high cost of distillate fuels, to consider alternatives which are about two-third the cost of Class 'A' and 'B' fuel oils. All residual fuel oils have to be heated, a system in a station having three important temperatures, which are:

1. The temperature at which the fuel is stored and/or transferred.

2. The temperature at which the fuel is centrifuged.

3. The temperature at which the fuel is admitted to the engine.

The higher the viscosity of a residual oil, the higher these temperatures must be. The maximum viscosity normally allowed for industrial engines is 3500 seconds Redwood No. 1 at 100°F (38°C) which fuel has to be heated to about 235°F (113°C) for admission to the engine.

These heating processes can be performed by heat recovered from an engine, the method depending on the viscosity of the fuel, and the cooling system. Fuels having a viscosity of 200 seconds can be heated up by 180°F (82°C) jacket water, as the required fuel temperature is less than 150°F (65·5°C) which is the economic maximum; all other fuels, up to 3500 sec viscosity, can be heated by 15 psig (1·03 bar(g)) steam which can be supplied from a latent heat cooling system or from an exhaust gas boiler. If an exhaust gas boiler is used, it is better to use a pressure of 50 psig (3·4 bar(g)) as this allows smaller and cheaper fuel heaters due to the higher steam temperature.

Unless a station contains a number of engines, it is not normally recommended that an exhaust gas boiler be installed just for fuel heating. The quantity of steam produced would be far in excess of these requirements, and it is not always practicable to condense surplus steam, arrange for short gas tubes to give a small gas temperature drop, or divert exhaust gases from the main pipe into a small boiler. In a multi-engine station, it is suggested that two adjacent engines exhaust into a double inlet, double outlet boiler, only one section of which need be steaming.

(g) *Refrigeration Plant*[149]

If two closed tanks, with a salt solution (lithium bromide) in one and plain water in the other, are connected, then the salt solution absorbs the water, and in being evaporated, the water is cooled. This is the basic operating principle of an absorption refrigeration cycle. The heat input section accepts either hot water or low-pressure steam, and the complete motor load of the unit is about 10 hp (7·45 kW).

(h) *Sewage Plant*

Sludge digestion is a most important process in sewage plant, and it requires a considerable quantity of heat. This heat, in the form of hot water, can be supplied to the sludge digestion tanks via sludge heaters, the sludge gas (methane) produced in the digestion tanks being used in a dual fuel engine. A typical scheme is illustrated in Fig. 7.14 in which jacket water, after leaving the engine, passes through an exhaust gas water heater and then on to a sludge heater.

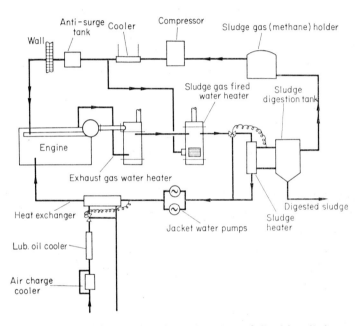

FIG. 7.14. Sewage plant serviced from waste heat of diesel installation.

It is impossible to give firm details of sewage installations, but the following approximate details may be of interest.

1. A minimum population to justify running engines on sewage gas is 50,000.
2. The net calorific value of sewage gas is 530–620 Btu ft^{-3} (19·8–23·1 MJ m^{-3}) at N.T.P.

3. Modern turbocharged dual fuel engines consume approximately 6600 net Btu hp^{-1} hr^{-1} (9·3 MJ kW^{-1} hr^{-1}) at full load, including pilot oil for ignition. Accounting for periods of low load, one could expect the average consumption of a station to be of the order of 7500–8000 Btu hp^{-1} hr^{-1} (10,060–11,200 KJ kW^{-1} hr^{-1}).

As previously explained, the quantity of heat that can be recovered from an engine is a function of engine load. It is useless, therefore, to depend on recovering the full-load dissipation figures, if engine loads fluctuate. By using an electrode boiler, however, an engine driving an alternator can be maintained constantly at or near full load, even though the basic load on the alternator varies. This is achieved by fitting the boiler with a device which is sensitive to the main load, and which alters the electrode boiler load in sympathy with rises and falls in the main load. For loads which vary widely, remarkable increases in thermal efficiency can be effected by using an electrode boiler; this presupposes that there is a demand for steam or hot water which is greater than the supply from the engine. Boiler loads can be supplied up to about 2000 kW, and approximately 3 lb (1·36 kg) of steam can be produced per kWhr.

Typical Applications

The following are four installations in Great Britain in which waste heat recovery has been successfully applied.

CASE 1. *J. & T. M. Greeves, Limited, Forth River Mills, Belfast*[67]

The pressure-charged engine is rated at 1470 bhp (1100 kW) at 428 rpm and coupled to a 1030 kW alternator. It is the main generating power unit and is in operation for 133 hr per week. In order that the cost of the power produced could be kept as low as possible it was decided that the engine should operate on 3500 sec fuel and full advantage should be made of waste-heat recovery. Before the installation of this power plant a steam-driven turbo-alternator was in service and the rooms throughout the mills were heated by low-pressure pass-out steam flowing through cast iron pipes suspended about 8 ft (2.44 m) from the floor. In the present installation heat is recovered from the engine water jackets, from the exhaust gases, which are passed through a boiler, economisers, air heater, and from the cooling water of the turbo-blower intercooler and lubricating oil cooler. The cooling of the engine is based on the latent heat cycle in which a small percentage of the water passing through the engine is flashed off into steam in a waste-heat boiler. This is supplemented by passing the exhaust gases through the tubes of the boiler after they have left the turbo charger. General arrangement is shown in Fig. 7.15. The steam produced in this boiler

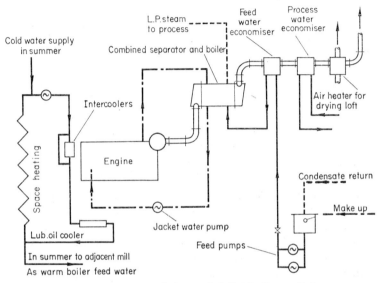

FIG. 7.15. Layout of plant at J & T. M. Greeves Ltd.

is at a pressure of 5 psi (345 mb) and is led into the main steam pipe supplying the mill. A large proportion of this steam is for process work. Based on the figures for the 12-month period between June 1964 and July 1965 the evaporation of this boiler averaged 2·26 lb (1·03 kg) per unit of electricity generated. It has been found by experience that the tubes of the boiler have to be cleaned every 3 months otherwise the evaporation falls away quite rapidly. To reduce deposits and water-side corrosion on the cylinder liners only condensate is used as the feed-water for the boiler. The feed pumps are electrically driven ram-type and the water level is maintained by level controllers which stop and start the pumps.

The Lancashire boilers which are now only used for stand-by purposes are fitted with two sets of economisers, one of which was used for the feedwater and the other for heating water process work. As these boilers are not in use their feed pipes were disconnected from the economiser and those of the exhaust heated boiler connected. The exhaust gases leaving this boiler are fed into the economisers. This results in the feed water temperature being increased to 213°F (100·5°C), an increase of about 85°F (47°C). The gases from the engine also raise the temperature of 11·2 ft³ (316 dm³) water per hour in the process economiser by about 70°F (39°C). The temperature of the gases at the exit from this economiser is about 230°F (110°C) and they are then fed into an air heater which reduces their temperature to 220°F (104·5°C) at entry to the stack. After 4 years in service there has been no evidence of corrosion on the gas side of the tubes of the economisers.

The water to the intercooler and lubricating oil cooler increases in temperature by 20°F (11°C) giving an exit temperature of 87°F (30·5°C) and a heat gain of approximately 900,000 Btu (950 MJ) per hour. In order that some of this heat might be used to advantage, the steam connections to the heating pipes in the rooms were disconnected and the cooling water pipes connected with suitable accelerators in the circuits. This modification was made in seven rooms of which six are now heated entirely by the hot water. The total floor area involved is approximately 54,000 ft² (5000 m²). It has been found that by circulating the water 24 hours per day, the rooms are kept at a comfortable temperature, although the water is at a comparatively low temperature. It should be understood that there is also a certain heat contribution from motors on the machinery installed in these rooms. During the heating season the cooling water is used in a closed circuit incorporating the heating pipes, whilst in summer the water leaving the coolers is used as feedwater for the Lancashire boilers in the adjacent mill.

CASE 2. *Pulrose Power Station, Douglas Corporation Electricity Department, Isle of Man.*

Until recently the generating plant at this station consisted entirely of steam turbines. In 1958 it became necessary to acquire additional plant and after a thorough investigation it was found that diesel plant would be more economical both as regards capital costs and running costs. This situation was mainly due to the increase in the cost of coal and the rapid development of larger diesel units during the past few years. Diesel plant had a further advantage in that it could be quickly started or stopped to meet wide variations of load during the 24 hours of the day. It was also appreciated that a combination of steam and diesel plant provided possibilities for waste heat recovery. A general arrangement is shown in Fig. 7.16.

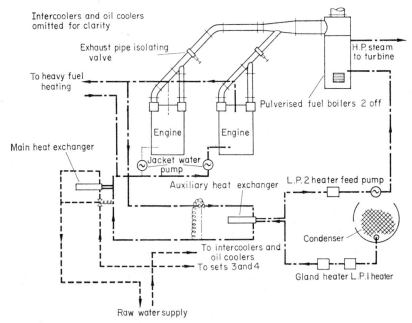

FIG. 7.16. Layout of plant at Pulrose power station.

Two engines were installed, each rated at 3096 bhp (2310 kW) at 428 rpm and coupled to 2200 kW alternators. Arrangements were made to pass the jacket water from both engines through an auxiliary heat exchanger to transfer heat from the jacket water to the condensate of a 5000 kW turbogenerator. A main heat exchanger was also provided in order to extract the necessary amount of heat from the jacket water by means of raw water circulation when the turbo-generator was not in operation. Both heat exchangers were fitted with by-passes controlled by thermostatically operated electro-valves which were set to maintain a constant temperature at the jacket water inlet and outlet.

The jacket water outlet temperature of the diesel engines is maintained at 180°F (82°C) with the inlet temperature at 168°F (75·5°C). Under these conditions, the feedwater from the condenser of the 5000 kW steam turbine is raised from 110°F to 170°F (43°C–80·5°C), a heat recovery to the boiler of 3 million Btu/hr (3·2 GJ/hr) when the turbine is at full load.

The exhaust system of the diesel plant is also designed to enable the exhaust gas heat to be recovered in the back end of the steam boilers. Each engine exhausts through isolating valves into a common exhaust duct leading to a high chimney and passing the steam boilers *en route*. Branch ducts with adjustable dampers are fitted to each of two 60,000 lb/hr (27,200 kg/hr) pulverised fuel boilers. The branch ducts enter the boilers at the rear bank of tubes and the diesel exhaust gas, together with the boiler gas, passes through the economiser and air heater. It is necessary, of course, to increase the induced draught to deal with the added volume of diesel exhaust gas. The heat recovery with a diesel exhaust temperature of 800°F (427°C) and a boiler outlet temperature of 350°F (177°C) is of the order of 2 million Btu/hr (2·1 GJ/hr). Due to gas-pressure limitations, it is not possible to pass all the exhaust gases through the boiler, and the above figure of 2 million Btu/hr (2·1 GJ) represents only about half of the total recoverable exhaust heat from one engine. To further reduce running costs, this station operates on Britoleum fuel oil, which has a viscosity of 200 sec Redwood No. 1 at 100°F (38°C).

CASE 3. *Messrs. Vernon & Co. Ltd., Textile Mill, Preston*

This textile mill is a good example of waste heat recovery combined with latent heat cooling for a relatively small generating plant in that it shows that full use can be made of recovered heat from the exhaust gases, lubricating oil and engine jacket water for heating and process loads.

The plant consists of a pressure-charged engine rated at 735 bhp (550 kW) at 428 rpm coupled to an alternator rated at 510 kW. Careful consideration has been given to the use of waste heat to meet the requirements of the mill where both steam and hot water are required for space heating and process.

The engine is designed to run on heavy Bunker 'C' fuel having a viscosity of 3500 sec Redwood No. 1 at 100°F (38°C) and is arranged for latent heat cooling. The exhaust gases are passed through to an exhaust gas boiler which also incorporates a separate oil-fired section. This boiler is designed to produce steam at 15 psig (1·03 bar(g)) alternatively 100 psig (6·8 bar (g)) the oil-fired section being automatically controlled to augment steam demands above that produced by the exhaust gases.

When the demand for steam at 15 psig (1·03 bar (g)) for either space heating or process work falls off, the exhaust boiler is isolated from the circuit and the steam pressure raised to 100 psig (6·8 bar(g)). Steam at this pressure is passed through to a converted Lancashire boiler which acts as a steam accumulator; when fully charged this is capable of feeding the space heating circuit at a reduced pressure of 15 psig (1·03 bar (g)) over a period of 5/6 hours when the main generating plant is shut down.

During the period when the heating load is reduced, steam at 15 psig (1·03 bar(g)) from the steam separator of the latent heat cooling system continues to pass out to process or space heating. In the event of no demand for heating load the steam from the steam separator is by-passed to a dump condenser, condensate returning to the primary condensate tank. It will be appreciated that considerable flexibility is achieved and with the additional load supplied by the oil-fired section of the boiler, which is capable of producing 5000 lb/hr (2260 kg/hr) at 30 psig (2·06 bar(g)), any combination of heating and process load can be met subject to operational requirements. In order to meet the demand for the hot water required for process and domestic use, an auxiliary lubricating oil cooler has been placed in series with the main lubricating oil cooler; water is circulated through the secondary side back to a thermal storage tank (converted Lancashire boiler) from which supplies are drawn off. Should hot-water requirements fall off giving rise to an increase in the returning lubricating oil temperature to the engine, a thermostatic by-pass valve comes into operation (controlled by the returning temperature) allowing cooling water to pass through the main lubricating oil cooler thus controlling the return lubricating oil temperature to the engine.

Figure 7.17 illustrates the general layout of waste heat equipment.

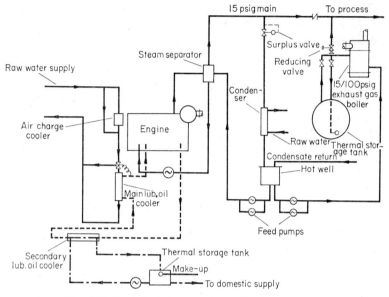

FIG. 7.17. Layout of plant at Messrs. Vernon & Co. Ltd.

CASE 4. *The Aldershot Military Town Installation**[58]

This station has an electrical capacity of 8·5 MW and can supply up to 100×10^6 Btu/hr (105 GJ/hr) to the district heating scheme of the military town. It is situated by the side of the Basingstoke canal approximately ½ mile (0·8 km) from the new Stanhope Lines barracks, which are connected to it by a twin pipeline system. The whole scheme was carried out by the London firm of Humphreys and Glasgow Ltd. and cost $2·65 million (new rate of exchange) in 1963. The main building comprises a boiler house, engine room and electrical annexe. Power is supplied from four Mirrlees diesel engines, each developing 3168 bhp (2360 kW).

The station has three functions. In addition to generating the 11 kV 8·5 MW power supply for the Aldershot military system, it also supplies the district heating scheme for the new barracks and supplies

*Material published originally in *Engineering*, 4 June 1965, pp. 730–1. Reproduced here by permission of the Editor and the Ministry of Public Building and Works.

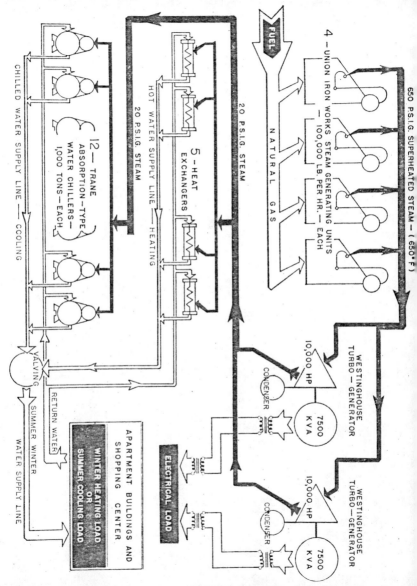

Fig. 11.3. Heat flow system, Rochdale Village. (By courtesy: Brooklyn

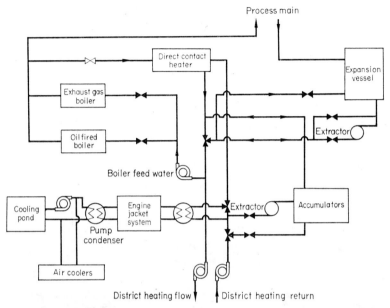

Fig. 7.18. Aldershot district-heating system using waste heat from diesel engines. (By courtesy of the Ministry of Public Building and Works.)

process steam to the Aldershot main. This latter supply is of saturated steam at 70 psig (4·8 bar (g)) with condensate return at 160°F (71°C) and could meet an estimated maximum demand of 40 million Btu (42 GJ) per hour. The district heating supply is of water at 270°F (132°C) in the outgoing main, returning at 160°F (71°C).

The main steam range is supplied by the four Richardson Westgarth oil-fired boilers, each with a maximum evaporation rate of 18,500 lb/hr (8400 kg) at 70 psig (4·8 bar (g)). The source of district heat is really the direct-contact steam/water heater and its associated storage tank. This acts also as a de-aerator, and is mounted in the highest part of the building. It has a maximum water flow rating of 900,000 lb/hr (408,000 kg/hr). Steam enters through two control valves regulated by a pressure recorder controller so that there is a constant pressure inside the steam space. This pressure can be varied in the range 40–50 psig (2·7–3·4 bar (g)). Water at about 160°F (71°C) returning from the district is pumped in through some or all of twenty-four spray nozzles so that it is heated to the saturation temperature of the steam; dissolved gases are expelled and the condensate is claimed to have an oxygen content better than 1 part in 100,000 by volume. The temperature in the storage tank is independent of the rate of flow of water into the heater.

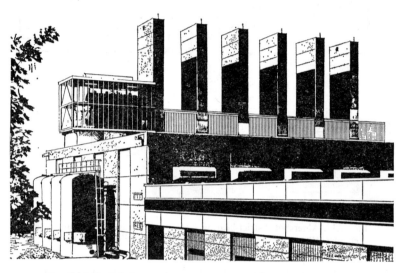

FIG. 7.19. Artist's impression of outside of Aldershot power station.

From this tank water passes into the district heating outgoing main. The flow is through either of two district flow pumps, or through a parallel non-return valve, according to the required pressure and flow rate in the main. The excess of incoming over outgoing flow to heater is returned to the boiler feed range by the boiler feed pumps, three in all.

The configuration of the district heating load, and the required flow rate, determine the pressure difference between flow and return mains. If, however, appropriate adjustments to the pump speeds or discharge valve settings are made to the flow and return pumps, the standing pressure of both mains will be raised, or lowered, simultaneously. This facility is necessary because the pressure in the return main must not exceed the rated 50 psig (3·4 bar (g)) of the radiators of the district heating load; and because the flow main pressure must exceed the saturation pressure of the water by sufficient margin to prevent flashing, particularly at those points in the load system which are above the level of the station.

Except for seasonal adjustments, and major changes in the load configuration, the rate of flow through the system will remain constant, hourly variations in heat demand being countered by varying the flow temperature. This is achieved by a temperature-recorder controller acting on a three-way mixing valve which by-passes the direct-contact heater. Variation of the flow temperature can be accomplished by varying the by-pass flow to restore it to the controller setting; it can be set manually anywhere in the range 200–280°F (93–138°C).

Hot-water Storage

Variations in demand may, on occasions, outstrip the available boiler capacity. Four hot-water accumulators, each of 12,000 gallons (45·5m³) enable the peak demand to be met without bringing an additional boiler into service, or supplement the boiler heat output when all four are in service. The accumulators are connected in parallel with the direct-contact heater and normally hold water at about 290°F (143°C). To release heat to the load, part of the return flow is diverted into the bottoms of the accumulators, easing the load on the boilers by reducing the input to the direct-contact heater, and causing hot water to be discharged from the tops of the accumulators into the outgoing main. Recharging the accumulators is a reversal of this procedure. Cold water is extracted by one of two accumulator extraction pumps and discharged into the district return main, whence it goes to the direct-contact heater, while hot water is diverted into the tops of the accumulators from the district outgoing main. Recharging is automatic when the boiler output exceeds the demand of the load; the pump is started automatically when the main steam pressure rises due to a fall in demand. When fully charged, temperature-control switches at the base of the accumulators cut out the extractor pump.

An expansion vessel is provided to accommodate the expansion of the system water in response to variations in its mean temperature. Control is initiated from the direct-contact heater tank, which, although it can accommodate some small variations in volume, is limited in size by its inherent design for a working pressure of 50 psig (3·4 bar (g)). If the water level rises above the centre line of the tank, a valve is automatically opened to divert part of the district return flow into the expansion vessel until equilibrium is restored. If the level falls, one of two extraction pumps automatically removes water from the vessel to the return main. The expansion vessel also provides a topping-up reserve to replace system losses, and serves as the return point for the condensate of the 70 psig (4·8 bar (g)) process steam main. It is important, therefore, that the level in the vessel be kept high enough to allow an adequate reserve against reductions in the mean system temperature and a temporary deficit of condensate return. Conversely, the level must not be so high as to cause wastage by overflowing.

Make-up water supplied to the expansion chamber comes from an 8 ft³/hr (0·23 m³/hr) line/filtration base exchange plant, drawing its supply from the cooling-water pond. A cross-connection is provided so that mains water can be used as an alternative feed. An auxiliary steam bleed for fuel warming and preheating the engine jackets also returns, through cleaning tanks, to the expansion vessel.

To safeguard the system, a master relay trips if an emergency stop is initiated from the station control desk, the return main pressure falls below the minimum working setting, or when the level in the direct-contact heater falls outside the limits of the level control operating the expansion vessel pumps or the boiler feed pumps, and isolates the direct-contact heater tank to prevent it being drained. If the pressure in the heater falls below the minimum setting a valve operates to release its air signal pressure and reduce the demand for steam by diverting water from the return main to the accumulators. Should the level in the expansion chamber fall below its minimum setting, the extraction pump is automatically shut down.

Additional Heat

Although the district heating load and process steam requirements are chiefly met by the oil-fired boilers, important contributions are made by utilising jacket cooling and exhaust heat from the diesel engine, thus greatly increasing the overall efficiency of the station.

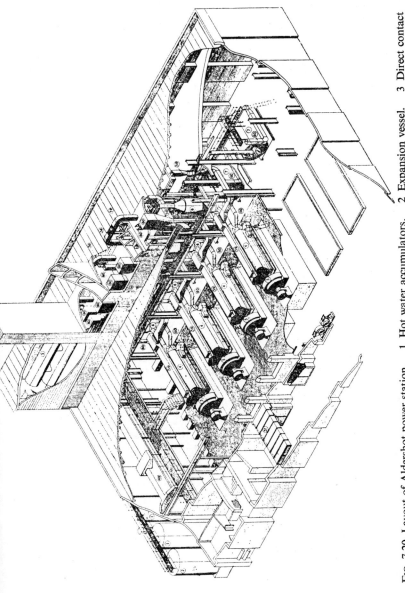

Fig. 7.20. Layout of Aldershot power station.   1 Hot water accumulators.   2 Expansion vessel.   3 Direct contact heater. 4 Diesel engine 3168 bhp. (2360 kW) 5 Alternator 2·14 M.W. 6 Exhaust gas boiler. 7 Maxecon oil fired boiler. 49 Overhead crane 20 ton.   57 Station ventilation air intake.   58 Station ventilation extraction.   59 Station ventilation extraction.   60 Air intake—Turbo chargers/boilers.

The exhaust-gas boilers discharge steam into the main boiler range, and are designed for a normal working pressure of 70 psig (4·8 bar(g)) at 270°F (132°C). Their output depends on the level of water in the shell, and the diesel-generator output, varying from 1085 lb/hr (494 kg) at 50% load to 3260 lb/hr (1480 kg) when the generators are on full load. The feedwater regulators normally maintain a constant water level, but, should the exhaust boiler output exceed the total demand for steam, the feedwater to one or more boilers can be shut off and the boilers blown down until the desired rate of evaporation is obtained. A boiler can be refilled on load provided that its level has not fallen below the safe minimum. There is an exhaust-gas boiler for each engine which also acts as a partial engine silencer.

A further fuel saving is obtained by recovering heat from the engine jackets. A pump for each engine circulates water under pressure through the jacket to an elevated steam separator, so that bubbles of steam which form in the jacket are released in the separator and pass into a common steam range, which is maintained at 15 psig (1·03 bar (g)). Thus the heat is available at the corresponding saturation temperature of 250°F (121°C) the temperature in the jackets themselves being about 10°F (5·5°C) higher at full load. The steam from the separators passes into a tubular condenser supplied with water diverted from the district return main at a nominal 160°F (71°C) and the condensate returns under gravity via a storage tank to the individual engines. The coolant flow in the condenser is regulated automatically to maintain a constant steam pressure. A dump condenser comes into operation to condense surplus steam if the main condenser cannot condense all the steam, i.e. if the district return temperature is too high or the flow is too low.

The diesel engines themselves are Mirrlees National KVSS12 each of which drives a 2677 kVA, 11 kV Brush alternator. The engines use the same heavy fuel as the main steam boilers, but are started up on a lighter grade of fuel. All fuels are fed from service tanks which are replenished from bulk storage tanks. The heavy oil service tanks have thermostatically controlled immersion heaters and incorporate level controls and protection devices for the engine and boiler system. The heavy fuel tanks for the engines are filled via a purification plant which removes solid matter and sodium salts from the oil, thus contributing to reduced cylinder wear.

The electrical system of the station falls into two main sections: 415 V, 3-phase supplied for pump motors, lighting, and other station auxiliaries, and an 11-kV supply to the Aldershot military system. Power requirements can be supplemented by importing from the 33-kV system of the Southern Electricity Board, for which purpose a 5000 kVA, 33/11 kV transformer is installed in a switch compound at the western end of the station. On-load tap changing is provided on the 33-kV side, which can be either manually or automatically controlled, and reverse power protection on the 11-kV circuit breaker prevents export of power to the SEB. The internal services of the station are supplied by two 500 kVA, 11 kV/415 V transformers.

The 11-kV switchgear has been so laid out as to provide completely centralised control of the system from the station control room and is mounted in three adjacent rooms on the same gallery. Provision is made both there and in the control room for future expansion of the station. The double-busbar switchboard is in three sections in separate chambers. Two generators are connected to each outer section while the centre section connects to the incoming feed from the SEB system and to a 3-MVA link to the old power station of the Aldershot system. The outgoing feeders and station auxiliary supplies are divided among the three sections. A neutral earthing switchboard is adjacent to the 11-kV board to enable any generator to be earthed through a non-inductive resistor.

The control board is similarly divided. A mimic diagram indicates the overall state of the hV system. In addition to indicator lamps and line current meters, there is a total load wattmeter, station frequency meter and an ammeter recording any current flow in the 11-kV earth connection. From the control desk can be initiated all the functions of the generators, incoming transformers, bus section switches and the district heating system. All synchronising functions are initiated from here; a key interlock between the synchroscope and the synchronising switches prevents synchronising being attempted from two positions.

CHAPTER 8

THE FUEL CELL AND TOTAL ENERGY

by

H. R. Espig

Energy Conversion Ltd. Basingstoke, England

It is estimated that nearly half the installations for non-industrial electrical energy require less than 100 kW. However, below 100 kW the cost of conventional generating equipment rises rapidly, the efficiency, especially on part load, falls and reliability is reduced. At present, there is no suitable generating plant capable of being economically applied in total energy installations of this size and the fuel cell is being developed specifically to fulfil this need.

Modern building complexes require electrical power and large quantities of energy for heating, cooling and, in commercial units, for process loads. The smallest unit that can be considered is the single house. Here, electricity is required for appliances, outlined in Table 8.1, plus washing machines, dishwashers, refrigerators, etc., where electricity is required for the motors only.[49, 50]

The energy requirements for a typical six-room house are outlined in Table 8.2. The average power consumption over the year, to operate those items for which electricity is essential, is 137 W. During the summer months the average daily rate decreases to approximately 100 W, rising during the winter months to nearly 400 W. These are typical Northern European figures, In the U.S.A. they would be much closer to each other due to air-conditioning needs.

The peak-power requirements generally do not exceed 3 kW for periods in excess of 20 min but can rise to a maximum of 5 kW for very short periods during motor starting. These figures assume that gas is used for cooking and space heating. Power requirements are limited to short periods during the day, mainly between 7 a.m. and

TABLE 8.1. ESSENTIAL ELECTRICAL POWER REQUIREMENTS[29]—
ALL-GAS HOUSE IN THE UNITED KINGDOM

Appliance	Watt
Light	up to 1000
Fan or heating pad	40 to 100
Radio	50 to 200
Television	200 to 500
Vacuum cleaner	200 to 300
Bathroom heater	250 upwards
Iron	600 to 1500
Coffee-maker, toaster	450 to 1200
$\frac{1}{2}$ in. electric drill	500 to 1000

Motor size (hp)	Running watt	Watt to start		
		Repulsion–Induction	Capacitor	Split phase
$\frac{1}{6}$	275	600	850	2050
$\frac{1}{4}$	400	850	1050	2400
$\frac{1}{3}$	450	975	1350	2700
$\frac{1}{2}$	600	1300	1800	3600
$\frac{3}{4}$	850	1900	2600	
1	1100	2500	3300	

TABLE 8.2. TYPICAL ANNUAL CONSUMPTION

Six-room house, four occupants, heat loss 52,000 Btu/hr (54 MJ/hr)

Use	Gas		Coal, tons	Oil	Electric, kWh
	10^3 ft^3	(m^3)			
Space heating	135·2	3860	7·5	1110 U.S. gallons (4300 litres)	29,719
Water heating	21·6	612			4200
Cooking	8·4	236			1200
Lighting, refrigeration, d.c.					1200

10 a.m. 12 noon and 2 p.m. and, in the winter months, between 7.00 p.m. and 10.30 p.m. The above figures obviously vary from house to house but indicate that for domestic application the total energy system has to operate with a peak load up to 50 times the average power level.

In large-scale total energy systems, a high overall operating efficiency is achieved by using the waste heat from the generator to provide heat for environmental control. In a house, the energy needed for space heating is over 80% of the total energy requirements and this is only required for approximately 6 months of the year depending on the climatic conditions. However, energy is also required for water heating throughout the year. This is in direct proportion to the electric demand. Thus, by coupling the fuel cell to a hot-water system high overall operating efficiencies can be achieved all the year round. It can be shown that the generating efficiency of the generating plant should exceed 20% to provide an efficient integrated system.

Thus the small-scale domestic total energy system with an overall thermal efficiency in excess of 66% is not limited to distinct climatic zones, as for large-scale industrial plant, but can show low overall generating fuel costs for a wide variety of installations. Because of the high peak loads it is necessary to provide batteries to smoothe the load in individual houses, and also storage vessels for hot water. For larger developments such as blocks of flats, the ratio

$$\frac{\text{Peak load}}{\text{Average load}}$$

is smaller so that the storage capacity is less, the efficiency is improved and the capital costs are reduced.

FUEL CELLS FOR DOMESTIC TOTAL ENERGY SYSTEMS

The Fuel Cell as a Power Generator

The fuel cell is an electrochemical device in which the chemical energy of reaction between a fuel and an oxidant is converted directly into electrical energy. The principle of operation is basically similar to a battery, but whereas the reactants in a battery must be renewed by recharging or by replacing the battery, the fuel cell continues to operate, provided the fuel and oxidant are supplied continuously.

In principle, any oxidation-reduction reaction may be used as the basis for a fuel cell, but in practice only a few reactions show promise. Of these, only that between hydrogen and oxygen is of practical importance and can be used to illustrate the basic principles of the system. The hydrogen is obtained from a hydrocarbon and the oxygen from the air.

The cell consists of two electrochemically conducting electrodes separated by an electrolyte, for example a solution of potassium hydroxide in water (Fig. 8.1). A fuel, such as hydrogen, is supplied to the outside of one electrode and oxygen or air is supplied to the outside of the other. When the two electrodes are connected together, a current flows, fuel and oxidant being consumed. Unlike conventional batteries, the electrodes are not consumed during the operation and the cell can

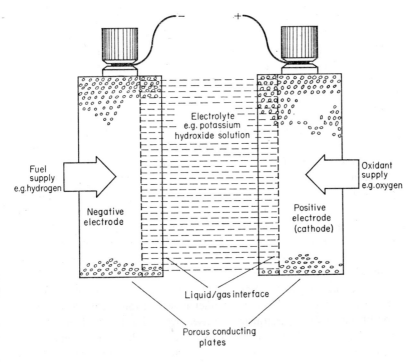

FIG. 8.1. Simple fuel cell.

continue to supply electrical power as long as the fuel and oxidant are supplied to the electrodes and the products of the reaction removed. Refuelling is simply accomplished by refilling the fuel tank.

The concept of a "black box" with no moving parts, in which electricity is generated as long as fuel and oxidant are supplied, is deceptively simple. Although such fuel cell systems have been developed, they have very low power densities. The more recently developed systems have high power densities and are more complex due to the need for subsystems to supply the fuel and oxidant, to remove the waste products, and to control the operating conditions over a wide variation in load. These functions are performed in different ways depending on the type and design of fuel cell systems considered.

The fuel-cell power plant has many advantages when compared with other generating systems. These can be summarised as follows:

(a) *High efficiency*[35]

The fuel cell operates at an invariant temperature and the efficiency is not restricted to the Carnot cycle which limits the efficiency of conventional internal-combustion engines operating between two temperatures.

Theoretical fuel cell thermal efficiencies can exceed 95%. However, in practice these are reduced to between 30% and 60% mainly due to the non-reversibility of the electrode processes and because power is required to drive the auxiliaries and control systems.

Thermal efficiencies of large internal-combustion engine powered generating plant varies from 25% to 35% if operated continuously at their rated output. Operations at low load factors reduces the efficiency (Fig. 8.2) whereas fuel cell systems maintain their efficiency over a wide range of load variations. In particular, the fuel consumption at "idling" is considerably less than for conventional generating equipment (Fig. 8.3).

In the majority of total energy systems the load varies considerably throughout the day. To enable efficient operation during peak-power conditions, several generators are used according to the load requirement. The fuel cell, because of its superior low-load performance, can be efficiently used over a wide range of loads, reducing the number of components and cost of the installation.

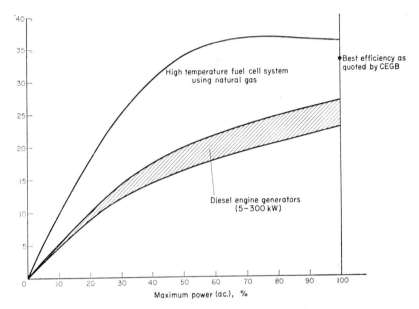

Fig. 8.2. Effect of load upon thermal efficiency of prime movers.

(b) *Maintenance and reliability*

The power generating part of the fuel-cell system has no moving parts. However, practical systems operating at high power densities require pumps, motors, air blowers, etc.

Simple fuel-cell systems have been shown to require virtually no maintenance, only needing refuelling once for periods of up to one year. More complex systems require maintenance, but because the auxiliaries are normally rotary low-power devices which operate continuously, usually at fixed speeds, long operating periods can be achieved without appreciable maintenance even in small sizes.

Because the moving parts are low-power rotary devices, they can be made quiet and reliable, allowing systems to be installed in domestic environments.

(c) *Clean exhaust*

The fuel cell oxidises the fuel electrochemically under controlled

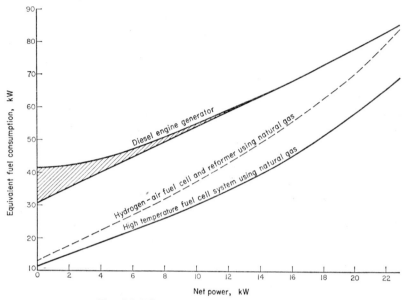

FIG. 8.3. Effect of load on fuel consumption.

conditions. The exhaust products depend on the type of system used. In the most highly developed systems using hydrogen as a fuel, the exhaust products are water vapour and air from which some oxygen has been removed.

However, hydrogen fuelled systems are not generally suitable for "total energy" installations, mainly because of high fuel costs. It is therefore necessary to consider systems operating on cheap hydrocarbon fuels such as natural gas. With these fuels the exhaust also contains oxides of carbon but because the combustion is continuous and controlled, the level of carbon monoxide is lower than for internal-combustion engines. Sulphur products have to be removed from fuels before being supplied to the cells to prevent contamination of the catalysts.

(d) Design[57]

The single cell produces power at low voltage. A typical voltage-current curve is shown in Fig. 8.4. In order to obtain higher voltages

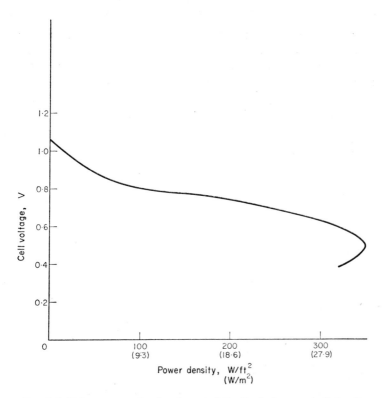

FIG. 8.4. Voltage-power density characteristics for hydrogen–air fuel cell.

and powers it is necessary to connect cells in series to form modules, which are used as building bricks to construct higher power systems. A typical module is illustrated on Plate 8. This consists of forty series connected cells and is capable of giving an output in excess of 7 kW at 28 volts d.c. The module weighs 90 lb (41 kg) and occupies 1·3 ft³ (37 litres). This modular concept allows systems to be designed for a wide variety of applications and enables plant to be optimised to suit space requirements and to reduce maintenance costs. Plate 7 shows a 5 kW system incorporating the above module and designed as a portable power plant.

Fuel Cell System for Domestic Generation

The cost of generating equipment rises rapidly for output powers below 100 kW (see Fig. 8.5). In order to exploit this market, TARGET, the "Team to Advance Research for Gas Energy Transmission Inc.", an organisation formed by twenty-seven gas companies in the U.S.A., has invested $21 million in a 3-year programme to provide a "fuel cell" power plant suitable for small-scale generation.[8]

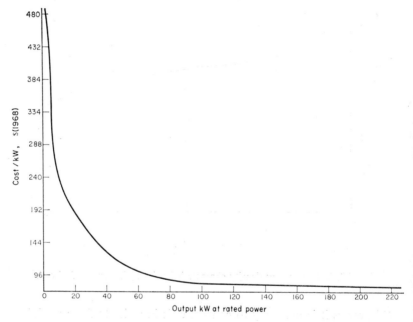

FIG. 8.5. Diesel engine generators. Capital cost as function of rated output.

The discovery of the principle of the fuel cell is attributed to Sir William Grove who demonstrated that the electrochemical dissociation of water was reversible. Development of a practical fuel cell from this stage was slow until Bacon demonstrated a 6 kW hydrogen–oxygen cell in 1959. This cell was the forerunner of the "Apollo" fuel cell plant which is used to supply the on-board power in the Apollo spacecraft. Hydrogen–oxygen fuel cell systems have now reached a

PLATE 1. Laying a street twin-pipeline district-heating network in Denmark. (By courtesy: Brun & Sorensen A/S, Denmark.)

PLATE 2. An 850-mm bore diesel engine. (By courtesy: AB Götaverken, Sweden.)

PLATE 3. The AEI 550-MW, Thorpe Marsh, steam power station. (By courtesy: AEI Ltd., Manchester.)

PLATE 4. The Warbasse total energy scheme on Long Island. (By courtesy: Brooklyn Union Gas Co.)

PLATE 5. Gas turbine rotor of a 1650-kW open-cycle gas turbine unit.
(By courtesy: Brown Boveri Ltd.)

PLATE 6. A small gas turbine plant used for total energy purposes in Germany. (By courtesy: Kraftwerk Vahr, Stadtwerke Bremen, West Germany.)

PLATE 7. 5-kW fuel cell system. (By courtesy: Energy Conversion Ltd., Basingstoke.)

PLATE 8. 7-kW fuel cell module. (By courtesy Energy Conversion Ltd., Basingstoke.)

stage where fully integrated reliable power plants are being produced for both space and underwater applications in outputs ranging from a few watt to over 100 kW. In these applications the direct and operating costs of the fuel-cell power plant are not of prime importance.

For a total energy system it is essential to use a cheap, readily available hydrocarbon as a fuel and, for domestic applications, one of the most readily available fuels is natural gas. There are several possible methods by which the hydrocarbon fuel can be used in the fuel cell and these are summarised in Fig. 8.6.

Most of the fuel-cell systems, which have reached a stage where they can be considered as engineering power plants, tend to use highly reactive fuel at a low temperature. These fuels are obtained from hydrocarbons by conversion in a large chemical plant. Of these, only hydrogen and hydrazine can be oxidised directly at the fuel electrode. The alternatives, methanol and ammonia are cracked and purified to produce hydrogen. The advantages of using hydrogen and operating at low temperatures include better stability of materials, longer life, cheaper constructional materials and quick start-up. The rate of reaction tends to be low at low temperatures and therefore electrode design and nature of catalysts are of overriding importance. However, the possibility of using a large chemical plant to produce hydrogen from natural gas and then piping this hydrogen to total energy installations should not be neglected particularly for new developments involving several small units.

An alternative to using the hydrogen directly in the cell, is to use a steam reformer to convert the hydrocarbon fuel into hydrogen and oxides of carbon. It is then possible either to feed this mixture directly into a cell with an acid electrolyte or to purify it and feed the resulting hydrogen into an alkaline electrolyte cell. Fully integrated fuel cell systems of these types have been developed but are at present not economic for total energy uses because of the high cost of materials at present required for acid environments, and the cost of small-scale hydrogen purifiers, required for alkaline electrolyte fuel cells. The rate of electrochemical reaction at the electrodes can be increased by increasing the temperature and the pressure. The latter produces other problems in the design of pumps and control systems; the former allows cheaper catalysts to be used but unfortunately produces other prob-

L

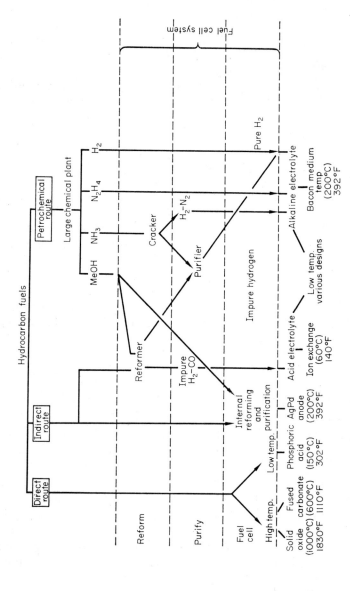

Fig. 8.6. Basic fuel cell systems.

lems in the use of materials and their stability at elevated temperatures. One of the earliest systems operating at high temperatures and pressures to be demonstrated was the "Bacon" cell which operated at about 390°F (200°C) and at pressures of up to 800 psi (56·3 bar). This cell produced 151 A/ft^2 (14 A/m^2) at 0·9 V and 1000 A/ft^2 (93 A/m^2) at 0·6 V. The system used aqueous potassium hydroxide as the electrolyte and nickel electrodes. This is ideal for hydrogen–oxygen systems, but can not be used for hydrocarbon–air reactions as the electrolyte would become contaminated with carbonates and the nickel electrodes poisoned. Alternative systems have been produced with high-power densities using sulphuric acid or phosphoric acid as the electrolyte and fuels such as propane, natural gas or impure reformed gas. However, the capital cost of the materials associated with the use of acid electrolytes is at the moment prohibitive and further development is required before a system can be produced at a capital cost suitable for a total energy installation.

The most attractive systems for direct conversion are high-temperature systems. The two main types are the molten carbonate electrolyte cell which operates between 930°F (500°C) and 1290°F (700°C) and the solid oxide fuel cell operating between 1650°F (900°C) and 2010°F (1100°C). The advantages of operating at high temperatures are the possibilities of using cheap catalysts and of integrating the fuel cell—reformer system. In total energy systems the high-grade waste heat allows economic design of heat-exchange systems. High-temperature systems with power ratings below 1 kW are not self-sustaining and would have to be operated inside a boiler or supplied with external heating.

Design studies based on the performance of single cells indicate that systems based on these two electrolytes would have efficiencies in excess of 30% at power levels ranging from full power to one-third of the nominal rating.

The solid oxide electrolyte system has the advantage of operating with air as the oxidant and of having an electrolyte that cannot leak out, whereas the molten carbonate electrolyte fuel cell requires carbon dioxide from the fuel exhaust to be added to the oxidant supply and has a semi-free electrolyte. Because of carbon deposition, both systems require a simple prereactor to convert the fuel to an acceptable feed gas.

The main advantages of using a high-temperature cell is that materials of construction can be cheap and that there is no need for expensive catalysts. Predicted capital costs range from $290 kW to under $30/kW (1968).

Direct hydrocarbon cells have not yet reached a stage where they can be applied directly to total energy systems. However, improved systems with high efficiencies, longer lives and lower capital costs are being developed continuously and will be capable of economic application in total energy systems in the near future.

CHAPTER 9

REFRIGERATION AND TOTAL ENERGY

IN THE United States and Canada, and also to some extent in central and southern Europe, where climatic conditions are more extreme than in the United Kingdom, the supply of air conditioning during summer is considered equally important to the supply of heating during winter. With the increase in living standards, the employment of air conditioning has tended to spread, however. For example, it is considered by many authorities in the United States that some refrigeration plant must be made operational whenever the ambient external temperature rises above 55°F (13°C). The reason for this is that even at such low ambient temperatures premises, which face south and have large picture windows, may become too hot at certain periods of the day.

There is no doubt that refrigerated air has its place even in countries such as Great Britain. Modern glass curtain wall offices often become unbearable in summer even in temperate areas, hospitals require an exact adjustment in temperature, stores and places of amusement get over-heated due to excessive lighting capacity and the heat given off by human metabolism.

There are considerable advantages in operating an air-conditioning system in conjunction with the production of power and heat.[132] During the summer, when heat requirements are low, the waste heat given off by the prime mover can be made use of in absorption refrigeration plant. This is, incidentally, how most American systems get the even heat load so needed for viable operation of a total energy system.

In addition, one can also use a compression refrigeration machine as a source of heat, The ratio

$$\frac{\text{Energy expended}}{\text{heating effect obtained}}$$

299

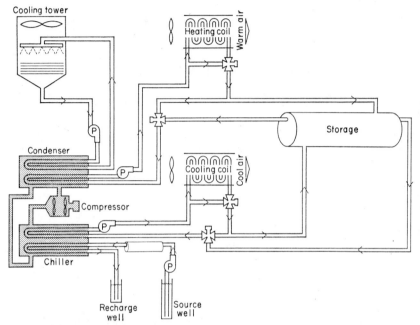

FIG. 9.1. Layout of a heat pump system. (By courtesy: Carrier International Inc.)

called the coefficient of performance, is always well above unity due to the thermodynamic considerations which apply, and which are explained below. This means that one gets a very high return from the energy spent in operating the reciprocating compressor or centrifugal refrigeration plants. The large heating and cooling loads that can be covered by a compressor refrigerator, which itself uses quite moderate quantities of steam, are an important factor in making such "heat pumps" an economic proposition. This is in spite of the high plant costs involved. Heat pumps are most economical to use if one requires a large amount of cooling for air-conditioning purposes, but at the same time needs the waste heat for such requirements as: domestic hot water, process heat for industry, flash evaporation of sea water, etc. It is also possible to store the hot water and to use it for space heating at night. Heat pumps are also employed in winter, using a source of

water (river, lake, sea, etc.) as a sink, to step up this heat to a temperature useful for space heating. As the coefficient of performance is
more than 1, such a process is once more economic from the fuel point
of view, which means that the power expended is less than the heating
effect obtained. As heat pump systems[142] either require electricity, or
at any rate high-pressure steam, their function can only be an auxiliary
one in a total energy system, useful for balancing out power, heating
and cooling requirements. Centrifugal compressor refrigeration plant
is often used with a feed of high-pressure steam from a main range, and
the waste heat from it is used for domestic hot water and other purposes.

REFRIGERATION THERMODYNAMICS[5, 6]

In a compression refrigerator, a gas or vapour is first of all compressed, using either a reciprocating pump or a centrifugal pump.
During this compression heat is evolved, which is taken off by means of
a heat exchanger. The compressed fluid then enters the expansion
chamber, where it is expanded to its original density. During the expansion heat is abstracted. When refrigeration machinery is used for
air-conditioning purposes, this heat is usually removed from circulating
cold water to produce chilled water at around 42°F (5·5°C).

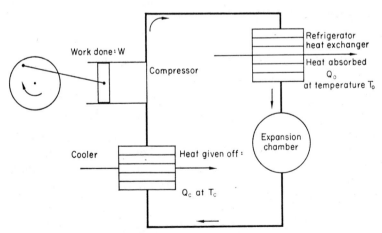

FIG. 9.2. Thermodynamics of compression refrigerator.

If a quantity of heat Q_0 is removed from the refrigerator at temperature T_0°R (°K) and if a quantity of work W must be done in order to be able to discharge a heat quantity Q_c at a higher temperature T_c°R (°K), then according to the first law of thermodynamics:

$$Q_0 + W = Q_c \tag{1}$$

But according to the second law of thermodynamics, the maximum amount of heat transferred may not exceed

$$Q_0 = W \left(\frac{T_0}{T_c - T_0} \right) \tag{2}$$

For any refrigerator, the coefficient of performance is the ratio between the amount of heat which is transferred in the machine and the work which is required for its removal.

This is given by

$$\frac{Q_0}{W} = \frac{T_0}{T_c - T_0}$$

with an ideal gas.

In practical refrigeration machines, the equation is not quite so simple, as there are two irreversible processes in the operation:

(a) The cooling of superheated vapour to saturation in the condenser.

(b) Expansion of liquid from condenser pressure to evaporation pressure.

In consequence the actual coefficient of performance is always well below the theoretical coefficient of performance. The efficiency of any refrigeration machine is defined as:

$$\text{Efficiency} = \frac{\text{Actual coefficient of performance}}{\text{Theoretical coefficient of performance}}$$

For a typical reciprocating compressor ammonia refrigerator, operating between the limits of 86°F (30°C) and a bottom temperature of 5°F (-15°C), the theoretical coefficient of performance works out at 5·74. The actual coefficient of performance, calculated from enthalpies, is 4·75, giving an efficiency of:

$$\frac{4\text{·}75 \times 100}{5\text{·}74} = 83\%.$$

RECIPROCATING AND CENTRIFUGAL REFRIGERATORS

There are three types of reciprocating compressors:
(a) Vertical single acting.
(b) Horizontal double acting.
(c) Compound compressors.

Vertical compressors require least floor space, horizontal compressors are most accessible and suffer least from vibration, while the multi-stage compressors have the advantages of reduction in the heat pressure due to the auxiliary cooling circuit between the compressors. Leakages are reduced as the pressure differences are minimised, and there is a reduction in inlet heating as the refrigerant enters a cylinder which has not been heated excessively previously.

The refrigerants used can be classified as wet, dry and superheated.

Wet refrigerants contain finely divided liquid droplets, while dry refrigerants are in their saturated state. Superheated refrigerants contain extra heat, above the saturation state. In general, it is best to avoid superheating of the refrigerant and this is normally avoided by intercooling between stages of compression.

Reciprocating compressor refrigerators are usually small in size, and can be designed for a variety of different refrigerants.

Centrifugal Compressors[85]

The disadvantage of reciprocating compressors, when used in refrigeration, is the difficulty of handling large quantities of gas and vapour. For refrigeration plants with a minimum size of 100 tons of refrigeration (1 ton of refrigeration = absorption of 12,000 Btu/hr or 3157 W (J/s)), centrifugal pumps are used to compress the refrigerant. As a centrifugal compressor has a much lower head than a reciprocating compressor, it is essential to use a number of these in series to achieve the desired head. The most common refrigerants used in connection with centrifugal machines are freon-11, freon-12 and freon-113.

Jet Compressors

It is possible to make use of waste steam directly for refrigeration

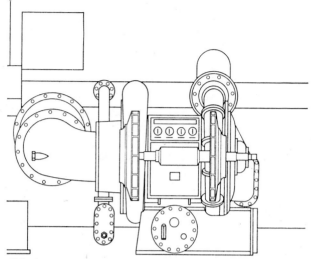

FIG. 9.3. A centrifugal refrigeration machine. (By courtesy: Trane Ltd.)

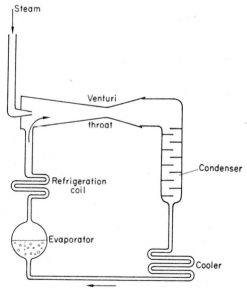

FIG. 9.4. Jet compressor refrigeration circuit.

purposes, by allowing it to pass through a jet into a Venturi throat, and thence to the compressor chamber and cooler/condenser. From there the water, which constitutes the refrigerant in such a case, moves to the lower pressure evaporator section, where heat is abstracted. Such a system has the advantage of simplicity and may well be used to employ low-pressure steam from total energy plants, which in winter is used for heating purposes, but which in summer can carry some air-conditioning load. The efficiency of such a system is poor, and for this reason it can only be used where there are only low and occasional demands for air conditioning, as for example in inherently cold northern countries. In addition, the refrigeration side must be kept well above 32°F (0°C), the freezing point of water.

REFRIGERANTS

By far the cheapest of all refrigerants is ammonia NH_3, which has excellent thermodynamic properties with a latent heat higher than that of any other refrigerant with the exception of water. Its disadvantages are mainly the fact that it attacks copper and copper alloys, as well as many lubricants, because it converts fatty esters into soaps. Ammonia is very highly toxic and leakages are attended by considerable dangers. It can form highly explosive mixtures with air. For these reasons, it is undesirable to use ammonia as a refrigerant in plant used in or near populated areas. It is hardly ever used in air-conditioning systems, but can be employed in industrial plant, provided adequate safety precautions are taken.

Apart from ammonia, the most common refrigerants used today are the freon group, consisting of chloro- and fluoro-substituted methanes and ethanes, methyl chloride, carbon dioxide and, last but not least, water. The main thermodynamic characteristics of these refrigerants are given in Table 9.1.

Methyl chloride is used in packaged refrigeration units up to a capacity of 10 tons (35 kW). Because of its lower vapour pressure it requires larger units than ammonia for any given capacity. Carbon dioxide is a safe fluid, but, because of its low critical temperature, the condenser temperature has to be kept below about 80°F (27°C) which is not always practicable. The condensing pressure is very high and

TABLE 9.1. PROPERTIES OF REFRIGERANTS

Refrigerant:	Water	Carbon dioxide	Ammonia NH$_3$	Methyl chloride CH$_3$Cl	Freon-22 CHClF$_2$	Freon-12 CCl$_2$F$_2$	Freon-114 C$_2$Cl$_2$F$_4$	Freon-21 CHCl$_2$F	Freon-11 CCl$_3$F	Freon-113 C$_2$Cl$_3$F$_3$
Boiling Point at one atm. pressure										
°F	212	—	−28	−11	−41	−21	38	48	75	118
°C	100	—	−33	−24	−40	−29	3	9	24	48
Critical temperature										
°F	705	88	271	289	205	233	294	353	388	417
°C	347	31	133	143	96	112	145	178	198	214
Critical pressure										
psia	3206	1070	1650	969	716	582	474	750	635	495
bar	221	74	114	67	49	40	33	52	43	34
Latent heat of vaporisation Btu/lb or kcal/kg (Multiply by 4·18 to obtain value in kJ/kg)	970	246	589	194	93	69	62	109	84	71
Toxicity	Nil	Nil below 4% conc.	Very toxic	moderate	fairly low	low	low	moderate	fairly low	low

therefore it is necessary to use heavy construction for the compressors. Water has excellent thermodynamic properties, except for a very high specific volume of vapour at atmospheric temperatures, which makes it quite impossible to use with reciprocating compressors. In addition, the high freezing point 32°F (0°C) of water provides a limit for its application. Water is used as a refrigerant in steam jet compressors. The evaporation side must be kept well above the freezing point of water.

The freon refrigerants cover a wide range of thermodynamic properties, are stable chemically and do not attack metals. Most are only very slightly toxic and then only when the concentration exceeds 10% by volume. The vapours are non-inflammable, but when in contact with burning carbonaceous matter, poisonous phosgene $COCl_2$ is formed.

ABSORPTION REFRIGERATION PLANTS

These are the types of equipment most widely used in total energy systems, because they are able to use low-grade heat as a driving medium. Absorption refrigeration systems are based on the same principles as compression machines, except that the compression process is being carried out by heat and not by mechanical energy.

Because absorption systems are completely closed ones, it is possible to use ammonia as the refrigerant with water as the compressing fluid or absorbent, or it is possible to make use of aqueous salt solutions such as lithium bromide, which absorb heat on dilution.

AMMONIA ABSORPTION SYSTEMS

The complete cycle of operations is as follows:

STAGE 1. Heat supplied from a heat exchanger causes an aqueous solution of ammonia to boil, and to drive off ammonia gas under pressure.

STAGE 2. The hot and compressed ammonia driven off is passed through a cooling coil, and is cooled in this to atmospheric temperature. This causes the ammonia to liquefy, the latent heat of vapourisation likewise being removed by the cooling coil.

STAGE 3. The liquid ammonia, which is now at room temperature, is brought into the refrigeration chamber, where it comes under greatly reduced pressure, This causes the ammonia to boil, thereby producing a cooling effect.

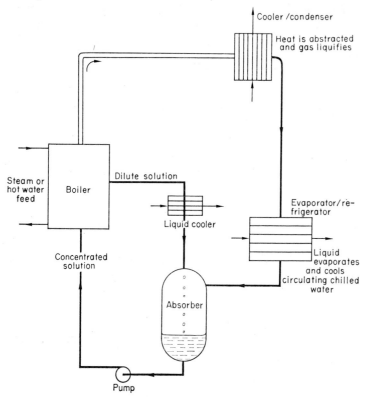

FIG. 9.5. Flow sheet of ammonia refrigeration plant.

STAGE 4. The ammonia, gas, which has emerged from the refrigeration coil, is dissolved in water. At about 80°F (27°C) and atmospheric pressure a volume of water can dissolve as much as 1000 volumes of ammonia. This produces the low pressure in front of the refrigeration chamber which causes the liquid ammonia to boil. As the ammonia dissolves in the water, the temperature of the water rises. This causes thermosyphon effects which help to induce the concentrated solution to flow into the heating chamber.

STAGE 5. The aqueous solution of ammonia is heated once more, driving off ammonia under pressure, and producing a weak ammonia liquor which, after passing through cooling coils, is used to absorb the ammonia as it comes from the refrigeration coil.

In all commercial absorption plants, the circulation of the water and ammonia solution is carried out by means of sealed pumps.

THE LITHIUM BROMIDE PROCESS

A typical absorption refrigerator of this type is the Swearingen absorption chiller,[113] described in the 1962 handbook of the National District Heating Association of Pittsburgh.

The cycle uses the lithium bromide–water pair in an absorbing system in which the means for regenerating the absorbent and the refrigerant are a two-effect evaporator, with extremely good heat economy. The basic circuit of the Swearingen absorption system, which is one of the most up to date, can be followed from Fig. 9.6. The refrigeration effect is generated by the evaporation of liquid refrigerant (water) and is passed on to the evaporator coil, which carries chilled water for the air conditioning system. The refrigerant vapour is absorbed by the rich lithium bromide solution as it flows over the cooling water coil in the lower right-hand vessel. This exhausts the absorbent solution and the resulting spent solution drains to the bottom, and is pumped through heat exchangers and through a steam-activated heater which is labelled "First effect generator". In this heater, enough heat is applied to evaporate about half the absorbed refrigerant. The spent solution becomes thus a half regenerated solution in the first effect generator and is then discharged from the heater into the upper compartment of the upper left-hand side vessel at about 1 psig (69 mbar(g)) where the half regenerated solution disengages the vapour. The vapour passes into the lower half of the vessel labelled: "Second effect generator". It condenses on the surface of the coil marked: "Second effect generator", and the condensate drops to the bottom.

The half regenerated solution which disengages the vapour in the upper compartment flows first into the upper heat exchanger and then

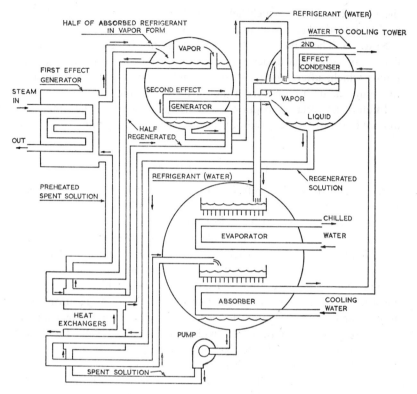

FIG. 9.6. Swearingen absorption chiller.

through a back-pressure valve into the coil of the second effect generator. The vapourisation of the other half of the absorbed refrigerant takes place there The refrigerant vapour outside the coil condenses at about 215°F (102°C) and heats the coil to near this temperature. The solution inside the coil boils at 190°F (88°C) because the pressure there is only about 1·6 psia (11 mbar) so that the remaining refrigerant distils out of the lithium bromide solution.

Thus in the second-effect generator the half-generated solution becomes fully regenerated. This steam enters the lower compartment of the right-hand vessel where the vapour and liquid disengage, and the liquid falls to the bottom. The vapour rises into the compartment labelled "Second effect condenser" and condenses on the cooling coil. The condensate sinks to the bottom of the compartment. The refrigerant which condenses in the second effect generator flows into the same compartment and joins this second portion of liquid refrigerant. The combined liquid refrigerant flows to the evaporator as shown and the cycle is repeated.

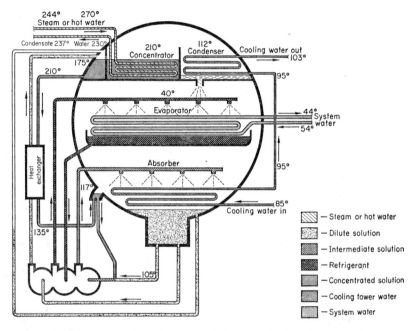

FIG. 9.7. Trane absorption chiller design. (By courtesy: Trane Ltd.)

The hot, fully regenerated solution at the bottom of the upper right-hand-side vessel flows back through the lower heat exchanger, where it is cooled. It returns to the absorber and the cycle is then repeated. In this refrigerator there is only one moving component, a totally enclosed pump which requires no maintenance. A lithium bromide plant of this type uses steam at about 100 psig (6·9 bar(g)). In addition, a 15-ton (53 kW) refrigeration plant uses $\frac{1}{2}$ kW of electric power to

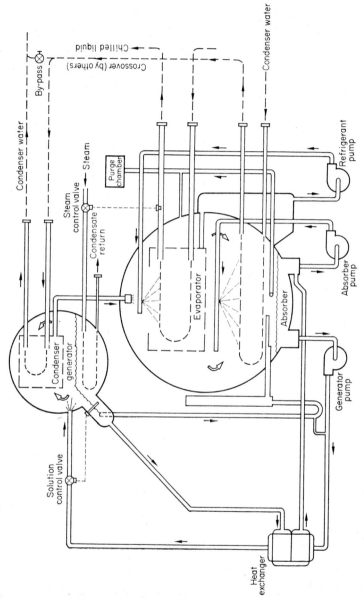

FIG. 9.8. Lithium bromide absorption chiller. (By courtesy: Garrett-AiResearch).

operate the pump. On average, the Swearingen type of lithium bromide absorption refrigeration plant produces 1 Btu (kJ) of refrigeration for every Btu (kJ) of steam heat absorbed. This works out at 13·5 lb (6·1 kg) of steam per ton of refrigeration effect (3·52 kW). Single-effect lithium bromide absorption refrigeration systems usually require 1·4 Btu (kJ) of steam per Btu (kJ) refrigeration effect or about 18–20 lb (8–9 kg) steam per ton (3·52 kW). Smaller ammonia-type absorption refrigerators have efficiencies much lower than this and may need as much as 2–2·5 Btu (kJ) refrigeration effect. Centrifugal machines using a steam feed of about 120 psig (8·2 bar (g)) into the turbine, need anything between 11–18 (5–8 kg) lb of steam per ton (3·52 kW) of refrigeration effect. Centrifugal plant is, however, more expensive than absorption plant.

Steam or hot water-driven absorption units are available in sizes from 50 to 1000 tons of refrigeration (176 kW to 3·52 MW). The units require more space and are heavier per ton of refrigeration effect than either centrifugal or reciprocating chillers of a corresponding tonnage. However, the absorption machines provide quieter operation, no vibration, high dependability and minimal maintenance. The quiet vibration

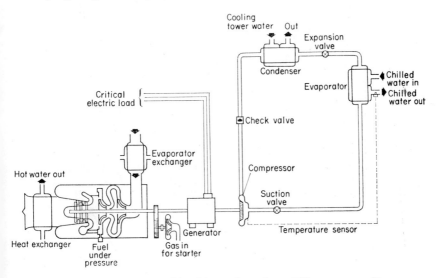

FIG. 9.9. Layout of turbine-driven absorption chilling system. (By courtesy: Garrett-AiResearch.)

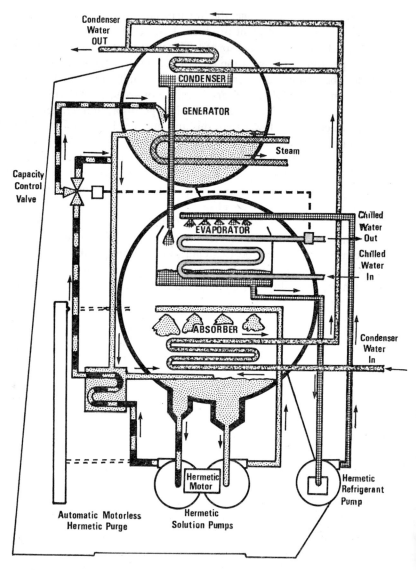

FIG. 9.10. Absorption cycle for cooling water used in air-conditioning practice. (By courtesy: Carrier Ltd.)

free operation is possible as the machines only require three small feed pumps. The absorption chiller plants also have efficiency capacity control. The absorbent is reconcentrated and circulated at a rate to produce the desired chilled water temperature. In consequence an absorption chiller can operate at as low at 10% of the full load and yet maintain a high efficiency. Absorption chillers are normally run by steam at between 8 and 12 psig (0·55–0·83 bar (g)) or by hot water pressurised to temperatures between 255°F and 400°F (124–204°C).

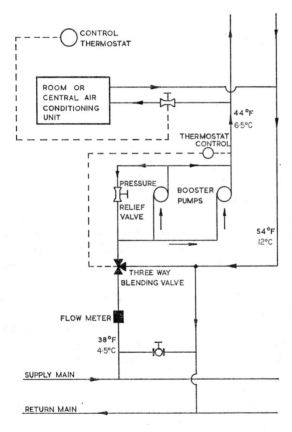

FIG. 9.11. Distribution system for cold-water circulator.

Absorption chillers need large cooling towers and a condenser water pump, as a greater amount of heat has to be dissipated than with the mechanically driven compressor systems.

ECONOMICS OF USING ABSORPTION PLANT IN CONJUNCTION WITH PRIME MOVERS[27, 28, 124]

One of the advantages of the absorption refrigeration plant is that it is able to use quite low-grade heat. In a scheme described by Bowman of the Carrier company, a steam turbine was coupled with an absorption refrigeration plant. For an extra expenditure of 38,000 lb (17,400 kg) of steam at 600 psig (41·3 bar (g)) per hour, enough waste steam at 20 psig (1·4 bar g)) could be produced at the back pressure end of the turbine to produce 4000 tons of refrigeration (14·1 MW), which works out at only 9·5 lb of steam per ton (4·3 kg/3·52 kW).

If direct steam heating had been used for the same plant, it would have been necessary to use 20 lb of steam (8·9 kg) per ton of refrigeration effect, so that an economy of 53% is achieved by running such absorption refrigeration systems on the "total energy" principle.

In this connection it is interesting to note that an electric-motor-driven centrifugal refrigeration system requires 0·83 kW of electricity per ton of refrigeration effect (3·52 kW). When the steam of the absorption system is provided as a by-product of power generation, the extra steam needed is equal to 0·83 kW worth of heat, i.e. it uses an amount of steam equal in calorific value to the electric power used in the centrifugal compressor machine. When the absorption system is operated by directly generated steam, the picture is not quite as favourable. In such a case 1·75 kW of heat are used, instead of 0·83 kW of electricity in the power-driven centrifugal machine.

If a centrifugal refrigerator is driven by a gas engine, the amount of gas needed to produce 1 ton (3·25 kW) of refrigeration is equal to 0·7 kW. As can be seen the directly driven centrifugal compressor plant therefore takes less fuel than the waste-heat-operated absorption plant in such a case. It may often pay to install centrifugal plants to carry the main load in a total energy system, using absorption plant merely to utilise the waste heat, which would otherwise have been thrown away.

CHAPTER 10

DISTRICT HEATING AND TOTAL ENERGY

SPACE heating of dwellings, industrial and commercial buildings, schools, hospitals and other urban buildings in cities situated in temperate regions is probably the best way of making use of the low grade heat produced as a by-product of electricity generation with most prime movers. Conversely, such waste heat can be obtained much more cheaply by the community than prime fuel, whether burned by individuals or in so called heating centrales. It has been found, for example, that in smaller district heating undertakings where heat is being produced by the direct combustion of coal in central boiler houses, the savings in fuel cost are only due to the following factors:

(a) cheaper grades of coal used;

(b) cheaper cost and transportation rate due to large quantities bought;

(c) improved efficiency of combustion in large undertaking as against smaller domestic boilers.

These savings are only marginally higher, if at all, than the very much increased plant and maintenance costs caused by the necessity of laying a long and complex underground pipeline network. The financial picture with regard to the oil-fired station is somewhat better, but again it is only possible to make district heating pay, provided the overall conditions such as density of supply, ground conditions, etc., are very favourable. When, however, the heat is being produced as a by-product of electricity generation, overall economic operation is found to be favourable even when pipeline-laying costs have had to be very high. These are cases when low thermal demand areas have to be supplied, where pipelines have to be installed in existing built-up urban areas or where water courses have to be crossed and special lines

317

laid in areas with unstable ground conditions or areas with a very high water table.

For most district heating schemes, the main suppliers of waste heat are normal condensing steam turbines,[157] able to run on an ITOC cycle (Intermediate take-off condensing), i.e. where it is possible to run the turbines as condensing stations when a peak demand of electricity exists, but where part of the steam is taken off at intermediate positions when the thermal demand warrants it. The average urban district

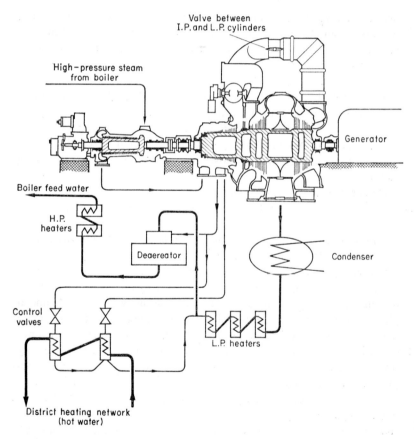

FIG. 10.1. Basic layout of an ITOC system.

heating systems used on the continent of Europe employ several prime suppliers of heat to the circulating hot water. These are first and foremost power stations, often converted from old-fashioned low-efficiency steam stations, but often also purpose-built gas-turbine plants, refuse incinerator plants either combined with power generation or alone, as

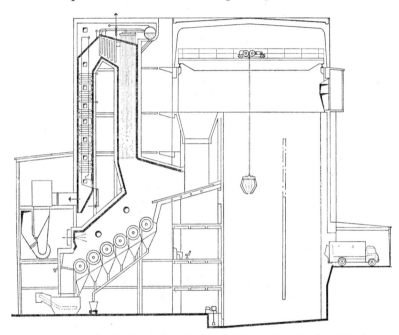

FIG. 10.2. Refuse incineration using the Vereinigte Kesselwerke, Düsseldorf system.

well as directly fired stand-by stations. A typical example of such a system is Germany's largest district heating network, the Hamburg system, which had a capacity during 1964 of 3860×10^6 Btu/hr (4,070 GJ/hr) with an annual heat supply rate of $10 \cdot 3 \times 10^9$ Btu (11 million GJ). The Hamburg system had a pipeline network of around 100 miles (160 km) in the form of twin mains, a supply and a return main. The bulk of the heat is supplied, as in most cases, by waste heat from power stations operating on the ITOC principle,

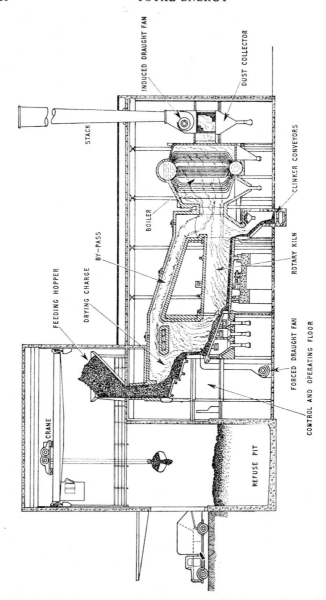

FIG. 10.3. Refuse incineration using the Danish vølund system.

but in addition there are auxiliary heating plants, which are fired directly using coal, oil, gas and refuse as fuel. A careful balance of heat and power requirement is set up to obtain the heat as economically as possible.

THE LENINGRAD SYSTEM[97-99, 103]

Leningrad has one of the largest of the Russian systems of district heating, and the system has been built out steadily since 1924.

Data in Table 10.1 are given with respect to the Leningrad system as applying on 1 January 1966

TABLE 10.1

Capacity of district heating network:	
11,000 × 10⁶ Btu	(11·7 TJ/hr)

Capacity of district heating network:
  $11{,}000 \times 10^6$ Btu $(11 \cdot 7$ TJ/hr)
Length of heating network:
  351 miles   (562 km)
Number of connected buildings:
  6427
Total volume of buildings supplied with hot water:
  $1 \cdot 42 \times 10^9$ ft³ $(40 \cdot 2 \times 10^6$ m³)
Total heat delivery during 1965:
  $3 \cdot 45 \times 10^{13}$ Btu   (36,400 TJ)
Total hot water delivery during 1965:
  $6 \cdot 63 \times 10^{13}$ Btu   (70,000 TJ)
Installed electrical capacity of ITOC turbines of system:
  656 MW
Heating capacity of turbine bleeds:
  6870×10^6 Btu/hr $(7 \cdot 23$ TJ/hr)
Percentage of total heat load which can be covered from turbine bleeds of the ITOC turbines:
  62%
Electrical power output of the ITOC turbines during 1965:
  $4 \cdot 346 \times 10^9$ kWh
The heat supply by combined heating and power stations to public and residential buildings amounts to $43 \cdot 7\%$ of the total heat delivered.

The Leningrad system operates as a composite whole using seventeen block boiler houses with a total heating capacity of 1900×10^8 Btu/hr (2000 GJ/hr) varying in capacity between 28 and 180×10^6 Btu/hr (29–290 GJ/hr), and three boiler houses with a total capacity of 1560 ×

10^6 Btu/hr (1630 GJ/hr). There are also some 356,000 ft³ (10,000 m³) of hot-water storage tanks.

But the bulk of the heat is supplied as waste heat from twenty-five district heating turbine plants of which six are low-pressure ones operating at less than 250 psig (35 bar (g)), fourteen are intermediate ones operating at 1300 psig (90 bar (g)) and five are high-pressure ones operating at 1900 psig (130 bar (g)). However, the high-pressure turbines account for 93% of the total electric capacity. The district heating turbines used operate both on the back-pressure principle and on the ITOC principle. In general, the back-pressure turbines have capacities of between 5 and 12 MW, while the ITOC turbines are larger, with outputs of up to 50 MW.

As the Leningrad system supplies not only heating but also hot water, it has been found that one of the main bottlenecks in the supply of the latter has been the capacity of water-treatment plants. At the beginning of 1966 the capacity of such water treatment plants was equal to 400,000 ft³/hr (11,500 m³/hr) which means that the requirements for hot water of a population of 500,000 can be covered.

At certain periods during the day maximum heating loads and maximum electrical loads coincide. Under such circumstances, the heating load is covered by hot water stored during periods of low power demand, and the stations are run for power generation purposes only. The net electricity output of the turbines then rises by around 100 MW or 15%.

Some 50% of the total power requirements of the Leningrad area are covered by the combined heating and power stations, i.e. stations operating on the total energy principle. The electrical capacity of these turbines is used on average for 6,740 hours per year with the bleeds being employed for 3910 hours of that time.

The fuel consumption of the Leningrad heating/power stations is given as 760 lb (342 kg) of coal per 1000 kWh delivered and the ratio of electrical output to heat supplied when the stations are operated in the heating mode averages at 80 kWh per 10^6 Btu (76 kWh'GJ) of heat produced.

Further technical developments are planned in Leningrad in order to improve the operation of the total energy system. One trend will be to replace the smaller back-pressure turbines by larger ones operating on the ITOC cycle, while the other is the installation of two 150-MW steam/gas units. It is planned that before 1980 all buildings of the city of Leningrad should be supplied by district heating from the central system. In addition it is intended to make extensive use of natural gas in the fuel balance of the city to eliminate air pollution. At the time of writing some district heating turbines operating at supercritical steam conditions 3500 psig (240 bar (g)) and 1070°F (580°C) with capacities of 100 and 250 MW were being erected.

COSTING OF DISTRICT HEAT AS SUPPLIED BY AN URBAN SYSTEM[15, 16]

In the costing of district heating system, one must always bear in mind that the operating authority must be in a position to provide heat to the consumer at a cheaper price then he could himself. The cost of

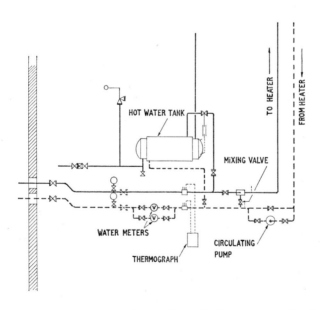

FIG. 10.4. Layout at consumer's end when using hot water as a heating medium.

heat to the consumer, if he has his own fuel combustion installation, is comprised by the following:

(a) The cost of his own plant in the form of an annuity charge which incorporates both payment of capital and depreciation.

(b) The cost of maintenance and repair of his plant.

(c) The labour cost of fuelling and firing his plant. In the case of a large consumer such as a block of flats, school, hospital, etc., this can be expressed in the form of cash, but in the case of private householders the cash value of this is not so easy to find.

(d) The fuel cost per useful therm or Gjoule, which is expressed as the purchase price of this fuel per thermal content at the consumer's premises multiplied by the average combustion efficiency of the appliance. This combustion efficiency varies from almost 100% for electricity down to around 60% for solid-fuel-fired boilers, and to about 15–20% for the open coal fires which are still being used in most of the older houses in the United Kingdom.

(e) The ancillary cost of having to use one's own appliance such as

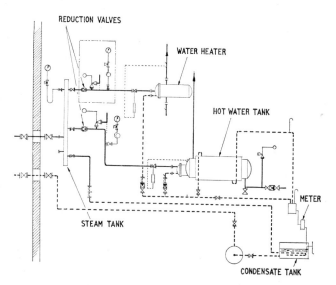

FIG. 10.5. Layout at consumer's end when using steam as a heating medium.

kindling materials, the cost of providing a boiler house fireproof
construction flue and flue lining etc.

In addition to these charges which are borne by the consumer himself, his community must also bear certain charges which are paid for
indirectly by the consumer in the form of higher local taxes, rates,
etc. These are:

(a) The cost of air pollution caused by individual combustion appliances. It has been estimated that district heating of thirty dwellings reduces the degree of air pollution by roughly 1 ton per

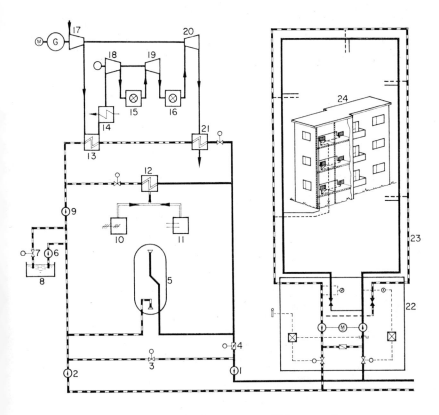

Fig. 10.6. Layout of distribution system at Vahr, near Bremen.
(By courtesy: Stadtwerke Bremen.)

annum, as against individual coal firing using even reasonably efficient small solid-fuel-fired furnaces.

(b) The cost of transporting fuel on public roads, and the collection, transportation and disposal of ashes from individual households.

When district heating is used, the plant at the consumers' premises reduces to the normal network of either hot-air or hot-water heating appliances, together with a number of auxiliaries such as heat exchanger for the supply of consumption water, valves of all types, a heat meter and other smaller items. The total capital cost of such equipment is far below the cost of combustion appliances needed for individual firing. As heat is being supplied from the central source in the form of hot water or steam, building regulations from the point of view of fire resistance can be relaxed considerably. No flue is necessary. The plant at the consumer's end requires virtually no maintenance. Because the

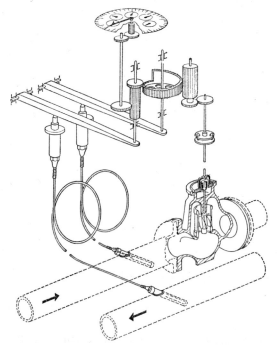

Fig. 10.7. An Aquametro type heat meter.

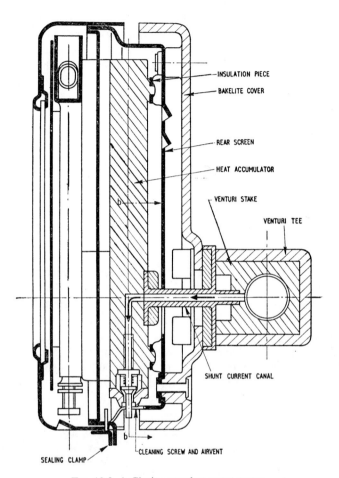

FIG. 10.8. A Clorius type hot-water meter.

siting of the centrales can be carried out with due attention to prevailing winds, etc., and often at some distance from residential areas, smoke pollution is very markedly reduced. In addition, large industrial combustion appliances can be run reasonably smokelessly by fitting centrifugal and electrostatic grit precipitators.

M

Many of the smaller district heating installations operate on direct combustion of fuel. Such schemes can only be defended economically when ground and distribution conditions permit the instalment of a very simple straight-forward and cheap network, and where the fuel supplied is very much cheaper in bulk than it would be if supplied to individual consumers. Usually such schemes have to be subsidised heavily by state or local authorities in the form of cheap interest loans, direct capital grants or in other ways, to make them a viable proposition.

When waste heat, produced by steam or gas turbines is used, its cost is so far below the cost of obtaining heat directly by the burning of prime fuel, that even quite unpromising schemes can be made to pay.

An example of this is the Hannover district heating scheme where a new $12\frac{1}{2}$ mile (22·5 km) network which cost $4·8 million in 1962–5 was installed in a fully built-up city. This system is fed from a central ITOC type steam turbine station.

In this scheme the cost of fuel works out at 6 cents/therm (56 cents/GJ) (1965 figures throughout) which was burned in the boiler installation of the power station. During the operation of the plant it was calculated that when the steam bleeds were being operated, the quantity of extra fuel needed, to bring power losses to zero amounted to 21% of the total heat supplied to the district heating network. In other words, the combustion could be considered to be 10,000/21 = 466% efficient. The fixed cost for fuel thus amounted to 1·26 cents per therm (13·3 cents per GJ). The share of the works costs of producing this heat (capital costs, maintenance charges, overheads, etc.) was calculated at another 2·10 cents per therm (22·2 cents per GJ), giving a total cost of 3·36 cents per therm (35·5 cents per GJ) ex works. An annuity of 10% of the pipeline network, pumping stations, etc., was assumed, which worked out at 6·6 cents per therm (69 cents per GJ). Pumping costs, heat losses, etc., amount to only 0·4 cents per therm (4 cents per GJ) giving a total cost at the consumer's end for the heat of 10·36 cents per therm. ($1·085 per GJ). The heat was sold to the consumers at a variable charge of between 14·5 and 16·5 cents per therm ($1·53 – $1·75 per GJ), which was a price high enough to cover administrative charges and make some profit, but low enough to compete easily with alternative forms of heating.

Relationship of Costs with Degree of Penetration of a District Heating System

District heating can only become economical in any given area provided a fairly high degree of penetration exists. In the case of public housing estates it is not difficult to achieve 100% penetration, as the nature of heating is obviously easily specified by the operating authority. This is obviously one of the reasons why district heating has been found to be such an enormous success in the Soviet Union and other communist countries.

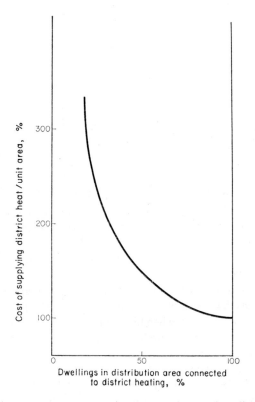

FIG. 10.9. Relationship between unit cost of supplying district heat and percentage area penetration.

When, however, privately owned dwellings are to be supplied, district heating must compete with other forms of heating. It can do so only upon convenience and price. The following figures are given regarding annual costs of supply of district heat per dwelling in Germany:

           20% connection $260·40
           70% connection $108·0
        100% connection $89·00

Obviously, when a district is only 20% connected the cost of district heating cannot compete with other fuels. In consequence the operating company must itself bear the initial losses until the system is sufficiently built out to become economical.

Choice of Medium Used

Two types of media are used for the transmission of heat from the heating/power station to the consumer, namely steam and hot water. The advantages of steam as a medium are the following:

(a) The latent heat of steam is about 965 Btu/lb (2250 kJ/kg) and in consequence the amount of heat carried by unit weight is much higher for steam than for hot water. The sensible heat contained by the condensate, assuming the steam is cooled down to 52°F (11°C), is only 160 Btu/lb (374 kJ/kg), which is around 15·5% of the total heat contained by the steam. In consequence it is often possible to save on condensate return mains. Even if such are fitted their dimensions are quite small and they are thus a good deal cheaper than the return mains needed when hot water is employed as a medium.

(b) Steam is far easier to pump than hot water. In consequence there is a considerable advantage in using steam supply lines rather than hot-water lines, when high-lying districts have to be supplied.

(c) Steam is very much preferred as a medium when industrial consumers have to be catered for. Steam is particularly useful for running air-conditioning plants.

(d) Steam is far easier to meter accurately than hot water. Simple flow meters or condensate meters can be fitted which assess the supply with considerable accuracy.

It should be mentioned that steam as a heat supply medium is particularly popular in the United States because of the relatively low cost of fuel applying there and also because the air-conditioning plants used during the summer are best run by steam. Return mains are rarely fitted, as the small quantity of heat carried does not usually warrant the extra expense. Where they are, careful dosing with hydrazine or the installation of stainless-steel condensate returns are needed. Usually the condensate from steam-heated district-heating schemes is returned not because of the sensible heat contained in it, but to save on water preparation costs.

In Europe hot water as a medium is the most popular.

Its advantages are the following:[36]

(a) Hot water can be obtained as a by-product of power generation at a much lower cost of fuel than steam. For example, when waste heat is produced from a back-pressure turbine operating with a feed of 1310 psia (90 bar) and 950°F (510°C) the reduction in power generation varied between 13·0% and 19·0% if hot water was extracted while if the same amount of heat in the form of steam was extracted, the reduction in power generation amounted to no less than 45·5%. On average the cost of heat per unit when in the form of steam varied between 338% and 228% of the cost of heat in the form of hot water.

(b) Heat can be supplied in the form of hot water far more flexibly than in the form of steam. Once steam conditions are fixed, the only variable in the supply is the actual rate of steam throughput. With hot water it is possible not only to alter the supply rate, but also the sensible heat content of the water by altering the supply temperature.

(c) Although the amount of heat stored by steam when calculated per unit weight is very high, the heat stored calculated per unit volume is not too good. For example, the total heat which can be stored in the form of steam at 80 psig (5·5 bar (g)) and 312°F (150°C) amounts to 265 Btu/ft³ (9·95 MJ/m). Assuming a difference in supply and return line temperature for hot water of 90°F (50°C) the heat stored by water amounts to 5600 Btu/ft³ (210 MJ/m³). Even assuming that steam can be pumped along pipelines at speeds up to 20 times as high as is feasible with hot water, the hot water still has the higher storage capacity, particularly if the temperature difference between flow and return line can be increased, which can easily be done during peak supply periods. In consequence water pipelines can be made smaller and also need not be insulated quite as well as steam lines, thereby saving in cost.

In Denmark, for example, 16 in. (40 cm) steam lines have an insulation cover of $9\frac{1}{2}$ in. (24 cm), while equivalent hot water lines only need $6\frac{1}{4}$ in. (16 cm) insulation cover. 8 in. (20 cm) steam lines have $6\frac{1}{4}$ in. (16 cm) insulation cover while the equivalent 8 in. (20 cm) hot water lines make do with 5 in. (12·5 cm) of insulation cover.

(d) In most district-heating systems there is a gradual build-out of the system, which takes place over a good number of years. When hot water is used as a medium, the heat carried by the system can be adjusted throughout by varying the temperature difference between supply and return line. No such flexibility is possible with steam systems.

Under European conditions of high fuel costs and variable heat requirement, it has been found that the advantages of hot water for district heating are overwhelming. Most of the larger and more recently commissioned district heating systems in Western Europe and in the countries of the Soviet bloc operate with hot water instead of steam. Exceptions are only found when:

(a) a large portion of the consumer circle consists of industry rather than residential premises;

(b) high-lying districts have to be supplied;

(c) steam can be supplied economically from gas turbines.

Types of Piping Systems used for District Heating Supply

Four different piping systems are currently being used for the supply of district heat to the consumer. These are

(a) the single-pipeline system;
(b) the twin-pipeline system;
(c) the three-pipeline system;
(d) the four-pipeline system.

THE SINGLE PIPELINE SYSTEM[34]

For most of the steam pipeline systems in the United States, no return line is envisaged, the condensate being simply discharged to the

Fig. 10.10. Layout of the New York steam system. (By courtesy: Consolidated Edison Inc.)

CONSOLIDATED EDISON CO. OF NEW YORK INC.
STEAM DISTRIBUTION SYSTEM

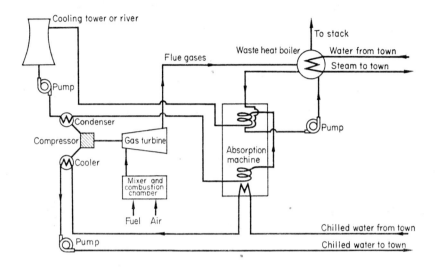

FIG. 10.11. Gas turbines as a source for district heat.

public sewers. This is not an ideal arrangement but under American conditions it is probably the cheapest. In New York steam is passed at a pressure of 125 psig (8·6 bar (g)) through 66½ miles (104 km) of single pipelines with diameters between 4 in. and 24 in. (10–61 cm). Steam is fed into the network at a pressure of 190 psig (15·1 bar (g)) and allowed to find its own level between the source and the remote points of the network.

There are three long steam mains, each with a diameter of 24 in. (61 cm) designed for a supply of 1,000,000 lb (454,000 kg) of steam per hour. The pipes are largely prefabricated sections with prefabricated man-hole assemblies. In 1967 there were some 2500 individual customers, mainly huge apartment blocks, commercial buildings and industrial consumers, who are connected to the distribution mains by 20 miles (32 km) of service pipe, varying from 1 in. to 20 in. in diameter (2·54–50·8 cm). The steam is metered to the consumer using either condensate meters, "shunt-flo" meters or differential pressure meters.[113]

The steam itself is produced in back-pressure steam-turbine plants, or during periods of peak demand, some is produced in boilers owned by the Consolidated Edison Co. or leased by them. After the steam has performed its function to supply space heating, or to drive large air-conditioning plants for the supply of the cooling load of large buildings such as, for example, the Pan-Am complex, the condensed water is discharged directly to the public sewers. As the heat content of the condensate is only around 15% of the total heat content of the steam supplied it is totally uneconomic under New York conditions to supply return lines for the condensate water.

The Soviet Single-pipe System[43]

In the Soviet single-pipeline system, the heating medium is water at a temperature of up to 392°F (200°C). The hot water is obtained as a by-product of power production using very large ITOC turbines. The feedwater for the system is ordinary river water or other natural water, which is first of all purified crudely by filtration, followed by passage through a magnetic field. This serves to change the dielectric nature of dissolved salt ions so that they precipitate out as a loose sludge rather than as a tough scale, as the water is passed in turn through the condenser of the turbine and then through a series of bleed heaters. The precipitated sludge is then filtered off and the hot water is transported through a single pipeline insulated with gas concrete, vermiculite concrete, etc., to the consumer's area. It has been found that it becomes economical to transmit hot water through immense distances when the single-pipeline system is used. Under Soviet conditions the maximum economic pipeline length between the supplying station and the sub-station on the consumer's side is as given in Table 10.2.

TABLE 10.2.

Rated capacity of station	Maximum economic pipeline length	
	miles	(km)
100 MW	60	(96)
200 MW	87	(139)
300 MW	106	(170)
400 MW	127	(203)
500 MW	140	(224)

Once the hot water is at the consumer's substation, it is usually mixed with a certain quantity of additional hot water at the same high temperature, from district boiler houses. The quantity of hot water supplied in this way depends upon the time of the year and the amount of hot

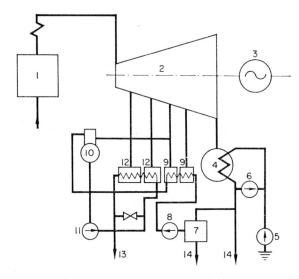

FIG. 10.12. Method of heating water with single pipeline heat supply from thermoelectric plant having non-regulated steam take-offs: 1. boiler, 2. turbine, 3. generator, 4. condenser, 5. circulating pump, 6. recirculating pump, 7. water-treatment plant, 8. first-stage network pump, 9. network low-pressure heat exchanger, 10. network water deaerator, 11. second-stage network pump, 12. network high-pressure heat exchanger, 13. single hot water main, 14. discharge water from condenser and after treatment (for washing and regeneration of agents.)

water needed by the consuming population centre for heating, hot water and industrial purposes. The district boiler houses are usually either oil, gas or coal fired. Water, dosed with lime, is sprayed into the flue gases to extract the sensible heat carried by these and also to remove obnoxious gases such as SO_2, CO_2 and suspended ash particles from them. This water is passed through a magnetic water-treatment

N

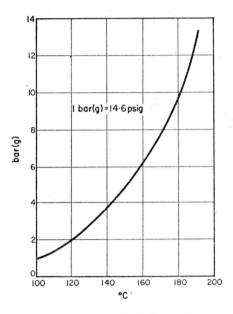

Fig. 10.13. Necessary static pressure in single pipeline to prevent boiling of water in networks.

plant, and the precipitates are filtered off. The water, which has already absorbed sensible and latent heat from the flue gases, is then used as boiler feedwater and added to the water which has been heated at the combined heating/power station. In this way efficiencies of over 90% of the *gross* calorific value of the fuel can be obtained. The high-temperature hot water is bled into the urban-district-heating circuit which circulates as a twin-pipe system to provide heating. However, it is naturally necessary to dispose of a volume of hot water equal to that supplied in the form of high-temperature water from the ITOC station and the district boiler houses. This hot water is used for the following main purposes:

    (a) domestic hot water for cooking, washing and baths;

    (b) municipal hot water used for public baths, swimming pools, hospitals, nurseries and schools;

(c) industrial process water supply for laundries, chemical industries, etc.

A careful balance has always to be made with regard to the quantity of heat required for space heating and the amount of hot water needed for consumption purposes. In general this balance is easier to achieve under climatic conditions which are not too extreme, and in communities where domestic and industrial demand are mixed.

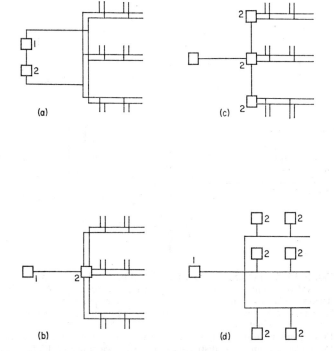

FIG. 10.14. Types of connection to single pipeline system; 1 = central station, 2 = substation.

The advantages claimed for the single pipe system are the following:

(a) *Pipeline costs are reduced very considerably*, due to the fact that no return main is needed, and also that the thermal capacity of water at 392°F (200°C) is very much higher than for water at a temperature just above the boiling point, which is the usual temperature of distribution employed for most district-heating networks. Although single pipelines have to be made from thicker material due to the increased pressure inside the pipelines, and insulation layers have to be thicker due to the high temperatures employed, it is estimated that a given single pipeline only costs roughly two-thirds as much as an equivalent twin pipeline.

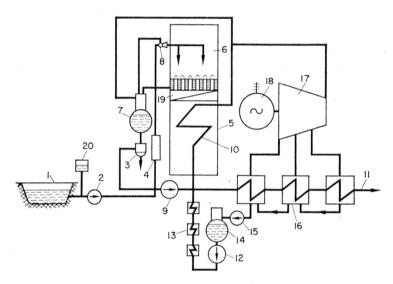

FIG. 10.15. District heating from a combined heat and power station with removal of sulphur and dust from flue gases. 1. Reservoir, 2. pumping station, 3. clarifier, 4. magnetic equipment, 5. boilers, 6. contact chambers, 7. de-aerator, 8. water ejector, 9. district-heating pumps, 10. boiler heating surface, 11. single pipeline district-heating mains, 12. feed pumps, 13. condensate heater using steam from turbine tappings, 14. de-aerator, 15. condensate pump, 16. district-heating system water heater, 17. turbine, 18. generator, 19. air heater, 20. Lime-dosing plant.

(b) *Running costs are reduced* as pipeline corrosion at such high temperatures is quite negligible, both inside and outside the line. If the external insulation should break down at any place, so that ground- or rain-water comes into contact with the pipe, the high temperature of the pipe ensures that the water boils off harmlessly without inducing corrosion on the surface. The low viscosity of the water at the high temperature employed and its comparatively small volume enables savings in pumping costs to be made.

(c) *There are considerable savings in water treatment costs*, as chlorination or other bactericidal treatment of the water becomes unneces-

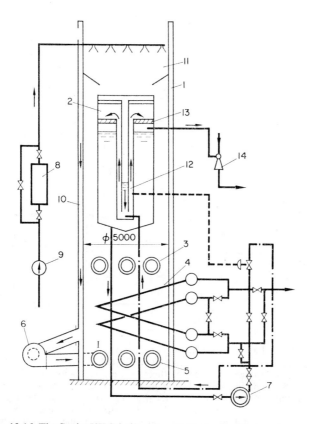

FIG. 10.16. The Soviet VKG boiler plant. 1. Boiler flue, 2. de-aerator tank, 3 upper burners, 4. convective tube bundle. 5. lower burners, 6. individual draught fans for burners. 7. district heating system pump, 8. water treatment plant, 9. cold water pump 10. air ducts to burners, 11. contact chambers, 12. hydraulic lock, 13. distributor, 14. water jet vacuum pump.

sary due to the high circulating temperature of the water. Ordinary river water can be used which is passed through suspension filters followed by magnetic or electromagnetic treatment and de-aeration, which is a very much cheaper process than is usually required for the treatment of normal town's water.

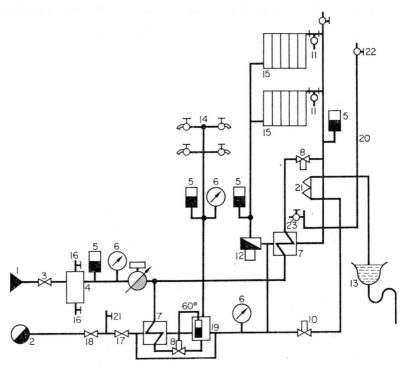

FIG. 10.17. Layout of single-pipeline connections at consumer's end. 1. Single-pipeline district-heating line, 2. cold water (town's water), 3. valve, 4. sludge chamber, 5. thermometer, 6. manometer, 7. water cooler, 8. regulating valve, 9. heat meter, 10. drain discharge valve, 11. thermostat, 12. low head valve, 13. drainage, 14. hot water supply, 15. radiators 16. valves, 17. check valve, 18. valve on water main, 19. bulb containing liquid butane, 20. oil pipe, 21. return line, 22. oil control valve, 23. valve for releasing oil and air.

(d) *It is possible to make use of the waste heat produced in large power stations* because it now becomes economical to transport the hot water to several urban areas from one single station. At the same time, the long distances between power station and urban area which become permissible make it possible to position the power station close to fuel supplies and without detracting from the amenities of the town. The local peak demand heating stations give off virtually no obnoxious fumes due to the operating characteristics using a combination of single-pipe working and magnetic water treatment.

THE TWIN-PIPELINE SYSTEM

The most common form of district heating practiced in Europe uses two mains, a flow main and a return main, and hot water as the heating medium. A twin-pipeline system is also sometimes used with steam, the condensate being returned to the station in a second, very much narrower pipeline. Whenever condensate return is practiced, usually to save on water preparation costs, it is necessary to install de-aeration equipment at the consumer's end otherwise rapid corrosion of the condensate pipeline is almost inevitable.

For normal operation of a twin-pipe system the pipes used are made from mild steel. Provided de-aeration of the circulating water is practiced, either by mechanical means or by addition of hydrazine, and the pH of the water is kept high, corrosion inside the supply and return mains is kept down to a very low level indeed. The flow temperature of the water varies with the time of the year, and the consequent heating demand. The maximum flow temperature is usually about 32°F (20°C) above the boiling point of water. The return temperature is usually around 140°F (60°C).

Two methods of hot water distribution are used:

(a) *Open systems*, in which hot water is being supplied directly from the town's circuit to the consumer, without using a heat exchanger on the consumer's side. Consumption water is provided by using a calorifier, which heats up town's water. Open systems have the advantage of simplicity and lower capital cost, but cannot readily be used for the supply of district heat at the top of tall buildings or for isolated consumers in high-lying areas. Similarly the control of open systems is not as flexible as that of closed systems. Open systems are controlled from the central station, while in the closed systems local control is possible.

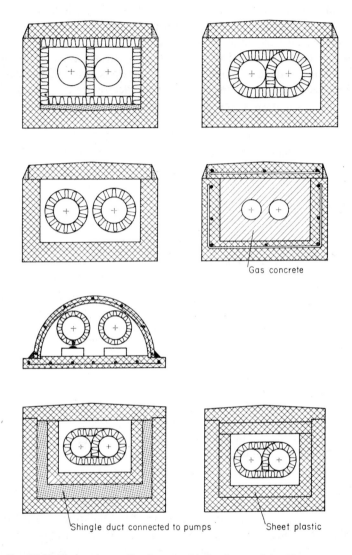

FIG. 10.18. Various types of underground twin-pipe conduits. (By courtesy: Danish Building Research Institute.)

(b) *Closed systems*. In this the supply of hot water and the return line from the station end at a substation. Heat from this primary supply is taken off via heat exchangers to heat up a closed secondary water circuit which has its own pumping and distribution system. Although the extra pumps and heat exchangers naturally cost additional money, the closed system has the advantage that one can have local stand-by boilers to heat the secondary water if the primary heat supply fails. In addition, closed systems are capable of catering for very different supply levels. Closed systems are essential when heat is supplied from a nuclear power station, as they prevent accidental leakage of radioactive materials into the circulating water flow.

Types of Insulated Pipelines Employed[76]

The most important factors which determine the nature of the pipelines to be laid are:

(a) the level of the ground water table;
(b) the nature of the soil and its stability;
(c) the presence of other pipelines in the vicinity and likelihood of future disturbance.

The most common method of all of laying insulated underground pipelines is to employ a concrete conduit and to embed the mild steel pipes in aerated (gas) concrete within this conduit. A rectangular section trench is dug, and the base is lined with *in situ* concrete followed by the casting of a concrete lining against the walls, using light shuttering. Gas concrete blocks are now laid on to the bottom of the concrete conduit and the twin mild steel pipes are positioned on top of them. Ends are butt-welded and at regular intervals expansion units are provided, which may be in the form of simple bends or "Z" connectors, bellow units or ball joints. Depending upon design, fixed points are positioned either at the ends or at the centres of each pipeline length. Access to the pipes is provided at the expansion chambers.

Next a concrete mix containing free lime and suspended aluminium powder is poured into the trench. The aluminium powder reacts chemically with the lime, liberating hydrogen gas, which causes the mix to rise as it sets. The final gas concrete which now embeds the pipes completely has a density of around 25 lb/ft^3 (400 kg/m^3). Once the gas

N*

concrete has set, the top is scraped flat and a precast concrete lid is positioned on top of the conduit, being suitably waterproofed so as to protect the gas concrete and the pipeline from rain water. Yet the connection is quite loose to permit moisture which gets into the gas concrete duct to evaporate readily. The top soil is then replaced.

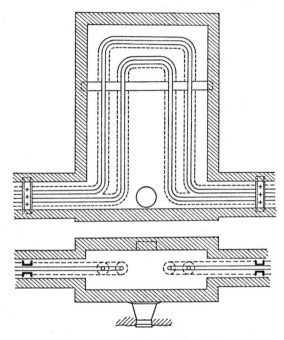

FIG. 10.19. Expansion chamber with U-shaped welded compensators and drainage duct. (By courtesy: the Danish National Institute of Building Research.)

For twin pipelines where each is 12 in. (30·5 cm) in diameter, the width of the conduit is 45 in. (114 cm) and its height is 31 in. (78 cm) with a distance between the pipes of 14 in. (35·5 cm). The heat transfer coefficient for such a pipeline system has been found experimentally to be 0·645 Btu/ft^{-1} h^{-1} °F^{-1} (1·11 Wm^{-1} °C^{-1}). Pipeline construction of this type is cheap and easily carried out, but requires a firm subsoil and the assurance that the ground water table never rises above the level of the sole plate.

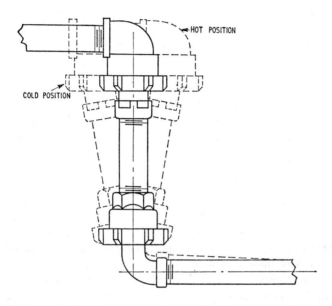

FIG. 10.20. Ball joints as expansion units. (By courtesy: Barrington Aeroquip Inc.)

A system which can be used with firm ground conditions but where just occasionally the ground water table may rise above the sole plate level, uses mineral wool wrapping for the pipes. The conduit design is as before with pipelines supported by means of steel fixed points and sliders, and being wrapped *in situ* with mineral wool. The mineral wool is protected further on the outside by means of either polyethylene or PVC sheeting which is wrapped around. In cases, where flooding may occur more frequently, the conduit is itself protected by being made of twin layers of concrete, the space in between being filled with ballast and connected to a pumping system. Gas concrete protects the surfaces of mild steel against corrosion, provided the gas concrete remains dry. Mineral wool, however, has no such protecting action and it is necessary to protect the steel pipe surfaces before insulating them. This is done by immersing the steel pipes in a chromate bath, followed by coating them with asphalt-impregnated felt.

Mineral wool insulation is also used, when pipes are run through cellar premises, as in the case where district heating mains are run through down-town areas of cities, or where water courses are traversed by tunnels, and district heating mains are led through them.

Prefabricated Mains

When ground conditions are rather more uncertain, prefabricated mains are often employed. In such a case the mild steel pipelines are protected by an external envelope of steel, asbestos cement or precast concrete. Asbestos cement protected pipelines usually carry the pipes in the centre, insulated with mineral wool and foamed polyurethane. Such lines are inexpensive but can only be used where there is no likelihood of the ground water table rising, and also where no traffic pressures occur which are likely to crack the rather brittle asbestos cement. An alternative method of laying pipelines is to wrap them singly with a succession of insulation materials and water exclusion membranes, such as bituminised sheeting, PVC etc. and to lay them directly into the soil. The pipes have to be protected against traffic pressures by placing precast concrete slabs on top. Such pipelines behave well if flooding is only occasional but cannot withstand permanent immersion.

A system of pipeline insulation which can withstand permanent immersion in water is the armoured pipeline, which consists of an inner steel pipe or pair of steel pipes, a layer of insulation and an external protective steel casing, which is spirally welded and protected against corrosion by thick layers of bitumen.

For small-diameter district heating mains a twin corrugated flexible piping system called the "Flexwell" system is used, where the space between the inner and the outer casing is filled with polyurethane foam. Such a district heating "cable" can be laid directly into the marshiest of soil, or even underneath water, needs no expansion units and is completely foolproof in operation. Its disadvantage is the fact that the inner pipe cannot withstand high pressures, which means that it is impossible to pump water at much more than 212°F (100°C) through it. Also the system is only suitable for pipes less than 1½ in. (3·8 cm) in diameter.

Loose-fill Insulation

There are a number of materials on the market which can be used in the form of loose fill to insulate district heating pipelines directly. These materials are usually coal tar products or similar materials which have a strong repulsive action to water. Common trade names for such materials are: Protexulate, Gilsulate, Mannolith, etc. Trenches are dug into the soil, and a layer of the material is spread, usually consolidated with paper sacks. The pipeline is laid on top and the rest of the powder is spread around being finally consolidated by vibration. Practical experience as to the effectivity of such methods has been variable. In many cases such loose fill has proved to be very satisfactory, but in others, cracks have appeared near the expansion joints or elsewhere, permitting moisture to cause rapid corrosion on the pipeline surface. In yet other cases slight soil slips or work on adjacent gas mains, water mains or power cables has caused the powder to be displaced, again producing exposure of the unprotected steel main.

TRIPLE- AND QUADRUPLE-PIPELINE SYSTEMS

Three-pipeline mains are fairly popular in Europe, the most notable example being the district-heating system in West Berlin. Such a system consists of two large-diameter and one small-diameter pipeline. During the winter, when heating demand is large, one of the large-diameter pipes and the small-diameter pipe constitute the flow mains, while the other large-diameter main constitutes the common return. In summer, when there is no heating demand, but hot water is still required for consumption purposes and as process heat for industry, the large-diameter supply main lies idle and the small quantity of hot water still needed is delivered by the narrow third pipeline. It returns via the normal return main, having given up its heat to town's water via calorifiers. Although the system is basically more expensive to install than the more common twin-pipeline system, it has several advantages over the latter.

A smaller-diameter pipeline loses less heat than a large-diameter line, and in consequence the supply of even small quantities of heat to the consumers is economical. The extra flow line also enables supply to be made in a more flexible way during periods of maximum heat demand. During the summer heat supply in conventional twin-pipe systems is often so uneconomical, that it is stopped absolutely. This however, often causes corrosion to occur in pipelines due to the presence of stagnant water. In the three-pipeline system water is always moving, even during the summer, and therefore corrosion is largely prevented.

Four-pipe systems are mainly used where both hot water and refrigerated water is supplied to the consumers, as in combined district heating and district cooling systems.

An example of such a system is the one at Hartford, Connecticut, U.S.A., which supplies steam through a 12-in. (30 cm) pipe and employs a 5-in. (12·7 cm) diameter stainless-steel return line for the condensate. Water is chilled at the plant to 38°F (3·3°C) and is circulated throughout the summer months through insulated steel mains and returns to the station via similar mains, but without insulation. Other such combined heating and cooling systems are to be found at Kennedy Airport, New York, Washington D.C., and in a number of other large European and American complexes. Often such four-pipe systems, which may incorporate hot-water pipes rather than steam pipes as in the Hartford scheme, employ prefabricated conduits which carry the pipelines needed.

Operation of European District-Heating Systems[146]

European district-heating systems are usually very large undertakings and use a number of primary heat sources. Not all these sources are in operation at the same time, because there is a considerable difference in demand during different parts of the day and different periods of the year.

The main primary sources of heat energy for European district heating systems are the following:

(a) Large condensing turbines operating on the ITOC (passout) system.

(b) Back-pressure steam turbines.

(c) Gas turbines, which may be either open cycle or closed cycle.

(d) Refuse incinerators, either alone or coupled with back-pressure turbines.

(e) Nuclear power stations using either back-pressure steam or closed-cycle gas turbines.

(f) Geothermic heat.

(g) Stand-by direct heating plants using a variety of fuels.

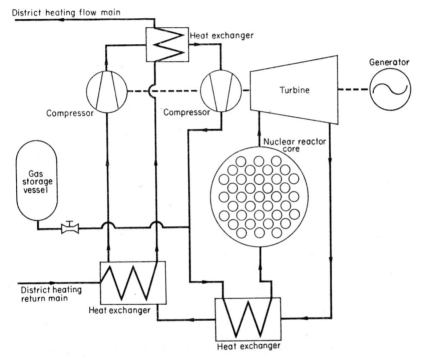

Fig. 10.21. District heating from nuclear power using a closed-cycle gas turbine.

Whenever possible, the heating demand is covered from either steam turbines, gas turbines, or refuse incinerators. Geothermic heat is used in one or two French schemes such as Carrieres sur Seine, where a bore-hole delivers water at approximately 140°F (60°C), but the best known schemes of this type are all found in Iceland, where geothermic heat provides the bulk of energy for both power generation and district heat. All district-heating systems have a number of direct-fired heating stations to cater for peak demand. However, in practice they are used as little as possible, as they provide the heat far more expensively than either the total energy steam and gas turbines, which utilise fuel more effectively, or the refuse incinerators, which obtain their fuel for nothing.

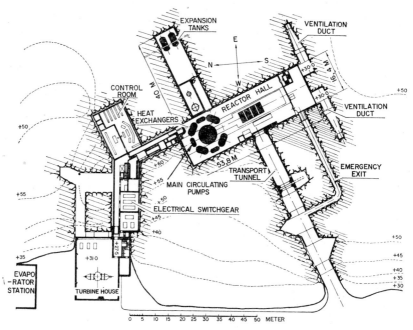

FIG. 10.22. Layout of the Agesta nuclear power station which supplies district heat to the town of Farsta, a suburb of Stockholm, Sweden. (By courtesy: AB Atomenergi.)

Steam Turbines

The ITOC turbines are normal condensing stations, usually positioned close to the city, which are able to supply low pressure steam by side-stream take-offs. Often such stations have been installed on the site of very old low-pressure sets, which have become obsolete. The com-

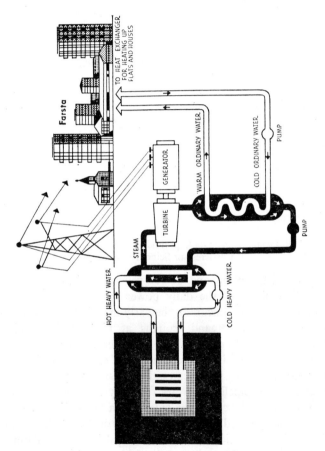

FIG. 10.23. Layout of the underground nuclear power station Agesta. (By courtesy: AB Atomenergi.)

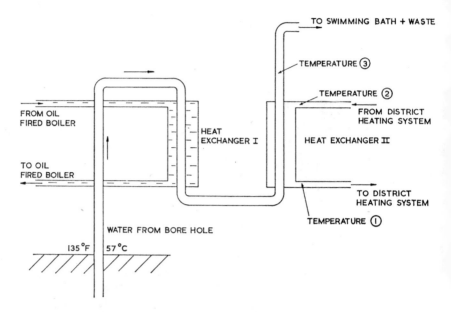

FIG. 10.24. Hot water from an underground source used for district heating
at Carrieres sur Seine, France.

bination of district heating and power generation has an important function in flattening out the daily power requirement curves. The maximum-power demand occurs in the early morning and in the early afternoon, with power-demand troughs at night and at midday. When ITOC turbines are employed, the slack period during the night is employed to bleed off a fairly large quantity of steam, in order to heat up circulating water. This water can either be stored in large accumulators, or even in the pipeline network of the system. When the period of peak power demand occurs, the side-stream take-offs are shut off, and the turbine is operated on pure condensing cycle. The heating load during this period is carried by the heat stored in the circulating hot water during periods of low power demand. As soon as the period of maximum power demand comes to an end, valves controlling the side-stream steam flow are opened once more, and the water is heated up again. Such operation gives a much better utilisation of the power plant than its operation for power production purposes only, even when night current is stored in underfloor heating systems, storage heaters and the like. The reason for this is that night current is produced at an efficiency certainly no higher than day current, yet it has to be sold to the consumer at a cost seldom exceeding 50% of the cost of day current. At the same time, night-current systems lack the flexibility of district heating which uses hot water as the medium.

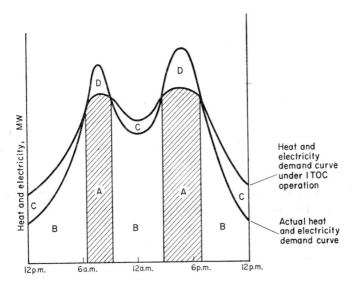

FIG. 10.25. Operating conditions for ITOC turbines.

When operating a district heating system using waste heat from power stations, it is advantageous to use as low a supply temperature as possible, as this reduces the cost of the heat in terms of electric generating capacity lost. Table 10.3 gives the relationship between flow temperature and power losses.

In this context the normal condensing operation envisages a back pressure of 0·6 psia (4·15 kNm⁻²), which corresponds to a temperature of 86°F (30°C).

In some cases hot water obtained from ITOC turbines can be made use of twice. The hot water is first of all circulated through standard radiator systems at its normal circulating temperature of approximately

TABLE 10.3

Back pressure		Temperature		% loss of power generation at a steam-supply temperature of 1200°F (650°C) and 2200 psia (51·5 bar) pressure
psia	(bar)	°F	°C	
7·35	0·5	185	85	20
14·7	1·0	212	100	27
29·4	2·0	250	121	34
44·0	3·0	273	134	39
58·6	4·0	291	144	42
73·2	5·0	306	152	44

176°F (80°C) and exits from such systems at about 122°F (50°C). In this form the hot water can be used for underfloor-heating systems using piping networks cast into concrete flooring slabs. Such heating systems are expensive, but as they are able to use water which is at a temperature which is too low for most other useful purposes, a low tariff is often charged for the heat supplied.

Table 10.4 gives the cost of fuel per unit heat as a percentage of producing the heat directly employing a boiler plant with an efficiency of 85%.

TABLE 10.4

Hot water				
194°F	(90°C) flow	158°F	(70°C) return	20·5%
230°F	(110°C) flow	158°F	(70°C) return,	25·6%
266°F	(130°C) flow	158°F	(70°C) return	30·6%
Steam				
88 psia (6 bar)				69·8%

These figures indicate the marked difference in fuel costs between ITOC turbines which produce hot water and ITOC turbines which produce steam as the heat exchange medium.

Gas Turbines in District Heating Practice[102]

As the exhaust gases of gas turbines are at a very much higher temperature than the exhaust steam of a steam turbine, there is not quite

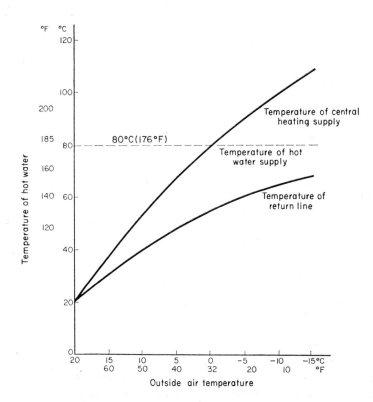

Fig. 10.26. Normal send-out and return temperatures of hot water as a function of the external air temperature.

the same drastic lowering in the power output of the turbine if heat is extracted at a somewhat higher temperature. In many cases, however, the waste gases from gas turbines are used to run steam generators, which themselves are used for current-generation purposes, in that they drive low-pressure steam turbines. Under such circumstances, however, their efficiency falls considerably if heat is extracted at anything but the minimum practicable value.

On the other hand, where a gas turbine is operated without waste-heat generation, its very high flue gas temperature in contrast to the low condensing side temperature of a steam turbine means that heat wastage is a good deal higher than with steam turbines.

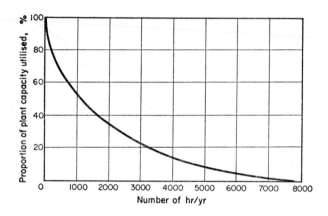

Fig. 10.27. Graph plotting hours of use against percentage plant capacity with most European district heating systems.

TYPICAL GERMAN DISTRICT HEATING PLANTS[7, 22, 38, 152-4]

At Sendling, near Munich, Germany, a district heating/power station with open cycle gas turbines is being used. If power production only is required, air at 88 psig (6 bar (g)) is first heated by the turbine exhaust gases which leave the turbine at 788°F (420°C). After exiting from the heat exchangers, these turbine flue gases are discharged at a temperature of 532°F (278°C) up the chimney.

If hot water is to be produced this can be done in various stages. First of all it is possible to pass the flue gases after exiting from the heat exchanger, into the hot-water generators. When the external temperature is 59°F (15°C) the power capacity of the plant is equal to 25 MW and the heating capacity 126 × 10⁶ Btu/hr (135 GJ/hr). If an increased heating demand exists, the heat exchangers are short-circuited so that the incoming air is no longer pre-heated by the flue gases. This increases the heating capacity of the plant to 220 × 10⁶ Btu/hr (230 GJ/hr). Additional heating capacity is also provided in the plant in the form of direct oil burners, able to raise the heating capacity of the plant to 280 × 10⁶ Btu/hr (295 GJ/hr). As can be seen the initial take-off of heat has no effect whatever upon the current generating efficiency of the gas turbine, although the second stage, when the heat exchanger is no longer used for preheating the external air but for district-heating purposes, does obviously reduce the efficiency of the gas turbine. For this reason, the heat exchanger is only disconnected during periods of low power demand, to store heat in the circulating hot water against the time when there is a peak demand of both power and hot water, Turbines similar to the Sendling one are operated in Germany at Bremen-Vahr[21] and at Braunschweig.

The Oberhausen Station

The Oberhausen station differs from the other ones mentioned, in that a closed-cycle gas turbine is being employed. While the power/ useful heat supplied ratio for steam back-pressure turbines is a maximum of about 100 kWh/10⁶ Btu (95 KWh/GJ), the figure rises to 110 kWh/10⁶ Btu (107 kWh/GJ) with open-cycle gas turbines and to 137 kWh/10⁶ Btu (130 kWh/GJ) with closed-cycle gas turbines.

In the Oberhausen station, the power output is a net quantity of 12·5 MW and under normal circumstances 48 × 10⁶ Btu/hr (50 GJ/hr) of heat are supplied to the district heating network. If the entry temperature to the compressor is raised, the heat supplied can be increased to 96 × 10⁶ Btu/hr (100 GJ/hr), but obviously at the cost of some power capacity. Again, this kind of operation is carried out at night when both heat demand and power demand are low, and the excess heat is stored in the form of hot water.

The heat requirement of the Oberhausen station is given as 12,120 Btu/kWh (12,700 kJ/kWh) with a compressor inlet temperature of 86°F (30°C) and 14,000 Btu/kWh (14,700 kJ/kWh) when the compressor inlet temperature is 122°F (50°C). Yet this slight difference in the overall efficiency of power generation produces an extra output of 48 × 10⁶ Btu/hr (50 GJ/hr) of heat. One of the characteristics of district-heating operation with closed-cycle gas turbines as against steam turbines is that the return temperature of the district-heating water considerably affects the efficiency of operation of the gas turbine. although its effect in the case of steam turbines is negligible. For this reason, district-heating systems using closed-cycle gas turbines should return the water at as low a temperature as possible. The normal flow and return temperatures of a district-heating system using steam turbines is of the order of 194°F (90°C) flow and 140°F (60°C) return. When closed-cycle gas turbines are used as a heating source it is advantageous to use instead 230°F (110°C) flow temperatures and 104°F (40°C) return temperatures.

The Mannheim-North District-heating Station with Refuse Incineration

This station is operated jointly by the oil refinery Mannheim GmbH and the municipal authority of the town of Mannheim, Germany. Its main functions are to supply power and process heat to the refinery, and district heating to the town of Mannheim, as well as acting as the municipal garbage-disposal unit for the town of Mannheim and its surrounding areas.

The plant consists of seven boilers with a total capacity of 448 tons of steam per hour, capable of being fired by oil or a combination of oil and garbage. Seven different turbosets are used, of which four are back-pressure turbines to provide low-pressure steam at pressures between 290 psig and 37 psig (20–2·5 bar (g)), while the remaining three are pass-out turbines. The supply temperature of the steam from the refuse incineration plant is 2000 psig (136 bar (g)) and 975°F (525°C). The total capacity of all the different turbines together is equal to 81 MW, and the maximum amount of heat which can be given off in the form of low-pressure steam and hot water is given as approximately 600 × 10⁶ Btu/hr (630 GJ/hr).

The refuse burned in the garbage incineration part of the plant is estimated to amount to about 85,000 tons of domestic garbage per annum and about 60,000 tons of industrial wastes. It is estimated that by 1975 the total quantity of garbage to be burned each year will be 220,000 tons, and an expansion of the plant to cater for such quantities is planned. Domestic refuse has a calorific value of 2260 Btu/lb (5200 kJ/kg) in summer and 1630 Btu/lb (3700 kJ/kg) during winter. As industrial waste materials have a higher calorific value the average heat content of the refuse has been found to amount to 2700 Btu/lb (6300 kJ/kg). When the garbage has a lower calorific value than about

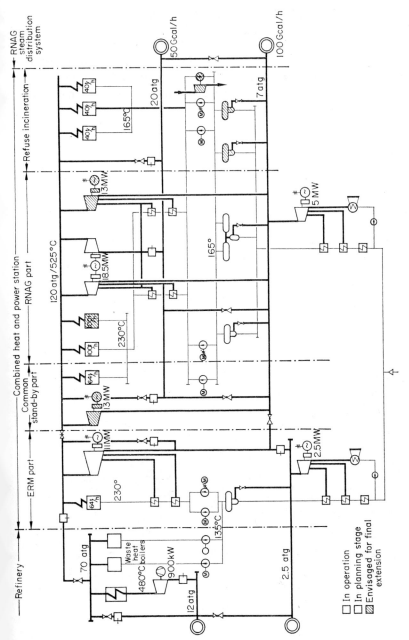

Fig. 10.28. Layout of Mannheim-Nord heat and power station. (By courtesy: Stadtwerke Mannheim.)

2050 Btu/lb (4800 kJ/kg) extra oil is added in order to keep the combustion temperature sufficiently high. At a calorific value of 1630 Btu/lb (3700 kJ/kg) some 1000 lb (450 kg) of oil are added per hour for a garbage throughput of 18 tons/hr. The Mannheim refuse incinerator uses a standard chain grate and reduces the volume of the feed refuse to about 10% of its original, giving a dense and sterile slack which can be used as hardcore for building purposes.

CHAPTER 11

EXISTING TOTAL ENERGY SCHEMES IN NORTH AMERICA

BECAUSE of special circumstances involving climatic conditions, difficulties of traditional power transmission, as well as the highly competitive nature of prime movers and other small-scale equipment produced in the United States, total energy has already made a considerable break-through there. It can be considered an expanding industry with very considerable potential.[141] The following are analyses of schemes in operation at the time of writing. With some 500 schemes operating satisfactorily by 1967, and an average growth rate of about 50% per annum, the schemes described here are only a very small number of an enormous field. They were selected to give a balanced picture of total energy in North America, but one of the criteria of selection was naturally the ready availability of information to the author.

A. TWO SCHEMES OPERATED BY THE BROOKLYN UNION GAS CO. OF NEW YORK[24, 42]

The Brooklyn Union Gas Co. is operating two total energy schemes, the Rochdale Village scheme, which serves twenty 14-storey apartment blocks containing 5840 dwelling units and two shopping centres with a total floor area of 300,000 ft² (28,000 m²), and the smaller Warbasse housing scheme in Coney Island, containing 2580 co-operative dwelling units and a 20,000 ft² (1870 m²) shopping centre. Both depend upon gas-fired high-pressure boilers, which supply 650 psig (44·5 bar (g)) steam at 650°F (343°C) to Westinghouse turbo-generators. The back-pressure steam, which is at 20 psig (1·37 bar (g)), is then used in summer for operating Trane absorption-type chillers, and in winter for the supply of circulating hot water to be used for heating. In addition the steam is used in heat exchangers all the year round to provide hot water for consumption purposes.

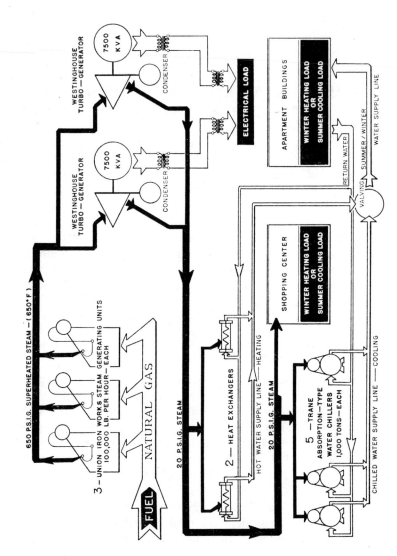

Fig. 11.1. Heat flow system, Warbasse houses. (By courtesy: Brooklyn Union Gas Co.)

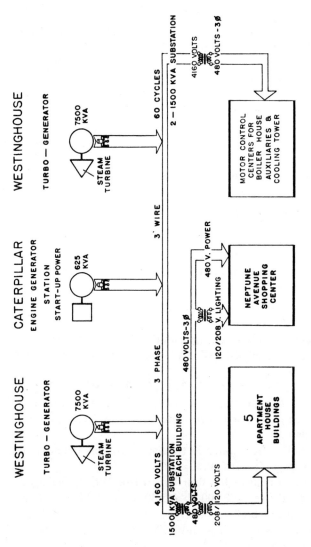

Fig. 11.2. Electrical system, Warbasse houses. (By courtesy: Brooklyn Union Gas Co.)

The Rochdale Village Scheme

The scheme comprises an area of 170 acres (69 ha.) which used to be occupied by the Jamaica race track in the suburb of Queens in New York. The entire housing complex is completely independent of grid electric current and is, in fact, not even connected to the grid system. The only fuels used are natural gas and some No. 6 grade oil for stand-by purposes.

All electric power is generated on site using two steam turbo generators, each with a capacity of 7500 kVA and two diesel gas engines each with a capacity of 3750 kVA. A total of 43,600,000 kWh is produced annually. The blocks of apartments are heated by a circulating hot-water system supplied through converters by the steam extracted at low pressure from the steam turbines. Air conditioning requires a maximum cooling capacity of 12,000 tons. The absorption chillers utilise the low-pressure steam extracted from the steam turbines which drive the electric generators. All the piping and the 25,000 fan coil units within the blocks are designed to serve the dual purposes of heating and cooling.

In addition there are heat exchangers used for the supply of domestic hot water.

Plant equipment

The Rochdale Village scheme uses the following plant:
1. Twenty No. 20,000 gallon (75 m³) oil tanks for the storage of Grade 6 oil.
2. Two Roots Connersville 270,000 ft³/hr (9500 m³) gas meters, to deal with the main gas supply which comes in through 16 in. (40·5 cm) pipes and is regulated down to 7 psig (0·5 bar (g)) at the plant.
3. The boiler feed water is treated at the plant and pumped in at 850 psig (58 bar (g)).
4. The water is heated in four Union Iron Works packaged boilers able to deliver 100,000 lb (45,400 kg) of high-pressure steam per hour. One of the boilers is on permanent stand-by.
5. There are two Westinghouse 7500 kVA 8 PF 4160 V 60 cps steam turbine generators 40% condensing autoextraction at 20 psig (1·37 bar (g)) employing 20 lb/kW (9·09 kg/kW) at full extraction.

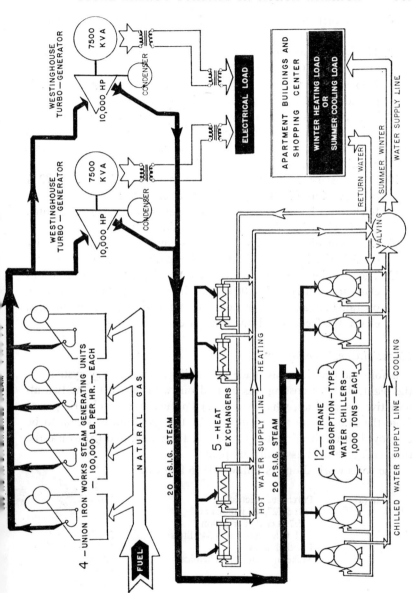

FIG. 11.3. Heat flow system, Rochdale Village. (By courtesy: Brooklyn Union Gas Co.)

6. Two Worthington Dual diesels 450 rpm, 3750 kVA able to use diesel oil or gas at 30 psig (2·06 bar (g)) pressure.
7. The heating system uses five exchangers to circulate hot water at 175°F (80°C) to the buildings.
8. Domestic hot water employs 80 psig (5·5 bar (g)) steam which is passed to each building where it feeds converters.
9. The cooling is carried out with twelve Trane 1000-ton absorption units, using a single shell and requiring less than 20 lb (8·08 kg) of steam per ton of cooling capacity. It is claimed that this constitutes the world's largest refrigeration installation.
10. Two Foster-Wheeler cooling towers measuring 38 × 48 × 72 ft (11·6 × 14·6 × 21·9 m) with three cells each are provided. Each tower has a capacity of 20,000 gallons (90·9 m³) per minute. One is winterised for turbine condensing steam.
11. One Worthington reciprocating gas compressor with a capacity of 65 ft³ (1·84 m³) per minute at 30 psig (2·06 bar (g)) is provided.
12. The switchgear comprises sixteen Westinghouse indoor metal-clad drawout-type 250,000 kVA interrupting duty electrically operated breakers, of which four serve the generator circuits, eleven the feeders and one is a spare.

Financial Considerations

Before the decision was made to employ a total energy system for the plant, detailed costing was carried out with regard to the two alternative possibilities, which were: (a) To purchase the electric power from the grid system and to use oil for the provision of steam to be employed in the heating and cooling of the estate, and (b) to use the total energy system as finally adopted.

The costs worked out as follows (1966 figures):

		$
Plan (a)	Purchased electricity:	810,742
	Oil: 5,727,000 gallons at	
	5·793 cents per gallon	
	(1 U.S. gallon = 4·546 litres)	331,765
	Fixed charges	528,716
	Make-up water and chemicals	22,302
		$1,693,525

Plan (b)	Gas: 1,188,244 thousand ft³ at 34·53 cents per thousand ft³	$
	(1000 ft³ = 28·32 m³)	410,300
	Oil: 855,180 gallons at 5·793 cents/gal.	49,540
	Electric generator: labour	50,000
	Electric generator: maintenance	32,000
	Mixed-up water and chemicals	27,292
	Fixed charges	750,984

Total $1,320,116

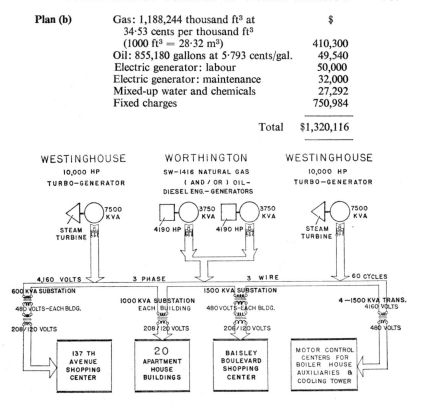

FIG. 11.4. Electrical system, Rochdale Village. (By courtesy: Brooklyn Union Gas Co.)

The saving in costs of no less than 337,409 dollars per annum was a strong inducement to go over to total energy. It should be mentioned that annual charges of 7·1% for interest, taxes and insurance are assumed in the calculations, and that the plant is amortized over a period of 30 years.

It was found during the operation of the plant that the average hourly use of gas amounted to 149,000 ft³ (4230 m³) while the maximum hourly use was 443,000 ft³ (12,600 m³).

Depending upon the season of the year, the total utilisation of energy varied between 60 and 70%.

o

B. REGENCY SQUARE, JACKSONVILLE, FLORIDA[39]

The largest total energy plant in south-east U.S.A. was installed in this 712,000 ft² (66,000 m²) shopping centre. The entire power, heating and cooling requirements of this complex were fulfilled by nine G398 Caterpillar natural-gas engines, each of which was coupled to a 450-kW electric set, and one 750 brake horsepower 567-kW Caterpillar natural-gas engine was used to drive a 650-ton centrifugal air-conditioning compressor. The waste heat of the engines is recovered by AMF Beaird Inc. Maxim Thermoflash heat recovery equipment. Except for the natural-gas-pipeline, the Regency square complex, which also has

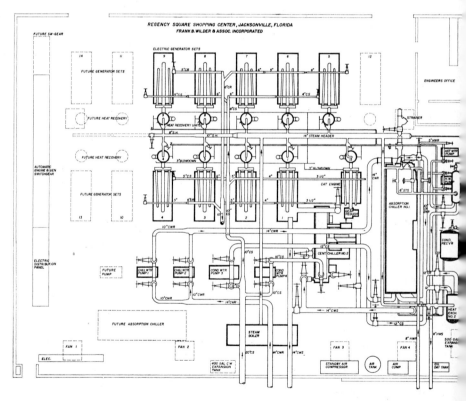

Fig. 11.5. Layout of Regency Square Total Energy Scheme.

its own sewage water-treatment plant and water supply, is completely self-contained and uses no mains electricity. Of the nine sets eight are usually required to supply peak-power needs during the day with one unit as stand-by. During off-peak hours and at night, only three sets are needed. The average day-time loading is 3200 kW which rises to 3600 kW during the peak period between 7.00 p.m. and 9.30 p.m. The late-night demand is only 900 kW. Five of the nine sets are the base load units and are started manually. Four of the generator sets are fully automatic and are programmed as automatic load-sensing units. To ensure that all the generators share the load equally, each of the electric sets has a Woodward EG 3C electronic load-sensing and sharing governor. These governors sense a load change before it reaches the generator and conditions in this way the engine governor actuator for a surge in load. Should an unexpected load change require additional power in excess of that supplied at the time, three breakers drop non-essential load in sequence. Each of these breakers is dimensioned for the capacity of one generator set. During normal operation, one of these breakers opens and stays open until a further generator has been started automatically. As soon as this is delivering, the breaker automatically closes again. Similarly, if one of the generators is out of action due to malfunctioning, the non-essential load breaker opens until another generator has been started to replace it. The usual time required for this is about 30 seconds.

Power is distributed throughout the centre at 480 V. Transformers are provided at the individual locations to step down the voltage to the one required.

Heat recovery

The heat is recovered from the ebullient cooled gas engines by means of the Beaird-Maxim TRP 25 Thermoflash heat package units, which consist of a heat-recovery silencer and a vertical steam separator with longitudinal finned tubes and surrounding shroud tubes to provide a high heat recovery for the exhaust from the engines. The steam separator section is of a vertical type and handles the steam/water flow from both the heat-recovery boiler and engine jacket. The steam/water mixture enters the recovery unit at 250°F (121°C) and strikes an impact plate which causes initial separation. The steam then travels

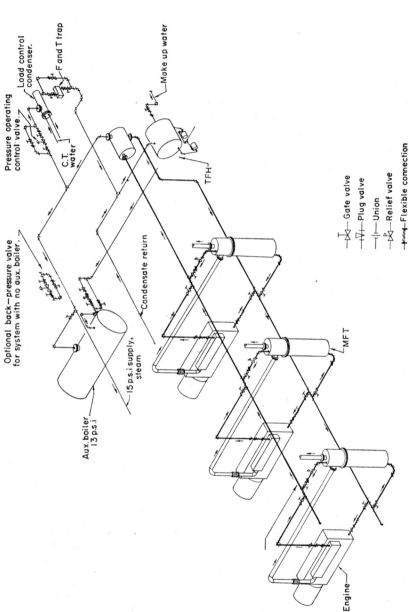

F and T trap

Load control condenser.

Pressure operating control valve

C.T. water

Make up water

Optional back-pressure valve for system with no aux. boiler.

Condensate return

15 p.s.i supply steam

Aux. boiler 13 p.s.i

TFH

MFT

Engine

—|◁— Gate valve
—|▽— Plug valve
—||— Union
—|◁— Relief valve
≻≺ Flexible connection
—◁— Motorized valve

Fig. 11.6 A forced circulation heat recovery unit. (By courtesy: AMF

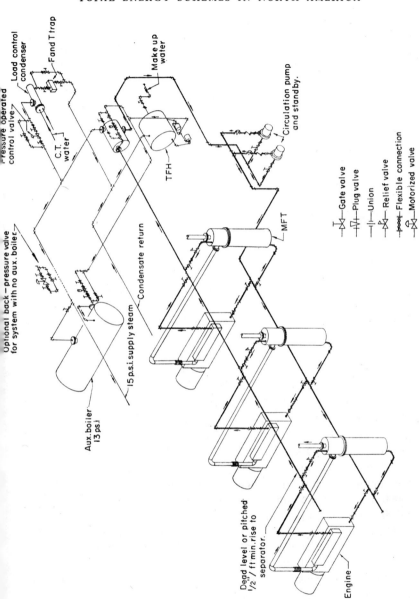

Pressure operated control valve

Load control condenser

F and T trap

Make up water

C.T. water

Circulation pump and standby.

TFH

Optional back—pressure valve for system with no aux. boiler

MFT

Condensate return

15 p.s.i. supply steam

Aux. boiler 13 p.s.i

Dead level or pitched ½"/ft min. rise to separator.

Engine

⊢▷⊣ Gate valve
⊢▽⊣ Plug valve
⊣∥⊢ Union
⊣△ Relief valve
⊨ Flexible connection
⊢⊗⊣ Motorized valve

Fig. 11.7. Natural circulation heat recovery system. (By courtesy. AMF Beaird Inc.)

through a series of baffles which remove all entrained water, which is then returned to the engine. The engine exhaust gas enters into the lower chamber, the shroud tubes and finally over the fins where the heat is removed. After this the gas passes to the atmosphere. This system also serves to silence the exhaust noise of the engines. The average quantity of heat recovered per engine is 2,432,000 Btu/hr (2·54 GJ/hr) at full load in the form of 2000 lb (908 kg) of steam at 12 psig (0·82 bar (g)).

A common steam header is used to feed the steam into a 16 HA 100 Carrier 1064-ton absorption chilling unit. A four-pipe distribution system is used with 14 in. (35·6 cm) chilled-water lines and 8 in. (20·2 cm) hot-water lines. In addition the tenth gas engine drives a 650-ton 17 CA 840 Carrier centrifugal compressor unit, which is employed for peak period supply. Even the gas engine driving this plant has ebullient cooling and exhaust heat extraction. Provision is made in the plant for future expansion to permit the installation of five more G 398 TA electric sets plus one extra absorption chiller. If there should be an interruption of natural gas, all engines can be switched over to liquefied gas. There is a 30,000-gallon (137 m³) tank in the utility area of the complex, which is adequate for five full days of operation.

C. THE PARK PLAZA SHOPPING CENTRE, LITTLE ROCK ARKANSAS[55, 55, 138]

Park Plaza is on a 24-acre (9·8 ha.) site and consists of a twin-storey construction with a total floor space of 240,000 ft² (22,000 m²). Peak-power demand is calculated at the rate of 4 W/ft² floor area (43 W/m²) amounting to 1150 kW in all. The load factor on the plant, peak demand to usage, is approximately 43%. It was also calculated that during the summer, steam requirements for cooling amount to 11,000 lb/hr (5000 kg/hr), while during the winter, heating would use 7000 lb (3200 kg) of steam per hour.

The installation consists of one Ruston-Hornsby 800 kW gas turbine and two Waukesha reciprocating natural gas engines each with an approximate capacity of 400 kW.

When fully loaded, the turbine-driven generator and waste-heat boiler give the following results:

Electric power: 14·5%
Steam to building: 47·25%
Heat losses, mainly as flue gases: 38·25%
Overall thermal efficiency: 61·75%

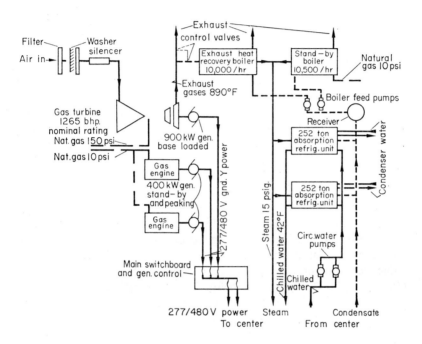

FIG. 11.8. Layout of Park Plaza Utility Center.

The flow diagram Fig. 11.8 shows the use of the gas turbine with exhaust-heat recovery. Inlet air is washed, filtered and passes through a silencer before reaching the compressor of the turbine. The natural gas is injected into the combustion chamber with the compressed air, fired, and passed through the machine to the exhaust. No silencer was required as the exhaust-heat recovery boiler provided adequate attenuation. Two stainless-steel butterfly valves, one in the main exhaust line and one in the by-pass of the boiler, are positioned automatically to provide 15 psig (1·03 bar (g)) steam pressure on the exhaust-heat-recovery boiler. Steam is passed from the exhaust-heat-recovery boiler and the stand-by boiler in parallel to the steam header. It is used either for heating in winter or, in summer, for employment in the two absorption refrigeration units.

The services furnished by this total energy plant are as follows:

(a) *Electric Power* is supplied at 277/480 V and individual transformers are used to provide 120/208 V power as needed. Fluorescent lighting is, however, operated directly by the 277-V supply and external areas use mercury vapour lamps at 440 V.

(b) *Heating and utility steam.* Steam from the central plant is supplied throughout the complex at a pressure of 10 psig (0·7 bar (g)).

(c) *Chilled water* is led throughout the building from the two 252 ton Carrier absorption refrigeration units of the complex. Further equipment is a 10,500 lb (4800 kg) per hour Erie City direct-fired boiler at 15 psig (1·03 bar (g)), which serves as an additional or alternative source of steam to the exhaust-heat boiler.

The excess cost of the plant over a system using purchased electricity was found to be about $200,000. This sum included all extra outgoings including space utilisation, lighting fixtures, plant, etc. For a total of 3693 MW produced over the year, the system uses 138,479 thousand cubic feet of natural gas at an average cost of 28·3 cents per 1000 ft³ (1000 ft³ = 28·32 m³). During its first year of operation, the gas turbine was on line for 8117 hours, and at one time the load upon it was 900 kW, which was catered for without trouble.

D. THE GARRETT AIRRESEARCH TOTAL ENERGY PACKAGE[66]

These provide the total power requirements for an office building, manufacturing plant, shopping centre or other industrial and commercial structures without the need for electric utility connections. The system employs a model 831 natural-gas-fired gas turbine which has a nominal rating of 400 shaft horsepower (298 kW) with an output drive pad speed of 8400 rpm. The engine weighs, complete with speed-reducing gearbox, 775 lb (350 kg) and measures 58 × 38 × 31 in. (1·47 × 0·97 × 0·79 m). It is fed by natural gas at a pressure of between 110 and 130 psig (7·5–8·9 bar (*g*)). The rotating group is a two-stage centrifugal compressor employing single-entry impellers mounted on a common shaft with a three-stage axial flow turbine.

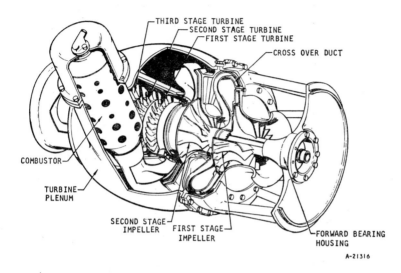

FIG. 11.9. Cutaway of typical Garrett-AirResearch Model 831–53 Power section.

One exhaust-heat-recovery boiler accommodates the maximum exhaust flow of the gas turbines and incorporates supplementary firing or exhaust afterburning provisions as required to achieve specific steam demands in excess of the rated capacity. The boiler is able to supply 2400 lb (1080 kg) steam per hour at a pressure of 15 psig (1·03 bar (*g*)) without requiring any supplementary heating.

The electrical output may be either 420-cycle power, standard (U.S.) 60-cycle power or a combination of both. A single module furnishes approximately 250 kW of electrical power. Any requirements in excess of this are provided by multiple-unit installation.

Operation of system

The typical total energy package marketed by the firm consists of

O*

two natural-gas-driven gas turbine sets either of which can provide the entire rated output of the system. There is also an exhaust heat recovery boiler and a condensate return and feedwater system for the boiler. Accessory equipment comprises batteries, a starter generator battery charging system, a lubricating oil system, engine intake air sound attenuators, intake air coolers, exhaust check valves, control and protection switchgear cubicles, instruments, switches and indicating lights necessary for starting, manual control and surveillance of the system.

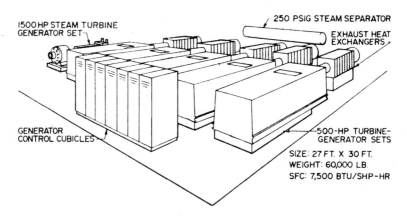

FIG. 11.10. Typical turbopower plant consisting of five gas-turbines and one steam turbine. (By courtesy: Garrett-AirResearch).

One of the gas-turbine-driven generators, operating singly, produces primary electrical power; 100% stand-by power capability is provided by the remaining set. In multiple installations there is, however, no such 100% stand-by capability. The gas-turbine engines are started by standard 24–30 V d.c. electric-starter generators in response to a manual signal, or automatically in multiple unit installations in response to system load. The engine fuel controls are designed for natural gas at a minimum pressure of 110 psig (7·5 bar (g)). Turbine exhaust gases are directed from the turbines through exhaust transitions to a common exhaust manifold and thence through the heat-recovery boiler. Single flapper check-valves in each exhaust transition isolate the stand-by turbine from the exhaust system. Matching the system steam output to the building steam demand is accomplished by regulating the boiler heat input. When turbine exhaust-gas heat content exceeds requirements, a portion of the exhaust is by-passed around the boiler to a discharge stack. Conversely when exhaust heat is insufficient, the turbine exhaust-heat content is raised to the required level by burning additional fuel in the exhaust stream or by firing an auxiliary burner in the boiler. These functions are accomplished automatically within the boiler by sensing steam pressure at the boiler discharge. The balance between steam load, steam-generating capabilities and electric load is accomplished automatically by circulating chilled water through cooling coils. These are installed in the intake ducts to cool the turbines compressor intake air. Boiler feedwater is pumped at 35 psig (2·4 bar (g)) from a 200°F (93°C) hot-well which collects return condensate from the building steam system plus treated make-up water. Boiler exhaust gas is discharged at a temperature of approximately 350°F (177°C).

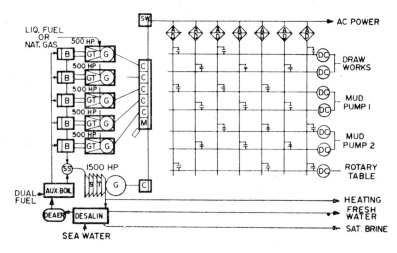

FIG. 11.11. Turbine power plant layout for a 4000 hp (3000 kW) drilling rig. (By courtesy: Garrett-AirResearch.)

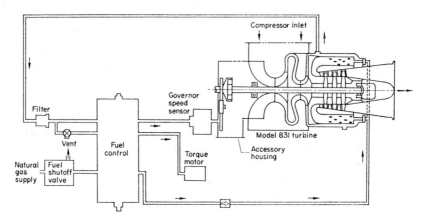

FIG. 11.12. Fuel and air flow schematic diagram. (By courtesy: Garrett-AirResearch.)

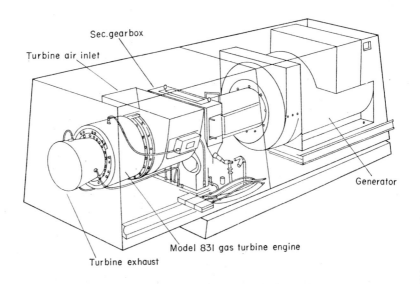

FIG. 11.13. Garrett-AirResearch turbogenerator.

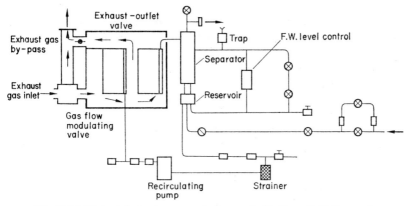

FIG. 11.14. Water tube heat-recovery boiler used with Garrett-AirResearch outfit.

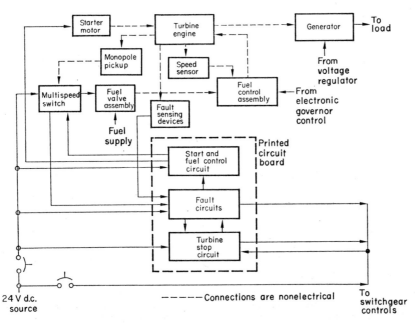

FIG. 11.15. Turbine generator set block diagram. (By courtesy: Garrett-AirResearch.)

Operating controls, protection equipment, all necessary switches, instruments, etc., are housed in two individual metal-clad cubicles. In general a basic system of two turbo-generator sets and auxiliary equipment needs a space 35 × 25 ft and 10 ft high (10·5 × 7·6 × 3m).

The system can be co-ordinated with an absorption cooling aggregate operated by the low-pressure steam of the exhaust-heat boiler. The capacity available with a single aggregate is 120 tons of cooling without requiring supplementary boiler firing.

The AirResearch total energy packages have been installed in various locations in the United States. Up to July 1968 twenty-two systems have been installed including:

Eight offices
Six service centres
Three computer centres
Two apartment blocks

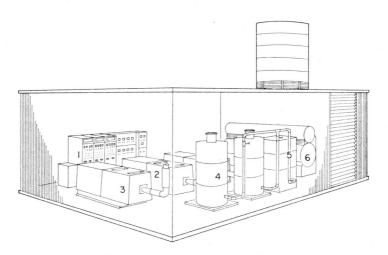

FIG. 11.16. Artist's drawing of an energy system recently installed in Los Angeles; 1 = control cubicles, 2 = turbogenerator modules, 3 = standby turbogenerator module, 4 = heat recovery boilers, 5 = steam separator, 6 = absorption unit.

Two industrial plants
One school
Three systems are also being installed on off-shore petroleum drilling rigs.

E. HILLCREST JUNIOR HIGH SCHOOL, EDMONTON, ALBERTA, CANADA[114, 127, 158]

This school has a total floor area of 67,447 ft² (6400 m²) and is supplied with power, heating and cooling by a total energy system using standard Caterpillar G 739 turbo-charged and aftercooled V-8 gas engines. These have a compression ratio of 10:1, 6·25 in. (15·8 cm) bore, 8 in. (20·3 cm) stroke and a displacement of 1964 in.³ (32·1 litres). The engine develops a maximum pressure of 143 psig (9·8 bar (g)) and 445 brake horse power (333 kW) at 1200 rpm 2500 ft (760 m) altitude with an ambient temperature of 90°F (32°C). Each of the two prime movers is connected to a revolving field a.c. Tamper generator, rated at 3·75 kVA, 300 kW, 1200 rpm, 277/480 V producing 452 A per terminal and operating at 60 cycles. The generator is capable of being overloaded by up to 10% for 1 hour. In practice, only one set is used at the time, the other acting as a 100% stand-by set.

Waste heat utilisation

The operation of the waste heat utilisation system can be followed from Fig. 11.18. The internal combustion engine (1) fuelled by natural gas provides shaft power to turn the generator (2) which in its turn produces electricity. Heat is rejected through the engine jacket water system (3) and in the form of exhaust gases (4). The heat rejected from the engine jacket is made use of by separating steam from the water in the steam separator (5) and returning the water to the cooling system. The exhaust gases pass through the heat exchanger (4) where water is heated to its boiling point or higher. This water and the steam also move on to the separator (5). The exhaust gases which leave the engine are at approximately 1100°F (594°C) and are cooled in this exhaust heat boiler to about 300°F (149°C).

If the steam supply from the engine set is adequate, the condenser

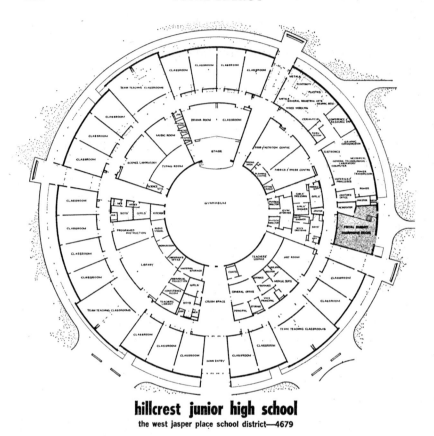

hillcrest junior high school
the west jasper place school district—4679

FIG. 11.17. Hillcrest Junior High School, Edmonton, Alberta, Canada.
(By courtesy: N-West Utilities Ltd.)

valve is closed as is the control valve on the boiler. If there is insufficient
steam supply to meet the heat load requirements, the pressure in the
steam line drops and the gas-fired boiler (6) cuts in at 14 psig (0·95 bar
(g)) to make up the deficiency. If all the steam supplied from the engine
cannot be utilised, the pressure rises. At 16 psig (1·1 bar (g)) the valve
to the condenser (7) opens and excess steam is condensed. Steam is also

utilised to power-absorption chillers (8) to produce chilled water for air conditioning. Steam or hot water can also be utilised (9) for process work, for space heating, hot water supply, etc.

General Data

The annual quantity of power produced is equal to 1·454 GW hours or 21·6 kWh/ft² (233 kWh/m²) with a peak loading of 260 kVA or 3·9 kVA/ft² (42 kVA/1000 m²). The gas generator was found to consume 14,400 Btu (16·2 MJ) per kWh and the annual heat recovery was calculated at 6085 million Btu (6·4 TJ). This amounted to 27·1%

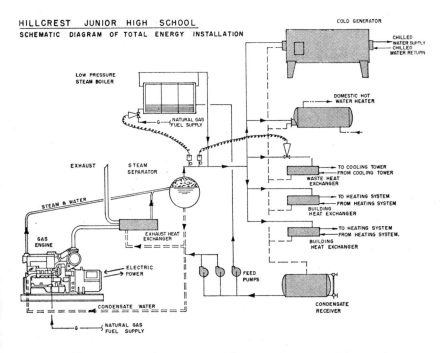

FIG. 11.18. Schematic diagram of total energy system at Hillcrest Junior High School. (By courtesy: Vinto Engineering Ltd.)

of the fuel input into the engines. The plant was in operation 8670 hours per annum with an average loading of 166 kW.

Costs. In Canadian dollars (1965).

The unit cost of gas supplied was equal to 20·4 cents/10^6 Btu (1 Btu = 1·05 kJ).

Annual cost of owning total energy plant

The installation cost of the plant was $68,400 but there were savings of $18,000 on boilers, reduced chimney size, etc. Thus the additional cost amounted to $50,400. The annual owning cost, assuming 6% amortisation over 20 years, amounts to $4394.

Running costs

The annual cost of the maintenance contract is $3,760. The gross natural-gas costs amount to $4,870 but as this cost includes the direct heating costs, amounting to $2,650, the net increase in fuel costs is equal to $2220.

Total Costs

	$
Annual owning costs:	4394
Maintenance:	3760
Fuel:	2220
	$10,374

The unit cost of power generation thus works out at
0·713 cents per kWh.
In the Edmonton area the average cost of power supply from central sources is between 1·2 cents per kWh and 1·5 cents per kWh.

F. BURNS BRICK CO. AT MACON, GEORGIA[18]

The Burns Company had in the past been purchasing gas for heating purposes and electricity for lighting, machines, cranes and hoists, etc. The annual charges had been $228,000 for natural gas and $48,000 for electricity. It was decided to go over to total energy instead and to suspend electric connections to the grid.

The prime movers for the installation are a Ruston and Hornsby TA natural gas turbine with a rating of 1260 brake horsepower (940 kW) at 80°F (27°C) ambient and a Waukesha natural-gas reciprocating engine coupled to a 250 kW generator which is used as a peak demand unit and for stand-by.

The gas turbine has an input fuel rating of about 20 million Btu per hour (21 GJ/hr) of which the exhaust gases contain 17 million Btu/hr (18 GJ/hr). The exhaust of the turbine, which is at 890°F (480°C) is led through insulated ducting to the four drier furnaces of the brick-works which have to be maintained at 500°F (260°C). Exhaust heat thus supplies some 95% of the heat required by these furnaces, the rest and heating during shut-down periods of the turbine being supplied by the old natural-gas burners installed in the drier furnaces.

The gas turbine drives a 1000-kVA Elliott generator with a power factor of 0·8, which normally supplies all power requirements of the plant. Peak electrical demand at the plant sometimes occurs during the day, when up to 1100 kW may be needed. Under such circumstances the Waukesha gas engine is started. At night and at weekends the load falls to about 250 kW, which is supplied by the Waukesha engine alone, and the gas turbine is then shut down. Cutting in and cutting out by the gas engine during the day, when loading increases, is completely automatic.

On average the gas supply may be expected to be interrupted for some 16 days per year, as the company is on a special interruptible rate contract with the Atlanta Gas Light Company. However, as there is a storage capacity of 44,000 gallons (165 m³) of liquefied propane at the plant which can be put into operation automatically as soon as the pressure in the gas burner falls below 90 psig (6·15 bar (g)) the continuous operation of the plant is assured.

The gas pressure is boosted from the normal supply pressure of 25 psig (1·7 bar (g)) to 120 psig (8·2 bar (g)) by a 75 hp (56 kW) Allis Chambers compressor. There are oil-wetted moving screens to filter the intake air and to cool it by evaporation cooling.

The Ruston and Hornsby gas turbine weighs about 7 tons but only occupies 200 ft² (18·5 m²) of floor space. In operation it was found that extra gas costs came to about $10,800 annually, but that naturally the $48,000 electricity power costs could be saved so that there was a saving in direct fuel charges of $37,200 per annum. The capital cost of a brand new plant complete with stand-by propane equipment and heat recovery units would have cost between $150,000–175,000. In the case in question the cost was much lower, as the gas turbine was second-hand and much of the equipment had been installed previously. Taking into consideration extra costs for maintenance and spares for the total energy system as against bought electricity, it was calculated that the simple pay-out period for the plant worked out at less than 5 years.

G. TOTAL ENERGY SYSTEM AT ENGINEERED PLASTICS LTD., EDMONTON, ALBERTA, CANADA[114]

The basic equipment in this case comprises two Caterpillar G 353 TA natural-gas-fired engines rated at 350 brake horsepower (260 kW) each at 1200 rpm which drive two 250-kW Electric Machinery Mfg. Co. generators for 480 V, 3-phase, 60-cycle power. Natural gas is piped in at 15 psig (1·03 bar (g)) pressure. The engine heat is recovered from the exhaust gases and through the engine jacket water system. Both exhaust and water pass into a vertical reboiler heat recovery unit. The exhaust gases enter the reboiler at approximately 1350°F (733°C), circulate through water immersed tubes and are cooled to about 275°F (135°C) before being exhausted outside. Engine water circulates into the re-boiler unit, giving out heat and is then returned for engine cooling. Steam is formed in the reboiler and is drawn off at the top at approximately 8 psig (0·55 bar (g)). This heat energy is used to heat the plant, generate hot water for plant requirements and to operate the absorption water chiller for process cooling. The layout can be seen from Fig. 11.19. The two complete power units are capable of operating independently or can be synchronised in parallel. Each unit generates 250 kW of electrical energy. During the second year of operation, 1967, the load factor of the total energy system averaged 68·5%.

Costs: In Canadian dollars (1967).

Capital costs:	$
Two prime movers plus two generators and insulation	65,000
Heat extraction system	10,500
Chiller absorption system	4961
Total	$80,461

Costs of owning: $
15% depreciation per annum on declining balance   10,200
Interest charges   4000

Total annual owning costs: $24,720

Operating costs:
Gas   3000
Water and water treatment   405
Lubricating oils   720
Maintenance materials   465
Maintenance services and overhaul   4960
Space rental (insurance and taxes)   970

Total annual operating costs: $10,520
Total annual costs: $24,720

The total energy cost per kWh worked out at 0·824 cents per kWh.

If purchased power is used, it was calculated that the cost of electricity would come to $30,600 per annum and the cost of heat energy to $32,960 per annum. Adding certain extra costs involved amounting to $4920 per annum, the total cost of using purchased power and a separate heating system would have come to $37,880 per annum.

Taking operating costs *only*, the savings amount to:

$22,440 per annum.

The simple pay-out period calculated is therefore:
(see Chapter 12)

$$\frac{\$65,000}{\$22,440} = 2 \cdot 78 \text{ years.}$$

H. CATTLE MARKETEERS INC., ST. CLOUD, FLORIDA

This is one of the first applications of the total energy concept to agriculture. The company specialises in the production of hay from coastal Bermuda hybrid grass, which is produced from sandy soil by the application of liquid fertilisers and is cut every 40 days. The grass is very wet when cut and some 570 gallons (2100 litres) of water are removed from every ton of hay to leave a high-quality finished product containing 15% moisture and 11–15% protein. A small drier of the plant is driven by purchased electricity and natural-gas-fired burners. However, it was decided to run a new large drier making use of the total energy concept. This drier is 267 ft (81 m) long and has a belt

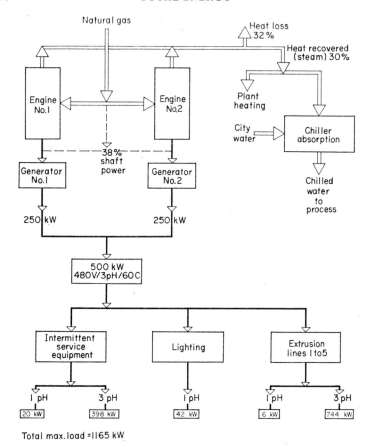

FIG. 11.19. Energy utilisation chart at Engineered Plastics Ltd. Edmonton, Alberta, Canada. (By courtesy: N-West Utilities Ltd.)

$10\frac{1}{2}$ ft (3·2 m) wide, operating at a variable speed of 9–28 ft/min (3–9 m/min). Special spreading arrangements are used to ensure that the hay is spread evenly over the whole belt. Fast circulation of air at accurately controlled temperatures is vital for the operation, and sixty-two motor operated fans are used for this purpose. A 430 brake horse-power (326 kW) Ruston gas turbine, coupled to a 300 kW generator provides all the electric power needs for the installation, including a safety margin for a 30 hp (22·5 kW) fire-fighting pump to provide water for the sprinkler system installed inside the drier.

The quantity of utilised electric power generated is about 270 kW. The price for this, including demand charge, would be about 1·8 cents per kWh. At this part load condition, the turbine exhaust has a mass flow of about 9·9 lb/sec (4·5 kg/sec) at 900°F (480°C), which represents approximately 7·3 million Btu (7·7 GJ) per hour. The input to the gas turbine is about 8·8 million Btu (9·2 GJ) per hour, and the operational efficiency is thus about 80%. The turbine exhaust is conducted to the drier and mixed with outside air to reduce the temperature to 375°F (190°C). There is also an exhaust to the outside air with a damper system which is interlocked with the main conveyor system. If the conveyor stops, or in the case of overheating from other causes, the damper automatically diverts the exhaust gases to the atmosphere. Three of the twelve zones are supplied with heat from the turbine, the rest having naturally aspirated gas-filled burners. The turbine exhaust gases are sufficiently clean to avoid contamination of the final product.

I. STUDENTS' HOSTELS AT OHIO STATE UNIVERSITY[32]

The natural-gas-fired total energy system used there was described by J. T. Coan and B. I. Routh in the July 1968 issue of *Air Conditioning, Heating and Ventilating*.

The power plant for each of the two 24-storey buildings consists of four 450 kW 4160 V generators each driven by a 690-hp natural-gas reciprocating engine. Heat is recovered as steam at 12 psig (0·83 bar (g)) from the engine jackets and exhaust systems, using ebullient cooling. The steam-recovery system is supplemented by four 100-hp (74·5 kW) steam boilers on the 24th floor, operating at the same pressure as the engines. In addition to the engine jacket and exhaust-heat-recovery system, heat released from the lubricating oil is recovered by means of shell and tube heat exchangers and used for the domestic hot-water supply.

Heat recovery, when all the heat is used together with shaft power, can provide approximately 70% system thermal efficiency, which approaches the efficiency of a gas-fired boiler. Nearly all the recoverable generated heat can usually be used, except during short fluctuating loads that allow overshooting due to lag in the system. The heating/cooling system is of the terminal reheat type, providing temperature and humidity control at practically no additional operating cost.

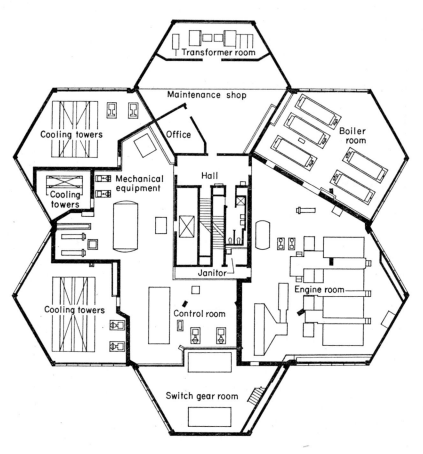

FIG. 11.20. Plan view of the 24th storey of the Ohio State University dormitory, showing location of major system components. (By courtesy: ACH & V).

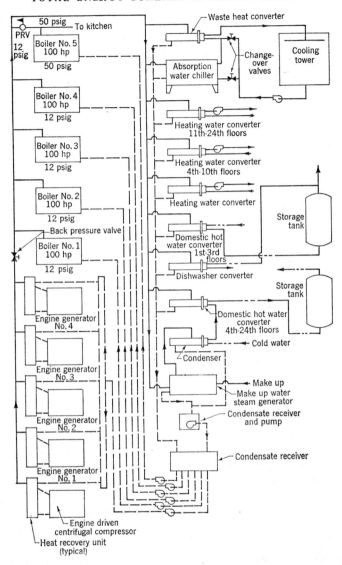

FIG. 11.21. Flow diagram of major mechanical equipment used in on-site power generation at one of the new dormitories at Ohio State University. (By courtesy: ACH & V.)

Chilled water is supplied from a 450-ton (1·6 MW) engine-driven centrifugal chiller and a 450-ton (1·6 MW) absorption chiller. Heat is recovered from the centrifugal chiller engine in the same way as for the generator engines. The two chillers are piped in series, allowing the centrifugal unit to lead and the absorption unit to trim and supplement the load with chilled water at a constant temperature of 44°F (7°C). Such chilled water is required whenever the outside temperature rises above 55°F (13°C). In the domestic water-heating system, the lubricating oil heat recovery exchanger receives the lubricating oil cooling water at 160° F (71°C) and transfers this heat to the domestic water. Any heat not used by the domestic water system is passed on to a cooling tower. If the domestic water temperature falls below 140°F (60°C) it is further heated by a steam generator and condenser that provides condensate for make-up water for the boiler feed and steam system. From the condenser the domestic water is further heated by the domestic hot-water steam converter to maintain the storage tank temperature. Figure 11.21 shows the steam-side recovery system which utilises between 30% and 33% of the engine input in the form of steam. The jacket water is heated to approximately 245°F (118°C), and delivered to a flash tank and separator to be flashed to steam. Heat is also recovered in an exhaust-heat-recovery boiler in the same jacket as the steam separator. Steam from the engines is delivered to a header and then distributed to the various steam consuming systems.

Economic Aspects of Systems

A detailed cost analysis was carried out which indicated a payback period of less than 10 years on the initial investment. Power costs for a conventional system were assessed on a flat rate of 1·1 cents/kWh, while gas costs for power generation were taken as 52 cents per 1000 ft³, and for boiler firing as 62 cents/1000 ft³ (1000 ft³ = 28·317 m³).

The following data applied:

Additional capital investment costs over conventional system:
$41,270 (1968).

Engine maintenance plus additional maintenance not required by conventional system less maintenance of conventional system not needed by
total energy system: $22,600 per annum
Fuel costs: $84,580 per annum
_____

Total $107,080 per annum

Energy costs of a conventional system:	$166,818
Savings of total energy system over conventional system:	$59,738

In the project in question, a very low interest was payable on the capital, amounting to only $3\frac{1}{2}\%$. Under those circumstances a pay-out period of 8·1 years was obtained. As the plant could be assumed to have a life of 30 years, this provided a very good factor (3·7).

Operating Conditions

The load profile of the system indicates that the hourly kW demand varies from 500 at 5.00 a.m. to a peak of 1400 at 7.00 p.m. As fuel consumption of an engine varies appreciably with load, the use of several engines is advantageous.

Engine sequence is as follows:

	Full load, kW	On	Off
Four engines	1800	1150	1050
Three engines	1350	700	600
Two engines	900	315	215
One engine	450		

Each engine, including the centrifugal chiller, has a separate recovery unit. All recovery units are tied together by a common equalising line which maintains the same water level in all units, eliminating the need for stop and check valves in the steam outlet of each boiler. The equalising line also provides circulation with the "off" engines, thereby keeping them warm and ready for immediate use when needed. The system is completely automatic, the additional cost of this over a manual system being $54,000. At $3\frac{1}{2}\%$ this amounts to only $2936 per year for a 30-year period and, in addition, gives the best heat-recovery conditions.

J. KANSAS CITY, MISSOURI, APARTMENT BLOCKS[46, 47, 79, 91, 111, 119]

Gas total energy installations are being installed in a number of apartment complexes in Kansas City. Since 1964 the Truog and Nichols Company has installed systems in the Georgetown development, which consists of 385 units, the Kings Cove development of 270 units, the

Mission Valley scheme of 90 units and the Kenilworth Garden apartments project comprising 246 units. In addition, there is a new scheme being planned at the time of writing for a project comprising 334 units, called the Belvedere Highlander.

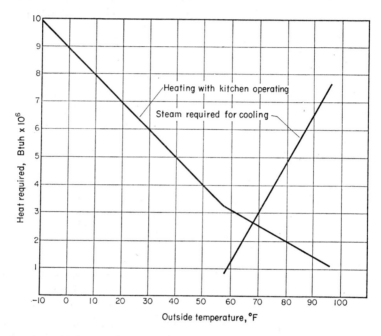

FIG. 11.22. Heating and cooling load curves based on building calculated loads. (By courtesy: ACH & V.)

Typical of these schemes is the Kenilworth project, which comprises nineteen buildings with a gross floor area of 310,000 ft² (29,000 m²) together with an additional 10,000 ft² (930 m²) clubhouse building, which encloses an indoor swimming pool, and is adjacent to a large heated outdoor pool. The total land area of the scheme is 17·5 acres (7·1 ha.). The total energy installation is accommodated in the clubhouse, and consists of two Caterpillar 450-kW natural-gas engine/generator sets and two Caterpillar 250-kW sets providing 60 Hz, 3-phase power at 480 V. At least one set is in constant operation with the remaining three on stand-by. The maximum demand has been estimated at 750 kW. A control system parallels the engines and generators and automatically operates the installation according to preset schedules.

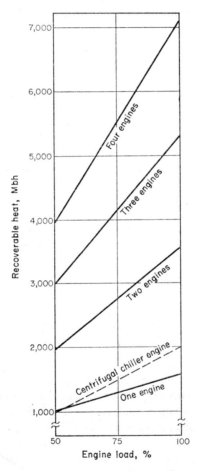

FIG. 11.23. Recoverable heat as shown from manufacturer's literature
(By courtesy: ACH & V.)

Heat recovery is by a vapour-phase system connected to each engine
and producing about 6 lb of 12 psig steam (2·7 kg of 0·83 bar (g))
for every kilowatt of power generated. The average power generation
figure is 640 kWh so that the heat-recovery system yields about 3900 lbs
(1770 kg) of steam per hour. In addition there are two natural gas-fired
low-pressure boilers in the system, each rated at 9·68 million Btu/hr
(10·2 GJ/hr) and a maximum production rate of 8000 lb (3600 kg) of
12 psig (0·83 bar (g)) steam per hour.

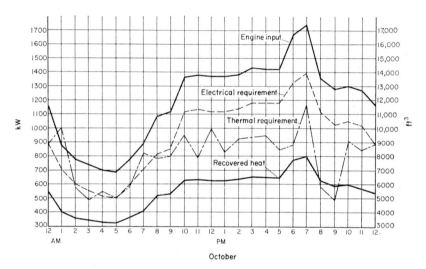

FIG. 11.24. A monthly profile of daily electrical and thermal requirements
for one dormitory. (By courtesy: ACH & V.)

During spring and autumn, the heat-recovery system tends to produce
more steam than is needed, and the excess is rejected to the atmosphere
through an excess steam condenser. Cooling is carried out by means of
two absorption machines, one rated at 275 tons (970 kW) and the other
at 250 tons (885 kW).

The individual apartments are served by a two-pipe system. Chilled
water is supplied at 45°F (7°C) and is returned at 55°F (13°C). Hot
water for heating purposes is supplied at a variable temperature, de-

pending upon the external temperature prevailing. The flow line temperature varies between 90°F and 160°F (32–71°C), and the return line temperature is some 20°F (11°C) lower. The changeover from the heating cycle to a cooling cycle takes place automatically, when climatic conditions warrant it, and takes about 30 minutes. The changeover from cooling to heating only takes 15 minutes. The cooling cycle is put into operation completely automatically whenever the external temperature rises above 75°F (24°C), and the heating cycle is put into operation when the external temperature falls below 65°F (18°C). Such a self-adjusting system is of very considerable value in the Kansas City area as temperatures in the district fluctuate between − 10°F (− 23°C) in winter and up to 100°F (38°C) in summer. The inside temperatures are kept at 76°F (24·5°C) dry bulb and 64°F (18°C) wet bulb both summer and winter.

Each apartment is equipped with an air-handling unit installed in the basement. Most units are rated at 800 ft³/min (22·7/m³ min), but larger apartments have units with a capacity of 1200 and 1600 ft³/min (34m³/min and 45·4 m³/min). Air supply to the first floor is through ducts and outlets at floor level on the perimeter walls of the dwellings, while the returns are high up on the inside walls. In the case of the second floors both inlets and outlets are on inside walls. All controls for the central system, as well as for the apartments themselves, are pneumatic. The compressed air required is produced by two compressors in the engine room.

30,000 ft³/min of external air (860 m³/min) is circulated over the engines and an evaporative cooler, which supplies the carburettor intake of the engines with air at a temperature between 80°F and 90°F (27–32°C). Exhaust is through the cooling tower. Because of the strong negative air pressure in the engine room, the boilers are screened off behind a glass partition so that the burner operation is not affected. There is an air supply to the boiler room with a balanced exhaust. The total electric load of the equipment room at peak operation is about 200 kW, including 50 kW for the cooling-tower blowers. The clubhouse load is about 45 kW.

To prevent a break-down, there are two of all critical pumps and controls, including the pneumatic controls and compressors, circulating pumps, boiler feed pumps and excess steam condenser pump. The engine room is sound-treated so that nothing more than a faint hum can be heard in the clubhouse, which lies immediately above it.

General Data (1966 figures)

The total cost of installing the generating equipment worked out at $217,200 and the cost of the heating and cooling equipment at $558,313.

This means that the actual cost of the generating equipment works out at 68 cents/ft^2 ($7·30 per m^2) floor area and the heating and cooling equipment at

$1.80 per ft^2 ($19·4/m^2) floor area.

The heating and cooling cost accounted for 11·9% of the total project cost, while the generating equipment accounted for 4·6%. The annual electrical output amounted to 3712 MWh or 11·6 kWh per ft^2 (125 kWh per m^2) floor area, giving an average load factor of 58·5% on the engines in use. The annual peak demand of 720 kW accounts for 53·6% of the total generating capacity, while the annual minimum of 270 kW amounts to 20% of the total capacity.

The total annual gas consumption amounted to 82·54 million ft^3 (2·34 million m^3) of which 67·7% was used in the gas engines, and 32·3% in the gas-fired boilers. The equivalent heat recovery from the gas engines, used for heating and cooling purposes, amounted to 26 million ft^3 (0·74 million m^3), equivalent to 31·4% of the total quantity of gas used.

Costs per annum	Heating and cooling equipment	Generating equipment	Total
Gas	$14,724	$8385	$23,110
Maintenance and service:	$12,736	$13,670	$27,406
Capital costs	$57,000	$22,100	$79,110
Total	$84,460	$44,155	$128,626

The total cost of power generated by the system worked out at 1·28 cents per kWh, and the total cost of operating the heating and cooling system worked out at 26·4 cents per ft² and year ($2·85 per m² and year). The annual cost of a ton of heating and refrigeration effect (3·517 kW) is assessed at $165 or 0·745 cents per kWh of heating and refrigeration effect.

The system made an annual profit of $102,675 so that the pay-out of the total energy plant amounts to 7·7 years, while that of the electrical generation part of the plant alone amounts to 5·25 years.

K. BERGAN HIGH SCHOOL, PEORIA, ILL.

This section was written based upon information supplied by Mr. J. Hunnicutt, publisher and editor of the journal *Total Energy*, of 522 Briar Oaks Lane, San Antonio, Texas 78216, U.S.A., and the author herewith acknowledges his indebtedness.

Bergan High School, which is operated by a religious order, has a capacity of 1600 students and a total floor area of 141,000 ft² (13,100 m²) The total energy plant for the school cost a total of $73,000 (1963) and the final contract costs for plumbing, heating, air conditioning and electrical work came to $5·06 per ft² floor area ($54 per m²). As can be seen from the flow sheet (Fig. 11·25) engine jacket water from the diesel engines is circulated through the exhaust-gas heat-recovery silencer and to the flash tank, where it is flashed to steam at 2 psig (0·14 bar (g)). This is used in the heating system converter or absorption chiller, with excess heat being dissipated in air-cooled rejectors. Condensate is returned to the flash tank, and pumped to the engine jacket by the jacket water pump. Water is also heated in an auxiliary electric heater (when generator loading and water temperature warrant it) and circulated through a 10,000 gallon (40 m³) insulated underground accumulator tank. During the heating season, hot water from this tank is mixed with water from the converter to maintain a predetermined temperature for heating the 180°F (82°C) domestic hot water and for supplying heat to the re-heat circuit. After use in these two applications this water is reused to add heat to two fresh air tempering circuits. It is then returned to the converter and/or heat tank to repeat the cycle. Cooling of interior spaces during winter operation is accomplished with tempered outside air.

P

During the cooling season the steam is used in the absorption chiller to cool water supplying the air-conditioning systems. Water leaving the chiller is circulated through a motor-driven reciprocating compressor-chiller unit, thence to the loads, with a portion being bled off into the gymnasium circuit as needed. Condenser water is circulated through the coils of ventilating units which are controlled to maintain desired humidity conditions. Heat supplied in the re-heat circuit is

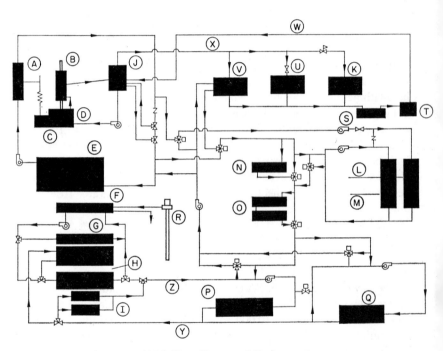

FIG. 11.25. Flow diagram of Bergan system.
A. Electric heater. B. Exhaust. C. Engine. D. Waste-heat recovery silencer. E. Heat-storage tank. F. Heat exchanger. G. Condenser. H. Absorption chillers. I. Chiller condensers. J. Flash tank. K. Heat rejecter. L. Residence load. M. Heating load. N. Hot-water heater, 180°F (82°C). O. Hot-water heaters, 140°F (60°C). P. Heating and cooling load. Q. Heating and cooling load. R. Well. S. Condensate cooler. T. Vacuum pump. U. Absorption chiller. V. Converter. W. Condensate return. X. Low-pressure steam. Y. Chilled-water return. Z. Chilled-water flow.

circulated through reheat coils to maintain the desired space temperature. The converter is not used when the absorption chiller is in operation. At such times, heat required for re-heat and domestic hot water is
supplied by the electric heater bank and the heat-storage tank.

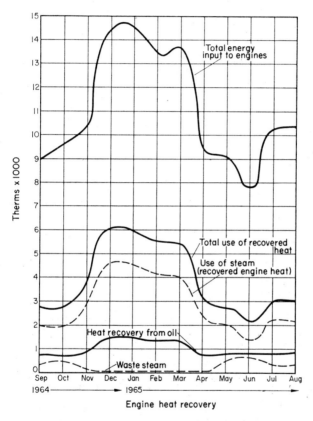

Engine heat recovery

FIG. 11.26. Engine heat recovery over year with Bergan system.

The electric-drive chilled-water system is used as a heat pump to
recover heat from well water by directing the chilled/hot water through
the condenser of the motor-driven compressor chiller, simultaneously

routing water from the well-water cooled heat exchanger through the evaporator side of the chiller.

Summary of Operating Data

The detailed data and load profiles were compiled during the 12-month test period and are shown in Figs. 11.26 to 11.29. The test period encompassed the full year starting on 1 September 1964 and ending on the 1 September 1965, during which time the total energy plant at Bergan high school generated a total of 1,124,160 kWh of electricity of which 554,395 kWh were consumed directly by the building, 423,600 kWh were used to operate the resistance heater bank, and 146,165 kWh were consumed in the electric chiller operation. During the same period a total of 6113 million Btu (6·5 TJ) were consumed by the school, of which 3724 million Btu (3·9 TJ) derived from heat salvaged from the

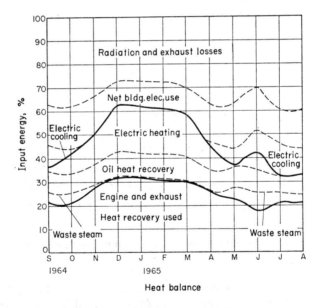

Fig. 11.27. Heat balance over year with Bergan system.

diesel engines, 1200 million Btu (1·25 TJ) were obtained from the oil cooler and the balance from the heater bank. In providing these quantities of energy, the total energy plant consumed 94,100 U.S. gallons of diesel fuel (358 m³) at 9·2 cents per gallon and 296 U.S. gallons of lubricating oil (1·15 m³) at $1·07 per gallon. The average heat rate was 11,700 Btu (12·3 MJ) per kWh of electricity generated before allowances for by-product heat were made.

The peak kW demand varied from a low of 175 during June to a high of 270 in January. The system load factor also varied with a low of 42·6% in October and a high of 73·2% in December with an average of 47·4% for the 12-month period. Comparisons were made between Bergan High School and another High School of practically the same floor area within the same city, which was built at the same time as Bergan. This latter school is electrically air conditioned.

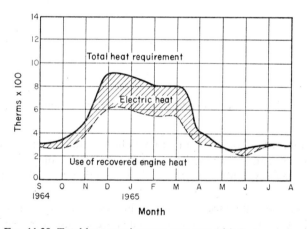

FIG. 11.28. Total heat requirement over year with Bergan system.

Bergan High School (1965)	$
Fuel cost at 9·2 cents/gallon	$8658
Lubricating oil at $1·07 per gallon	700
Maintenance	1500
Labour	2000
Purchased energy	1672
Total	14,530

Neighbouring school (1964)	$
Purchased electricity	23,615
Oil (stand-by fuel)	2346
Gas	9063
Total	35,024

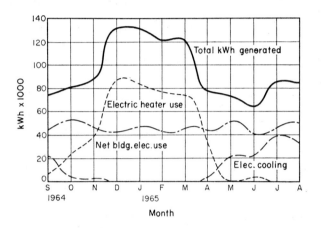

FIG. 11.29. Total power generated over year with Bergan system.

In addition, while the Bergan High School total energy scheme is fully automatic and is only visited occasionally by the sole janitor of the complex, the conventional system needs no less than ten full-time attendants.

Much of the difference in costs is, however, due to the fact that Bergan is a compact and well-insulated design, while the neighbouring school has a more open plan and larger window areas. For this reason the real cost advantages of total energy would probably not be quite as large as would appear from the figures given above, although they would still be appreciable, as the purchased power cost in the area amounts to 2·6 cents per kWh.

CHAPTER 12

ECONOMIC ASSESSMENT OF
TOTAL ENERGY

by

The Energy Economics Section, Market Development Dept.,
Northern Natural Gas Co., Omaha, Nebraska, U.S.A.

MEASURING ECONOMIC WORTH BY SIMPLE PAYOUT

The desirability of a proposed investment can be related to any commonly used measure of economic worth. To appraise capital investment opportunities many managers and investors use the concept of simple payout or the number of years to "payout" the investment cost. Simple payout is here defined as:

$$\text{Payout in years} = \frac{\text{Incremental investment}}{\text{Annual operating savings less maintenance cost}}$$

Incremental investment is the additional cost of a gas engine over the price of an electric motor of equal capacity. Annual operating savings is the cost savings accruing from the use of natural gas in an engine instead of electricity in a comparable motor, less an incremental maintenance expense chargeable against the engine.

The objection may be raised that simple payout as opposed to payout after taxes or rate of return is not an accurate measure of investment profitability and should not be used. The concept, however, of simple payout is adequate for the purposes of this study because it affords a first approximation or screening of alternate investment possibilities.

The formula that is used to calculate payout years is

$$\text{Payout in years} = \frac{C}{H[E - (M + G - H_r)]} \qquad (1)$$

where:

C is the difference in first cost between an engine and a motor in $/kW,

405

H is the number of annual operating hours,
E is the cost of electricity in $ per kWh,
M is the engine maintenance cost in $ per kWh,
G is the cost of gas in $ per kWh,
H_r is the value of the recoverable heat in $ per kWh.

The calculation of simple payout is based on a knowledge of the incremental cost of a gas engine over an electric motor, the applicable gas and electric rates, the number of engine running hours per year, a specific fuel consumption of the gas prime mover and an average maintenance cost of operating the gas engine, and value of recoverable heat. Some of these items are fixed approximately and values for them can be assumed as characteristic of all gas engines. Typically, these machines are priced about $100 per kW above motors, require 13,500 Btu (14,300 kJ) of fuel per kW hour to run, and need $0·0027 per kWh to be maintained. If the exact percent of recoverable heat is unknown, but there is some use for the waste heat (building heat, pre-heating, process heat), a reasonable conservative assumption is an H_r of 50%.

The annual engine running hours used in the payout equation depends on the application of the prime mover. If exact engine hours are not known, an approximation can be used based on data from Table 12.1 which shows average annual operating hours for the major categories of driven equipment.

TABLE 12.1. ESTIMATED ANNUAL OPERATING HOURS OF SELECTED DRIVEN EQUIPMENT

Application	Average annual operating hours
Air compressors	3400
Refrigeration and air-conditioning compressors	2600
Generators	
Stand-by	0
Non-Stand-by	3600
Pumps	5300
Others	3700

Source: Batelle Report for GATE.

The average number of operating hours for each of the four kinds of driven equipment was found by a weighted average of the number of operating hours for the units in each Standard Industrial Classification category.

TOTAL ENERGY FEASIBILITY EQUATION

The economic feasibility of a total energy installation is dependent upon a number of variable factors including equipment costs, gas and electricity rates, load factors, maintenance costs, stand-by requirements, use of recoverable heat, taxes and financing arrangements.

The rate of return on the capital committed is probably the most useful of the criteria employed. This rate of return is computed as the compounding rate which will discount the net receipts from the operation of the investment over the useful life of the project to a value equal to the first cost of the equipment. A knowledge of the uniform present worth factor and the economic life of the equipment is all that is required to determine the rate of return.

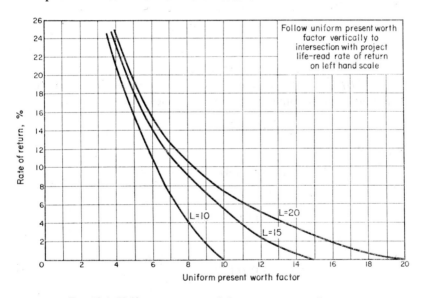

FIG. 12.1. Uniform present worth factor versus rate of return.

The uniform present worth factor (UPWF) can be obtained from the following equation:

$$\text{UPWF} = \frac{I}{GS + HRS - ME - FE - IT} \qquad (2)$$

where I = investment,
GS = generator savings,
HRS = heat recovery savings,
ME = maintenance expenses,
FE = fixed expenses,
IT = income-tax.

(a) Investment (I)

I can be determined from the following formula:

$$I = PBD \times IPR \times (1 + SP) \times DKW \qquad (3)$$

where PBD = peak billing demand,
IPR = instantaneous peak ratio,

$$\left(\frac{\text{instantaneous demand}}{\text{billing demand}}\right),$$

SP = fraction stand-by plant,
DKW = installation cost in dollars per installed kilowatt.
From preliminary studies the following values were obtained:

$$IPR = 1 \cdot 10 \qquad SP = 0 \cdot 33$$

Equation (3) therefore reduces to:

$$I = 1 \cdot 475 \times PBD \times DKW. \qquad (4)$$

(b) Generation Savings

These can be expressed as:

$$GS = KWH \left(ER - \frac{GR}{EGE \times LHV} \right) \qquad (5)$$

where KWH = annual kilowatt hour usage,

ER = electric rate (dollars per kWh),

GR = gas rate (either dollars per ft³ or dollars per m³),

EGE = engine generator efficiency given as a fraction of unity,

LHV = lower (net) calorific value of gas quoted in Btu/ft³ and divided by 3·413 or as kJ/m³ and divided by 3600 to give answer compatible with kWh values.

The following values are assumed:

$$LHV = \frac{920}{3\cdot413} = 269 \text{ (British units)},$$

$$\frac{34{,}700}{3600} = 96\cdot5 \text{ (SI units)},$$

$EGE = 0\cdot26.$

Therefore:

$$GS = KWH \, (ER - 0\cdot0146 \, GR) \text{ British units,} \tag{6a}$$

$$GS = KWH \, (ER - 0\cdot0398 \, GR) \text{ SI units.} \tag{6b}$$

(c) Heat Recovery Savings

$$HRS = \frac{KWH \times PHR \times PRU \times GR}{LHV \times EGE \times BE} \tag{7}$$

where BE = conventional boiler efficiency = 0·80,

PHR = fraction heat recoverable = 0·45,

PRU = fraction recoverable heat used = 0·80,

also assuming that $LHV = 269$ (Brit. units) or 96·5 (SI units).

$EGE = 0\cdot26$, equation (7) reduces to:

$HRS = 0\cdot00643 \, GR \times KWH$ (Brit. units),

$HRS = 0\cdot0179 \, GR \times KWH$ (SI units).

(d) Maintenance Expenses

$$ME = KWH \times MD \tag{9}$$

where MD = maintenance costs in dollars per kWh produced. Assuming this value at 0·004,

$$\text{ME reduces to } 0·004 \; KWH. \tag{10}$$

(e) Fixed Expenses

$$FE = I \times FER,$$

where FER = fixed expense ratio = 0·03,

so that $FE = 0·03 \; I.$ (11)

(f) Income-tax

$$IT = ITR\left(GS + HRS - ME - FE - \frac{I \times DF \times INT}{2} - \frac{I}{EL}\right) \tag{12}$$

where ITR is the income-tax rate,

         EL is the economic life = 20 years,

         DF is the debt fraction = 0·70,

         INT is the interest rate.

IT therefore amounts to:

$$ITR \; (GS + HRS - ME - FE - 0·35 \; I \times INT - 0·05I) \tag{13}$$

Inserting equations (4), (6), (8), (10), (11) and (13) into equation (2) we get, using British units,

Uniform present worth factor = UPWF =

$$\frac{DKW}{5990 \; LF(1 - ITR) \; (ER - 0·0079 \; GR - 0·004) + DKW \; (ITR(0·08 + 0·35 \; INT) - 0·03)} \tag{14}$$

The factor is thus dependent upon six variables which are:
1. Income-tax rate, ITR;
2. Dollars per installed kilowatt, DKW;
3. Average electric rate, ER;
4. Load factor, LF;

5. Average gas rate, GR;

6. Typical interest rate INT.

Let us assume that these six variables are as follows:

$$ITR = 0{\cdot}24, \quad DKW + \$150, \quad ER = \$0{\cdot}02/kWh,$$
$$LF = 0{\cdot}50, \quad GR = \$0{\cdot}50 \text{ per } 1000 \text{ ft}^3, \quad INT = 0{\cdot}07.$$

UPWF can thus be evaluated at 5·62 years, which gives an approximate rate of return of 17%.

To simplify these calculations, the Northern Natural Gas Co. issues a special slide rule to its potential customers, with which the UPWF can be evaluated with considerable simplicity.

When equation (14) is to be used for conditions where the price of gas is quoted per 1000 m³ instead of 1000 ft³, the equation must be modified as follows:

$$\text{UPWF} = \cfrac{DKW}{5990\,LF(1 - ITR)\,(ER - 0{\cdot}00022\,GR - 0{\cdot}004) + DKW\,(ITR(0{\cdot}08 + 0{\cdot}35\,INT) - 0{\cdot}03)} \quad (14)$$

Naturally, any other currency can be used instead of dollars in the above equations, provided its use is consistent throughout.

PRIME-MOVER PAYOUT CALCULATION

When calculating the feasibility of a prime-mover application, one method that is frequently used is the simple payout method, i.e. how long will it take to recover the investment.

The equation for the simple calculation is as follows:

$$\text{Payout (years)} = \frac{\Delta C}{H[E - (M + G - H_r)]} \quad (16)$$

ΔC = incremental engine cost (gas engine over electric motor)
= \$/hp,

H = operating hours per year,

E = electric rate (average) = cents/kWh,

G = gas rate = \$/MCF (10^3 ft³) (1 ft³ = 0·0283m³),

M = maintenance cost = \$/hp-hr (1 hp = 745·7W),

H_r = value of recoverable heat used = \$/hp-hr.

To use this equation for calculating prime-mover payout, all the terms must be reduced to common units as follows:

$C = $/hp$—no conversion required.

$H =$ operating hours/year—no conversion required,

$$E = \frac{(\text{cents/kWh}) \, (\text{kWh/hp}) \, (\$/100 \text{ cents})}{\text{Gen. eff.}} = \frac{(\text{cents/kWh}) \, (0 \cdot 746) \, (1/100)}{0 \cdot 90}$$
$$= 0 \cdot 0082889 \, (\text{cents/kWh}),$$

$$G = \frac{(\$/\text{MCF}) \, (\text{Btu/hp-hr})}{(\text{Btu/MCF})} = \frac{(\$/\text{MCF}) \, (10,000)}{10^6} = 0 \cdot 01 \, (\$/\text{MCF})$$
$$(\text{MCF} = 1000 \text{ ft.}^3)$$

$M = $/hp-hr.

$$H_r = \frac{(\$/\text{MCF}) \, (\text{Btu/hp-hr}) \, (0 \cdot 45 \text{ recoverable}) \, (\% \text{ used})}{0 \cdot 80 \text{ boiler eff.}) \, (\text{Btu/MCF})}$$

$$= (\$/\text{MCF}) \, (10,000/10^6) \, (P) \, (0 \cdot 45)/(0 \cdot 80)$$
$$= (G) \, (P) \, (0 \cdot 5625)$$

This results in an equation as follows:

$$\text{Payout} = \frac{\Delta C}{H[E - (M + G - H_r)]} \qquad (16)$$

Substitute expression for H_r

$$\text{Payout} = \frac{\Delta C}{H[E - M - G(0 \cdot 01 - 0 \cdot 005625P)]}$$

where P equals the percent of recoverable heat used. The equation with all conversion factors appear as follows:

$$= \frac{\Delta C}{H[(0 \cdot 00829) \, (\text{cents/kWh}) - (\$/\text{hp} \cdot \text{hr}) - (\$/\text{MCF}) \, (0 \cdot 01 - 0 \cdot 005625 \, P)]} \qquad (17)$$

To solve this equation one needs only to substitute in the appropriate values for annual usage in hours, electric rate in cents/kWh, maintenance charge in $/hp-hr (annual basis), gas rate in $/MCF and the percent of recoverable heat that will be used.

If we consider the same values for the variables as previously, the equation and calculation would be as follows:

Payout (years) =
$$\frac{75}{5000\,[(0{\cdot}00829)\,(2)\,-\,(0{\cdot}002)\,-\,0{\cdot}50(0{\cdot}01\,-\,(0{\cdot}005625)\,(0{\cdot}50))]}$$

$$=\frac{75}{5000\,[(0{\cdot}01658)\,-\,(0{\cdot}002)\,-\,0{\cdot}50\,(0{\cdot}0071875)]}$$

$$=\frac{75}{5000\,[0{\cdot}01658\,-\,0{\cdot}00559]}$$

Payout (years) $=\dfrac{75}{5000\,(0{\cdot}01099)}=\dfrac{75}{54{\cdot}95}=1{\cdot}36$ years.

Pay-out Calculation using Nomograph

The average electric rate is shown to be 2·0 cents/kWh and the average gas rate is $0·50/thousand cubic feet. The electric motor driving the air compressor operates 5000 hr annually. Data from the manufacturer shows an engine cost of $75/hp (over the cost of the same size electric motor) and a maintenance cost of $0·002/hp-hr. For this example it is assumed that 50% of the recoverable heat is usable. Shown below is the step by step solution of the payout calculation using the nomograph and the values mentioned above (Fig. 12.2).

1. Connect recoverable heat used (50%) with gas rate ($6.50/MCF) and locate reference point on (1), axis.
2. Connect reference point (1) with maintenance cost (0·002 $/hp-hr) and locate reference point (2).
3. Connect reference point (2) with electric rate (2·0 cents/kWh) and locate reference point (3)
4. Connect reference point (3) with annual operating hours (5000) and locate reference point (4) (yearly savings — $/hp) — $55/hp.
5. Connect yearly savings ($55/hp) with incremental engine costs ($75/hp) to determine prime mover payout—1·36 years.
   Because of the orientation of the payout line on the nomograph, it is sometimes difficult to read the value to the desired accuracy.

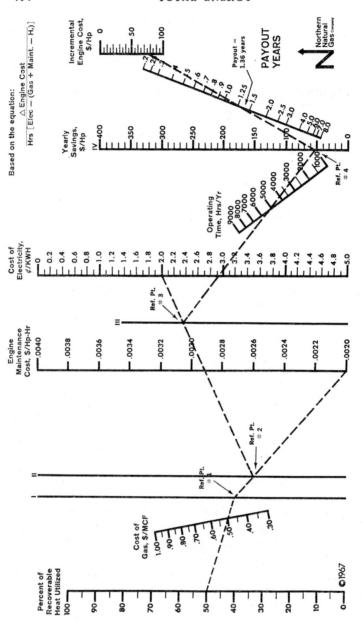

Fig. 12.2. Nomograph for Prime Mover Payout based on the equation:

$$\frac{\triangle \text{Engine cost}}{\text{Hrs. (Elec} - (\text{Gas} + \text{Maint.} - \text{Hr}))}$$

Once the yearly savings have been determined from the nomograph, the payout can be calculated by dividing the incremental engine cost by the yearly savings. In this example, the calculated payout—$85/$55 is 1·36 yr.

Application of Penetration Factors

To illustrate the meaning and use of the penetration factors, consider the following example:

A market survey in a utility service area has been completed and the information regarding the size, application, etc., of the electric motors has been categorized and totalled. From this information it has been determined that there are forty electric-motor-driven air compressors larger than 100 hp in the area. How much of this replacement market one could reasonably be expected to capture?

In order to estimate the expected prime mover share of this market, the following penetration factors have to be determined:

Payout penetration factor

It has been determined that the payout period for this size engine is 1·53 years. Referring to Table 12.2, it is indicated that the expected penetration for this payout period is 0·8.

Size penetration factor

All of these motors are larger than 100 hp (74·57 kW) and therefore the expected penetration factor would be 1·0 (Table 12.3).

Installation factor

Since the application for these motors is driving air compressors, the expected penetration factor is 0·7 (Table 12.4).

Replacement factor

The replacement factor as discussed in this text is 0·5.

The expected market penetration for this particular application would be the product of all these factors:

$$\begin{matrix} \text{Expected} \\ \text{market} \\ \text{penetration} \end{matrix} = \begin{matrix} \text{Number} \\ \text{of} \\ \text{units} \end{matrix} \times \begin{matrix} \text{Payout} \\ \text{factor} \end{matrix} \times \begin{matrix} \text{Size} \\ \text{factor} \end{matrix} \times \begin{matrix} \text{Installation} \\ \text{factor} \end{matrix} \times \begin{matrix} \text{Replacement} \\ \text{factor} \end{matrix}$$

Expected market penetration $= 40 \times 0.8 \times 1.0 \times 0.7 \times 0.5 = 11.2$ units.

From this example, one could reasonably expect to replace eleven of these electric motors with gas engines.

TABLE 12.2. ESTIMATED PENETRATION FACTOR FOR GAS PRIME MOVERS BASED ON PAYOUT IN YEARS

Payout, years	Probability of customers' acceptance (penetration factor)
Under 1	0·9
1–2	0·8
2–3	0·7
3–4	0·6
4–5	0·5
5–6	0·4
6–7	0·3
7–8	0·2
Over 8	0·1

Source: Battelle Report for GATE.

TABLE 12.3. ESTIMATED PENETRATION FACTORS BASED ON SIZE CLASSIFICATIONS

Size		Penetration factor
Under 100 hp	(74·57 kW)	0·5
Above 100 hp	(74·57 kW)	1·0

Source: Battelle Report for GATE.

TABLE 12.4. ESTIMATED PENETRATION FACTORS FOR GAS PRIME MOVERS
BASED ON INSTALLATION CHARACTERISTICS

Application	Penetration factor
Air compressors	0·7
Refrigeration and air-conditioning compressors	0·5
Generators	
Stand by	0·5
Non-stand-by	0·4
Pumps	0·6
Other	0·4

Source: Battelle Report for GATE.

BIBLIOGRAPHY

THIS bibliography comprises most of the sources from which data on "Total Energy" have been obtained, although many of the industrial contributors of this book have also drawn upon the internal documentation of their firms, and as such complete references are not available. Readers wishing to know more on specific points are advised to write directly to the authors of the individual chapters.

The author has made full use of the many hundreds of abstracts provided by the GATE abstracting service of the South-West Research Institute, San Antonio, Texas 78228, which, together with the Institute of Gas Technology, Chicago, Ill. 60616, has abstracted and are abstracting virtually all information on Total Energy published in English-speaking countries. Russian work is covered by *Teploenergetika*, of which a cover-to-cover translation service exists in the form of the journal *Thermal Engineering*, published by Pergamon Press Ltd. Most other journals dealing with Total Energy are abstracted in *Fuel Abstracts* published by the Institute of Fuel, 18 Devonshire Street, Portland Place, London, W.1.

This book deals with the technical developments in Total Energy up to the end of November 1968. To obtain more recent information on the subject the reader will have to consult the sources, given above, regularly.

LITERATURE REFERENCES

1. AEI Ltd., technical brochures (1968). Chapter 2.
2. *Air Conditioning, Heating and Refrigeration News* (Anon.). Hospital gets emergency power source without stand-by generator, Nov. 19 (1965). Chapter 1.
3. AMERICAN GAS ASSN. INC., New York, *Gas Total Energy* (1968). Chapter 1.
4. ANDRESEN, C. E. Horseshoe Lake Station Unit No. 7. Combined cycle steam generator design and operation, *Combustion*, Vol. 36, No. 6, Dec. (1964). Chapter 5.
5. ASHRAE Guide and Data book, *Refrigeration Applications*, New York (1964). Chapter 9.
6. ASHRAE Guide and Data book, *Refrigeration Fundamentals and Equipment*, New York (1963). Chapter 9.
7. BACHL, H. and DICHTEL, C., Heizkraftwerk Sendling, *Stadtwerke München* (1968). Chapter 10.
8. BACON, F. T., Fuel cells, *J. Inst. Fuel*, Sept. (1965). Chapter 8.
9. BAMMERT, K. Turbosätze für heliumgekühlte Reaktoren, *OECD Dragon THTR assessment meeting* Brussels, May (1965). Chapter 6.
10. BAMMERT, K., Zur Erwicklung des kohlenstaubgefeuerten Lufterhitzers, *VDI Zeitschrift*, Vol. 100, No. 20 (1958). Chapter 6.
11. BAMMERT, K. and BOEHM, E., Auslegung von Kernkraftwerken mit Gasturbinen, *Atomkernenergie*, Vol. 7, No. 8 (1964). Chapter 6.

419

12. BAMMERT, K., GEISSLER, TH. and NICKEL, E., Pulverized coal firing in closed-cycle gas turbines, *Sixth World Power Conference*, Paper 9 11131/6 (1962). Chapter 6.

13. BAMMERT, K., KELLER, C. and KRESS, H., Heissluft-turbinenanlage mit Kohlenstaubfeuerung für Stromerzeugung und Heizwärmelieferung, *Brennstoff, Wärme, Kraft*, Vol. 8, No. 10 (1956). Chapter 6.

14. BAMMERT, K. and TWARDZIOK, W., Kernkraftwerke für grosse Leistungen, *Atomkernenergie*, Vol. 9, No. 10 (1967). Chapter 6.

15. BECK, K., Fernwärmeversorgung der Gemeinden, Sigillum Verlag, Cologne (1964). Chapter 10.

16. BELINSKII, S. Y., Raising the effectiveness of using district heating turbines in power systems, *Teploenergetika*, Vol. 14, No. 2 (1967). Translation in *Thermal Engineering*. Chapter 10.

17. BERMAN, P. A., A gas turbine for a helium-cooled reactor, *Journal of the Franklin Institute, Philadelphia*, Monograph 7 (1960). Chapter 6.

18. BLAKE, J. W. and TUMY, R. W., 3500 kW gas turbine raises station capability by 6000 kW, *Power*, Sept. (1948). Chapter 5.

19. BOEHM, E., Gasgekühlte, durch Berylliumoxyd moderierte Hochtemperaturreaktoren mit Gas-turbine für den Schiffsantrieb, 3. *Jahrbuch der Kernenergiegesellschaft*, Hamburg (1964). Chapter 6.

20. BOEHM, E., Hochtemperatur-Reaktoren mit Gasturbine Paper No. 4/7, presented at Internationale Fachmesse für die Kerntechnische Industrie, Sept. (1966). Chapter 6.

21. BRANDERS, A., Nachbarschutz und sicherheitstechnische Massnamen beim Kraftwerk Vahr. *Technische Überwachung*, Vol. 5, No. 8 (1964). Chapter 10.

22. *Brennstoff-Wärme-Kraft* (Anon.). Spitzenstrom aus Wasserkraft und Erdgas, Vol. 13, No. 7 (1961). Chapter 10.

23. BRETT-LITTLECHILD, R., Latent heat cooling and waste heat recovery, *Diesel Engineers and Users Assn. Report*, Oct. (1960). Chapter 7.

24. BROOKLYN UNION GAS CO., Technical information and brochures (1967). Chapter 11.

25. BROWN, F. H. S., Development of modern steam power station plant, Parsons Memorial Lecture, Inst. of Mech. E., Dec. 12 (1962). Chapter 5.

26. BROWN-BOVERI, technical brochures (1968). Chapter 2.

27. CARLYLE INTERNATIONAL CO., technical information and booklets (1968). Chapter 9.

28. CARRIER LTD., technical information and booklets (1968). Chapter 9.

29. *CEGB Statistical Yearbook*, London (1967). Chapter 8.

30. CENTRAX LTD., technical brochures (1968). Chapter 2.

31. CLAY, P. E., Heat recovery systems, *Actual Specifying Engineer*, Vol. 14, No. 5 (1965). Chapter 7.

32. COAN, J. T. and ROUTH, B. I., Total energy for campus dormitories, *Air Conditioning, Heating and Ventilating*, July (1968). Chapter 11.

33. CONNEL, W., Gas turbine burns coal slurry, *Gas Turbine Magazine*, No. 3 (1961). Chapter 6.

34. CONSOLIDATED EDISON CO. INC., New York, technical information and brochures (1967). Chapter 10.

35. CONSUMER'S GAS COMPANY, Toronto, statistical information (1954–65). Chapter 8.

36. COPENHAGEN POWER AUTHORITY, technical information and brochures (1966). Chapter 10.
37. CRAIG, H. R. M. and JANOTA, M. S., The potential of turbochargers as applied to highly rated 2-stroke and 4-stroke engines, Cimac Congress (1965). Chapter 5.
38. DENGLER, F., Das Coburger Heizkraftwerk "Coburg", *Energie*, Vol. 11, No. 9 (1957). Chapter 6.
39. DENNIS, E., 10 engines, 4000 kW for shopping center, *Diesel and Gas Turbine Progress*, June (1967). Chapter 11.
40. DEUSTER, G., *Die Heissluftturbine in der Heizkraftwirtschaft und das Heizkraftwerk Oberhausen Schweizerische Bauzeitung*, Vol. 80, No. 88 (1962). Chapter 2.
41. DEUSTER, G., *Die gescglossene Gasturbine im Heizkraftwerk Mitteilungen der Vereinigung: Industrielle Kraftwirtschaft* (1964). Chapter 2.
42. DIAMANT, R. M. E., District heating in the U.S.A., *Electrical Review*, No. 23, Dec. (1966). Chapter 11.
43. DIAMANT, R. M. E., Single pipeline hot water transmission in Soviet district heating systems, *Heating and Ventilating Engineer*, Dec. (1967), Jan. (1968), Feb. (1968). Chapter 10.
44. DIAMANT, R. M. E., Methods of centralised heat generation. Paper read at IHVE symposium on district heating, London, March 21st–22nd (1967). Chapter 1.
45. DIAMANT, R. M. E. and McGARRY, J., *Space and District Heating*, Iliffe, London (1968). Chapters 1, 2, 10.
46. *Diesel and Gas Turbine Progress* (Anon.). Remote system combines total energy plant, Dec. (1966). Chapter 11.
47. *Diesel and Gas Turbine Progress* (Anon.). TES plant will serve expanded inn, convention hall, Aug. (1967). Chapter 11.
48. *Diesel and Gas Turbine Progress* (Anon.). 14,000 kW from sewage gas, Jan. (1968). Chapter 1.
49. DIESEL ENGINEERS AND USERS ASSN. Publication 318. Working cost and operational report, Apr. (1968). Chapter 8.
50. DUGDALE, I. and SUDWORTH, J. L., Assessment of the future of fuel cells and rechargeable batteries for rail traction. Paper No. 20, *Sixth International Power Source Symposium*, Sept. (1968). Chapter 8.
51. DYHR, F. and HOLZAPFEL, H., Heissluftturbinen für Heizkraftwerke. Heizkraftwerk Oberhausen, *Energie*, Nov. (1961).
52. ECABERT, R. J., Combined steam and gas turbine plants producing electricity and process steam simultaneously, *Combustion*, Aug. (1964). Chapter 5.
53. ECABERT, R. J., Steam generators for combined steam and gas turbine plants, *Trans. of ASME, Journal of Engineering for Power*, Oct. (1966). Chapter 5.
54. ELDRED, C. L., Installation and operation of a gas turbine at Little Rock, Arkansas. Paper read at Houston, Texas, Mar. 4–8 (1962). Chapter 11.
55. ELDRED, C. L., Shopping center utilizes total energy concept package, *Diesel and Gas Engine Progress*, Aug. (1963). Chapter 11.
56. ELMENIUS, L., Gasteam—a combination of gas and steam turbines, ASME paper No. 66 GT/CMC70 (1966). Chapter 5.
57. ENERGY CONVERSION LTD., Internal reports and memoranda (1968). Chapter 8.
58. *Engineering* (Anon.). From new power station—district heating, June 4th (1965). Chapter 7.

59. *Escher-Wyss News*, Special issue on closed cycle gas turbines, Vol. 39, No. 1 (1966). Chapter 6.

60. FLEUR, J. K. LA., Description of an operating closed cycle helium gas turbine, *ASME paper* 63 *AHGT* 74 and *Gas Turbine Magazine*, July/Aug. (1963). Chapter 6.

61. FORTESCUE, P., General atomics Europe, Zurich; Gas cooling for fast reactors, Geneva Atom conference, Sept. (1964). Chapter 6.

62. FOSTER-PEGG, R. W., Trends in combined steam-gas turbine power plants in the U.S.A., *Trans. of ASME Journal of Engineering for Power*, Oct. (1966). Chapter 5.

63. FRUTSCHI, H., Oekonomische Energie- und Wärmeerzeugung, *Technische Rundschau (Schweiz)*, No. 30 (1965). Chapter 6.

64. FRUTSCHI, H., 10 Jahre Heizkraftwerke mit geschlossenen Gasturbinen, *Technische Rundschau*, No. 31 (1966). Chapter 6.

65. FRUTSCHI, H. and HAAS, W., 25% thermal efficiency with a pulverised coal fired gas turbine plant of 2000 kW output, *Escher-Wyss News*, No. 2/3 (1959). Chapter 6.

66. GARRETT-AIR RESEARCH CORPORATION, technical brochures (1967) and (1968). Chapters 1, 11.

67. *Gas and Oil Power* (Anon.). An efficient private power and heating plant, Jan./Feb. (1967).

68. GAS TURBINE ASSOCIATION, *Annual Gas Turbine Catalogue* (1967). Chapter 5.

69. *Gas Turbine Magazine* (Anon.)., Gas-cooled reactor combined with closed cycle gas turbine produces a mobile low power level nuclear power plant, Nov/. Dec. (1960). Chapter 6.

70. *Gas Turbine Magazine* (Anon.).The nuclear gas turbine, July/Aug. (1965). Chapter 6.

71. GATE Inc., San Antonio, Texas, *Gas Total Energy* (1968). Chapter 1.

72. GATE Inc., San Antonio, Texas, Total energy abstracts (1964–8). All Chapters.

73. GAUTHIER, C. J., Marketing total energy, *The Inst. of Gas Engineers* 33rd *Autumn research meeting*, Nov. (1967) Chapter 1.

74. GEPPERT, H. and KUPER, K. D., Kernkraftwerk mit Gasturbine im Direktkreislauf, *Technische Rundschau*, No. 31 (1966) Chapter 6.

75. GETHING, F., Heat recovery boiler developments, *Diesel and Gas Turbine Progress*, No. 34, Feb. (1968). Chapter 1.

76. GFELLER, M. *et al.*, Total energy in Berne, *Engineering and Boiler House Review*, Vol. 83, No. 1, Jan. (1968). Chapter 10.

77. GOEBEL, K., "Hohe Wand" Gas turbine/steam turbine power station, *Siemens Review*, Vol. 33, No. 5 (1966). Chapter 5.

78. HAAS, W., The use of low grade coal in closed cycle gas turbine plants, *Escher-Wyss News*, Vol. 35, No. 2 (1962). Chapter 6.

79. HALEY, E. C., Add-on total energy plant serves apartment complex, *Diesel and Gas Turbine Progress*, Apr. (1966). Chapter 11.

80. HASELER, A. E., Total energy systems, *The Steam and Heating Engineer*, Mar. (1968) and Apr. (1968). Chapter 1.

81. HAYS, R., Gas turbine supplies both heat and power, *Southern Power and Industry*, Mar. (1963). Chapter 11.

82. *Heating and Ventilating Engineer* (Anon.). What is total energy?, Feb. (1968). Chapter 1.

83. HENDRICKSON, R. L., Thermodynamic cycles. Paper presented at General Electric gas turbine engineering seminar, Schenectady, New York, June (1967). Chapter 5.

84. HIEDL, H., Concerning the thermodynamics of combined thermal power cycles, *Wärme*, Vol. 70, No. 3, Apr. (1964). Chapter 5.

85. HOFFMAN, R. V., Turbine generated critical power. Paper read to Petroleum Industry Electrical Assn. April 24th (1968) at Galveston, Texas. Chapters 2, 9.

86. HOFFMANN, F. DE, Der gasgekühlte Hochtemperaturreaktor als Schiffsantrieb. Lecture held at Hamburg to Kernenergie Studiengemeinschaft, Oct. 4th (1961). Chapter 6.

87. HOHL, R. and FRUTSCHI, H., Combined production of electric power and heat with steam turbine and gas turbine plants, World Power Conference, Lausanne, Paper 95/11b-4 (1964). Chapter 6.

88. HOLLANDER, L. J., Total energy spells precise power, *American Gas Assn, Monthly*, Vol. 50, No. 20, Feb. (1968). Chapter 1.

89. HOLLIDAY, J. B. and KEENAN, J. G., Turbo machinery for high temperature gas cooled reactors. Paper read at OECD gas turbine meeting, Paris, May (1965); also *The Engineer*, June (1965). Chapter 6.

90. HUNNICOTT, U., Bergan High School T/E plant sets new high for oil, *Total Energy*, Vol. 3, No. 4, Apr. (1966). Chapter 11.

91. *Industrial Gas* (anon.), TE/KC = OK, Jan. (1967). Chapter 11.

92. INSTITUTE OF GAS TECHNOLOGY, *Gas Engine Handbook*, Chicago (1967). Chapter 2.

93. JONES, D. R., Gas turbine added to existing steam plant increases efficiency, *Power Engineering*, Aug. (1965). Chapter 5.

94. KELLER, C., Die geschlossene Gasturbine für Kernkraftanlagen, *Neue Technik*, No. B4 (1965). Chapter 6.

95. KELLER, C., Ein Beitrag der Schweiz zur Atomtechnik, *Schweizerische Handelszeitung*, No. 27 (1965). Chapter 6.

96. KELLER, C., The nuclear gas turbine, *Gas Turbine Magazine*, July/Aug. (1965). Chapter 6.

97. KIRILLOV, I. I. *et al.*, Selection of optimal parameters for the TsKTI-LPI high temperature gas-steam plant, *Thermal Engineering*, No. 1 (1967). Chapter 5.

98. KNIGHT, J. C., District heating in the USSR, *Engineer*, No. 224, Nov. 24 (1967). Chapter 10.

99. KOMISSAROV, V. A., Experience gained in introducing low pressure economisers to power stations in the Novosibirsk power system, *Teploenergetika*, Vol. 13, No. 10 (1966). Translation available in *Thermal Engineering*. Chapter 1.

100. KORNEEV, M. I., PRUTSKOVSKII, E. N. and ROMANOV, A. A., First results of setting up and operating a steam/gas plant with a high pressure steam generator of 120 t/hr output, *Teploenergetika*, Vol. 11, No. 9 (1964). Chapter 5.

101. KRESS, H., Anwendungsmöglichkeiten der Gasturbine im Ramen der Heizkraft-Kupplung, *Praktische Energiekunde*, Vol. 5, No. 1/2 (1957). Chapter 6.

102. LANGNER, W., Fernwärmeversorgung in Verbindung mit Gasturbinen, *Technische Mitteilungen*, Vol. 60, No. 8, Aug. (1967). Chapter 10.

103. LANIN, I. S. and KUTSKO, E. A., Development of district heating in Leningrad, *Teploenergetika*, Vol. 14, No. 2 (1967); translated in *Thermal Engineering*. Chapter 10.

104. MANCUSO, N., ASME paper No. 56 GT/CMC, Mar. (1966). Chapter 1.

105. *Marine Engineer and Naval Architect* (Anon.). Gotaverken's 850 mm bore engine, Dec. (1966). Chapter 2.

106. MARR, P. A. D., *Gas Turbines for Improved Process Economy*, Ruston and Hornsby (1968). Chapter 2.

107. McCLURE, C. J. R. and CLARK E. L., Total energy plants. *Actual Specifying Engineer*, Vol. 10, No. 2 (1963). Chapter 1.

108. MEIJER, R. J., The Philips hot gas engine with rhombic drive mechanism, *Philips Technical Review*, Vol. 20, No. 9 (1958/9). Chapter 2.

109. MEIJER, R. J., Philips Stirling engine activities, *Philips Research Laboratories Publication* (1967). Chapter 2.

110. MESCHINO, R. G., New energy systems for building services, Trans-Canada Pipelines Ltd. (1967). Chapter 1.

111. MICHIGAN CONSOLIDATED GAS CO., news release (1967). Chapter 11.

112. MORIMOTO, K., The first closed cycle gas turbine power plant in Japan, *Fuji Denki Review* Vol. 4, No. 3 (1958). Chapter 6.

113. NATIONAL DISTRICT HEATING ASSN., PITTSBURGH, PENN., *Annual Proceedings* (1960, 1961, 1962, 1963, 1964, 1965, 1966, 1967). Chapters 9, 10.

114. NORTH WESTERN UTILITIES, LTD., CANADA, news releases (1964). Chapter 11.

115. NUCLEAR POWER GROUP LTD., Dual purpose power/salination plant (1968). Chapter 1.

116. *Oil Engine and Gas Turbine* (Anon.). Packaged plant for fish meal production Oct. (1957). Chapter 1.

117. *Oil Engine and Gas Turbine* (Anon.). Unique record of service in British sewage works, Sept. (1963). Chapter 1.

118. *Oil Engine and Gas Turbine* (Anon.). Turbo-compressor in industrial service, Aug. and Oct. (1963). Chapter 5.

119. OKUN, M., Total energy facts, Mission valley apartments—Kenilworth apartments. J. C. Nicholls Co., Kansas City, Mo., Oct. (1966). Chapter 11.

120. ORLIK, V. K. and TKACHEV, V. V., The TsKTI 200,000 kW (PGU 200/210) steam/gas plant, *Thermal Engineering*, No. 11 (1966). Chapter 5.

121. POPE, J. A. and LOWE, W., The development of highly rated medium speed diesel engines, *Trans. Inst. Marine Engineers*, Vol. 78, No. 8, Aug. (1966). Chapter 7.

122. PRATT and WHITNEY LTD., technical brochures (1968). Chapter 2.

123. PFENNINGER, H., Arbeitsverwertung und Kombination der Gasturbinen mit Dampfkraftwerken in der Hüttenindustrie, *Stahl und Eisen*, Vol. 80, No. 22, Oct. (1960). Chapter 5.

124. RATAI, W., School planning and the heat pump, *Actual Specifying Engineer*, Vol. 12, No. 6 (1964). Chapter 9.

125. RIETDIJK, J. A. *et al.*, A positive rod or piston seal for large pressure differences, *Philips Technical Review*, No. 10 (1965). Chapter 2.

126. ROBINSON, W., The total energy factory, *The Heating and Ventilating Engineer*, Nov. (1967). Chapter 1.

127. RONDEN, C. P., Total energy systems, Paper read at the annual meeting of the association of professional engineers of Alberta, Edmonton, 29 Mar. (1968). Chapter 11.

128. ROVER LTD., Engine catalogue No. 2 (1968). Chapter 2.

129. ROLLS ROYCE LTD., technical brochures (1968). Chapter 2.

130. RUEGG, R., Industrielle Wärmeversorgung und Fernheizung mit und ohne Wärmekraftkupplung, Schweizerische Bauzeitung, Vol. 77, No. 5, 5 Nov. (1959). Chapter 6.

131. RUSTON AND HORNSBY LTD., press releases, Mar. (1965). Chapter 2.

132. SALMON, J. E., New look at heat pump systems, National Engineer, June (1962). Chapter 9.

133. SENECHAUT, P., Combined cycle may show substantial economy, Power, Feb. (1968). Chapter 5.

134. SCHMIDT, D., CCGT for combined production of electricity and fresh water, Escher-Wyss News, No. 1/2 (1964). Chapter 6.

135. SEARS–ROEBUCK CO., Catalogues. Chapter 8.

136. SHAVE, R. E., Total energy and the gas turbine, Steam and Heating Engineer, Nov. (1967). Chapter 5.

137. SILBERRING, L., The supercharged steam generator, Suzler Technical Review, Vol. 47, No. 3 (1965). Chapter 5.

138. Shopping Center Age (Anon.), The economics of gas energy, Nov. (1963). Chapter 11.

139. SPILLMAN W., The closed cycle gas turbine for non-conventional applications, ASME paper 66-GT/CLC-8/Gas Turbine meeting of the ASME at Zurich (1966). Chapter 6.

140. STEINER, W., The application of flash evaporators for industrial purposes, Dechema Monographien, Vol. 47 (1962). Chapter 1.

141. STERRETT, E., Total energy plant power El Paso shopping center, Diesel and Gas Engine Progress, Oct. (1963). Chapter 11.

142. TAMBLYN, R. T., Bootstrap heating for commercial office buildings, ASHRAE· Journal, (1963). Chapter 9.

143. TECHNOLOGICAL UNIVERSITY OF DELFT, Proceedings of a one-day symposium Total Energy gas and the gas turbine, Sept. (1966). Chapter 5.

144. TRANE, LTD., technical information and brochures. Chapter 9.

145. UNITED NATIONS, Dept. of Economics and Social Affairs (anon.), Small Scale Power Generation. Chapter 2.

146. VEREINIGUNG DEUTSCHER ELEKTRIZITÄTSWERKE (Anon.), Richtlinien für Wärmemessung und Wärmeabrechnung, Frankfurt (1966). Chapter 10.

147. WALKER, G., Stirling Cycle Engines for Total Energy Systems, IGT publication, Chicago (1967). Chapter 2.

148. WEIR-WESTGARTH LTD., technical information (1968). Chapter 1.

149. WERDEN, R. G., Heat pumps condition year round in large factory warehouse, Heating, Piping & Air Conditioning, Aug. (1961). Chapter 7.

150. WILSON, J. G., Energy recovery pays off at three Shell refineries, The Oil and Gas Journal, 18 Apr. (1966). Chapter 1.

151. WILSON, W. B. and HINIKER, T. G., Cost and performance of gas turbine exhaust heat recovery boiler systems, Combustion, April (1965). Chapter 5.

152. WINKENS, H. P., Die Wirtschaftlichkeit der Fernwarmeversorgung über Heiz-kraftwerke im Rahmen der Energieversorgung über leitungsgebundene Ener-gie-träger, *Technische Mitteilungen*, Vol. 60, No. 8, Aug. (1967). Chapter 10.

153. WINKENS, H. P. and EBERT, F. H., The Mannheim–Nord combined heat and power station with refuse incineration, Stadtwerke Mannheim (1965). Chapter 10.

154. WINKENS, H. P. and GEIPEL, W., Planung und Bau der Mullverbrennungsan-lage in Mannheim, *Mitteilungen der VGB*, Vol. 100, Feb. (1966). Chapter 10.

155. WITTEVEEN R. A. J. O. VAN, *The Philips Stirling Engine*, NV Philips, Eindhoven (1966). Chapter 2.

156. WOLF, M., Städteheizung und städtische Stromversorgung rationeller durch die Heisslufturbine, *Energie*, No. 8 (1955). Chapter 6.

157. WOLF, M., Neuere Heizkraftwerke, *Elektrizitätswirtschaft*, Vol. 65, No. 4 (1966). Chapter 10.

158. WORKUN, M., Hillcrest Junior High School, technical information. Chapter 11.

159. YOUNG, C., *Proceedings of the Diesel Engineers and Users Assn.*, June (1967), Publication 314. Chapter 7.

160. ZUND, L., An interesting configuration for a 26,000 kW thermal power station. *Sulzer Technical Review*, Vol. 48, No. 2 (1966). Chapter 5.

INDEX

Absorption refrigeration plants 307
Agesta system 351
Aircraft engines for industrial purposes 172
Air heaters 209
Aldershot district heating system 278
Alternator load limiter 139
Ammonia absorption systems 307
Apollo fuel cell 294
Armoured pipelines 346
Asynchronous alternators 105

Back pressure
  governing system 145
  turbines 61, 64
  turbine/diesel plant 69
Bacon cell 297
Ball joints 345
Beaird-Maxim heat recovery units 369
Bergan High School, Peoria, Illinois 399
Bleed point pressure control 132
Boiler pressure and temperature 75
Brooklyn Union Gas Co. 361
Burns Brick Co. Macon, Georgia 384

Calorific value of fuels 11
Carnot's equation 1
Carrieres sur Seine system 352
Cattle Marketeers Inc., St. Cloud, Florida 387
CEGB stations, efficiency 54
Central generation vs. total energy 12
Centrifugal compressors 303
Closed cycle gas turbines 209
  coal fired 214
Coefficient of performance 300
Compensators 344
Condenser vacuum, choice 78

Condensing turbines 59
Consumer connections (district heating) 323
Coolers 222
Cooling water requirements 50
Cost of fuel per unit heat 354

Dead band 114
Diesel and gas engines 251
Diesel engines 25
  heat balance 251
  utilisation of waste heat 265
Direct drying 16
Distribution pipework, steam turbines 80
District cooling 348
District heating 317
  choice of medium 330
  closed systems 343
  costing 328
  degree of penetration 329
  open systems 341
Double pass-out condensing turbine 71

Economic assessment of total energy 405
Economic worth 405
Electrical governors 151
Electrical power requirements 287
Energy losses in pipes, bends, etc. 230
Engineered Plastics Ltd., Edmonton, Alberta, Canada 386
Engine recovery system, design of 261
European district heating systems 348
Exhaust gases 253
Export power controller 152

Feasibility equation for total energy 407

427

Feasibility of total energy 12
Feedwater heating 73
Feedwater temperature, choice 77
Flash evaporation 19
Flexwell system of pipelines 346
Four pipeline system 348
Free piston generators 35
Freon 306
Fuel, cost 7
Fuel cell modules 293
Fuel cells 286
  for domestic purposes 288

Garrett Air Research TE package 374
Gas/air heat exchangers 199
Gas/hot water heat exchangers 199
Gasolene driven plants 29
Gas/steam cycles 182
Gas turbines 29
  for district heating 354
Geothermic heat for district heating 349

Hartford, Connecticut system 348
Heat exchangers 218
  and waste heat boilers, design of 197
Heat exchanger surfaces 232
Heating costs (U.K.) 13
Heat meters 326
Heat recovery savings 409
Heavy fuel heating 269
Helium gas turbine 224
Helium, physical data 228
High frequency current generation 14
Hillcrest Junior High School, Edmonton, Alberta, Canada 381
Hydrocarbon fuel cell 295
Hydrogen fuel cells 292

Induction alternators 105
Inlet alternators 105
Inlet pressure governing system 141
Insulated pipelines 343
ITOC turbines 4, 65, 318, 352

Jacket water, heat recovery 253
Jet compressors 303

Kanasa City, Missouri apartment blocks 393

Latent heat cooling 258
Leningrad district heating system 321
Lithium bromide absorbers 309
Lead/fuel consumption curves 292
Lead/thermal efficiency curves 291
Loose fill insulation 347
Lubricating oil, heat recovery 253

Mach number 232
Mannheim, Germany plant 358
Methyl chloride 306
Mixed pressure turbine 72
Mollier diagram 56
Motoring, prevention of 154

Noise of gas turbine equipment 15
Nomograph for pay-out calculation 413
Nuclear power for district heating 349
Nuclear power plants 224
Nusselt number 232

Oberhausen, Germany plant 357
Ohio State University System 389
Open-cycle gas turbines 155
  choice of fuels 169
  fluids other than water 195
  small machines 177

Parallel operation with public electricity system 61, 98
Park Plaza, Little Rock, Arkansas scheme 372
Pass-out back pressure turbine 71
Pass-out condensing turbo-alternator 136
Pass-out governing systems 127

Pass-out turbine 56
Penetration factors 415
Petrol driven plants 29
pH values of boilers 207
Plant, cost 6
Power failure, U.S.A. 7
Power obtainable from process steam
    flow 81
Power stations, efficiency 3
Prandtl number 232
Prefabricated mains 346
Prime mover pay-out calculations 411
Process steam 53
Process steam supply 16
Pulrose power station 274

Reciprocating refrigerators 303
Refrigerants 305
Refrigerated water distribution system
    315
Refrigeration 270
    economics with TE 316
    thermodynamics 301
Refuse incineration 319, 358
Regency Square, Jacksonville, Florida
    scheme 368
Reynolds number 232
Rochdale Village scheme 365

Sealing
    of casings and pipes 233
    of machine shaft 233
Sea water distillation 268
Sendling, Germany plant 356
Sewage disposal 18
Sewage plant 270
Simple payout 405
Single pipeline system 332
Speed droop 111

Speed governing systems 108
Speed governors, isochronous 116
Speed regulation 111
Steam conditions 74
Steam costing 94
Steam/gas cycles 180
Steam plants, cost 52
Steam power ratio 59
Steam separator 261
Steam turbines 46
    for district heating 350
Steam turbine/gas turbine systems 15
Stirling engine 38
Sulphur-containing fuels 198
Swearingen system 310
Synchronous alternators 105
System stability 1q5

TARGET 294
Thermodynamics 55
    first law 3
Three pipeline systems 347
Topping turbine 70
Total energy schemes, North America
    361
Total energy system
    at J. and T. M. Greeves Ltd. 272
    at Vernon and Co. Ltd. 276
Transportation of power, cost 5
Twin pipeline system 341

Uniform present worth factor 407
United States, total energy 4

Warbasse houses scheme 362
Waste heat boilers 202
West Berlin district heating system 347